The Secret of Islam

LOVE AND LAW
IN THE RELIGION OF ETHICS

ALSO BY HENRY BAYMAN

The Station of No Station: Open Secrets of the Sufis

The Secret of Islam

LOVE AND LAW
IN THE RELIGION OF ETHICS

Henry Bayman

North Atlantic Books
Berkeley, California

Published by
North Atlantic Books
P.O. Box 12327
Berkeley, California 94712

www.northatlanticbooks.com
Cover and text design by Susan Quasha
Printed in Canada

The Secret of Islam: Love and Law in the Religion of Ethics is sponsored by the Society for the Study of Native Arts and Sciences, a nonprofit educational corporation whose goals are to develop an educational and crosscultural perspective linking various scientific, social, and artistic fields; to nurture a holistic view of arts, sciences, humanities, and healing; and to publish and distribute literature on the relationship of mind, body, and nature.

Library of Congress Cataloging-in-Publication Data

Bayman, Henry, 1951-
  The secret of Islam : love and law in the religion of ethics / by
Henry Bayman.
       p. cm.
Includes bibliographical references and index.
  ISBN 1-55643-432-4
  1. Islam. 2. Islamic law. 3. Faith (Islam) I. Title.
  BP50 .B393 2003
  297.2—dc21
                                                    2002154400

1 2 3 4 5 6 7 TRANS 07 06 05 04 03

Contents

Preface

———— ❧ ————

This book started out as a translation of a Turkish anthology titled *Spirit and Body,* by the renowned Sufi Master Ahmet Kayhan—who, as I have written elsewhere, defies description or any simple categorization.

I first met Master Kayhan[1] in the early spring of 1978 at his flat in Ankara, Turkey. By profession I am an engineer and I had been studying Sufism for a number of years with a master in Turkey, who brought me to visit Master Kayhan that day. My life was completely changed by that meeting and as I have described my relationship with the Master elsewhere, I will here provide only a bit of background in order to clarify why I have taken it upon myself to publish his teachings and the writings he considered worth translating.

If there is one thing all the thousands of people—from the most diverse backgrounds—who have been graced with his presence would probably agree upon, it is that the Master is indescribable. He was unique—one of a kind, even among Sufi masters—and so, incomparable. I find myself saddled with the thankless job of describing him to a world scarcely equipped with the tools necessary for an adequate comprehension of such a person.

As I have written in *The Station of No Station,* the bare bones of the Master's biography are quickly told. The closest I can make out is that he was born in late winter or early spring, 1898. He was a hundred years and seven months old when he passed away on August 3, 1998.

Because vital statistics were not conscientiously collected in those years, however, he was registered together with his half-brother when the latter was born several years after him. On his ID papers, his birthdate is given as 1903 (1321, reckoned by the lunar calendar, which was then in use). His birthplace was the small village of Mako (Aktarlar, as it is now known) near Poturge in the province of Malatya in Turkey. He lost his father when he was only a year old, and his mother remarried, but died when he was seven.

He was basically unschooled. He learned to read and write only during his military service, in his twenties. But that has to be set against the fact that he was trained by the greatest Master of them all: Hadji ("Pilgrim") Ahmet Kaya Effendi, his master, who was called "Keko" (Kurdish for "Father") by his followers.

Ahmet Kayhan settled in Ankara in the 1930s and married Hajar (March 25, 1937), who remained his wife until his death. His master, Keko, passed away on May 7, 1944, and was succeeded by Musa Kiazim, who had been Keko's fellow disciple during and after the First World War. With the death of Kiazim Effendi in 1966, Ahmet Kayhan, my Master, "donned the mantle."

Up to this time he had taken various odd jobs in Ankara, opened three shops, finally settling down as a government employee at the State Waterworks, from which he retired for reasons of health. All this he did in order to support his family. He had four children, two girls and two boys. They, in turn, have lived to see their grandchildren.

From the sixties onward, Grandpa conducted the activity of enlightening the people. Since he was retired, he was able to devote his full time to this effort. I once counted forty-seven visitors on an average day, but in recent years this number increased substantially as more people came to know him.

The facts of a saint's life, however, rarely tell us much about who s/he was. I have related the above only because it is necessary, not because it is helpful for an appreciation of Effendi.

His Line of Descent

Master Kayhan's chain of transmission is traced through the Prophet, his close associate and first Caliph Abu Bakr, Abdulqader Gilani, Bahauddin Naqshband, Ahmed Sirhindi, Abdullah Dehlewi, Khalid Baghdadi, Sheikh Samini, Osman Badruddin, and Ahmet Kaya Effendi (Keko). I have omitted most of the names in the Golden Chain from the list and concentrated only on the most illustrious.

It is said that the line of Prophethood started as a light in the forehead of Adam. Down through the ages this light was transferred from the forehead of one prophet to another, until it reached Mohammed, the last prophet. Mohammed combined the attributes of prophethood and sainthood within himself.

Now although prophethood had come to an end, the light of saint-hood again continued down through the ages, passing from one great master to another. It emerged from Mecca with the Prophet, passed on to Baghdad with Sheikh Gilani (founder of the Qadiri Order), traveled to Bokhara in Central Asia and devolved on Shah Naqshband (founder of the Naqshbandi Order, to which my Master belonged), went south to India with Imam Rabbani (Sirhindi) and Abdullah of Delhi (later to be known as New Delhi), returned to Baghdad with Maulana Khalid, fi-nally traveling north to find itself in Eastern Anatolia. This circuit of the light of sainthood continued for hundreds of years, and will be com-pleted only at the end of time—so it is said.

The Sufi Orders are, in Effendi's words, "spiritual schools"—a fact recognized by Peter Ouspensky. Of course, the fact that the "Saintlight" moves on doesn't mean that its former abode is left neglected. The Naqshbandi (Naqshi for short) Order's spiritual schools and training continued after the departure of the Saintlight. It was to the tail end of these that George I. Gurdjieff latched on towards the end of the nine-teenth century, and many of the unique elements in his teachings are imported direct from the Central Asian Sufi schools. John G. Bennett, a student of Gurdjieff, traced the migration of the schools to Turkey, but died on the verge of discovering the precise whereabouts of the Saintlight.

The long and short of it is, the Master was squarely at the center of the highest expression of traditional Islamic Sufism, in the line of the Samini Branch of the Naqshbandi Order. This was Grandpa's spiritual pedigree, yet he was beyond all orders, sects, or schools. And though he was a devout Moslem, he embraced people of all religions.

The Views of Others

I could draw on many accounts from eyewitnesses, and perhaps in the future I shall do so. For now, however, I have confined myself to the following excerpt from an American friend who is attached to another Sufi master: "Ahmed Effendi is certainly unique and special, but it is a uniqueness which has nothing foreign about it and nothing that separates…For me it is a quality which I can only call intimacy. I do not know any other more respectful term for the quality. What I mean is the degree to which Effendi seems to be within one's own self, one's own being, and the complete ease and directness of his communication, literally transcending speech and language and culture and time and history, while at the same time establishing, confirming, and justifying them…there was never a need to speak, and my increasing knowledge of Turkish, which did add immeasurably to the relish of conversation with Effendi, never seemed to increase the intimacy of the presence of Effendi in my heart, or the hearts of any of my friends who love him…Although I am upset [over his loss,] I feel a deep and profound joy and happiness in knowing that I can not be separated from his love in any way whatsoever."

The Master's Teachings

Ahmet Kayhan was a Man of Knowledge, or a Man of Wisdom. With him there was no distinction between Moslem, Christian, Jew, or Buddhist. He was far beyond drawing distinctions in the ordinary manner. For him there were only human beings, and to all he counseled the same teaching: God exists, and God is One. Abide by the Divine Law. Work for the establishment of peace on Earth, love one another, and devote yourself to serving your fellow humans. Feel compassion for all creatures, even a fly.

As you can see, his teachings were independent of time, space, or geography, and so, truly universal. His pamphlets on world peace—their structure and important parts were dictated by him—aroused favorable responses from a former French president, from the Pope, and from both the then-president and prime minister of Israel. (One of these is reproduced in Appendix E.) If he had survived longer, his intention would have been to continue to call all people to peace on Earth. He was against all weapons of mass destruction. But this was only the beginning of his comprehensive teaching.

Methodology

The methods of the Master in teaching his students varied, yet there were discernible trends. He would not tax a pupil beyond his or her capacity. In accordance with the saying of the Prophet, he would speak to the level of understanding of his listeners. He had the knack of explaining the most complicated things in the simplest terms. If, despite this, the person didn't understand, he would repeat himself, as many times as necessary. He would keep at it until the listener understood, and once he saw he had communicated his message successfully, he would say no more about it.

The Master was an inexhaustible repository of Sufi teaching-stories and anecdotes. He would select the most appropriate for a given occasion, sometimes relating events from his life history. He had infinite love and respect for his own Master and would sometimes fondly relate a memory of the times they had together.

What was outstanding about the Master's use of teaching-stories, however, was his ability to string them together in the appropriate order to achieve exactly the desired result. In this respect, he had the virtuosity of a composer with them.

He would quickly identify the *forte*—the strongest virtue—of a person. He once told me that only a moment was enough for a true *murshid* (Islamic guru) to take the snapshot of a person—I'm inclined to call it a kind of spiritual X-ray. He would then cultivate that virtue of the person, also supplementing this with whatever "vitamins" were deficient in a student's constitution.

When a question was asked of him, he always answered it, even if he appeared to refuse at first. At times, he left his students without explicit guidance. It might be surmised that some activity, some energetic effort, was expected of them during such periods.

The analogy has been suggested to me that the Master was giving each one of us a handful of seeds. It was our duty to plant these seeds, cultivate them, and see them through to maturity and the bearing of fruit. Another analogy is that he was giving us keys to unlock the secret chambers of our brains.

Formal Organization

The Master had no formal organization to speak of. Although he was in the Naqshbandi line of descent, there were no dervish convents (*takkas*), no ceremonies, no special rituals, and no formalities. The convents were disbanded in 1928 by the newly-formed Turkish Republic, but with the Master I learned that there was no need for them. True spirituality could be exercised and conveyed without any formal structure at all—all that is necessary is acceptance on the part of the teacher, and devotion, sincerity, and effort on the part of the student. Having served their purpose, the *takkas* had passed into history as defunct sociological institutions.

Instead there were ad hoc discussion groups, which came into existence on the spur of the moment with whomever might be present at that time. Visiting the Master and participating in these discussions were very important. A leaflet or pamphlet distributed by the Master might be read, which he might interrupt at any time in order to clarify or emphasize a certain point. Even this might not be necessary, as the *baraka* (spiritual action or power) of the Master could work in total silence. When one's spiritual "battery" was "discharged," one could go back to the Master for a "recharge." If love can be defined as "giving without receiving—or asking for—anything in return," then the Master loved his following.

Although he himself never wrote any books, in keeping with the oral tradition of the Sufis, Master Kayhan had an excellent command of teaching stories. He also collected volumes of Sufic lore (e.g., teaching-stories, poetry, and aphorisms) and other works that he considered essential to an understanding of Islam. Being an accomplished Master, he himself was not in need of any of these. Rather, they were for the edification of his students—namely, us. I helped him compile four important Turkish anthologies: *Adam and the Universe* (1989), *Spirit and Body* (1991), *I Found What I was Seeking* (1992), and *Study in the School of Wisdom* (1994). All were published in Turkish and still remain untranslated, though the present book constitutes a beginning towards bridging that gap.

Because his talks were not usually recorded and his speech was characterized by brevity, I have had to reconstruct his teachings as I remember them and, in some cases, I have tried to translate certain concepts/issues into Western terms using his teaching methods. To summarize his principal methods, I would say that they were:

1. ad hoc discussion groups or private conversations in which he answered disciples' questions, as shown in the Sage and Disciple section

("Moses, Jesus, and Mohammed," some parts of which illustrate the quality of these conversations). Sometimes too, he used the Socratic method, asking questions of us;

2. relating traditional Sufi tales and personal anecdotes to clarify a point;

3. instructing his followers to read or translate certain texts that he considered essential, especially when they addressed an issue of particular concern to the disciple (in some cases I have used what I consider Western equivalents, e.g., Carlyle, to the Turkish texts he recommended). As will be shown in this book, love of knowledge is one of the characteristic aspects of Islamic society and some of his favorite works in Turkish were those by Gilani, Ibn Arabi, and Misri;

4. teaching by the example of his own behavior which was always characterized by that quality so admired by Turks, "courtesy" (see Appendix A for a list of sayings about courtesy). Like the Prophet Mohammed, he lived a highly ethical life, wanting nothing from his followers. His life was an example of loving, thoughtful, and ethical behavior that produced inspiration and joy in those around him;

5. direct transmission, in which he would work in total silence, sending us knowledge and strength through *baraka* (spiritual action or power).

Translation

As I began working on the literal translation of *Spirit and Body,* I felt challenged by the words "Sufism" and "Islam," and the conceptions these give rise to in people's minds.

"Sufism" has come to be understood in a variety of ways. Properly, it is the esoteric aspect, the highest expression, of Islam. Yet it cannot be divorced and considered in isolation from the exoteric aspect: the former is the content and the latter is the form which contains it.

In the case of the term "Islam," the word has become associated with so many connotations that different people using the same term rarely mean the same thing. One thing is clear: *what you understand from the word is almost certainly not what "Islam" really means.* This holds no less true for many Moslems than for non-Moslems, given the sorry state of religious instruction in so-called "Islamic" countries. If this is the case even with Moslems, just think what the situation must be for non-Moslems. This book aims to disabuse readers from such misunderstandings, and it is hoped that by the time you finish it, you will have gained a more accurate impression of what "Sufism" and "Islam" really mean.

The more I applied myself to the task, however, the less tenable it became to remain content with a literal translation. For one thing, the anthology did not proceed in linear sequential order; it presumed a certain amount of knowledge concerning Islam and Sufism in the reader, and a relatively simple chapter might, for example, be preceded by a difficult one. This knowledge could not be taken for granted in the average Western reader. Hence new, introductory chapters had to be written that incorporated material dispersed throughout the Master's other anthologies and his talks.

The result is a book that evolved from *Spirit and Body* remotely resembling the original. I, of course, must bear responsibility for all its shortcomings, and in light of this I would like to say a few words about my main concerns in preparing it.

1. *Universality.* Islam is a universal religion, a religion for all humanity; it always has been. The original book assumed an Islamic cultural background in its readers. From the start, Islam has found roots predominantly in the Middle East, and naturally it has been imbued with the culture of that region. But a Western reader may rightly wonder how Islam can be called universal if no way can be found to relate it to his or her own cultural background.

Western culture is based on the Judeo-Christian tradition, and Islam has so much in common with Judaism and Christianity that there should be no reason why Western readers should find themselves unable to relate to it. Hence, I have interspersed the text with quotations from Western sources wherever an affinity suggested itself. These are mostly absent from the original book, but I hope the general readership will find the book more accessible and appealing in its present form. Being a universal religion, Islam has expressed universal truths, and some of these truths have been the property of the Western religious and intellectual tradition as well. Wherever a Western source is referred to, therefore, it should be noted that Islam in most cases already contains that truth quite independently, and the reference is given only in order to ease the reader's comprehension.

A Sufi teaching-story told by Rumi beautifully illustrates this point. A Greek, an Arab, a Turk, and a Persian once came together, and when they were hungry they pooled their money to buy something to eat. At that point a difficulty arose, however, because the Greek wanted to buy *stafil,* the Arab wanted to buy *inab,* the Persian wanted *angur* while the Turk wanted *uzum.* They finally began to quarrel, and at that moment a wise sage passing by interrupted them. "Tell me what you want," he said, and taking the money from them, soon came back with some grapes. They were amazed to see that they all had wanted the same thing. So it is with human beings everywhere: although we all fundamentally want the same things, we call them by different names, and in doing so imagine they are different.

Well, then, here are the grapes.

2. *Unification.* As will be discussed in this book, Islam is the religion of unification. At the most immediate level, of course, this refers to the fact that God is One. Yet there are other dimensions to it. Ideally, Islam aims to unite science, philosophy, religion, and art—no field of human knowledge or perception lies outside its ken. The "grand synthesis" which some have aimed at but failed to achieve because they weren't looking in the right place can only be achieved within the purview of Islam.

Mathematics has been called the queen of sciences, and in a similar vein it may be said that Islam is the crown of religions. The true facets of all religions—and they all contain truth, even the most unexpected—are proper subsets of Islam. Hence, in order to help the reader, I have attempted to show parallels with other religions where these exist.

And finally, Islam ideally aims to unite all humanity. I find it unnecessary to belabor the importance of this point in the "global village" we inhabit today.

The Master's speech and his writing style in the original text are lucid and conversational, but there is a difficulty in translating some of the more esoteric ontological concepts into English. Therefore, in order to add to the understanding and the translation of the concepts discussed here, efforts were concentrated on the following points:

Translations from the Koran: I have not adhered to any single translation of the Koran, although the best-known translations have been consulted. As elsewhere, I have not hesitated to sacrifice accuracy for clarity where called for.

From Turkish, Arabic, and Persian to English: Spirit and Body was in Turkish, with frequent use of Arabic and Persian words. However, in order to help the reader, I have—except on a few occasions—tried to use Arabic equivalents of the Turkish and Persian words scattered throughout the original text.[2]

Translation of the words "Allah," "zikr," and "salat": In Islam, "Allah" is the proper name, the personal name of God. In English we use the capitalized form, "God," to refer to the Deity, who is One. The lowercase form refers to fictitious deities whose existence has been assumed in the previous history of humanity. Even when it indicates one of a kind, however, "God" is still a generic, not a specific, name. There was once only a single specimen of *homo sapiens*, yet he had a name and it was Adam.

Absolute Reality, being all-encompassing, has both personal and impersonal aspects, but in Islam He is addressed as a person. And "Allah" is the name He has chosen for Himself. He desires, even demands, to be called by this name. This is similar to the way in which the Hebrews address God by the "tetragrammaton," the unpronounceable YHWH. Although it was forbidden to vocalize this word, we know that they probably pronounced it as "Yahweh" or "Jehovah."

As an interesting and significant aside, it may be mentioned that this word is also of Arabic origin. According to Professor T. James Meek, author of *Hebrew Origins*, the name was foreign to the Hebrews, and in their attempts to explain it they associated it with *hayah*, "to be," from which they derived the meaning usually ascribed to Yahweh, "I am." Professor Meek himself deems an origin from the Arabic root HWY, "to blow," more probable. Thanks to the Master, however, we are now able to give the correct form and meaning: *Ya Huwa*, which may be translated as "O He," another name by which God likes to be called in Islam. The third-person singular form refers to the absolute transcendence of God, and is the ethically proper form of address in certain contexts. The upshot is that even before Moses, the Arabs already possessed a second name for God of great importance which was adopted by the Hebrews.

The name "Allah" carries within it the power of the presence of God, so that many Sufis have achieved an experience of God by constantly calling upon His name. Indeed, "Allah" is the most comprehensive and Supreme Name of God. Hence, God is almost always referred to by the name He prefers, Allah, in the original text. In view of the unfamiliarity of this name to non-Moslem readers, however, the word "God" has been used in its place to express clearly what we mean, in almost all occasions except where it is absolutely unavoidable.

Concerning *zikr,* this refers to the continuous repetition of a religious formula, such as one of God's names discussed above. This may be done either vocally (verbally, externally) or silently (mentally, internally). This technical term has overtones of remembrance, incantation, invocation, and the best way to describe it, perhaps, is as the repetition of a keyword, "keyword" in the present case meaning a sacred word or formula assigned by a perfect master that unlocks the doors of inner space. In order to be consistent, I have tried to use "invocation" for *zikr* as far as possible throughout the text.

Salat, which is *namaz* in Persian, poses a problem in translation that could not finally be resolved here. Although generally translated as "Prayer(s)" into English, it is so different from what is ordinarily meant by the term that an alternative is called for; yet in the end, I had to opt for retaining this customary form of translation. (Other possibilities are Active Prayer, Formal Prayer, and Ritual Prayer.) *Salat* is different from any other kind of worship. One is tempted to call it "Islamic Yoga" in order to convey a sense of its nature to the West, but this too falls miserably short of the mark. Ultimately, the only solution may be for the West to become familiar with these terms, *zikr* and *salat/namaz,* and to use them in the same way—freely and without fear of being grossly misunderstood—as Yoga and Mantra are now used. In this book, *I distinguish Islamic Prayer from ordinary supplication by capitalizing the "P."*

Gender solutions: Turkish is delightfully free of gender associations in the third person. The singular form, "o," can mean "he," "she"—even "it." Hence, whenever we are speaking about people, it is automatically understood that both sexes are included. I have attempted to carry this over into English. Thus, I have tried to use the form "s/he," "his or her," and "human" rather than "man."

Editorial and translation comments have been added as notes, within brackets in the main text, or in italics at the beginning and/or end of a text. Since this is an anthology, with each chapter initially designed to be self-contained, a certain amount of repetition could not be avoided.[3] In part, these repetitions serve the purpose of what would be handled as hyperlinks on the Internet. Primary sources have been given in the notes where possible; I have sometimes had recourse to secondary sources.

Why an Anthology?

Being based on the Master's books, this book naturally inherits their structure. It is essentially a compendium of works that the Master himself referred to in his teachings or excerpts from Western sources that I consider the equivalent of the Turkish works he used. I have also included examples that I myself have constructed to illustrate the methods the Master used with his disciples. (I have had to create these out of whole cloth. They are sometimes reconstructed from my memory of a given teaching and constitute a rough approximation of the style in which he taught or the subject matter he addressed.) In keeping with the oral tradition of the Sufis, attribution is only given where the author is a famous Sufi or poet (other sources are unattributed, part of the shared body of knowledge, as they are in the teachings).

Not all selections in the Turkish original lent themselves to translation with equal ease. Some of them had, therefore, to be omitted entirely. Others had to be, not just translated, but also adapted to the English language and Western culture. The Master gave permission to use a selection of texts from his other publications, which an English-speaking readership would, it was hoped, find to be of the greatest benefit and interest. This applies not merely to entire texts, but to portions of texts that have been interspersed throughout the book where required. Hence, many texts were substantially rewritten, and completely new texts were added where necessary. The fruit of these efforts was an online book titled *The Meaning of the Four Books.*

After that, I prepared another online book, *Science, Knowledge, and Sufism* (taking some of the Master's brief utterances and expanding upon them). The present book contains selections from both. In preparing this publication, further changes, improvements, and additions have been made. The result is a wholly new book which, however, remains faithful to the spirit of the originals.

Since those books were written, recent events have overtaken us in the form of September 11, 2001. Hence, a new Prologue has been added to clear away the cobwebs before we start off in earnest: it analyzes such matters as fundamentalism and neo-fundamentalism in detail. I cannot emphasize enough that terrorism, the slaughter of innocents, has nothing to do with Islam. This point has been dealt with in sufficient depth in the Prologue. Consequently, rather than constantly repeating myself over what has already been said there, in the remainder of the book I shall try to explain what Islam *is* and *is for* rather than what it *is not* or *is against.*

The Mother Lode

Perhaps it will not be apparent to many—and so needs to be stated at the outset—that what we have here is the Mother Lode, the living core, of authentic Sufism. Some of the material here may strike you as familiar, even mundane. Yet tucked away in corners are small nuggets that have been handed down through the ages by the famous oral transmission of the Sufis, and have as far as is known never before seen print. The explanation about *Ya Huwa* above is a case in point.

The book is organized into roughly two parts. The first part deals with the exoteric path—that is, the Divine Law. Initial chapters provide introductory information. Later chapters dealing with democracy and women address social subjects and provide sorely-needed answers to some questions.

The second part deals with the esoteric path, or mainly Sufism, and thus with matters of a spiritual and mystical nature. Here we are allowed to see how the spirit can truly soar in Islam, using the concepts and methods of the religion. But the two parts are not mutually exclusive: the book nicely weaves the two threads of exoteric/esoteric all along the way, so that they are treated as parts of a single whole, which is as it should be.

Last but not least, the appendices reproduce a significant part of the teaching material used by the Master. These include pamphlets or sheets he used to distribute; for example, a pamphlet by the Master on the subject of world peace is included as Appendix E. Other appendices are translations from selections that went into his anthologies. Careful study of these appendices will reveal a great deal about the emphases and general thrust of the Master's teachings—but then, so will the rest of the book.

Because this is an anthology, a few words to provide orientation may be helpful. Like a many-gated city, you should enter by whichever door attracts you. The fundamental Truth at the heart of Islam is being approached from different angles and always reflects the same truth. A linear approach, reading through the texts in the order of presentation, may prove frustrating for the reader. For example, there are a number of topics that are covered in more than one text. This is inevitable and to a certain extent intentional, because the same topic is being approached from other perspectives that lend depth and breadth to earlier conceptions.

It is my hope that these teachings will provide you with an approximation of the kind of experience that those of us lucky enough to sit in the Master's living room in Ankara experienced: complete immersion in timeless Islamic teachings that very gradually began to seep into one's consciousness. Over and over we asked him questions about the right path and various other aspects of Islam. Through his patient teachings, through his loving example, and through his encyclopedic knowledge of Sufi stories and understanding of the Koran and the life of Mohammed, the deep beauty of Islam began to illuminate our lives—as I hope it will illuminate yours.

Special thanks are due to Tim Thurston and Peter Murphy for their proofreading, suggestions, and invaluable help in bringing the book to completion. Gail Hanlon did a great job editing the two online books into the present form. My thanks also to all others who contributed to it in any way.

H. Bayman
Summer 2002

Foreword

—————— ﯼ ——————

Perhaps one of the most important points that I would like to make in this book is that Islam (when it incorporates the contributions of Sufism) is a religion that fully encompasses the whole spectrum of human thought, from rational scientific thought to intuitive and mystical understandings of the universe. There is, in Islam, no dichotomy between reason and faith. As Westerners, we are accustomed to consulting science for answers about the meaning of life. We often forget that our greatest scientists have often journeyed back to spiritual explanations upon entering realms of mystery. As will be shown in this book, Islam is, I venture to say, the one religion that truly synthesizes rationality and mysticism, the mind and the heart, social life and interior life in a way that makes it the "crown of religions," the Grand Synthesis or metareligion. (Whether or to what extent this is true should be judged only after the reader finishes the book, not before.) Because it is chronologically the last of the major religions, it has recognized earlier contributions and incorporated some of their best attributes as well. As I see it, Islam heals the split between heart and mind, so I will begin with a brief foreword on how contemporary society with its secular bias is in need of the spiritual healing available through Islam.

Western Science and Spirituality

"A little science leads one away from God, a great deal of science leads one back to Him."[4] According to noted historian Paul Johnson, as much as eighty percent of scientists believe in God. Among them have been the greatest scientists the world has ever seen. Scientists who believe in God run through the whole spectrum of scientific disciplines, from physics, which studies the external world, to psychology, which studies the inner world of humans.

The founders of modern science—Kepler, Descartes, Barrow, Leibniz, Gilbert, Boyle, Newton, et al.—were all deeply and genuinely religious thinkers, for whom God was the chief mathematician, beyond rigid scholastic frames and more mystical and Pythagorean in nature. Both Newton—the father of British empiricism—and Descartes—the originator of French rationalism—were profoundly religious thinkers. Albert Einstein, one of the greatest physicists of the twentieth century and certainly the most famous, explained his faith as follows:

"The most beautiful thing we can experience is the mysterious. It is the source of all true art and science...

"To know that what is impenetrable to us really exists, manifesting itself as the highest wisdom and the most radiant beauty, which our dull faculties can comprehend only in the most primitive forms—this feeling is at the center of true religiousness. In this sense, and in this sense only, I belong to the ranks of the devoutly religious men...

"It is enough for me...to reflect upon the marvelous structure of the universe which we can dimly perceive, and to try humbly to comprehend even an infinitesimal part of the intelligence manifested in nature."

In Einstein's vision, the Lord God manifests Himself in nature with the highest wisdom, the greatest beauty, and with infinite intelligence, subtly but not maliciously. And true religiosity is the source of all true art and science. It takes a scientist of Einstein's stature to recognize the deep beauty, profound order, and magnificent intelligence manifested in "blind nature."

Einstein was firmly of the opinion that "God does not play dice with the universe." His detractors on this point, Niels Bohr and Werner Heisenberg, were the founders of the "Copenhagen school" of quantum mechanics, which favored a probabilistic interpretation of quantum events. Yet in relation to God, Bohr and Heisenberg, too, found it necessary to speak of "the central order of the universe," for probability, too, has its mathematical laws—so much so, in fact, that the illustrious mathematician John von Neumann—who also helped invent the modern computer—once remarked: "Probability is black magic." There are laws that govern even chance, and all order, and all laws of mathematics—including laws of probability—and of science, are the design of the Divine Lawgiver.

On the other end of the spectrum, Carl Gustav Jung, the psychologist who delved deepest into the human unconscious in the twentieth century, replied to the question: "Do you now believe in God?" as follows: "I know. I do not need to believe. I know." In the face of such testimony, the efforts of those who strive to deny God are petty and misinformed. Just how petty is highlighted by Jung's following remark: "A man can know less about God than an ant can know of the contents of the British Museum."

The same view of God as chief mathematician has been shared by eminent scientists in the twentieth century. "From the intrinsic evidence of His creation," wrote the renowned physicist James Jeans, "the Great Architect begins to appear as a pure mathematician." Paul Dirac, the Nobel Prize-winning quantum physicist and discoverer of antimatter, observed: "God is a mathematician of a very high order, and He used very advanced mathematics in constructing the universe."

The views of all these scientists—and many others—have encouraged me to write this book. Alfred North Whitehead, the great mathematician and philosopher, expressed his thoughts as follows: "Religion is the vision of something which stands beyond, behind, and within, the passing flux of immediate things; something which is real, and yet waiting to be realized; something which is a remote possibility, and yet the greatest of present facts; something that gives meaning to all that passes, yet eludes apprehension; something whose possession is the final good, and yet beyond all reach; something which is the ultimate ideal, and the hopeless quest."

On this last point, I would beg to differ with Whitehead. The final good is not beyond all reach, and the quest is not hopeless. For the mystics, as Josiah Royce said, "are the most thorough going empiricists in the history of philosophy," and Sufism represents the summit of mysticism. And just as there is physical science, there also exists such a thing as "spiritual science." There exists a religion, moreover, where spirituality and science—knowledge of the inner world and knowledge of the external world—do not clash, but complement each other, and that is Islam, the Grand Synthesis.

✳

Even though we live at the peak of technological civilization—with air travel, skyscrapers, and the Internet—many have begun to acknowledge that the world we live in constitutes a spiritual desert.

Human scientific and technological capability has been stretched to the utmost. Yet our emotional life has become progressively stultified, our moral life increasingly barren.

But this is not the true stature of human beings. A person is a complete organism in which all the parts are equally important, and fine-tuned, this totality is the most wonderful thing in the universe, with a destiny that beggars the imagination.

We treat the brain as a machine for reasoning, and nothing more. Yet if the human totality were to be developed harmoniously, that is in a truly holistic manner, then we would discover abilities of the brain that, in our present deplorable condition, cannot even be guessed at. This lopsided development stands in need of correction. We need to achieve a balance that will fulfill more—ideally, all—of our potentials, and if we are able to do so, we will be happy, for happiness lies in the realization of the purposes for which we have been designed.

This does not entail throwing our present achievements to the winds. We need not forsake our knowledge, our technology, or our civilization. Nor need we become hermits and live in mountain caves. What needs to be done is to bring our neglected aspects up to a par with those which are already highly developed. In terms of the human entity, the focus for this is the heart and the spirit. In social terms, it is morality, or ethical conduct. The fact that we have seldom realized, however, is that these two are coupled, to an extent that one cannot exist without the other. Moreover, moral conduct is the foundation, the infrastructure, for the elevation of the spirit. No spiritual improvement is possible without salutary conduct.

Traditionally, these fields have fallen within the domain of religion, and in contemporary society many of us have rightly distanced ourselves from religion. But suppose we had thrown out our reason and knowledge in a similar way—where would we be now? "Science without religion is lame," Albert Einstein said; "religion without science is blind." We need both.

The truth is that we have become alienated from our spirits. And this estrangement has progressed to such an extent that some of us even deny that we possess spirits at all. But the spirit is nothing other than that which animates the body. To say that spirit does not exist in a living being is like saying that a TV set can work without electricity. Suppose a man born blind came to you and said: "Eyesight cannot exist, because I have never experienced its existence." Would you believe him? In this vein, philosopher David Hume claimed that he had conducted lengthy introspection and could not find any trace of a human soul. But in order to find something, one first has to look in the proper place, and in the right way.

Here, a story told often in the Middle East may serve as further analogy. Nasruddin Hodja (also know as Mullah Nasruddin, the humorous sage of the Middle East) was once looking for something in the middle of the street. He was down on all fours, searching. A man who knew him came by, and asked him what he was looking for. "I've lost a key," the Hodja replied. So the man began to help him. After a while, though, unable to find anything, the man asked: "Hodja, where did you say you dropped the key?" "Down in the basement of my house," the Hodja said.

The man laughed. "Why, Hodja," he exclaimed, "in that case we're looking in the wrong place. Why aren't we looking in your basement instead?" "Ah," said the Hodja, "it's too dark in my basement. This is where the light is."

If we deny even the existence of the spirit, then we are certainly bound never to find it. If we believe that a thing does not exist, of course there is no need even to go looking for it, so the possibility of discovering—or recovering—it is reduced to zero. Those who haven't the slightest inkling of what the spirit is tell us: "Spirit does not exist," and we believe them. Those who haven't the slightest notion about God tell us God does not exist, and we believe them too. Clearly, if we choose a crow as guide, our noses are sure never to be free of mud.

Humans are amphibious creatures. We live in the material world with our body and in the spiritual world with our soul. A person shorn of one aspect cannot soar, any more than a bird with one wing can fly.

We have starved the heart of nourishment, until it has entered suspended animation, and we have denied sustenance to the spirit, until it has fallen into a coma. Yet the heart and the spirit, in spite of their apparent lifelessness, are neither dead nor nonexistent; they await our tender loving care in order to be revived—they live dormant, waiting for springtime.

Our material achievements are unmatched in recorded history, yet as a civilization, we have failed to complement our material progress with moral—and, by implication, spiritual—progress. We have conquered outer space whilst forgetting and deserting our inner space. And because we have failed to strike this balance, the whole edifice is trembling uncontrollably before our very eyes, as evidenced in even the everyday media.

What we witness today is the plaster falling from the ceiling. Those who can remember the last thirty years will not fail to recognize how we have regressed. Violence has spread throughout the world until there's no safe place left. What is needed is a *solution*. We need a methodology that can be practiced by everyone.

For the first time in history we have a civilization that is truly global. Furthermore, all the knowledge and, more importantly, all the wisdom distilled drop by golden drop by all the civilizations in history, are at our fingertips, if only we would choose to avail ourselves of them. We need a faith that is truly global to complete our global civilization—a faith that takes into account and coordinates all the religions of the past. In its absence, our metropolises and all our accomplishments will sink into a quicksand of violence, ruthlessness, and destruction.

We think that intelligence, which we value so highly, is centered in the mind. The Sufi sages, however, held (and continue to hold) a different view. Like the ancient Chinese and Egyptians, they considered true intelligence to be based in the heart; according to them all, the seat of the intellect was not the mind, nor indeed the heart alone, but the "heartmind." We have severed the connection between the mind and the heart, and as long as it is not reestablished, all our attempts to achieve wisdom will be in vain.

Many have lamented a world that has not only differentiated but polarized the mind and the heart, so that the two are mutually exclusive. This schizoid split between reason and emotion has yielded precisely what one would expect: uncontrolled oscillation between the poles of heartlessness and mindlessness. Either we have hard-boiled rationalism and science, which exclude affection and spirit altogether, or spiritualism and similar fringe beliefs, which require us to throw away our intellect. What we need is a harmonious synthesis of the mind and heart.

The emergence of fringe cults, soothsayers, and fortune-tellers calls to mind the end of another great civilization, that of Rome. Historians are still debating the reasons for the fall of Roman civilization, but the result was the Dark Ages. Today we cannot afford to give up our present civilization, for the cost would be far too great. If this civilization goes, humanity goes with it.

Can we have the best of both worlds? Can we both save this civilization, and carry it to loftier heights? The answer to both questions is yes.

In the hectic rush of contemporary society, few of us have the time or the resources to carry out a prolonged investigation of religions. For this reason, most of us rely on hearsay or superficial impressions in judging a religion. The problem is compounded by two other factors. First, the differences between religions are not matters on which the poorly informed layperson can easily pass judgment. And second, what a religion demands of its adherents and what those all-too-human adherents do in real life are two different things. The merits of a religion should be judged on the basis of its precepts, not on the failures or inabilities of its followers. Yet, at the same time, a religion should cause a noticeable improvement in the average person who practices it, something that may be difficult, though not impossible, to assess.

A religion may be broadly termed a system of beliefs. But if a person claims to believe one thing and yet acts otherwise, their actions speak louder than their words. As the Ottoman poet Ziya Pasha wrote,

Deeds are a person's mirror, mere claims do not heed;
The level of one's intellect is apparent in one's work.

If actions and beliefs are in synch with each other, then we can truly say that a person lives according to the lights of his or her faith. As Rumi, the mystic, rightly said: "Either appear as you are, or be as you appear to be."

In this book, I would like to give the reader a glimpse of a faith that, if implemented correctly, is a foolproof algorithm for success and happiness. If a person applies it properly, that person will succeed. If a nation applies it correctly, that nation will succeed. Look closely at people and nations that have been successful, and you will discover that they have applied a small subset of the precepts of this faith. Look at those that have failed, and you will find that they have failed to apply those precepts, even, in some cases, in spite of their claim to profess that very faith.

Untruth can only lead to error. Even those tenets which at first glance one would regard as metaphysical are true, for metaphysical principles, if pursued long enough, will lead to concrete outcomes in the physical world.[5]

By now many of us have experimented with a variety of religions and philosophies. Some have appealed to us more than others. Yet the comprehensive one still eludes us—or rather, we elude it. Many accounts of Sufism have been published in the West, but without taking into consideration the various cultural differences.

For a long time, our attention in the West has been focused on the religions and philosophies of the East. We have tried to temper the extreme rationalism, materialism, and mechanism of the West by the equally arid (because nontheistic) spirituality and asceticism of the East. Herein lies the crux of the problem. Aware that sitting at one end of the seesaw has landed us in a fix, we seek salvation by going overboard and trying to sit on the other end. But the seesaw will then be as unbalanced as it was originally. From the mind we seek to go over to the heart, yet the heart by itself is as helpless as the mind in isolation. *What is needed is a synthesis*—in order to balance the seesaw, we need to go over to the middle, not to one or the other extreme. We need a system that equally embraces our materiality and our spirituality; that synthesizes our hearts and our minds—and even then, without the presence of God the two are still empty. What we need is a synthesis, like that of hydrogen and oxygen, which combine to yield water—the sparkling water of life, a substance entirely different from oxygen or hydrogen taken alone. We need to fuse the best of the West with the best of the East. Today we have the opportunity to build on the best of our civilization—to become truly "civilized." And geographically as well, the solution between East and West is to be found in the Middle. As the Koran puts it, "a lamp... kindled from a Blessed Tree... an olive that is neither of the East nor of the West, whose oil wellnigh would shine, even if no fire touched it; Light upon Light" (24:35). And this light, because it belongs to neither, can illuminate both East and West. Islam is that light.

Prologue:
Rescuing Islam from the Hijackers
—————— ✳ ——————

Ignorance is the mother of all evils.
—MOHAMMED, THE PROPHET OF GOD[6]

The nafs—*or ego—is the ultimate terrorist.*
—ELIZABETH DEBOLD[7]

Never in Islam's entire history
has the action of so few of its followers
caused the religion and its community of believers
to be [perceived as] such an abomination in the eyes of others.
—ANWAR IBRAHIM[8]

How sad that all future historians will date the beginning of the twenty-first century—not to mention the third millennium—from September 11, 2001. And how sad that we should be forced to deal with those dreadful events in the context of Islam, a religion that ought to be as far removed from such vile deeds as day is from night.

In what follows I shall be concerned to show that the modern currents of so-called Islamism, fundamentalism and neo-fundamentalism (all of these labels pose semantic problems, but we have to start somewhere) are products of our times (of modernity and postmodernity). Furthermore, they are not merely products but offspring, in the sense that they bear the genetic traits of modernity and postmodernity. Thus, even as they are reflexive, i.e. arise as apparent reactions to (post)modernity, they also suffer from the same encumbrances that ail their parents. But at the root of all these movements is ignorance.

Marxism and the "Islamic State": The Omission of Spirituality

Nowhere is this ignorance more obvious than in the Islamists' approach to politics. Islam, traditional Islam, was never a political ideology. It addressed certain political issues, but only to the extent that they pertained to virtuous conduct. The problem with Marxism, a direct offshoot of modernity, is that it collapsed the spiritual dimension of religion directly onto the material. Because it had no eyes with which to see the spiritual, it interpreted religion as a solely material construct. Religion was nothing but a political ideology; its purpose was to manipulate people on the basis of its less provable claims.

Decades of communist propaganda in the twentieth century seem to have taken their toll on the leaders of Islamist movements, because, even if they do not share the jaundiced view of communism regarding the basic tenets of religion, they have finally, in effect, agreed with its conclusions. For them, Islam has become a political ideology.[9] It is both an instrument and goal of politics. It is to be used to attain power, and that power is to be used to fortify Islam. This is not much different from the position of communists vis-à-vis communism. Although the first great event in recent history to exemplify this was the Shiite revolution of Iran, Sunnis have not proved immune to the allure of this approach either. Other parallels between the so-called "Islamic revolution" and communism have been drawn, notably by Middle-East historian Bernard Lewis.

The vision of modern-day Islamists is thus one with all the spirituality bleached out. This is an error of such monumental proportions that it seems puzzling it has not been more widely remarked, although it has been noted by a few scholars such as William Chittick and Sachiko Murata, as shown here:

> Modernist Islam typically rejects the intellectual understanding of the tradition, unless it is posed in political terms...In some cases, the celebration of God's wrath and anger is used to justify methods of warfare—such as mass killing and terrorism—that are explicitly forbidden by the Shariah.[10]

Although Islam does have a social and legal aspect, a material and a public dimension, it is first of all a matter of private faith, personal observances, and inner growth. The claim that "in Islam, religion and politics cannot be separated" is a huge fallacy that cannot be substantiated from either the Koran or the Prophet's Way. Quite the contrary, they cannot be easily combined. In the Koran, in fact, God tells the Prophet quite explicitly: "You are only a reminder. You are not one to govern/rule over them" (88:21–22).[11]

The very concept of a "state" is extra-Koranic. Nor was there any state apparatus to speak of during the Prophet's lifetime, that Age of Bliss to which all fundamentalists yearn to return—which must make of them political anarchists in theory but totalitarians when it comes to practice, the same ailment that afflicted the communists. (To add a Sufic touch to the analysis, these are all modes the Base Self assumes in expressing itself, regardless of whether it is Marxists or Islamists who are involved.) Political structures worthy of being called a "state" developed later on. To compare the Prophet with ordinary political rulers is to radically misinterpret the office of prophethood. People obeyed the Prophet out of their own free will, because they were convinced of his authenticity. What the Prophet accomplished by love and gentle persuasion, the clueless seek to impose by force, as if coercion could ever substitute for love.

The total neglect of spirituality for the sake of political power and/or legalism actually serves the Marxist definition by making it come true. It reduces Islam to a political ideology, and while this may vindicate Marxism, it cuts the very basis of Islam out from under it. Fools rush in where angels fear to tread, and the attempt to fiddle with the basic parameters of a religion ends in the resounding failure of those who make the attempt. In the process, a harsh image of Islam has been projected that actually has nothing to do with the religion as taught by the Prophet, reflecting only the impoverished vision of its propounders.

Even if we accept that the "Islamists" (advocates of a politicized Islam)[12] are trying to come up with a response to the challenge of modernity, they are using the exclusively secularist tools of modernity to do so, which dooms their efforts from the start. (Nor am I against secularism per se, because the world is composed of both a material and a spiritual aspect. It is only when the material is emphasized to the total neglect of the spiritual that problems arise.)

In the social arena, most people seek guidance from their spiritual leaders, but they do not want a social straitjacket. What people want today is an algorithm (a set of instructions to achieve a certain purpose) that will help them answer the fundamental questions of existence, enable their spiritual growth, and guide them through the vicissitudes of life. This is exactly what Islam is and always has been, and it is precisely what the Islamists' version is not.

The Saint and the Terrorist

In some respects, Islamists are modernists. They share the "single vision" of modernity, its one-dimensionality, its "my version is true, all other versions are false" attitude. Whereas postmodernism, like the actual world, allows for many truths to coexist.

Traditional Islam sought to remake human beings in the image of God and the Koran. "In the traditional view, reform of society depended upon reform of the individual, and reform of the individual depended upon observance of Islam...Individual perfection was always connected with nearness to God, [i.e. with] actualizing the divine form within each and every person."[13] The Islamist project, instead, tries to remake the Koran in the image of the Islamists, who read whatever they like into or out of the Koran. What cannot be accepted is their totalistic claim that theirs is the only true reading, when in fact it is patently wrong. Their failure to see the multidimensional complexity/beauty/mystery of the world is the result of ignorance, but if we don't help them disabuse themselves of this ignorance, we risk falling into the same pit with them.

The highest goal of Islam is to produce the Perfect Human Being, the spiritually enlightened individual, who is the dazzling incarnation of divine qualities, in whom all human potentialities have flowered to perfection. The highest stage of enlightenment is the realization of "unity in diversity, diversity in unity"—all are One and One is all. God created the entire universe out of love, giving existence to a dizzying variety of beings.

At the level of mundane truth (referred to as the "realm of Multiplicity" by the Sufis, i.e., the ordinary world in which we find ourselves), no two things are identical. Physicists have shown that you cannot clone even a photon—i.e., make an exact copy of a particle of light.[14] All creatures are unique, and this uniqueness needs to be respected precisely because God created them that way. As the Turkish Sufi poet Yunus said, "Because of the Creator, be tolerant to the creature." But whereas the enlightened human being—the Perfect Human of Islam—loves and cherishes all, despite their individual failings and errors, the fundamentalists cannot tolerate any other view except their own. They cannot accommodate the multidimensionality, plurality, or democracy that are the true legacy of Islam. To see this, one need look no further than the mutual respect the founders and followers of the Four Schools of jurisprudence have had for each other.

Opposites come into being together, so it was perhaps inevitable that they gave rise to their mirror image, the "axis of evil" approach: "You're either with us or against us." It needs to be understood that both sides are ultimately using the same phrase. It is to the extent we can transcend this dichotomy that we will be able to avoid being engulfed by the black hole that now tugs at us.

A polarization has occurred so that each side regards its opposite as the "radical other," and this way lies madness. Here is where the highest reaches of Islamic mysticism can help us to heal the breach. We must ask each group to contemplate the following question: "Why do you see only the other—when there is no other!" One wonders whether they are finding fault with God.

If pluralism (at the level of Multiplicity) were not part of the Divine Order, God would not have employed it in creating the universe. This is stated clearly in the Koran: "If your Lord had willed, He would have made humankind a single nation, but they will not cease to be diverse... And for this God created [humankind]" (11:118-9), and "O humankind! We created you from a male and a female[15] and made you into nations and tribes that you may know each other [not that you may despise each other]" (49:13). What a joyful celebration of diversity these verses portend, if one but reflects!

Moreover, at the level of higher truth (ultimate Unity), the Other is Us. So a bit more compassion (coupled with humility) is required—on both sides. This stance would breed better self- and mutual understanding, and begin to eradicate the roots of error. All sides should heed the words of the great Sufi poet Niyazi Misri:

I used to think that in the world, no friends were left for me
I left my me behind and knew: no others[16] are left for me.

Taliban, bin Laden, and the Wahhabis

Earlier, fundamentalism was characterized by the desire of some Moslems to create Islamic states in their own countries. We could say that it all began with Ayatollah Khomeini in Iran and his call for Islamic revolution. After his initial success in 1979, Iran attempted to export its revolution abroad. Similar to Trotsky's view of Russian communism, it was theorized that the "Islamic revolution" would spread geographically to other Moslem countries. This did not happen, partly because Iran was Shiite, a sect which constitutes a minority of ten percent among the world's Moslems.

But while the revolution did not spread, the ideas engendered by it found an echo even in some Sunni circles.[17] The notion of an Islamic state, ruled in accordance with *sharia* law, proved too attractive to be dismissed out of hand. So it was that Islamic movements spread to obtain political power, by peaceful means where possible and violent means where not.

By about 1996, however, the forces of political Islam were spent. They had not been able to win trust or attain power, and even the Iranian revolution was deteriorating. It was at this stage that a strain of fundamentalism appeared which, though superficially the same as what went before, on closer inspection reveals traits that necessitate distinguishing it from its predecessor. Olivier Roy, the shrewd observer of political Islam, has termed this new current "neo-fundamentalism," and I concur with him that a new label does seem called for. Whereas the older fundamentalism belonged to the age of modernity, neo-fundamentalism appears to be a product of, and reaction to, conditions of the postmodern world, especially to post-colonialism and globalization.

I would like to summarize the salient points made by Roy regarding this new phenomenon. First, it is based on Wahhabism, founded by one Abdel Wahhab who lived in the eighteenth century, calling for a rigid application of the *sharia* and a return to the Golden Age of the Prophet. Second, Roy links it to deculturization. One of the consequences of globalization has been the capitulation of entire cultures before the onslaught of the dominant material culture, especially in its American incarnation.

Suffering the effects of post-colonial instability and under further threat from the massive inroads made into all cultures by the development of the global market economy (which has become synonymous with *Western* culture in most people's minds), many Moslems have become uprooted, culturally dispossessed. Flung worldwide by the slingshots of outrageous fortune, they have found themselves strangers in strange lands that have filled them with existential *angst*. They now fear for their very faith: in their view, their religion is on the verge of being swamped by Western culture.

As a response to this deculturization and loss of identity, even exile, the neo-fundamentalists have come up with a minimalist package of global utility. This first-aid kit is limited to specific obligatory life rules prescribed by the *sharia*. This simple set of rules is intended to be applicable everywhere—in the Asian wilderness or at an American college. We are faced with a version of Islam that favors a puritan and literal reading of the Koran, that is privatized rather than sociopolitical as was the earlier fundamentalism. According to Roy: "This neo-fundamentalism wants only to impose the *sharia* as the norm of all human and social behavior…It defines the whole world as a virtual *umma* [religious community] that only asks to be realized through the engagement of all Muslims…[It aims at] the reconstitution of one universal Muslim community…Insisting on the *umma*, [the neo-fundamentalists] effectively address a universality lived by Muslims who identify neither with a territory nor with one specific nation."[18] After all, as a world religion, Islam is capable of accommodating this aspect of globalization.

But this reduction of the religion to its simple basics also has the effect of fostering a black-and-white approach. A superficial literalist/"textual" reading of the Koran leads to a view where the differences between self and other—"us versus them"—are accentuated rather than diminished. This reduced version of Islam yields negative results when coupled with ignorance and frustration. What counts isn't just what you find in a religion, it's also what kind of baggage you bring to it—the *quality and depth* of your understanding.

Roy is careful to point out that neo-fundamentalism does not automatically lead to terrorism. Nevertheless, this state of affairs provides fertile ground for both. According to Roy, neo-fundamentalism becomes prone to violent action when it is radicalized by anti-imperialist discourse.

(It should be mentioned in this context that Roy sees bin Laden as an anti-imperialist. If the fundamentalists earlier seemed to be speaking the language of Marx, the neo-fundamentalists thus appear to have progressed to the discourse of Lenin.)[19]

A Hybrid Ideology Causing Cultural Schizophrenia

To all this, Malise Ruthven adds the detail that the "Islam" of the terrorists is actually a hybrid strain spliced with modern Western memes (cultural "genes"), leading to religious and cultural schizophrenia:

> This was far from being the received Islam or what scholars of religion call "cumulative tradition," but a brand-new, invented Islam that drew on selected elements of this tradition but also incorporated, without acknowledgement, many "western" ideas—from the revolutionary puritanism of Robespierre to the "propaganda of the deed" advocated by the Baader-Meinhof gang.[20]

Clearly, revolutionary elements from the Western cultural tradition have been grafted onto a reduced version of Islam, and the result is a chimera. The components are incompatible: atheism and hatred are being mixed in with religion and love. (*The Revolutionary Catechism* [1869]—written by Sergei Nechayev, the first modern nihilist who was also the inspiration for Dostoyevsky's *The Devils*—alone is proof enough of this.) It is inevitable that either of the two sides should cave in.

Further, revolution itself is about politics. And where there is talk of war, one need only remember Clausewitz's dictum that "War is a continuation of politics by other means" to again discern politics not far behind.

Take the *Al Qaeda Training Manual,* for instance, which blends episodes from Islamic history with CIA covert operation methods.[21] It looks like something straight out of a South American guerrilla handbook of the 1970s. The way the Islamic component is used has been termed "wooden language" by experts for the case of communist propaganda—that is, exhortative and manipulative language that aims to control the reader's behavior in a certain way. It seeks not to enlighten but to robotize, surreptitiously subverting the clear Koranic verse, "There is no compulsion in religion" (2:256). (As my Master asked me shortly before his demise, "You've been with me for fifteen years. Have you ever seen me give an order to anybody?" He never went beyond gentle suggestion on any topic.) Politics is the main concern, religion is important only to the extent that it can be used to further political goals. What has all this got to do with Islam? Islam itself is being abused and victimized here. The terrorists use it only as a pretext to achieve their political goals by inhuman means. The *Manual* also discloses the political agenda: "to establish a caliphate." We shall soon have occasion to deal with this subject in greater depth.

Anti-Culture, Anti-Civilization

We have said that globalization brings with it a dissemination of the dominant world culture, i.e., Western culture with a progressively increasing American tinge. Whereas American culture and traditional Islam are pluralistic, however, the neo-fundamentalists are profoundly nihilistic. Where the "melting pots" of the former welcome all cultures, the vision of the newcomers tolerates none, including their own. This is a blatant contradiction in view of the fact that their ideology itself tacitly incorporates elements of modern culture. Thus, as Roy points out,

> Transforming Islam into a mere system of behavior norms, refusing all that concerns culture in favor of an emergent Islamic code adaptable to any situation, from the Afghan desert to the American campus, neo-fundamentalism is simultaneously a product and an agent of modern deculturization. The Islam of the Taliban, like Saudi Wahhabism or the radicalism of bin Laden, is hostile to all that concerns culture, even Islamic culture: from the destruction of the Prophet's tomb [attempted in 1925 by] the Wahhabis to that of the Buddha statues in Bamyan or the Twin Towers of New York, the refusal of every concept of civilization and culture is again found constantly...[22]

From people who show such singular disrespect towards their own Prophet, it is futile to expect courtesy for anyone or anything else. Indeed, the views of al-Qaeda and the Taliban, in Afghanistan, are also predicated on Wahhabism. All three may be considered under the more general term of Salafism, in which the Age of Bliss, the period of Mohammed's rule in Medina, is held up as a puritan and utopian social ideal. There is, of course, a deep contradiction in trying to eradicate all memory of the Prophet while simultaneously trying to resurrect the "ideal society" of his time, just as there is in reducing his tolerant religion to a totalitarian ideology. If there is one lesson the history of the twentieth century has taught us, it is that all utopian projects seem to be plagued by the totalitarian temptation, and this one is similarly crippled.

Interpreting the Koran:
Omission of the Prophet's Example

One of the problems confronting the neo-fundamentalists is that they wish to read the Koran and make sense of it without recourse to the Prophet's example. But the Koran itself discourages such an approach, stating that the Prophet should be loved and taken as role model, for it was he, before and beyond all others, who gave living expression to the written word of the Koran. Leave him out and you leave out a crucial ingredient, because everyone will then interpret the Koran in their own way: like Protestantism, there will be hundreds of different denominations. The sorry state which they will then end in is only too apparent from the deeds of those already extant. Thus do those who set out to return to the original purity of the Koran end up in an altogether different space.

As a matter of fact, behind every attempt to divest the Prophet from his rightful place as role model in Islam, we may discern the Base Self of the party involved trying to elevate itself to that role: "There is no god but God, I (whoever that "I" is) am the Prophet of God"—*I* am the model, what *I* say is true. Removal of the Prophet—even partially—creates a void, and the Base Self rushes in to fill that void. Overt or covert repudiation of the Prophet is where everything goes wrong, never to be straightened out again. This is why the Way of the Prophet is second in importance only to the Koran itself. It is the one protection against a disease that has infected many claiming to speak in the name of Islam in recent decades.

Moslems are not free to interpret the Koran according to their own whim. (This is not meant to deny freedom of independent judgment in ambiguous matters, but rather to affirm that there is no need for it in unambiguous areas.) They must do so on the basis of the Prophet's words and deeds. The Prophet was a *well-rounded* character, full of wisdom, tolerance, and love. It is his character and judgment informed by real presence that is the crucial changing factor. *This* is what matters. And it is where any *political* project founders, for the latter tries to usurp that goal, to take its place. In its ethical—and most important—dimension, the *sharia* is the path that leads to the induction of the Prophet's noble character traits in every Moslem, that leads them to emulate and ultimately exhibit superb conduct. If it does not yield this result, something must have gone wrong with the process. We have documented evidence of the Prophet's behavior with which to judge such self-proclaiming Moslems. But of course, these days Moslems seem to be as unaware of such facts as non-Moslems, since ignorance is rampant everywhere.

Further, there is a magisterial tradition reaching back to the beginning in which those more knowledgeable spent lifetimes in the study and contemplation of such matters. To disregard this vast resource and to strike out on one's own is reckless. This path can only lead to disaster, because hungry wolves lie in wait for stray sheep. The epigraph above by the Prophet explains why the ignorant are so hell-bent on trying to destroy his legacy. For, in designing a minimal package, they have undercut the subtleties of the Koran and jettisoned the baby with the bathwater. Little do they realize that in doing so, they are destroying Islam itself. Roy denies the Huntingtonian claim[23] that all this has anything to do with a "clash of civilizations":

> [T]he neo-fundamentalists are simultaneously agents of deculturization related to globalization, and a consequence of this globalization. While endeavoring to define a pure religious identity, exclusive of any cultural influence, they allow the uprooted Moslem, the product of globalization, to build an identity adaptable to all societies, because detached from the idea of society. The modernity of bin Laden is this hatred of culture and of history, it is this Islam in kit form, exportable to the desert of

Kandahar or to the suburbs of New Jersey (...) [F]or the neo-fundamentalists, there is no Islamic culture: they are the first destroyers of all Islamic culture (...) If bin Laden and Mullah Omar as well are heralds of the death of culture, they are initially heralds of all death. They are far from incarnating a clash of civilizations, because they kill their own civilization.[24]

In his choice of the concept "hatred," Roy has, perhaps inadvertently, put his finger on the crux of the matter. For the heart of all religion is love, and Islam being a religion, its essence too is love. Hate is an emotion that is egotistical and diabolical, and as soon as you begin to mix poison in your soup, it becomes inedible. The destruction of the Twin Towers, the slaughter of innocent thousands, can only be informed by a massive hatred, and this is precisely the point where the terrorists forfeit their right to speak in the name of religion—not just Islam but *any* religion.

The Seeds of Mistrust

In *The Consequences of Modernity* (1990), Anthony Giddens pointed out that one of the salient properties of modernity is trust. In a highly specialized, technological society such as America, there has to be implicit trust in "the expert," whether this be a doctor, engineer, lab technician, or even a cab driver. Moreover, most of the transactions of the global market economy are based on trust. Even on the Internet, millions of orders are routinely tossed into a limbo called "cyberspace," with the implicit trust that the purchased article will materialize in the mail a few days later.

It is this trust, without which modernity would be much diminished if not abolished entirely, that the terrorists have sabotaged. They have engendered a crisis of confidence in American society, and in this respect their influence has been deeply subversive. Reactions bordering on the paranoid have not failed to manifest themselves. While they have not succeeded in destroying the tolerant, hard-working, and good-hearted nature of most Americans, the damage inflicted on trust is continuing to lead to increased security measures that endanger civil liberties and may yet spell doom for democracy.

But if the terrorists are anti-modern in the context of trust, how "Islamic" can their influence be regarded as? Because Islam and all authentic religions place a premium on trust—on trusting others and being trustworthy oneself. Even before he became a prophet, Mohammed was known by his nickname "the Trustworthy." And the Master always instructed us: "Don't deceive, don't be deceived." The Moslem has traditionally been defined as "That person from whose hands, tongue, and sexuality other people are safe."

One of the reasons why America is the most modern nation in the world is because it is also deeply religious, in certain ways representing the best aspects of the Judeo-Christian heritage. When they dive-bombed trust and honesty, then, the terrorists targeted not just modernity but all three monotheisms, which are at one—and, unsurprisingly, entirely in accord with modernity—in these respects.

Indeed, a prominent reason why Moslems in many countries have met the 9/11 attacks with rank disbelief—attributing the events to the CIA, Mossad, or some similar high-level conspiracy—is because being Moslems themselves, and knowing what being a Moslem entails, they are absolutely convinced that such acts cannot be perpetrated by one of their kind. These go against such deep grains of Moslem sensibility that they have refused to even consider the possibility, taking refuge in conspiracy theories instead.

Fascism or Democracy?

Eliminate spirituality, substitute politics for that, cut out the Prophet's example, erase genuine Islamic culture and civilization—enlivened by the presence of the Prophet—eradicate love and substitute hate, and where do you end up? A story of Nasruddin Hodja that is well-known in the Middle East, a variation on the bed of Procrustes, seems a good analogy for fundamentalist attempts to transform Islam: Nasruddin saw a hawk for the first time, but his previous experience of birds had been confined to sparrows. "You poor bird," he said, and proceeded to trim off its beak, talons, and feathers. "That's better," said Nasruddin viewing his masterpiece when he was done, "now you look more like a bird."

In like manner, the self-styled "vanguards" of Islam have succeeded only in pruning it into a "bird." If they keep it up, soon nothing much will be left. The irony is that this is being done by the same people who sincerely wish to return to the "days of old, days of gold." In other words, the people who should be in the forefront in opposing an "Islamic Reformation" are precisely the ones who are unwittingly carrying it out.

The fundamentally anti-culture stance of the neo-fundamentalists is reminiscent of the stance of Nazi General Hermann Goering, who was very fond of the phrase: "When I hear the word 'culture' [and hence of fully developed, cultured, individuals—like the Prophet], I reach for my gun."[25] Here is yet another link to what has been designated as "Islamic fascism."[26]

Throughout history, there have been many faces of Islam. Lamentably, some versions have been less palatable than others. This is why strict adherence to the Prophet's example is needed, but it is often other things to which people "strictly" adhere.

Fortunately, these other forms of Islam are no more than a small minority: as the Prophet himself said, "My community will never unite on an error." Recent research has shown that in the support of democratic ideals, "there is minimal difference between the Islamic world and the West."[27] This is another argument against Samuel Huntington's "clash of civilizations and/or cultures." The egalitarianism inherent in Islam even places the Islamic world ahead of the West in some respects: as the study concludes, "contrary to Huntington's thesis, compared with Western societies, support for democracy was marginally slightly *stronger* (not weaker) among those living in Islamic societies."

The Purpose of *Jihad*

Where, one might ask, do the Islamist movements want to go? What is their goal? There does not seem to be a single unified aim, precisely because they are so diverse and sometimes even at odds with each other. But we can gain insight into one of their approaches by examining the "last will" of Ayman al-Zawahiri, the right-hand man of Osama bin Laden. A battle-hardened warrior who has waged a long campaign against the Egyptian government, Zawahiri has no conception of the war ever ending, as illustrated below:

> [T]he earth-shattering event, which the West trembles at the mere thought of[,] is the establishment of an Islamic caliphate in Egypt.

If God wills it, such a state in Egypt, with all its weight in the heart of the Islamic world, could lead the Islamic world in a *jihad* against the West. It could also rally the world Muslims around it. Then history would make a new turn…

[The *jihad*ist] Islamic movement will not triumph against the world coalition unless it possesses a fundamentalist base in the heart of the Islamic world.

The establishment of a Muslim state in the heart of the Islamic world is not an easy goal or an objective that is close at hand. But it constitutes the hope of the Muslim nation to reinstate its fallen caliphate and regain its lost glory.…

Liberating the Muslim nation, confronting the enemies of Islam, and launching *jihad* against them require a Muslim authority, established on a Muslim land, that raises the banner of *jihad* and rallies the Muslims around it. Without achieving this goal our actions will mean nothing more than mere and repeated disturbances that will not lead to the aspired goal, which is the restoration of the caliphate and the dismissal of the invaders from the land of Islam.[29]

This extract distills the essential thought of Zawahiri: one first does battle in order to establish an Islamic state and reinstate the caliphate, preferably in Egypt, and then the caliphate wages war against the West. Since the latter is identified with a world coalition, this in effect means a *jihad* against the whole world.

This is just plain wrong. First, because it is immoral according to the teachings of Islam. In Arabic, *ahlaq,* which derives from *hulq,* means ethics, innate constitution, and character traits. That is, perfect ethics are synonymous with praiseworthy character traits, which are those of the Prophet. Now the Prophet (1) never declared *jihad* against the whole world, and (2) opted for peace whenever possible. In fact, his invitations to the Eastern Roman Emperor Heraclius, the Persian Emperor Kavadh and the Chinese Emperor Taizong all had the purpose of securing peace on earth. Hence, such an action is Islamically immoral because it does not square with the example of the Prophet.

Second, it is wrong because it is not one of the requirements of being a Moslem. And third, because it goes against the message of Islam, whose very name means "peace" or, more correctly, "pacification" ("surrender" to God being one of the meanings of "Islam"). Hence, a proper Moslem is nonviolent, peaceable, and amiable. Such a person wouldn't even—consciously and willingly—step on an ant.

Further, global *jihad* is nothing but a pipedream, since no single power, not even America or China, could win a war against the rest of the world. So what we have is a senseless war without end, with terrible loss on all sides and with no well-defined feasible goal in sight. The lives of untold Moslems and non-Moslems are to be thrown away for nothing but the personal grudge of some people. Their vindictive agenda has already made life more difficult for millions of human beings, with Moslems—supposedly their brethren—suffering the greatest loss. As for the "invaders" (U.S. troops in Saudi Arabia), they are in "the land of Islam" almost by invitation, because Saddam invaded Kuwait in 1990. They are not an occupying force. Thus, truth and falsehood become confused in a delusion that would sweep all before it.

The Caliphate

The resurrection of the caliphate is a desire that seems close to the heart of some Moslems, including Osama bin Laden.[30] According to recent reports, he intends to establish an Islamic empire and caliphate by destabilizing and toppling the secular regimes in Central Asia.[31] (Guess who the next caliph is going to be?) The goal of al-Qaeda itself is to "unite all Muslims and to establish a government which follows the rule of the Caliphs."[32] This is the reason why they are waging war. After the expulsion of the former Soviet Union from Afghanistan, this is the new pastime the former *mujahideen* have found for themselves.

The caliphate was formally abolished in 1924, and sufficient time has now elapsed that people with a short sense of history regard it in a rosy hue of nostalgia. But what *was* the caliphate, actually?

Let us first attempt to understand what the caliphate (as a concept) is *not*. It is *not* the Islamic counterpart of the Papacy, and a Caliph would not be the equivalent of the Pope. The reason is that there is no clergy in

Islam, no spiritual bureaucracy with its own hierarchy. So the caliphate, contrary to the conceptions of many Moslems and non-Moslems alike, has nothing to do with *spiritual* authority, although of course it was always venerated.

Rather, the caliphate is a *political* institution. It is like the presidency in modern nation-states. The caliph is the political leader of the world's Moslems and the head of their state. Note how this differs from the Papacy. One has to have a geographically contiguous country in which all the Moslems live, and a society with a single state. The caliph is then the person at the helm of such a state. Following the time of the Prophet, as well as for a long time afterwards, it was a viable institution, and fulfilled its purpose historically.[33]

The Prophet himself foresaw the end of the caliphate, saying: "After me, the caliphate is thirty years." This was the period of the Four Rightly-Guided Caliphs, the only true period of the caliphate. After that, it continued until 1258, when the Mongols sacked Baghdad. And then it survived until 1924, more as a nominal title than an actual force. Long before, caliphs had fallen under the influence of military leaders, and it was only the power of the Ottoman sultans that gave the institution an added lease on life. At one point, there were two or three caliphs ruling simultaneously across the Islamic world, just as there were two or three contending Popes in Christianity at a certain time.

But what of today? Moslems are spread all over the world, and the unit of political organization today is the nation-state. Now if the so-called "Moslem countries" were to form some kind of federation, and then to elect a chief executive with powers to govern and represent them all, then perhaps one might be justified in calling that leader a "caliph." But short of that—and it is a long, long way off—there is no sense at all in discussing a caliphate. No nation-state is about to surrender its authority to a single person, especially anyone from a different nationality. It's that simple.

Besides, what purpose would it serve? What led to the abolition of the caliphate in the first place was the fact that it had outlived its historical purpose, and it had fallen into a position of great weakness as a result. Those who desire caliphal rule have great expectations, perhaps a return to the glory and grandeur of its heydays, yet in the end it was not able to save even itself. In short, the caliphate died of old age. What would be gained by exhuming the corpse?

Nowhere among the injunctions of Islam is there a requirement to create an Islamic superstate. There is no reason—deriving either from the Koran or the Prophet—that compels a Moslem to work toward such a goal.

This discussion leads to the following conclusion: the issue of the caliphate is but another attempt to reduce Islam to a political ideology. The wish to resurrect the caliphate is a case of political powerlust, and a misplaced one at that. Indeed, the reason why the period of Rightly-Guided Caliphs ended was because the fifth caliph fell victim to precisely this temptation of worldly power, in effect replacing the caliphate (based on appointment by a committee) with monarchy and dynastic rule. ("Ali invited to Islam," said the Master, whereas his opponents "invited to the Base Self [to egoism].") Modern-day Islamists ought to stop using Islam as an instrument for their political purposes and start obeying it as the religion it is instead.

Obtaining state power is not a panacea, a cure-all, as the communists eventually found out and the mullahs of Iran are discovering. Islam will be strengthened, not by building an Islamic state or superstate, but by more diligent faith and practice on the part of its adherents, including those who fancy they're serving the religion by politicizing it. This is simply ignorance, and the first step necessary is to shed ignorance.

From its very beginnings down to the Iranian experiment, the history of Islam demonstrates that religion and politics do not mix well. Whenever there has been a close encounter of Islam with politics, Islam has emerged bruised and battered from that encounter. There is always a Machiavellian streak to politics and Islam gets obscured by that cynicism.[34] The real thrust of Islam must always be ethics: as the Prophet said, "I came to perfect character traits." No particular political project is *required* by Islam in any way.

There are others besides bin Laden who covet the position of caliph. As the Master observed, "One [only] becomes Caliph with [outstanding] ethics. Without ethics, one will be Pharaoh." As a rule, all recent candidates share the "endearing" characteristic that the less worthy they are to become caliph, the more fervently they crave that title. If one of them succeeds, Moslems at some future date may well be forced to adopt the motto, "History is a nightmare from which I am trying to awake."[35] These errants would build their caliphate over the corpses of thousands of innocent victims, including Moslems, their brothers according to Divine Law. How can one expect any good spin-off from the dawn that follows such a night?

Some Moslems may look at the Pope and long for a comparable high-profile spiritual leader, but the caliph is not that leader, and everyone is actually better off without such a leader. We must never forget that the essence of Islam is direct communion between the individual and God—there is no need to import a churchlike hierarchy and its political agenda into a religion where these were banned from the first day.

The Place of Religious Law

There are those who say, "Islam is a total system, it has an answer for everything, including politics." No! Islam is not a total system, it is primarily an *ethical* system. More precisely, it is a method to obtain happiness and peace in both this world and the next. Islamic law developed because it was deemed proper to have laws based on Godly ethics.

Religious law had nothing to do with politics. Its development was the affair of civil society, not of the state, and hence it was a sociological and not a political phenomenon. (I follow Immanuel Wallerstein in describing sociology as the study of civil society.) The learned scholars or legists always tried to hold those in power at arm's length because they feared the purity of religious law would be compromised. Lord Acton's principle, "Power corrupts," was well understood. The sovereigns (secular lawgivers, including the caliphs) and those who derived religious laws (by which the sovereign was also bound) were two distinct entities in Islam—a kind of "separation of powers" and "separation of religion and state" arising from ethical necessity, long before Montesquieu separated powers for the West in 1748. This represents a divergence from the Western way of doing things, where law-making was exclusively the province of the state. The *sharia* was more of a cultural institution—a civilizing influence—than a penal code, informing the conduct and homogenizing the customs of civil societies throughout the Islamic world. Here, for example, is the testimony of Joseph Schacht, one of the foremost authorities on Islamic law in the West:

> In the field of penal law, it is easy to understand that the Qur'an laid down sanctions for transgressions, but again they are *essentially moral and only incidentally penal,* so much so that the Qur'an prohibited wine-drinking but did not enact any penalty, and the penalty was determined only at a later stage of Islamic law...This feature of Qur'anic legislation was preserved by Islamic law, and the purely legal attitude, which attaches legal consequences to relevant acts, is often superseded by [moral exhortation—] the tendency to impose ethical standards on the believer....Islamic law is in the first place concerned with laying down ethical rules for the behaviour of the individual...it was weakest, and in some respects even non-existent, on penal law...[36] (Emphasis added.)

When religion and politics are mixed, religion inevitably becomes politicized. The state then becomes both the maker and the enforcer of religious law. This is why those who long for a *sharia* state are mistaken. Even in classical Islamic society, the state did not have a say in legislating religious law. It is best to maintain this separation. If the state—as the possessor of legitimized violence—is granted that power, it will be expanding its domain at the expense of civil society, and the result will be abominations of the kind we have all beheld in some so-called "Islamic" countries.

It is expedient in our day to return to emphasizing the ethical over the legal aspect of the Divine Law, just as it used to be—to stress that it provides private guidelines for each individual conscience. If religion does not find a place in hearts, it will find no place at all, as witness the alienation of the Iranian people by the strictures of mullahs imposed from above.[37]

Misinterpreting the Koran

The way in which the extremists interpret the Koran and the concept of *jihad* (meaning "struggle" in general, but also "war") is likewise of interest. First, note that according to the Koran (4:75, 22:39-40), *jihad* is war *against religious persecution.* It should not be treated as implying any and every kind of war in general. The famous Turkish Islamic scholar Ahmet Hamdi Yazir has noted that *jihad* is waged for freedom of religion, so that the Koranic verse, "There is no compulsion in religion" (2:256) may be satisfied.

All those seemingly suspect verses opponents usually quote from the Koran need to be read in this context, plus the dangers facing the Prophet in his time. They all need to be evaluated in the light of the following verses: "God does not forbid you from friendship with those who do not wage war against you because of (your) religion, who do not evict you from your homes (on account of that), from dealing kindly and justly with them; for God loves those who are just. God only forbids friendship with those who fight you for (your) faith..." (60:8-9). In other words, do not make friends with enemies of your religion who fight against you. You can be friends with anyone else. Here is the ultimate criterion for *jihad:* is someone forcing you to abandon your religion, or not? Are you being subjected to forced religious conversion? Obviously, then, *jihad* in the Koranic sense is neither ordinary war, nor a war of conquest, nor mass murder, nor terrorism.

Second, verse 5:32 unequivocally declares: "One who [unjustly] kills a person has killed all humankind, and one who saves a person has saved all humankind." Furthermore, many of the verses regarding warfare in the Koran are concluded (or followed) by statements of the kind: "If they desire to make peace with you, seek not a way against them." In the face of the Prophet's known rules of combat, such as sparing women and children, men of religion and property, it is impossible to see how the Koran could be misappropriated to support terrorism of any sort.

One in-depth study has asked the question: "How does Osama bin Laden interpret the Koran?" As sources, it uses bin Laden's long, three-part "Declaration of War" (October 12, 13, and 14, 1996) and his so-called *fatwa,* the "World Islamic Front's Statement Urging Jihad Against Jews and Crusaders" (February 23, 1998). I will not burden you with the details, but go directly to the conclusion: "Bin Laden's reasoning depends upon two techniques: (1) taking parts of Qur'anic verses out of context [e.g. by omitting their lenient conclusions] and (2) defining the enemy and the enemy's supporters, actions, and property in such a way as to include them in the category that deserves the very worst of punishments...He accepts Faraj's and Ibn Taymiyyah's assertion that *jihad* is more important than anything except belief in God, and that allows him to define away what most Muslim legal scholars consider to be war crimes, such as the killing of noncombatants."[38] Only a feat of mental sleight-of-hand can yield a rabbit where there is none. (It may be noted that Ibn Taymiyyah's works are happy hunting grounds for Islamic extremists of all stripes.)

Any such attempt to reinterpret the Koran according to one's own lights yields a lesson in self-delusion. Where does someone who has no credentials as an Islamic scholar find the audacity to issue a *fatwa*? How can such a *fatwa* be the diametrical opposite of clear statements in the Koran? If this path is opened, what is to prevent anyone from issuing *fatwas* right and left? Or is it their purpose to open such a path? Is the intention to drag the world of Islam, if not into *jihad,* then at least into chaos? One is justified in asking such questions when surreal atrocities are being justified in the name of such *fatwas.* Therefore, I strongly urge the non-Moslem reader to use the character of the Prophet to judge such individuals before accepting the idea that all who speak in the name of Islam are *truly* speaking in the name of God.

Not a single Islamic authority of note condoned the events of 9/11. After 1517, the Ottoman sultans were both sultan and caliph, which made them (for a while) the most powerful rulers on earth. Yet *even they,* when they needed a religious ruling (*fatwa*), did not issue one themselves but applied to the Sheikh of Islam, who was the person properly authorized in such matters. The perpetrators of 9/11 invested themselves with an authority which not even the caliphs or sultans enjoyed—a situation that graphically demonstrates what happens when you try to mix religion with politics in the crucible of ignorance. If they had consulted the best—or even mediocre—Islamic scholars instead of trying to write their own *fatwa,* they would have avoided falling into error. They have no notion of legitimacy or due procedure of law, since they play the judge, the jury, the prosecutor, and the executioner rolled into one. This alone is enough to disqualify them from pronouncing on legal matters.

The events of 9/11 violate so many ethical principles in or out of Islam that one scarcely knows where to begin. Take just a single pronouncement of the Prophet: "Don't kill any living thing by burning it alive." Now picture not just any living thing but a human being, and not just one human being but scores of them, being roasted alive in a thousand-degree furnace of jetliner fuel. (See where we're headed when we omit the Prophet?) Let's get this straight once and for all: Islam does not support terrorism, and terrorists do not represent Islam. Even the very suggestion is abominable.

Terrorism as Nihilism

The more extreme extremists become, the further away they move from the vast majority of "the people of the Middle Way" (*ummatan wasatan*). As Gilles Kepel—another astute observer of fundamentalism—has noted, their very success in committing extremist acts betrays the way in which they marginalize themselves: their actual failure to rally widespread support, to offer anything substantial to the masses.

The blatantly nihilistic streak in the events of 9/11 did not escape the attention of either Moslems or non-Moslems. Muhammad Khatami, the president of Iran, was one of the first to express it in the clearest terms:

> [W]hat we are witnessing in the world today is an active form of nihilism in social and political realms that threatens the very fabric of human existence...Vicious terrorists who concoct weapons out of religion are superficial literalists clinging to simplistic ideas. They are utterly incapable of understanding that, perhaps inadvertently, they are turning religion into the handmaiden of the most decadent ideologies. While terrorists purport to be serving the cause of religion and accuse all those who disagree with them of heresy and sacrilege, they are serving the very ideologies they condemn....[39]

Suicide is prohibited by Islam as a form of murder—it is self-murder (its German equivalent, *selbstmord*, is quite revealing), no matter for what purpose, and is sharply distinguished from martyrdom. To be slain by the will of God and to slay oneself along with others by one's own will are two different things. God's commandment in the Koran is: "Believers, do not kill (or destroy) yourselves" (4:29). The fundamentally un-Islamic nature of suicide attacks is underlined in the following words: "The idea that martyrdom is a pure act of worship, pleasing to God, irrespective of God's specific command, is a terrifying new kind of nihilism."[40]

Suicide attacks are not just un-Islamic, they are profoundly anti-Islamic. Historically, they had no place at all in Islamic culture. Suicide bombing was invented by other parties and began to be used by so-called "Moslems" only during the last two decades. Its use in the Middle East is due not to a religious but to a territorial, i.e. political, dispute. Religion is not the topmost concern on the minds of those who advocate it. Once again, this is robbing religion to pay politics. Along with other social aberrations such as serial killing, the suicide attack is distinctly a phenomenon of postmodern times. This drastic departure from what has been the Islamic norm for fourteen centuries can only be explained by a lack or distortion—not an excess—of Islamic sensibility.

> The new *jihad* is not only apocalyptic; it is nihilistic. Osama bin Laden's statement that his men love death as much as the Americans love life is an expression of superb nihilism. The eroticization of death…by the destruction of one's own body in an act of supreme violence which dismembers and pulverizes it, is remarkable…As many Koranic scholars have pointed out, there is no theological justification for this: it is one thing to die in war and yet another to make the destruction of one's body along with those of others the supreme weapon.[41]

In his *Dostoyevsky in Manhattan* (2002), the French philosopher André Glucksmann finds it necessary to paraphrase Marx: "A specter is haunting the world: the specter of nihilism." Though nihilism may not be invincible, superpowers are superpowerless against it. The battlecry of the nihilist is "I kill, therefore I am!" No one expressed this desire to gain immortality by way of destruction better than Dostoyevsky. The nihilists he denounces are initially atheists bent on destroying religion and—please note—religious culture. This enmity has a very good reason, for religion and culture are the two things that impose restrictions on human misconduct. As Glucksmann observes:

In general, one defines nihilism by the formula of Dostoyevsky: "If God is dead, everything is permitted." [Glucksmann is here aptly combining Nietzsche's famous phrase with Dostoyevsky's.] But I believe that the exact formula would be rather: "Everything is permitted, therefore God is dead." The cogito of nihilism is the fact of recognizing that there is an at least equal pleasure in doing evil as there is in doing good. This nihilism is not specific to modernity.

Glucksmann traces the course of nihilism from the beginnings of Western culture. Thus, the seemingly postmodern version of terrorism turns out to belong to a venerable, time-honored tradition. Others have already noted that in the Middle East, it had its precursor a thousand years ago in Hassan Sabbah and his sect of Assassins. The present nihilism, however, has reached the Islamists through the medium of modernity, through a secularism so powerful that they fall under its sway even when they are consciously opposed to it.

But what is truly terrible is that whereas the nineteenth century Russian nihilists killed in order to prove that God is dead, the present-day terrorists kill in order to prove that God is Great (i.e., they purport to kill in the name of God).[43] This demonstrates a mind-boggling disorientation on the part of the latter. For they have set out for Paradise and landed in the other place—started out with monotheism and arrived at atheism. They have adopted its methods. (Like the communists, they preach that the ends justify the means.) They *say* they are monotheists, but they *act* like atheists, and actions always speak louder than words. When there is a discrepancy between the two, it is the former and not the latter that count. Hence, they have become *unconscious* nihilists—blinded by their ego, their *nafs,* the ultimate terrorist, and also deluded by others who mislead them for their own particular aims. Why is ignorance so dangerous? Because it enslaves you to the interpretations of others, since you lack the intellectual formation to trust your own understanding.

This betrays such a fundamental confusion of values in the minds of the fundamentalists that words fail to take its proper measure. They have their priorities all mixed up, confusing death with life, hate with love, evil with good, and illicit with licit (as defined in the Divine Law). It is this categorical failure to discriminate between black and white that frees us from any obligation to take whatever they may say about Islam—or indeed anything else—seriously.

The Moral Challenge for America

Finally, is there a moral lesson for us in all this? I believe there is.

A recent movie[44] ends with the superhero's words: "With great power comes great responsibility. This is my gift, this is my curse." That remark is no less true of nations than it is of individuals. As the sole remaining superpower—or "hyperpower," to use the French term—the United States is, like it or not, an Atlas bearing the burden of the world on its shoulders.

We still think the president of the United States is the president of the United States. But this is only superficially true. After the fall of the Berlin Wall around 1990, he has become the de facto president of the world. This is a whole new situation, enjoyed by a very few civilizations throughout the known history of the world—and never to this extent. But are we really aware of this? Can we truly see that this also makes every single American the representative of, and therefore responsible for, twenty human beings in other parts of the world?

The world tacitly acknowledges the leadership of the United States, but it expects us to act with justice, with consideration for others—even for the most insignificant ant—which is the mark of true leadership. The lion, the king of the jungle, must not tread the path of the lone wolf. Our responsibility is great; and if we fail to fulfill it, the consequences too will be great. When faced with adversity, we must not lose our cool, we must not overreact. For example: if a few gnats or mosquitoes bother you, do you go on a rampage and leave your house (the world as well as domestic life) in ruins?

The task before America is to become "a light unto the nations." But for this, it must look beyond its traditional foreign policy of self-interest and watch out for the good of all humankind, in a way that *genuinely answers the needs of others.* It must gear its policies to the win-win option.

This calls for a broadening and deepening of vision on all sides, by acknowledging complexity rather than promoting simplistic understandings and solutions. We should not be surprised when people bring their griev-ances to our door. Rather, we should try to heal those grievances, to turn them into gratitude. To care for others is a requirement of Godliness, whether one be a Christian or a Moslem. Moreover, this is in our own interest. The rich have a duty to help the poor become educated.

The world out there expects great things, great leadership, from us. Moreover, I am optimistic: I believe we can rise to this challenge. We have the power to do it, it all depends on the will and desire for wisdom, peace, and love. In philosopher Slavoj Zizek's wise words,

> Whenever we encounter such a purely evil Outside, we should gather the courage to remember the Hegelian lesson: in this pure Outside, we should recognize the distilled version of our own essence...

> Either America will persist in, even amplify, the attitude of "Why should this happen to us? Things like this don't happen *here*," leading to more aggression towards the threatening Outside, just like a paranoiac acting out. Or America will [make] the long-overdue move from "A thing like this should not happen *here!*" to "A thing like this should not happen *anywhere!*" America's "holiday from history" was a fake: America's peace was bought by catastrophes going on elsewhere.

> Therein resides the true lesson of the bombings: the only way to ensure that it will not happen *here* again is to [work to] prevent it from going on *anywhere else*.[45]

Introduction

———— ❦ ————

My Master, Ahmet Kayhan, often spoke of the importance of having a "sound mind, sound heart." The two had to be united if God was to be found. The intellect alone or the heart alone would not suffice. To paraphrase Seyyed Hossein Nasr, "Reason divorced of knowledge of the divine burns into itself, like acid." For the Master and for his disciples, this form of Sufism represents the central core of Islamic teachings, synthesizing the exoteric and esoteric ends of the spectrum. As I wrote in my book, *The Station of No Station,* he used the word "Islam" and I tend to use the term "Sufism" to mean the same thing. In this book, I will use "Sufism" and "Islam" interchangeably to mean this kind of Sufic-infused Islam that the Master taught. As the Master explained, both the spirit and the law are fully represented in true Islam, but it is rare that these two are wholly combined in practice. He emphasized the great importance of this synthesis of exoteric and esoteric teachings. Properly defined, Islam is the Law (Divine Law) plus Sufism. Each is tempered by the other.

Islam as Love

Especially in light of September 11, 2001, and the political climate that has ensued (I write this in the summer of 2002), it seems to me that the Master's teachings about love are critical to our survival on Earth. As one of the Master's disciples so eloquently summarized his teachings about social justice, "If you love someone, you cannot violate that person's rights."

In my opinion Islam can be boiled down to two words: Law and Love. The first refers to the exoteric rules and observances an adherent must follow, the second to the spirit that should infuse all our actions. Although we tend to regard Islam as exoteric and reserve the esoteric sphere for Sufism, thus calling it by another name, both are part of Islam. Segregating and compartmentalizing the two in the usual fashion actually serves to perpetuate the misperception that they are two different things. Then by a curious invention, some people, not only those outside the religion, but also within it, reach the erroneous conclusion that if Sufism stands for spirituality and love, Islam (as the Divine Law) must be associated with rigidity, vindictiveness, anger, and hate. Nothing could be further from the truth.

As can be seen, while some humans are by nature more predisposed to formality and others to mysticism, something within the human constitution shrivels when one side is emphasized to the total exclusion of the other. Focusing on a dry legalism while neglecting the spiritual, for example, results in the kind of distortion of the human psyche being discussed. So the two aspects of Islam actually balance and complement each other; that balance is lost when one side is missing.

"My hate is my religion." Well, in that case your religion is hate and not Islam, which is love and compassion and moderation and tolerance and goodwill combined, the very opposite of hate. This mistake of confining Islam solely to the exoteric has got to end if we are to avoid dragging down Islam and everything along with it. When he said "Islam," Master Kayhan always meant both the external and the spiritual, and I submit that we need to adopt the same convention.

There should be no confusion in anyone's mind: religious identity, national identity, ethnic identity, and cultural identity are all different things, although there may be significant overlaps. While an expression like "the nation of Islam" does exist, this is meant in the sociological sense of religious community, not in the political sense of nation state. In terms of culture and civilization, to represent Islam and the West as implacable opposites is absurd. Modern Western civilization is based on the Renaisssance, which took its life-breath from scientific advances in Islamic civilization during its heyday. And being a Moslem in no way entails being against science, technology, democracy, free markets, or famous brand-name commodities.

Almost every chapter of the Koran begins with "In the name of God, the Compassionate, the Merciful." Why is God compassionate and

merciful towards human beings? Because He loved humans so much
that He created the entire universe for them. God wishes the best for us,
which is why He has sent prophets and holy books—like Ariadne's
thread,[46] they help us pick our way through this maze and lead us to
Paradise. As the Master explained, God's wish is that human beings should
love Him too, and should love each other. The Prophet said, "You cannot enter Paradise…unless you love one another." Indeed, we should
love all His creatures great and small. It has been remarked that "Love is
the explanation of the mystery of the Koran," which proclaims: "For
those with faith and good works, the Compasionate has assigned love"
(19:96). A Turkish Sufi hymn asks,

> *If you love God, won't God love you?*

To which the Koran responds:

> *They love Him and He loves them (5:54).*

This aspect of things gets so neglected that it seems worthwhile to
state it loud and clear right at the beginning. This also means that those
who neglect it are missing something crucial.

The Master's own life was an example of the completely ethical life
(outlined in the Koran) and his love radiated outward to be felt by all
who met him. In his presence, all of us felt inexplicably happy. It seems
to me that his supreme teaching—his secret, if you will—was love. He
was, to me and almost everyone who met him, an example of what the
Sufis call "The Perfect Human" (*al-insan al-kamil*). He was as close as a
human can come to Godliness, and that level of perfection is the goal of
the true Islamic path, as I will explain in the final chapter of this book.

It is my purpose in this book to show how love infuses all Islam—no
Islamic teaching, *properly understood,* can be used to justify harsh laws
and cruel and unjust punishment. Even at its most exoteric, true Islam
should foster love, kindness, and compassion. About Islamic fundamentalism and other misinterpretations of Islamic law, it cannot be stated
more clearly than this: where cruelty (*zulm*), injustice, and terrorism (unjust murder of innocents) begin, Islam ends.

A Brief Overview of Islam

What follows is a brief historical overview of Islamic culture with considerable emphasis on Western observations about that culture. I hope this will provide the reader with some understanding of the many contributions of Islam to Western culture, the high level of civilization and political tolerance exhibited during fourteen hundred years of Islamic civilization. Ottoman culture, in particular, represents the highly cosmopolitan and tolerant society characteristic of Islamic culture in its full bloom. In cases where Islamic culture has fallen short of this ideal, it is vital to recognize the extent to which pre-existing cultural milieux have influenced the versions of Islam we see today. Many facets of culture, both good and bad, predated the Prophet Mohammed's life or the spread of Islam, infusing and shaping the cultures in which Islam unfolded. The practice of Islam in the United States, for example, has taken on its own local color, even setting aside some of the practices in Turkey and elsewhere in the Middle East. Edward Said has recently written that in this sense, there are many Islams: "As the religion grew enormously in the century after Muhammad's preaching and career, the faith spread into hundreds of different regions and cultures…Each region and people who came under its sway developed its own kind of Islam. Thus, Islam is a world of many histories, many peoples…cultures, and countries."[47]

The Islamic Legacy

Speaking on the Islamic legacy to Europe, Prince Charles has said:

> We have underestimated the importance of eight hundred years of Islamic society: a culture in Spain between the eighth and fifteenth centuries. The contribution of Muslim Spain to the preservation of classical learning during the Dark Ages, and to the first flowering of the Renaissance, has long been recognized. But Islamic Spain was much more than a mere larder where Hellenistic knowledge was kept for later consumption by the emerging modern world. Not only did Muslim Spain gather and preserve the intellectual content of ancient Greek and Roman civilization, it also interpreted and expanded upon that

civilization, and made a vital contribution of its own in so many fields of human endeavour—in science, astronomy, mathematics, algebra (itself an Arabic word), law, history, medicine, pharmacology, optics, agriculture, architecture, theology, music. Averroes and Avenzoor, like their counterparts Avicenna and Rhazes in the East, contributed to the study and practice of medicine in ways from which Europe benefited for centuries afterwards.

Islam nurtured and preserved the quest for learning. In the words of the Prophet's tradition: 'The ink of the scholar is more sacred than the blood of the martyr.' Cordoba in the tenth century was by far the most civilized city of Europe. We know of lending libraries in Spain at the time [of] King Alfred...It is said that the four hundred thousand volumes of its ruler's library amounted to more books than all the rest of Europe put together. That was made possible because the Muslim world acquired from China the skill of making paper more than four hundred years before the rest of non-Muslim Europe. Many of the traits on which Europe prides itself came to it from Muslim Spain. Diplomacy, free trade, open borders, the techniques of academic research, of anthropology, etiquette, fashion, alternative medicine, hospitals, all came from [Cordoba,] this great city of cities. Mediaeval Islam was a religion of remarkable tolerance for its time, allowing Jews and Christians to practice their inherited beliefs, and setting an example which was not, unfortunately, copied for many centuries in the West. The surprise…is the extent to which Islam has been a part of Europe for so long, first in Spain, then in the Balkans, and the extent to which it has contributed so much towards the civilization which we all too often think of, wrongly, as entirely Western. Islam is part of our past and present, in all fields of human endeavour. It has helped to create modern Europe. It is part of our own inheritance, not a thing apart.

More than this, Islam can teach us today a way of understanding and living in the world which Christianity itself is poorer for having lost. At the heart of Islam is…an integral view of the Universe [that] refuses to separate man and nature, religion and science, mind and matter, and has preserved a metaphysical and unified view of ourselves and the world around us.[48]

The Copernican Revolution

It is well known that Islamic scholars preserved the scientific writings of ancient Greece at a time when Europe was living through the Dark Ages. The scientists and scholars of Islam have often been regarded merely as middlemen, translating and preserving the texts of Greek astronomy, medicine, and philosophy, until Europe would awaken from its slumber to carry the light. Recent research, however, has shown that the medieval Islamic astronomers did far more: they actually corrected and improved on Greek astronomy. Finding discrepancies in the system devised by Ptolemy, they invented new mathematical tools to account for the motions of heavenly objects. Ptolemy's model involved a construction that made such motion physically impossible. The thirteenth-century Islamic astronomer Mu'ayyad al-Din al-Urdi solved this problem, and Copernicus borrowed Urdi's theorem in his models of planetary motion. Copernicus also made use of the "Tusi Couple" (a mathematical theorem for obtaining linear motion from circular motion), named after the famous astronomer and polymath, Nasir al-Din al-Tusi, who first proposed it in 1247. Thus, Copernicus apparently built his heliocentric cosmology using the mathematical tools devised by Islamic astronomers. In this new light, the medieval Islamic astronomers played a fundamental role in the European scientific revolution and the Renaissance.[49]

Recognition of Mohammed and Islam in the West

Many scholars from the Judeo-Christian world have researched and examined Islam, testifying to the wisdom of the Glorious Koran and the greatness of the Prophet Mohammed. For example, Fritjof Schuon, the acknowledged expert of Grand Tradition in our time, has written: "If the Prophet had so wished—supposing Islam were the product of his mind— he could also have declared himself the son of God; he could have declared the Arabs a people elect; he could have founded a…cult which would have included his own person, the Archangels, some pagan divinities and, possibly, one or more of his wives, along with God; and he would certainly have done so if he had had the character still all too readily attributed to him in the West. That he did not do so proves in any case two things, namely a character of absolute integrity, and an authentic message from God; both things—the human qualification and the divine intervention—are necessarily combined, for the Messenger must be in conformity with the Message, he must in some manner anticipate it by his character and by his gifts....[T]he absolutely honest, simple, upright, disinterested, and generous personality of the Prophet—we speak as a historian and not as a 'believer'—reveals proportions that transcend the commonly human."[50]

In his *Decline and Fall of the Roman Empire,* Edward Gibbon stated that the Koran provides a magnificent witness to the unity of God. In statements such as the following, he supported not only the Prophet but also the Koran, God's miracle:

"It is not the propagation but the permanency of his religion that deserves our wonder; the same pure and perfect impression which he engraved at Mecca and Medina is preserved, after the revolutions of twelve centuries by the Indian, the African, and the Turkish proselytes of the Koran...The Mahometans have uniformly withstood the temptation of reducing the object of their faith and devotion to a level with the senses and imagination of man. 'I believe in One God and Mahomet is the Apostle of God' is the simple and invariable profession of Islam. The intellectual image of the Deity has never been degraded by any visible idol; the honors of the prophet have never transgressed the measure of human virtue; and his living precepts have restrained the gratitude of his disciples within the bounds of reason and religion."[51]

The Christian missionary, Rev. Bosworth Smith, stated: "By a fortune absolutely unique in history, Mohammad is a threefold founder—of a nation, of an empire, and of a religion. The Quran is a book which is a poem, a code of laws, a book of common prayer, all in one, and is reverenced by a large section of the human race as a miracle of purity in style, of wisdom, and of truth. It is the one miracle claimed by Mohammad—his 'Standing Miracle,' he called it; and a miracle indeed it is." Of Mohammed he also said, "He was Caesar and Pope in one; but he was Pope without Pope's pretensions, Caesar without the legions of Caesar: without a standing army, without a bodyguard, without a palace, without a fixed revenue. If ever any man had the right to say that he ruled by the right divine, it was Mohammad, for he had all the power without its instruments and without its supports."[52]

In his *History of Turkey*, the famous French author and historian Lamartine expresses his admiration for the Prophet of God in the following way: "Philosopher, orator, apostle, legislator, warrior, conqueror of ideas, restorer of rational dogmas; the founder of twenty terrestrial empires and of one spiritual empire, that is Mohammed. As regards all standards by which human greatness may be measured, we may ask, is there any man greater than he?"[53]

The Englishman John Davenport, who emphasized the justice of Islam and was a student of the history of world religions, eloquently testified to the nonviolent history of Islam (an important history to remember in view of recent violent incidents associated with so-called Islamic actors). As Davenport said, "Islam has never interfered with the dogmas of any faith—never persecuted, never established an inquisition. It offered its religion, but never enforced it." Islam has introduced itself to the world, but has never abased human beings by forcible religious conversion, court trials or the torture of the Inquisition. He continues:

> Europe is still further indebted to the Musalmans. For, not to mention that to the struggles during the Crusades we mainly owe the abolition of the onerous parts of the feudal system, and the destruction of those aristocratic despotisms on the ruins of which arose the proudest bulwark of our liberties, Europe is to be reminded that she is indebted to the followers of Muhammad, as the link which connects ancient and modern literature; for the preservation, during a long reign of Western darkness, of the works of many of the Greek philosophers; and for the cultivation of some of the most important branches of science, mathematics, medicine, etc., which are highly indebted to their labours. Spain, Cassino, the Salernum were the nurseries of the literature of the age; and the works of Avicenna, Averroes, Beithar, Abzazel, and others gave new vigour and direction to the studies of [Western scientists]....Muhammad himself said that a mind without erudition was like a body without a soul, that 'glory consists not in

wealth but in knowledge;' and he charged his followers to seek learning even in the remotest parts of the globe.[54]

The American psychoanalyst Jules Masserman, in stating his views on leadership,[55] reached the following conclusion: "The greatest leader of all time is Mohammed." Although he himself was Jewish, he assigned Moses to second place, which is quite extraordinary. Michael H. Hart, the American astronomer, historian, and mathematician, also accorded Mohammed first place: "Muhammad...was the only man in history who was supremely successful on both the religious and secular level."[56]

Sir James Jeans, the famous physicist and author of *The Mysterious Universe,* was a devout churchgoer. Yet when told about the Koranic verse: "Among His servants, only men of knowledge (scientists) fear God" (35:28), he exclaimed: "This is terrific! At the end of fifty years of scientific investigations and observations, I was forced to believe in God, to love Him and fear Him. An uneducated person living fourteen hundred years ago could not have uttered these words. If the truth you mention is in the Koran, it must be the Book of God, and Mohammed must be a prophet."

Edouard Montet, professor at the University of Geneva, says in his introduction to his work *A Translation of the Meanings of the Glorious Koran:* "If we were to choose only one of the invaluable reforms that the Prophet Mohammed introduced to humanity—forbidding the practice of burying female children alive—this would be enough to place his service to humanity at the forefront of the annals of history."

Roger Garaudy, a Frenchman, was the head of the Communist Party, the director of the Institute for Marxist Research, a writer on Marxist philosophy, a member of parliament and a senator, and even a candidate for the French Presidency. Sent to prison in Algeria as a political agitator, he had the chance to study Islam at first hand, an enterprise which took him some forty years. In 1981, at the age of sixty-eight, he announced to the world that he had become a Moslem, saying: "Islam is the choice of the times. All the answers sought by man are in Islam." Garaudy found that Islam combined Christianity's concern for the individual with Marxism's emphasis on the social.

Such examples can be multiplied indefinitely. The point is that having studied Islam in depth, no fair-minded commentator has come away from this encounter without being favorably impressed. Recently, for example, Karen Armstrong, a former nun and writer on Islam and the three monotheistic religions, observed:

> Islam…is not the intolerant or violent religion of western fantasy. Mohammed was forced to fight against the city of Mecca, which had vowed to exterminate the new Muslim community, but the Koran, the inspired scripture that he brought to the Arabs, condemns aggressive warfare and permits only a war of self-defence. After five years of warfare, Mohammed turned to more peaceful methods and finally conquered Mecca by an ingenious campaign of non-violence. After the prophet's death, the Muslims established a vast empire that stretched from the Pyrenees to the Himalayas, but these wars of conquest were secular, and were only given a religious interpretation after the event.[57]

And so the testimony continues.

As we have seen in this brief sketch, violence and coercion have no place in Islam. The Koran clearly states: "There is no compulsion in religion" (2:256). In view of this legacy, can one truly say that what one already "knows" about Islam is based upon an *unbiased* and *informed* judgment and not upon misinformation? Is one's knowledge based on the teachings of the Koran, and on the example set by the Prophet Mohammed? If not, then there is much to be gained from the study of this book.

PART I

❧

The Exoteric Path: Divine Law

A Faith for All Seasons

—— ✳ ——

(What follows is a brief discourse [of a kind the Master often gave] on the subject of Islam as the archetypal or metareligion that has synthesized and superseded all others, even as it expresses tolerance for diversity in religions. Although it addresses many theoretical issues, it ends, as so many of his discourses did, with a call to apply the principles of Islam in one's daily life. For the Master, any discussion of abstract principles or theories was offset by a corresponding discussion of how to live an ethical life. For example, he often spoke with us about the fundamental importance of "Courtesy" [defined as "splendid moral conduct"— see Appendix A] and learning to control what the Sufis call the "Base Self"—refraining from even the thought of "forbidden lust" and "forbidden gain," as described in this section. Closing these "two doors" was the one thing the Master was most particular about—he would repeat this over and over at every opportunity. The chapter concludes with a discussion on global synergy and the alms-tax.)

"There is only one religion on earth," said George Bernard Shaw, "but there are a hundred versions of it," and William Blake was of the same opinion: "All religions are one." Islam claims to be that archetypal religion. Many of the prophets mentioned in the Koran are referred to as "Moslems," which means that the prophets of earlier religions submitted to God, the One and the same God, even though the religious precepts

3

revealed to them were localized rather than universal. Adam, the first man, was also described as the first prophet, the first to embrace Islam (translated as "submission to God").

In time, however, the teachings of the earlier prophets became obsolete, because the times and circumstances for which they were valid were superseded; and also corrupted, because the original teachings were unable to survive untampered. As people mistook the manifold attributes of God for God Himself, they began to call these attributes "gods," thus slipping from monotheism into polytheism. Entropy is a cosmic law ordained by God, and human affairs are not exempt from it. Such degeneration necessitated the renewal of true religion from time to time, a reiteration performed by the many prophets.

Finally, God sent the perfect religion that is valid for all mankind as long as it exists: they are coterminous. He chose Mohammed as the vehicle for conveying this religion. As the Prophet remarked: "I was sent to complete admirable conduct." Here is the great contribution of Islam to spirituality: the recognition that spirituality is dependent on ethics, and that perfecting one's ethical conduct leads to a perfect spirituality.

In the view of Moslems, Islam was not different from all the other true religions, as is evidenced by its acceptance of all earlier prophets, such as Moses and Jesus; it was merely their most mature, most perfected, and streamlined form. For example, just as Christianity was a continuation and—in certain respects—a consummation of Judaism, Islam is a continuation and consummation of both Judaism and Christianity. Similarly, it is an extension of and improvement upon Buddhism, and so on. And although the earlier religions were tribal and local, addressing a small part of mankind for a restricted period of time, Islam was intended by God to be truly universal—as valid for an American, say, of the twenty-first century as it was for the little Arabic community to which it was revealed fourteen centuries ago. God has made this unmistakably clear by the following verse: "Today I have perfected your religion over you" (5:3).

Although God, having revealed the final and most perfect religion, has abrogated all earlier manifestations of religious devotion—and in this sense other religions will not be accepted by God—Moslems recognize that it is part of the divine purpose to maintain diverse religious communities in coexistence. Because: "We would have created you in one faith if We had so desired," God states in the Koran (5:48, 10:99, 11:118); "We made you of diverse faiths so that you might get to know each other" (49:13). Ultimately, the decision to enter Islam is a private, individual choice, made on one's own free will after proper investigation. But Islam recognizes in all religions its earlier forms, its predecessors, its ancestors. And this is why Islam is the "religion for all seasons:" it encompasses and embraces all earlier religions and traditions, because they are its own.

Nevertheless, Moslems also reserve the right to point out their errors in cases where they have strayed from the true path, since it is the most developed version of the best aspects of all religions. In our age, when a truly universal community is needed to unite the "global village," a truly Islamic society has to be characterized by its tolerance for other faiths and its acceptance of diversity, testified to by the history of Islam which spans fourteen centuries.

Bearing Witness

Entry to the religion of Islam is extremely easy. One need only repeat the Word of Witnessing (*Kalima al-Shahada*) or the Word of Unification (or Unity) (*Kalima at-Tawhid*).

The Word of Witnessing is: "I bear witness that there is no god but God, and that Mohammed is His servant and Messenger." The Word of Unification is: "There is no god but God; Mohammed is His Messenger." Anyone repeating these Words (especially the first) wholeheartedly and with a sincere belief will enter Islam.

Let us pause for a moment to consider what their recitation entails.

The first part of both formulas is the faith of monotheism: there is only One True God, the Lord of all Being. In ancient times, people used to worship stones, trees, and many other deities. They idolized these objects; that is, they attributed to them properties superior to what they intrinsically possessed. They projected upon them godlike attributes, and from this it followed that obeisance was owed these objects. The thesis of monotheism, on the other hand, was that only the supreme power, the Creator of the Universe, deserved the unconditional allegiance and worship of human beings.

Although we may believe that we are very far from such an unsophisticated mentality today, our emancipation and education may have blinded us to certain facts, and led us to underestimate the power with which the human psyche tends to deify various kinds of entities. The truth is that even in this day and age, we tend to invest things with a significance they do not possess. This deification is all the more insidious because it is largely subconscious. We may not worship a tree, but we have our own idols and superstitions that hold comparable sway over our thought processes.

In order to bring to light what is involved here, it is necessary to make the following definition: anything which a person loves in excess and/or fears in excess is that person's god, or idol. (This also includes attribution of power to that thing.)

When considered in terms of this definition, it will easily be seen that even the most confirmed atheist might well be, in real life, a polytheist or idolater.

Love and fear are two basic components of the human psyche. Even if you believe in One God, if you love or fear something more than Him, that thing is your god. That is, you are setting up another god, you are associating a partner, with God. If you do not believe in God, your deification is all the more total and indefensible.

Looked at in this light, it at once becomes apparent that we all pay allegiance to various pantheons of idols. The movie star, the rock musician, the sports figure, or the politician to whom we are overly attached may all be considered our gods, a fact recognized even in common speech where such persons are referred to as "idols."

A man may be so deeply in love with a woman that he "worships" her. A person who washes and polishes his or her car excessively is, without realizing it, "deifying" that car. At the very least, s/he is making a fetish out of it, which is already in the realm of the sacred. Another who has a great fear of his or her boss, debtor, or local bully, has unconsciously taken these as idols.

In this sense, almost anything can serve as a deity: money, science, a work of art, alcohol, political power, sex, oneself, one's reason, or even one's TV set, to name but a few. These are all false gods, however; they usurp our devotion without being worthy of it.

All this goes to show that if you do not worship the sun, the moon, or the stars, you are not automatically disqualified from idolatry or polytheism. In fact, there are indications that ancient and primitive peoples understood this broader definition of a god quite well; they were just more prosaic in their choice of idols.

Now the basic tenet of monotheism in the face of all this is that there is only one Being worthy of such adoration and fear, who commands man's absolute allegiance and respect; and that is the One and only True God, the Creator of the Universe and everything that is in it.

Another danger is that even though we believe in God, we might show excessive reverence to something that we fancy will draw us close to Him. This may be an icon, an object, an angel, or a human being. All of these have their proper place; it is only when we go too far that we run the risk of associationism.

We should, in that case, avoid associating anything with God. We should dissociate Him from and glorify Him above everything else, for He is so far beyond all finite things, no matter how great, that He simply does not bear comparison with any of them.

This, then, is the meaning of "There is no god but God," and from what has been said it can be seen that it is as valid a claim in our modern age as it was in ancient times, for it is timeless.

This claim, however, is equally the profession of a Jew or a Christian, who also believe "there is no god but God." The second part of both formulas is exclusive to the Moslem: "Mohammed is the Messenger of God."

Now what do we mean by this? This means that we accept Mohammed as the true guide, exponent, and conveyor of religious knowledge. It means that we willingly accept—and undertake to carry out—all the commandments and prohibitions of God as revealed through His Prophet.

These two formulas (the two Words), then, constitute a pact, a covenant (the final covenant, in fact) between humans and God. Their recitation is not an end, but a beginning—the beginning of many obligations which a Moslem is required to fulfill. By doing so, one will earn merit. It means that we accept the Koran, as revealed to Mohammed via the angel

Gabriel, and the Prophet's additional explanations, advice, and example (his Way, or *Sunnah*) not contained explicitly in the Koran.

The latter, though not included in the Koran, have come from the same blessed mouth that delivered the Koran. If we accept the veracity of the latter, we are duty-bound to do the same for the former, provided it is an established fact that a certain word has issued from him. Such sayings (*hadith*) of the Prophet are called Traditions.

The Koran itself testifies to the absolute trustworthiness of the Prophet: "He does not utter anything of his own accord" (53:4); "Take what the Prophet gives you, and beware what he prohibits" (59:7); "If you love God, love and obey [His Prophet], and then God will love you" (3:31); and "You have a good example in the Messenger of God" (33:21).

Indeed, Islam rests on two legs that are inseparable: the Koran, and the Way of the Prophet. And just as the Koran is the constitution for all humanity, the Messenger of God is the prophet of all human beings—though they may not know it.

It has been remarked that there are two versions of the Koran: the first is "the silent Koran," which is the written Koran we all know. The second, "the Koran that speaks," is the Prophet himself. For try as we might to fathom certain parts of the Koran and behave accordingly, we cannot do so without the concrete example of the Prophet, of whom his wife Aisha once remarked that "His conduct is the Koran."[58]

Furthermore, Islam has to be accepted in its totality: "Do you accept a part of the Koran and deny another part?" (2:85) That would be similar to accepting only certain parts of a whole, living person. The living example of the Prophet, therefore, has found divine sanction in the Koran itself, and it is noteworthy that movements (such as fundamentalism) which refuse part or all of his Radiant Way have invariably become harsh and intolerant (a prime cause for lamentation in the West), for they thereby unwittingly reject his legendary gentleness and tolerance.

A Global Faith with Local Applications

Islam is a universal religion: it is not the religion of one nation or race, but all humanity. Of course, it had to be revealed somewhere on earth, and this happened to be an Arabic community in the seventh century

A.D. But God has explicitly indicated that henceforth, Islam is to be a religion for all humanity, not for this or that tribe, race, or nation. This means that anyone can practice it, anywhere and at anytime, no matter what nation or culture one belongs to.

Care should be taken at this point not to confuse Islam per se with the cultural and historical milieu in which it has traditionally been embedded. With all due respect to its birthplace and the noble people who live there, we should be careful to segregate the religion and its precepts from elements of local custom. We cannot all become Arabs or ride on camels, but then Islam does not require us to. What it does is set down precepts that will lead to the present and future happiness of human beings regardless of locale. It is natural that every locality and culture will find its own expression. But beyond a plethora of ramifications, the basic rules are what count. Einstein's Theory of Relativity does not state that everything is relative. It states that there are things and relationships which remain invariant under transformations, and seeks to understand them. In the same way, Islam is invariant and of perennial use to human beings, and should not be confused with the countless individual actualizations which cannot help but differ.

A Churchless Faith

There is no church in Islam, no clergy, and no monasticism. Between a person and God, there stands nothing. Religious scholars may deal with legal or exoteric matters, and spiritual teachers may give esoteric instruction; but they are human beings like ourselves, and do not mediate between God and human beings. They do not constitute a clergy. No one has the right to come between any human being and God or to exercise power in God's name. This is the most intensely private of relationships, and since God has, with this religion, made known to humanity His requirements concerning the most important things, everyone knows what to do without the intermediary of a church. One can be clean and pure and practice one's faith without a church, for one is accountable to God, and to God alone, who stands in no need of any other representative.

Closely related to this is the idea that Islam does not sacrifice matter for spirit, or vice versa. Both are of equal importance. Both are part of the human makeup, and humans will be crippled if they neglect one side for the sake of the other. Spiritual advancement does not entail renunciation of the world, nor do worldly possessions—provided we possess them and they don't possess us—preclude spiritual/afterworldly progress. The two must go together. Extreme asceticism—like all extremes—is not advocated by Islam, which points to the "Middle Way."

A Religion of Hope

Islam is a religion of hope. Its stance as regards humans and the universe is basically optimistic. Original Sin, an ineradicable residue of sin that is genetically passed on down the generations, does not exist in Islam.[59] Furthermore, sin and evil do not have the connotations in Islam that they possess in other religions. Sin is not a source of irremediable guilt; it is rather in the nature of faults, errors, or mistakes which may issue from a human being as a matter of course—provided, of course, it is not intentional and deliberate. Unmitigated "evil" as the term is understood in the West does not exist in Islam—the closest term to it would be "ill" (*sharr*).[60] Badness is entirely manageable in Islam. Even the Devil, who in some religions is powerful enough to rule this world, only has the power to whisper and suggest treachery to those who heed him; beyond this, the Koran teaches that Satan cannot actually compel us to do anything.

Two sayings of the Prophet will serve to clarify the optimistic position of Islam. "Every child is born a Moslem; it is only afterwards that his parents and environment make him the follower of another religion." This means that every child is born *already saved*—not already damned. It is only actions in later life that may cause the fall of a person, who comes into this world pure and untainted. ("Born a Moslem" here means born with Islamic morality and beautiful conduct, rather than any conscious acknowledgment of Islamic precepts on the part of the child; i.e., Islam is that childlike pureness.)

The Prophet also said, "Suppose you want to plant a tree, and you know for certain that the End of the World is near (in other words, that that tree has no chance of growing). Nevertheless, *go ahead and plant that tree.*" No matter how bad a situation may appear to be, one is encouraged to act with hope. God has declared: "My mercy is greater than My wrath," and the Prophet has explained: "I was sent as a mercy to the worlds." No matter how sinful a person may be and how destitute s/he may feel as a consequence, the door of sincere repentance and the resolve not to consciously repeat a sin will most certainly lead to divine mercy, absolution, and salvation.

A Natural Religion

As we can see, Islam is a religion tailored to human needs. It fits Arthur Koestler's description of a religion whose essence is "perennial but not archaic, which provides ethical guidance, teaches the lost art of contemplation, and restores contact with the [divine] without requiring reason to abdicate." It does not go against the grain, and dovetails with the natural disposition and requirements of human beings. For this reason, it is referred to as "the religion of natural disposition." (It should not, however, be confused with the historical Deism of Voltaire and Locke, which, in Pascal's famous phrase, brings the subject up to "the God of the philosophers," but cannot take the step to "the God of Abraham." Philosophy might bring us to God's doorstep by accepting His existence, but we need a revealed religion to pass beyond the threshold and learn anything further.)

As in all matters, here, too, the Prophet must stand as the model for Moslems. Where you're able to, give advice, help others, show them the Good. Where you can't, pray for them and try to help them. Never argue; only discuss in the most appealing way.

How can one help those who do not share the faith?

People who do not use the revealed Scriptures as a guide have an impossible task ahead of them. Instead of picking the fruit from the tree that has been presented to them, they have chosen to "build the tree" from scratch! Where can they start? The only certainty is that they will try to construct their own morality—a system of values to live by.

If you know there is no possibility of their hearts responding to the Divine, you can at least help them in the following two respects. For these will go some way in saving them from misery, and will save others from falling victim to their ignorance.

Reining in One's Desires

1. *Forbidden Gain.* Whatever you gain by illegitimate means—and here I mean illegitimate in God's sight—will sooner or later be a curse on you for which you must pay. No good will come of it, no matter how easily or how surreptitiously it is obtained. In the final analysis, illicit profit is never in one's own best interest. I'm not just talking about outright stealing or embezzlement here. Islam is so strict about this point that it warns you not to drink a cup of tea or coffee if you visit a person whose earnings are suspect in your eyes—that cup will be tainted.

Let me make this crystal clear. Suppose you're flat broke, and you decide to go over to your friend to borrow some money. Now on your way, you find that the streets are strewn with thousands of dollars. It's there, it's yours for the taking, you didn't steal it, and it's all free!

Under these conditions, you *must not take the money.* Don't even touch the bills. Just wade through them as if they never existed, and continue on your way to ask your friend for the measly sum you had in mind.

I know that's a difficult proposition—it sounds exaggerated and counterintuitive, but you'll be better off in the end than if you'd done otherwise.

Don't eat an illicit morsel, and don't allow your family (or those under your care) to swallow one. This does not mean that we're condemned to poverty, and that legitimate wealth is ruled out. You can be as rich as you like, so long as you earn it by honest means.

2. *Forbidden Lust.* "Do not approach fornication," says the Koran. What is meant here is not simply that you should not indulge in illicit sex, but that you should refrain from even the slightest movement, the slightest thought, in that direction. (Here's where Jesus' figurative expression: "If your eye offends you, pluck it out" takes on meaning.) Except for your lawfully wedded spouse, regard all other human beings as your brothers or sisters, mothers or fathers, or children (it goes without saying that this rules out incest).

Sex is probably the strongest impulse in human beings. If handled unwisely, it is powerful enough to shatter them. In its proper place, it will lead to worldly and marital happiness. It promises the fulfillment and contentment of a warm family life. Experimenting with illegitimate relationships, on the other hand, can only bring on disaster. It can cause the collapse or destruction of an entire civilization. Fornication, adultery, and all forms of sexual perversion and depravity put an end to one's psychic assets once and for all. It doesn't make any difference if "two consenting adults" are involved—this is just an excuse to bypass the hurdle. There is a God-given trust, a lease, in each human being that must remain inviolate and which s/he is forbidden to give to another even by his or her own consent, unless in proper wedlock with a member of the opposite sex.

When God created Adam at the dawn of human history, He was engaging in the production of His most marvelous, most complex, creature. This is well-nigh a sacred act. Thenceforth, He entrusted the creation of further human beings, the propagation of the race, to us. In other words, we are participators in God's creation of each new human being. This is a tremendous responsibility. And, like it or not, this is the purpose of sex. We may think only about how pleasurable it is, but it is there for procreation.

Now consider what it takes to obtain a well-formed human being: a minimum of twenty years of nurture, of tender loving care by both parents. And this is best achieved within a healthy marriage. Sex, therefore, is a social event. A sexual wrong is a social wrong affecting everybody, even future generations.

This is compounded in the case of a married couple. Adultery is the most common cause of marital breakdown. The person found to be attractive is nothing but a menace to one's spouse, one's innocent children and, ultimately, to oneself. But this lesson is most often learned the hard way, because of the refusal to benefit from other people's experiences. The sanctity of marriage must be preserved.

Now these last two points—forbidden gain and forbidden lust—are so crucial that they can elevate a person to the heights of sainthood, or plunge one into the depths of misery. All the techniques of mystics throughout history served only one purpose: the control of the Self. And yet, self-control is actually predicated on these two critical points alone: illicit pecuniary interest and passion. This is true not merely for Moslems, but for everyone. Control these two, and you have no need of all the other ascetic practices mentioned above. Fail to do so, and none of them will save you. For the ultimate aim of all asceticism is to tame these two selfish drives, to keep them within permitted, legitimate limits.

The annihilation of mankind will be the direct or indirect outcome of failure to hold these two in check. No matter who you are, by reining them in, you will not merely save yourself, but will also contribute to the survival of humanity. It is imperative that those "beyond the fold" of Islam should understand this. The duty of a Moslem, where possible, is to carefully and intelligently make this known to them.

Synergy and Society

In order to better appreciate the kind of individual and society envisioned by Islam, let us explore an important byway of the social sciences. This involves the application of the concept of synergy to human culture.

Anthropologist Ruth Benedict drew a distinction between cultures of low synergy and cultures of high synergy. It was Benedict's insight that human personality bears the stamp of its specific culture, and that there is a correlation between social structure and character structure, especially aggressiveness. Aggression, she said, is marked in societies where the interests of the individual and the group are at odds with each other. "The problem is one of social engineering," according to Benedict: "Nonaggression occurs not because people are unselfish and put social obligations above personal desires but because social arrangements make these two identical."[61] Using synergy in its meaning of combined action (where the whole is greater than the sum of its parts), she distinguished between cultures of low synergy, in which the social structure provides for acts that are counteractive and counterproductive (borrowing a term from physics, we might call this "destructive interference"), and cultures of high synergy, in which such acts are mutually reinforcing ("constructive interference"). Life in low-synergy societies is a zero-sum game; when one person wins, everybody else loses. In high-synergy cultures, on the other hand, the name of the game is "non-zero sum;" there is no true loser because everybody wins.

Benedict found that in societies where institutions did not exist to redistribute wealth, which has a natural tendency to become concentrated, life was difficult and individuals were predominantly anxiety-ridden and aggressive, and vice versa. This had nothing to do with the level of economic or technological development; people might lead a happy and fulfilling life even in the most primitive society, while widespread suffering—with consequent fear, aggression, and violence—might exist even in the most advanced one. In short, high synergy means high peacefulness and low aggression, while low synergy means the opposite. Because high-synergy societies foster win-win situations and victory for all, their peoples are generous, naturally friendly, and benevolent.

Now what has all this to do with Islam? Everything. For this religion aims to take society at whatever level it finds it and to transform it into a high-synergy society. It provides the social institutions for what Benedict called "the syphon system"—an economy where wealth is constantly channeled away from points of concentration and spread throughout the community. Where everyone is provided for, poverty is not a word to fear, and people can be much more secure, easygoing, and hence, peaceable. In an age when senseless violence and sexual depravity is being pumped into our cultural bloodstream by the media (as if there weren't enough to go around to begin with), we could do worse than take the heed of Islam, with its prescription for nonaggression and peace.

Ottoman Ethics

In the past, Islamic societies exhibited concern for social and ecological issues because this was built into the very fabric of their religion. The Ottomans, for example, had practices of a resoundingly ecological nature, long before ecology was ever heard of in the West. The quintessence of ecology was, of course, first expressed by the Koran: "Eat, drink, but do not waste" (7:31).

As we well know, the earth's resources will provide enough for everyone, as long as they are not squandered mindlessly. The "green" choice is primarily an ethical choice; the science of ecology may tell us that the destruction of the environment will lead to the destruction of humanity, but it does not tell us why such self-destruction is wrong or bad.

In accordance with the Islamic precept to "show compassion and tolerance towards not merely human beings, but all of God's creatures," the

Ottomans saw to it that hungry wolves in the wild were fed carrion. This not only protected villages from being raided, but prevented the predator from entering the "endangered species" list because, according to their conception, "every living being is precious." The means for this was a unique institution they called the "foundation." Thus the Ottomans had foundations for the preservation of birds, cats, mongrels, wildlife, et al.— a delicate ecological sensibility informed all their actions. Looking at all the funds and foundations devoted to the preservation of nature in the West today, one cannot help but remember their predecessors in a less ecology-conscious age.

Indeed, Islam teaches us to save even a scorpion in distress, so long as it does not intimidate us directly. The reason for this is not the ecological precept that diversity of species leads to more stable ecosystems. It is that these creatures possess the gift of life, which is worthy of respect in itself.

One of the areas in which Ottoman culture excelled was security against poverty. What I am about to relate may sound like a fairy tale today, yet it is the truth, and provides a graphic example of Benedict's "syphon system." The Ottomans had "charity stones," pillars in the middle of the street, slightly taller than a human being, on top of which a rich person might place a donation for the poor. A needy person coming along could then reach up and collect it. In this way, donor and receiver remained anonymous to each other, and the dignity of the poor was preserved from injury. No one was reduced to begging. Since theft was unheard of, there was no danger that the money entrusted to the mute stones would vanish. What they accomplished as a matter of course, we cannot even dream of today. The equivalent in this day and age would be an open bank account; but can you imagine the deposits not being stolen before the poor and needy got to them?

The essence of Ottoman ethics was this: *treat every human being as if s/he were a jewel.* This means that a person should be handled delicately, as a being of infinite worth. You will not find this stated in history books, which seldom do justice to this aspect of Ottoman life, but such was in fact the ideal, and—more often than not—the practice. And this is the kind of morality we need today. In an overcrowded world we stand even more, not less, in need of such conduct.

The Alms-Tax

We cannot go into all socially and ecologically oriented Islamic observances here, but shall consider, in conclusion, that most social form of worship, the alms-tax institution—the archetype of all syphon systems.

Among the aims of Islam are social justice and the fair distribution of wealth, and the alms-tax is the primary—though not the only—means to achieve this goal. Everyone who is rich beyond a certain measure (*nisab*) is required to give one-fortieth of their holdings—not just income—to the poor. This measure is ninety-six grams of gold, or the equivalent amount in cash (roughly one thousand dollars as of this writing—the figure fluctuates) and/or valuables, and one must have been in possession of this amount for at least one year, *over and above one's debts and daily requirements.* Of course, this does not preclude other forms of charity, such as the "end-of-fast" (*fitr*) alms given at the end of the month of Ramadan, or individual handouts or donations.

Let us now take a closer look at what is involved in the alms-tax, and how it is considered in Islam. The word for alms-tax, *zakat,* literally means "cleansing" or "purification." The implication is that money or property, even when honestly earned, is unclean; it contains a residue which makes it "filthy lucre." It is, if you like, contaminated, almost radioactive, and unless it is decontaminated it will harm its owner. Now this impurity can only be cleaned away by giving it to the poor. That portion of one's wealth is their *rightful property.* One's earnings are then cleansed, and the "uncleanness" drops away from the money given—but only if the recipients are poor. If, for instance, a well-to-do person withholds, accepts, or takes the alms-tax, it will jeopardize his or her entire fortune in the sight of God.

In order to understand more clearly what this means, let us return to Benedict's syphon system, and compare the social body to the human body. This is a valid comparison, because human beings living in a society are connected to each other by multifarious ties. In our present-day atomistic societies, which sociologist David Riesman once characterized as "the lonely crowd," there is a tendency to compare society with the molecules in a gas. But that is not a society; that is instead "a bunch of people living at the same address."

Just as wealth has a natural tendency to become concentrated in society, blood in the body is always being drawn in by the heart. But just think what would happen if the heart did not pump this out again. Moreover, this blood that is drawn in is spent blood; it is contaminated with waste matter and toxic materials, and has to be circulated through the lungs (and also the kidneys) for aeration or "purification." This oxygen-enriched blood is then redistributed to all parts of the body through capillaries. Extremities of the body, such as the hands, feet, ears, and nose, are the first to get cold in bad weather.

Now picture what would happen if such extremities were to freeze. The heart, being centrally placed, would not be affected directly, yet it, too, would suffer because the entire body would suffer. And if fresh blood could not reach cells that are the end users of oxygen, anoxia and rapid death would set in.

In our analogy, then, the alms-tax serves the dual function of the lungs plus kidneys, and the capillaries; it both purifies the money circulating in the economy, and siphons it to those parts of the social body that receive the least "blood." Thus, not even the lowliest person will starve for want. This does not mean, however, that Islam advocates shiftlessness. Islam frowns upon laziness and begging, and encourages everyone to work to the best of their abilities. The alms-tax is not intended to operate like the welfare system in the United States.

In the Koran, the alms-tax is mentioned in the same breath as Prayer, and is accorded equal importance. The following saying of the Prophet serves to highlight its priority:

"If the alms-tax of the rich were not enough for the poor, God would have given them other means of sustenance. If there are any poor who go hungry, this is only because of the cruelty of the rich."

This is borne out by the period of Omar Ibn Abdulaziz, sometimes called "the Fifth Rightly Guided Caliph" or "the Second Omar." His rule lasted no more than two-and-a-half years, ending with his death in 719 A.D. During this brief period, Omar ruled with such exemplary justice that everyone under his reign prospered. Those were the times when the alms-tax was collected and distributed officially. Finally, one of his alms-tax collectors, Yahya Ibn Said, said: "Omar Ibn Abdulaziz sent me to Africa to collect the alms-tax. After collecting it, I sought poor people to give it to, but I couldn't find any poor worthy to receive it. Because Omar had made everyone rich."

This provides historical proof that, if the alms-tax were given with due care, it would put an end to hunger and want. Hard as it may be to imagine, the alms-tax points the way to nothing less than a peaceful revolution. The concept of a "negative income tax" to be given to the poor, entertained some years ago in the United States, shows that modern social thinking on poverty is finally catching up with the alms-tax, instituted fourteen centuries ago.

The alms-tax is usually given on a person-to-person basis, although there have been times in history when it was collected and dispensed by the state (increasing, if necessary, the customary two-and-a-half percent). This enhances the probability that the donation will reach the truly needy, while the inherent "uncleanness" involved makes corruption unlikely in a country keeping the faith.

A few other sayings of the Prophet will help clarify the status of the alms-tax:

> The alms-tax has been made obligatory in order that property be cleansed and beautified. Whoever does not give the alms-tax has defiled his property, and is in hellfire in the afterlife. A society that does not give the alms-tax will be plagued by droughts and crises. Property for which it is not paid will be ruined on land or at sea. Whoever pays the alms-tax protects himself from the evil of his property. After Prayer, the most virtuous worship is the alms-tax. If a person does not pay it, neither will his Prayer be accepted.

It is not simply the dirt of money that is swept away, however: hardness of heart, the contamination of greed and callousness, is removed from the donor, giving way to feelings of charity and compassion. Like Charles Dickens's Ebenezer Scrooge, the giver undergoes a reform and conversion. It begins to dawn on the giver that ever-increasing consumption, consumerism, and anthropocentrism are not what being human is all about.

The Day of the Dictator

In our age, the top twenty percent of the world's population controls eighty-six percent of the globe's wealth, and the bottom twenty percent controls one-and-a-third percent. It is not too much to say that even today, the effects of world poverty can only be eradicated by an imaginative application of the alms-tax within the world community—i.e., on a global scale. The social ills of the world, the polarization between the haves and the have-nots, can only be curbed by a similar donation on the part of the rich in rich nations to the poor in poor nations. A worldwide application of the alms-tax charity would lead to a significant increase in global synergy and reduce the negative impact of globalization that has caused so many complaints. An insignificant amount to the rich would mean a lot to the poor. Giving the poor buying-power would also oil the wheels of the world economy. The "peaceable kingdom," all humankind living together in peace and harmony, would then become possible.

"If a wolf slaughters a lamb in [some far-off land]," said Omar, the second Caliph of Islam, "Omar is responsible." It is only by such a sense of responsibility that we can resolve our global problems. "Our true nationality," noted H.G. Wells, "is mankind." No matter what nationality we belong to, we are human beings first and members of that nationality afterwards. We need to bear this constantly in mind, and to take the precautions necessary for preserving our "global village." The Prophet's saying: "If a person dies of hunger in a land, the whole country is his murderer," should now be reconsidered with the whole world in mind. To recall Benedict again: "One's life experience is different if economic institutions make it impossible to be hungry as long as anyone in one's world has food at all..."[62] The four hundred richest Americans alone command a wealth of more than one trillion dollars.[63] "The fortunes of the world's three richest individuals now exceed the total wealth of the inhabitants of its forty-eight poorest countries."[64] God knows we have the wealth, the technology, and the wherewithal to achieve this, were we but to set our minds to it and to examine our consciences carefully.

Unless this is done, and unless per-capita GNPs are drawn toward a median point amongst the rich and poor nations, crises will be inevitable not merely domestically, within nations, but on an international scale. It is a trivial exercise to observe that if Benedict's high synergy correlates with low aggression, the opposite holds as well—low synergy corresponds to high aggression. Beyond a certain threshold, revolutions and wars will spread like wildfire. What was not given freely, with compassion and charity, people will seek to wrest by force. And that can only pave the way for the day of the dictator, the time of the terrorist—the day when only the cruel and merciless will rule. The true way to preempt them is to relieve the distress of the destitute. For it is in giving to God's creatures—and our human brothers and sisters rank foremost among these—that we receive from God. Another saying of the Prophet is: "Unless you desire for others what you desire for yourself, you cannot enter Paradise." The thanksgiving for plenty is charity to others. Failing that, all the bombs and weapons in the world won't help us.

It does not take great intelligence to see this. But the solution is primarily a matter of the heart, and a heart is what we in the world seem to be lacking most today.

What Does "Islam" Mean?

In order to avoid misunderstandings, it is perhaps worthwhile to look at the meaning of the word "Islam."

Islam means "surrendering to and obeying" God. But the full meaning of the word can only be brought out by looking at the other words deriving from the same root, SLM. For in Arabic, words derived from the same root possess meanings that complement and complete one another. For this reason, they constitute a constellation centered around that root and are "nearest neighbors" or "relatives"—the offspring of that root, as it were. It is through them that the word gains dimension and depth. This is one of the reasons why the Koran can never be translated fully into other languages.

It is impossible to exaggerate the importance of this constellation of words associated with Islam. For they provide us with the key to the most realistic assessment of what Islam is and is not. We can obtain the shortest and closest approach to the truth and living essence of Islam by examining their content.

Moslem or *Muslim* means a person who has surrendered, who obeys God and His commandments. *Taslim* means surrendering, and also "giving the trust to the right place, to be safe from disasters and calamities." *Salaama* is "safety, security, wholeness, perfection, to be free from fears and anxiety, salvation, liberation, and happy outcome."

Similarly, *salaam* is "peace, comfort, auspicious results, freedom from mortality, friendship." To *salaam*, i.e., "salute," a person is to wish him well, to wish peace, comfort, and completeness (shedding faults and attaining perfection) on him. The Koran speaks of Paradise as *Dar as-salaam,* or "the Abode of Peace."

Salim bears the meaning of "firm, complete, fearless, secure, trusted, completed, fortified," as well as "strong, perfect, true." *Aql as-salim* is "common sense, wisdom, sound judgment, right and balanced thinking."

Sullam, again from the same root, is synonymous with *miraj* (ascension, ladder), and its meaning of "staircase" points to the method that purifies and elevates man, that exalts him and leads him upwards to Truth. *Musallam* is "that which has no doubt, whose truth and rightness is acknowledged by everyone."

Musalama is "to be in peace, peacefulness, tranquility, to be gentle, well-tempered, and compassionate." These attributes summarize the Way of the Prophet, and point to the adoption of Mohammedan morals by Moslems.

Taslim and *tawaqqul* (trust in God) have been traditionally misunderstood in many cases. It has become a habit to use these as excuses for laziness and a blind fatalism. But these words were never intended to mean sloth, lethargy, or surrender to the caprices of our ego and obedience to the devil. Rather, they signify living in harmony with the laws of the universe which are the commandments of God, and acting in accordance with them. They mean "not to force," not to use force, not to violate the unfolding of the universe by opposing its flow. More clearly, they imply that human beings should not try to force or bend the laws of the universe for their own self-interest, and should revise—or transform—their relationship with the universe and its Creator *from being one of egotistical benefit into a relationship of wonder, admiration, and love.*

To summarize the details given above, *to be a Moslem—the one who lives 'Islam'—is to achieve tranquility, peace, security, and happiness; to be well-mannered and to possess splendid moral conduct; to attain perfection, liberation, and fulfillment by purifying oneself and unification.* It also expresses the path—the truth and rightness of which is beyond doubt—that leads to these goals.

Moses, Jesus, and Mohammed

———————— ✻ ————————

(What follows is a dialogue of the kind the Master might have engaged in to teach us about Islam, in particular about the conduct of the Prophet [known as "the Way"]. Having a teacher or guide is considered essential in Sufi tradition and every teacher's ultimate guide is, of course, the Prophet Mohammed.[65] The Master spoke to us often about prophets and saints, "seed personalities" as I have called them here. He encouraged us to become fully human [like them], able to use all of our faculties to their highest capacity, the goal of the Islamic path. And he told us many stories about the Prophet, to illustrate to us the Prophet's ethical code and the way of life we should emulate. I offer you then this fictitious dialogue between a sage and a student in the hopes that it will help enlighten you.)[66]

Prologue

"Come on, son," said the sage, "you don't expect to get anywhere by yourself, do you? The road is fraught with pitfalls, and no one can make it on his own. Where did you get this notion: 'If you meet the Buddha on the road, kill him'? You can't make the trip without a guide, and the founder of a religion is the guide of all guides."

"Was the Buddha a prophet too, sir?" the disciple asked. He was well-meaning and polite, but young and a little foolish.

"He's not mentioned in our Book by name," said the sage, "so we can't say for sure. Legend has it that there have been 124,000 prophets, only a few of whose names are known. The holy texts would have to be some kind of phone book if they were to name them all. In any case, the Buddha is widely recognized as nothing less than a founder of a religious philosophy, and what applies to him certainly applies to the prophets as well."

"I had this notion that I could go it alone," said the disciple. "I don't want to get entangled in all this religious stuff. Besides, I want to attain enlightenment, not the Christian notion of salvation."

"That's absurd," said the sage. "Besides, liberation, salvation, and enlightenment all mean the same thing."

"Probably what is meant when they speak about killing the Buddha," observed the disciple, "is that one should stop at nothing when on the road."

"Perhaps. But it's still extremely bad form to speak of him in that way."

The Prophets

"Tell me," the sage asked, "is there anyone you admire at all?"

The student thought for a moment, and gave the name of a popular rock star.

"Not that I have anything against rock stars, or indeed against movie stars or ball players or great politicians," said the sage, "but you have to set your sights higher. A good deal higher."

"You have come to me in search of Truth," the sage continued. "But I must warn you that your expectations about Truth will prevent you from perceiving it. For Truth exists independently of anyone's perceptions about it; it is not *your* truth or *my* truth, but *the* truth, the whole truth, and nothing but the truth, as they say." He smiled.

The student pondered, but only for a few seconds. "Sir," he said, "having come this far, I think it's my duty to lay aside my preconceptions and hear you out, at least."

"Very well," replied the master. "Truth is One, yet it presents many facets, like a polished diamond. One facet is science, another philosophy. Art, music, literature are all aspects of Truth, and you can probably think of others.

"In all ages," he continued, "there have been superior human beings who have enriched the heritage of humanity by their attempts to get closer to the Truth. Human beings of exceptional genius and discernment, too numerous to be recounted here, are veritable mountain tops when compared to the common run of humanity.

"Our voyage, or rather yours, must begin with the realization that there have been people in history who stand in the same relation to these peaks as they, in turn, stand in relation to the rest of humanity. Superior human beings had to strive every inch of the way to reach the pinnacle of a certain facet of Truth. Yet there have been others to whom Truth has revealed itself, not through one of its facets, but directly. Sometimes they, too, have striven greatly to achieve this vision. Sometimes it has come upon them unexpectedly, all of a sudden. In all cases, however, the vision they received has served the improvement and happiness not merely of themselves, but hundreds of millions of human beings. These are the ones I choose to call *seed personalities:* out of whom great good has grown, who have galvanized countless people with their presence.

"This is the Age of Technology," he went on. "Science and technology are both aspects of Truth, and who can deny the boons they have granted us? Yet at the same time, emphasizing them to the exclusion of everything else has blinded us to many other things that our ancestors realized much more clearly than we do today. As a result, everybody is lost—lost, because we can't find the golden thread to lead us out of the labyrinth. You yourself, for instance, are tossed like a piece of driftwood on the high seas; you feel like a leaf in the wind, being hurled wherever it blows. A person needs to be anchored in something solid to survive the vicissitudes of life without being fazed by them."

He got up and removed a dusty tome from a shelf. It was *Heroes and Hero-Worship,* dated 1841, by Thomas Carlyle.

"Why don't you read aloud the passages I indicate to you, and we'll take it from there," he suggested. "I know the language is a bit dated, but we'll be well rewarded, you'll see." So the student read:

> The thing a man does practically lay to heart, and know for certain, concerning his vital relations to this mysterious Universe, and his duty and destiny there, that is in all cases the primary thing for him, and creatively determines all the rest. That is his

religion: or, it may be, his mere scepticism and *no-religion:* the manner it is in which he feels himself to be spiritually related to the Unseen World or No-World: and I say if you tell me what that is, you tell me to a very great extent what the man is, what the kind of things he will do is.

Answering of this question is giving us the soul of the history of the man or nation. The thoughts they had were the parents of the actions they did: their feelings were parents of their thoughts: it was the unseen and spiritual in them that determined the outward and actual: their religion, as I say, was the great fact about them.

"Skip a few pages and read on," said the sage. The student continued:

In all epochs of the world's history, we shall find the Great Man to have been the indispensable saviour of his epoch; the lightning, without which the fuel would never have burnt. The History of the World, I said already, was the Biography of Great Men...

Innumerable men had passed by, across this Universe, with a dumb vague wonder, such as the very animals may feel; or with a painful, fruitlessly inquiring wonder, such as men only feel; till the great Thinker came, the *original* man, the Seer; whose shaped spoken Thought awakes the slumbering capability of all into thought. It is ever the way with the Thinker, the spiritual Hero. What he says, all men were not far from saying, were longing to say.

The disciple looked up. "Please don't think it rude of me," he said, "but I'm worried about all the charlatanism, the broken promises, the shattered dreams."

"Ah," said the sage, "Carlyle has the answer to that, too. Don't imagine he was uncritical, taking everything without a pinch of salt. Give me the book." He turned back a few pages and said, "Read."

Quackery and dupery do abound: in religions...but quackery was never the originating influence in such things; it was not the health and life of such things, but their disease, the sure precursor of their being about to die!

Quackery gives birth to nothing: gives death to all things.

"That'll be enough," the sage said, and replaced the book to its shelf.

"Humans are always bound by their nature, society, and culture," he resumed. "Animals, too, are bound by their natural needs—and their social needs, if they happen to be social animals. But there is something in human beings that strives to transcend the merely animal level of subsistence—to exist, to *be;* to be not simply an animal, which is what all animals are doing all the time anyway, but to be a *human.* Today, living as we do in such luxury as even the emperors of old never dreamed of, even today the greatest part of our efforts are geared to the acquisition of mere creaturely comforts.

"Now in history, there have been singular moments when an individual has broken through to another level of being, or that level has reached out and contacted him or her. As a result s/he has acquired a new self, has been transformed into a *person.* S/he breaks the bounds of his or her specific circumstances, natural and social, and becomes—to a greater or lesser extent—a universal human, part of a universal community.

"It is a fact, as astounding as it is singular, that all such persons have testified to a separate reality, a different level of being, even in cases where they did not speak about God as such.

"This person then feels it an obligation, indeed duty, to inform others of this discovery. Many recoil in horror and incomprehension; but on a few open minds s/he makes an impression they will never forget. S/he is the person they all sat down to supper with for many a night, yet s/he is not the same person, somehow. For s/he has been transfigured by that experience, and they have at last seen an example of something they never expected to see: *a Human.*

"This person has now become an embodiment of ideas, whether totally new, or venerated or long forgotten. And this embodiment is so wonderful, so captivating, so lovable, that people who can sense this difference seek to emulate the principles they see ensconced in every move, every breath of this person, and by at first pretending, to *become,* in the end, like the person they admire. And so, they are attracted to him or her like iron filings to a magnet.

"That is the kind of person I call a prophet, or, if one is an accomplished follower of such, a saint.

"The prophet or saint superimposes on the physical body and the social dimension of humans an invisible force-field, a subtle envelope, a new, purified self, within which true human nature might flower. This envelope is the totality of their teachings. Yet those teachings are none other than the expression in words of the reality that the prophet embodies in real life. The prophet lives the life, in order that the followers may know the doctrine; and in order to understand the doctrine, you too have to live the life. For while the do's and don'ts may be easy—and they aren't always so—not all aspects of the doctrine are readily comprehensible.

"And so, this person acts as a seed for mankind, just as we use cloud-seeding in order to precipitate rain, or a 'seed' brings on the crystallization of a saturated chemical solution."

"But sir," protested the student, "the people you're telling me about all lived in ancient times. They were all shepherds at one time, and most of them didn't even know how to read or write. How can such persons be taken as examples in our day?"

"Too much book-learning is what makes you say that," replied the sage drily. "Very well then, consider this: In our digital age, we are fast approaching the point where, in the future, information may be beamed directly and instantly into one's brain. Now suppose that this were in fact realized, would you consider reading books an inferior or a superior form of information input?"

"Inferior, of course," came the reply.

"Exactly. Now what I am talking about is very similar to this." He pointed to his head. "The Guarded Tablet is right here," he said. "If the Omniscient decided to impart to you a portion of His knowledge, do you think He would necessarily need the medium of a book? He would merely unlock a door of the Akashic Records, and that would be that. The prophets may have been unlettered shepherds, but they had one great advantage that we don't—they had God behind them."

Moses

"Moses," he went on, "was one of the greatest prophets. He lived in the thirteenth century B.C., and conversed with God so much that he earned the title: 'Speaker with God.' I shall not bore you with the details of his life, since I assume you know them already. His birth, recovery from a basket in the Nile, and upbringing under the nose of Pharaoh, his arch-foe; God's appearance to him in the burning bush; his contest with Pharaoh, and the Exodus by which he led his people out of slavery; the parting of the Red Sea; God's delivery of manna from heaven; Moses' meeting with God on Mount Sinai for forty days and nights; the forty years in the desert before they could enter the Promised Land—all these, I'm sure, are too well-known to need repetition. Moses is an all-too-human figure. He is aware of his shortcomings, especially his difficulties of speech, but that's another story—and a beautiful one, too," the sage added, "remind me to tell you sometime."

"I will," said the student.

"Moses is also the pivotal figure in Jewish history. He was more than a prophet; he was a messenger of God, meaning that he was a lawgiver and not just a renewer of law earlier revealed. Moses hated injustice, and may be considered the father of all earthly utopias. He was a giant aqueduct through which the law and light of God poured into the minds and hearts of his people. His actions were decisive, his resolve unshakable; yet at the same time, he had to appear sterner than he was in order to hold his group together.

"There was nothing Moses loved more than communion with God, for at bottom he was a devoutly spiritual man. Great historians have always recognized that humankind sometimes progresses by a giant step, thanks to the earth-shaking influence of a seed personality. And Moses was such a man. He effected a revolution of the mind and spirit, and brought such a perspective on things that old ideas could never be the same again.

"The duties God charged Moses with were truly gargantuan. He accepted them reluctantly, but tried with all his might to fulfill the task set for him. And in his desperate struggle he succeeded, though he never saw the Promised Land himself. The Torah is quite right to conclude: 'Never [before or] since has there arisen a prophet in Israel like Moses, whom the Lord knew face to face. He was unequaled for all the signs and wonders that the Lord sent him to perform in the land of Egypt, against Pharaoh and his servants and his entire land, and [unmatched] for all the mighty deeds and all the terrifying displays of power that Moses performed in the sight of all Israel' (*Deuteronomy* 34:10-12)."

"He was an imposing figure, all right," the disciple agreed.

"Yet there is another dimension to the Biblical account that has escaped almost everyone," the sage continued. "The whole chain of events has by and large been read as history, and nothing more. But when you look at it from an esoteric angle, the Exodus is also the sacred history of the individual soul. Pharaoh is the pharaonic, egotistical self that holds the spirit in slavery. The journey to the Promised Land is precisely what the Sufis call 'the journey to the homeland.' And the trials in between, the forty years in the desert, are the tribulations that the spirit undergoes along the way. And so it is with the life of every other prophet—what we can only grasp intellectually as allegory or metaphor was, for them, *reality actually lived*."

"I hadn't heard of that before," said the student.

"Let me just tell you this much," said the sage, "even the fact of Moses' demise just when his people were about to enter 'the land of milk and honey' has deep esoteric significance."

The student frowned. "What about Jesus?" he asked.

Jesus

The sage smiled. "Jesus certainly needs no introduction," he said. "A noted historian has observed that Moses was beyond the power of the human mind to invent, and I think the same thing may be said of Jesus. Of course, his story has been embellished, because there is a dark tunnel of about two decades after his death that historians, in spite of all their efforts, have been powerless to illuminate. Innumerable rumors flourished as a result, some true and some spurious. Yet there had to be a Jesus, because he complements Moses in so many ways."

"How so?" asked the disciple.

"Well, Moses is by and large an exoteric figure. Overemphasis on the purely legal aspect of his teachings had, by Jesus' time, obscured any spiritual element they might have possessed originally. Jesus had to come, in order to restore the spiritual dimension of man. Besides, Moses is still a tribal prophet, and the decrees revealed to him are still specific to a small segment of humanity. Jesus' teachings, in contrast, were destined to reach a much wider audience.

"Every action, every word of Jesus radiates authority," he went on. "So much, in fact, that those who have confused him with God may perhaps be excused for doing so. Yet Jesus himself never claimed to be God; in fact, he explicitly denied it: 'Why do you call me good? Only God is good' (*Matthew* 19:17, *Mark* 10:18, *Luke* 18:19), or: 'My Father is greater than I' (*John* 14:28), if you remember your Bible. Even Paul, who made so much of Jesus' end—not even he claimed that Jesus was God, though he came dangerously close. When Jesus says: 'I and my Father are one' (*John* 10:30), therefore, he means this in a metaphorical and not a literal sense, otherwise he would be contradicting himself."

"I'm not a theologian," the student admitted.

"Nor do you have to be, it's all there in the Bible," said the sage. "Moses was the moralist, the judge, the hygienist, whereas Jesus was the psychologist and mystic. Jesus was love, humility, and sacrifice personified. These qualities shone through all his actions, for he went about doing good. He healed the sick: restored sight to the blind, speech to the dumb, the use of their legs to the crippled. He helped the poor, freed the oppressed, fed the hungry. Being a prophet of God, he did all these miraculously; but one does not have to be a miracle worker in order to do these things in one's own small way, with one's limited human means, or to recognize that they are admirable virtues in themselves.

"When we turn from Jesus' deeds to his words, the transparent meaning of his actions evaporates. That's why they've been debated for centuries. Some of his sayings are clear enough, and it would take us a long way if we could practice even them alone faithfully. For example: 'In all things, do unto others as you would have them do unto you; for this is the Law and the Prophets' (*Matthew* 7:12). Or: 'You shall love the Lord your God with all your heart, and with all your soul, and with all your mind. This is the first and greatest commandment. And the second is like it: You shall love your neighbor as yourself. On these commandments hang the Law and the Prophets' (*Matthew* 22:37–40). Note the reference to the Law (Hebrew *Torah*) and the Prophets (*Naviim*) in both cases, which together with the Books (*Ketuvim*) make up the Old

Testament. Jesus is here establishing his continuity with the tradition of Moses, and his advice is clear and simple.

"But other sayings of his are quite complex. We then have to discard any notion that he was a simple man preaching a simple doctrine. Part of the problem is that people have tried to interpret his sayings by applying the tools of Greek philosophy to them. When that was done, the pure, clear life-water of his teachings became frozen into the stark stalactites and stalagmites of dogma—whereas the only way to understand them is to take the mystical approach.

"One example should suffice: 'He who loses his life shall find it' (*Matthew* 10:39, *Luke* 9:23-4, *John* 12:25). Here, if anywhere, is an esoteric statement belonging to Jesus. Now what do you suppose he meant by this paradoxical remark?"

"What, indeed?" echoed the disciple.

"Well, let's apply the tools of Islam to it and see what we come up with. This refers to the death-rebirth experience of the soul. A saying attributed to Mohammed puts it more clearly: you have to 'Die before you die,' for unless one dies and is reborn, one cannot enter the Kingdom. This Kingdom of God—or Heaven—is the spiritual counterpart of the Promised Land which we were talking about (also the 'Pure Land' of Amida Buddhism, if memory serves) and, as everyone knows, 'is within you' (*Luke* 17:21).

"Now, how is this to be achieved? The Bible states that Jesus 'emptied himself' (Greek *ekenosen*), in order to let God's light shine through (*Philippians* 2:7). For the thoughts, the desires, the caprices of the ordinary self only obstruct that light. Self-emptying (*kenosis*) leads to Unity or Union (*enosis*), in other words. Now this is precisely the perception of Unity or Union (Arabic *wahdah*) of the Sufis, which is achieved through (spiritual) poverty (*faqr*). 'Poverty is my pride,' said Mohammed, yet at another time he remarked: 'Poverty is blackness of face (i.e., a disgrace).' It's clear that he's speaking about two different kinds of poverty: spiritual poverty in the first case and material poverty in the second. And what does Jesus say to that? 'Blessed are the poor in spirit, for theirs is the Kingdom of Heaven' (*Matthew* 5:3). The explanation and the explained fit each other like hand and glove.

"This goes to show that only a mystical, Sufic interpretation will explain some of Jesus' sayings. But we can't all be mystics, so that door will remain closed to a great majority of people."

"I've never heard of this 'kenosis leads to enosis' idea before within Christianity," observed the student.

"Probably," the sage smiled, "this is because Christian theology focused on the uniqueness of Jesus, rather than the availability of his experience to all adepts."

"Does this mean that the Sufis took their doctrine from Christianity, as some have claimed?" asked the student.

"It means," corrected the sage, "that Mohammed took what was Jesus' and completed it, just as Jesus said he would. If we love Jesus enough, we should take heed of his directions."

The Essence of Christianity

"I think," said the sage, "Angelus Silesius summarized the ultimate core of Christianity admirably:

> *Though Christ a thousand times in Bethlehem be born*
> *But not within thyself, thy soul will be forlorn;*
> *The cross on Golgotha thou lookest to in vain*
> *Unless within thyself it be set up again.*

"If you truly understand what that means, you have reached the limits of what you can learn from Christianity. In Sufism, this is called *fana,* the extinction or termination of the little local self. Sufis have compared the death-rebirth experience of the soul to the birth of Christ. Like the Virgin Mary, we should give birth to the Jesus, that is, the spirit-child (*tifl al-maana*) within ourselves. One can give birth to only one spirit-child, and only once (*monogeneton*). Because according to the Prophet, 'Who dies once, does not die again,' and according to the Koran, 'They won't taste death, except for the first death…That is the great liberation' (44:56-57). That's also one meaning St. Paul intends when he advises his readers to 'clothe yourselves in Christ.' Unfortunately, almost all these inner meanings were lost long ago."

A Question

"Why is it," asked the sage, "that intelligent people lament 'the spiritual vacuum that exists all over what once was Christendom'? And what is the reason for the unsettling, ominous silence that echoes down church corridors through the centuries?"

"I have no idea," said the disciple. A shiver ran up his spine.

"Let me put this another way," said the sage. "Have you read Umberto Eco?"

"No, but I've seen the movie," replied the disciple, remembering *The Name of the Rose.*

"That book ends with the sentence: 'Once there was a rose. Now, there is only its name,'" said the sage. "Do you have any idea what this rose is?"

"No."

"It is Jesus," the sage continued. "And every prophet is a rose. Moses, Jesus, Mohammed are all roses. The saints in a religion are roses, too, but lesser roses than its prophet. The reason that we cannot smell the fragrance of Jesus is that his term is over. His time is up."

"How do you mean?" asked the disciple.

"Well, look at it this way. Suppose you're an American, or an Englishman, or a Frenchman, or a German. We all know that Eisenhower, Churchill, de Gaulle, and Adenauer were great leaders of these nations. Now suppose you wanted to write a petition to your president or prime minister. And suppose you began your letter: 'Dear Mr. Eisenhower,' or 'Dear Mr. Churchill,' or 'Dear Monsieur de Gaulle,' or 'Dear Herr Adenauer,' and sent it off. What do you think would happen?"

The disciple laughed. "I don't know," he said. "It'd probably end up in the wastebasket."

"Exactly," said the sage. "And why is that? Because none of these people are in office any longer. You would have to address your present prime minister or president in order for your petition to be considered valid.

"Now it's exactly the same thing with the prophets," he continued. "If you remember, Jesus said: 'I am the way and the life. No one comes unto the Lord, except by me.' And well he might, for this statement is true of all prophets, *so long as they are in office.* In Abraham's time, for instance, no one could go to the Lord except by Abraham. In Moses' time, no one could go except by Moses, and so on. In every age it's the prophet of that time that's going to ferry you to the other shore, and once you get there, the customs inspectors say: 'Who's your ferryman?' It's all right to answer Moses or Abraham if you lived in their term, but not if you haven't.

"Each prophet is in office until the next one comes along. It doesn't matter if a prophet is alive or not when his successor arrives. However, since no prophet will come after Mohammed save the fakes and impostors, he will be in office till the end of time. There will be no further Revelation, because God has stated His case to humanity in the final form He desired."

"Does this mean that only Mohammed's community is eligible for salvation, that all the earlier religious communities were somehow inferior?"

"Not at all. Each prophet was the spiritual—and sometimes also the worldly—king of his age, and as long as his people obeyed him, they were assured of God's grace. Every religion is the Islam of its age. Judaism is the Islam of its time, Christianity is the Islam of the Christian Era, and so on. They may differ from the final version—Islam as we know it—in detail, but not in the essential points. Mohammed's distinction resides in the fact that his message addresses not this or that tribe or community, but humanity at large. Because it was so universal, there is no need for another prophet to come with further revelation. Of course, the final revelation abrogates earlier revelations, just as today's newspaper supersedes yesterday's daily, or the current version of a computer program updates its earlier versions. This doesn't mean the earlier versions are bad or all wrong, they're just out-of-date."

"I don't know, sir," said the disciple. "It would be better if Jesus had left some indication about his successor."

"Oh, but he did. He said: 'As long as I am in the world, I am the light of the world' (*John* 9:5), and 'I will ask the Father, and he will give you another Paraclete, to be with you forever' (*John* 14:15). He also said, 'The Paraclete...will teach you everything, and remind you of all that I have said to you' (*John* 14:26), and 'When the Paraclete comes, whom I will send to you from the Father, the spirit of truth who comes from the Father, he will testify on my behalf' (*John* 15:26). Many other times he mentioned the Paraclete as well: 'It is to your advantage that I go away, for if I do not go away, the Paraclete will not come to you; but if I go, I will send him to you' (*John.* 16:7), and 'I still have many things to say to you, but you cannot bear them now. When the spirit of truth comes, he will guide you into all the truth; for he will not speak on his own, but will speak whatever he hears, and he will declare to you the things that are to come. He will glorify me, because he will take what is mine and declare it to you' (*John* 16:12-14)."

The sage paused. "Jesus," he said, "could not have given a clearer indication that he would have a successor. I myself couldn't have said it better if I had wanted to. First of all, note that there are two Paracletes, not one: because Jesus says 'another Paraclete' like himself, he is one and Mohammed is the other. Further, the Bible explicitly calls Jesus 'a Paraclete' (1 *John* 2:1), so that there are, presumably, other Paracletes— and 'Paraclete' now begins to sound an awful lot like 'prophet.' Let's not go into the deeper matter of what 'Paraclete' means; let me just say that I would again be vindicated.

"Jesus calls the Paraclete the 'spirit of truth'; indeed, Mohammed was a spirit of truth, just like Jesus. Jesus makes it plain beyond words that his teaching is incomplete and will be completed by another like him. When he came, Mohammed gave instructions on all the things that Jesus, on his own admission, could not elaborate. He dictated the Koran just as he heard it, without addition or omission. As the Koran itself points out, he did not speak of his own accord (53:3). And because he guided us into all the truth, he will be with us forever, for God's Revelation is now complete. Moreover, Mohammed both testified on Jesus' behalf and glorified him, for he called Jesus 'my brother,' which also dovetails with the notion of two Paracletes. And the Koran glorifies Jesus as the Messiah (Christ), son of Mary (5:72, 75)."

The disciple mused. "I don't know," he said. "I thought the Paraclete was the Holy Spirit. It says so in the Bible."

"Don't forget," countered the sage, "that the Paraclete is *another* Paraclete, just like Jesus. There are two Paracletes, not one, and one of them is Jesus. Whatever Jesus was, the other has to share the same characteristics. If Jesus was a human being, the Paraclete has to be a human being, too. If Jesus was a prophet of God, then so is the Paraclete. If you can speak about Jesus as a spirit that is holy, which I can readily grant, one can say the same thing about Mohammed. The point is that each of them is *a* holy spirit, not *the* Holy Ghost.

"There's another thing," he continued. "When Jesus appeared to the disciples later on, he breathed on them and said to them, 'Receive the Holy Spirit' (*John* 20:22). This shows that the Holy Spirit either *is* Jesus' breath, or is contained in his breath. In either case, the Holy Spirit is something intangible. Ever hear of a breath that hears and speaks physically? Only a human being can do those things.

"Further, we can see here that Jesus and the Holy Spirit are *both present simultaneously.* But as Jesus himself explains, the Paraclete can only come in his absence. This proves to us that the Holy Spirit is not the Paraclete."

The disciple sighed. "All this theology is making me dizzy," he explained. "Can you tell me a bit more about Mohammed? I don't know much about him except for his name, and that he founded a religion called Islam."

Weakly-Coupled Religions

"The problem with Moses' teachings and those of Jesus," the sage continued, "was: first, that they still were not universal enough, and second, that they were *weakly coupled.*"

The disciple frowned. "I don't get it, sir," he said.

"Well, let's tackle one at a time. Recall that Moses' precepts addressed a small portion of humanity; they were specific to Jews alone. Jesus' beautiful teachings, on the other hand, were only for adepts of mysticism, and these too are always in a minority. Yet there had to be a religion for all humankind: one that would embrace everyone, of whatever temperament, inclination, or calling in life. This is why the two were not universal enough.

"We now come to the second point. The Church Fathers were well aware of this difficulty. They knew that Moses' exoteric teachings left out spirituality, while the esoteric teachings of Jesus omitted the legal aspect which is a must in social life. They tried to remedy this situation by *combining the two*—which is why you have both the Old Testament and the New in the Bible.

"But in the end, it was a makeshift arrangement. Certain interpretations grafted onto Jesus' original doctrine proved as incapable of mixing with Moses' as water with oil. Moreover, even if that had proved possible, the limitations of both which we've just discussed precluded a truly universal synthesis.

"There are other contrasts as well. Judaism is a worldly religion, whereas Christianity—as it developed later—reviled the body and concentrated exclusively on the spirit. The Jewish God is a wrathful God, whereas God is love in the Christian conception, and so on. Now each of these conceptions excludes the other; a human being, for instance, is not just a disembodied spirit (in which case one would be a ghost), nor simply a body (in which case one would be merely a corpse), but a unique, living combination of the two. Religion needs to recognize both sides of the coin, and it ought to address and answer the needs of both aspects. Where would night be without day, or vice versa? What was needed was a religion that radically combined the two, a synthesis—and not merely a mixture—that transcended both. And that is why Mohammed had to come.

"Take the Koran, for example. It seamlessly integrates the exoteric with the esoteric. A saying of the Prophet states that 'Every verse in the Koran has simultaneously an esoteric and an exoteric meaning,' and goes on to explain that the esoteric meanings are to be found to a depth of seven levels. We've already seen an example of this above (44:56–57). Both the exoteric and the esoteric meanings are true, but because the esoteric meanings are comprehensible only to a few, the exoteric has primacy. The result is a text that is deceptively one-dimensional, especially in translation, but is in reality incredibly rich and textured in meaning. That's why the language of the Koran isn't just Arabic. More to the point, it's God-ish.[67] Otherwise, any Arabic speaker would immediately understand all its meanings."

The disciple was silent for a while. "I can't be hearing all this," he said at last.

"Oh, but you are," the sage said gently. "You wanted to hear the Truth, didn't you? I told you it wouldn't be easy. We don't have to go on if you don't want to. It's against our rules to force anyone."[68]

"Please continue," said the disciple, after a period of thoughtful silence. "Do you mean that Mohammed concocted a new religion out of Judaism and Christianity?"

"No," the master explained patiently. "Religion and philosophy are two different things. You and I could perhaps sit down and construct a new philosophy, for instance, because philosophy depends on human reason alone. But this is not the case with religion, for it depends on a direct revelation from God, and comprises both rational and surrational aspects. And a philosophy can generate new ideas, but it cannot generate *a Human.*"

"Surrational?" the student interjected.

"Well, since you ask, it's time for some definitions. 'Nonrational' is, obviously, that which is not rational, and this can be divided into two subsets: irrational and surrational. By 'irrational,' I mean something that is illogical, that contains a logical contradiction. For example, 1=3 or 3=1 is a mathematical impossibility. 'Surrational'[69] or 'superrational,' on the other hand, is a higher degree of rationality. In other words, we would find a surrational thing to be supremely rational, *if only we were in possession of all the facts.* The surrational is as far above the rational as the irrational is below it. For example, Moses' adventures with Khidr related in the Koran are of a surrational nature: Moses found that there were perfectly logical reasons for Khidr's actions which he was previously unable to make sense of, once the facts were explained to him. The commandments and the ways of the Lord may be mysterious, but they are not illogical once you know the inside story.

"Now I said that revelation contains both rational and surrational elements. Every true religion was originally composed of these two, but irrational elements also crept in with the passage of time. Only Islam is immune to this process, which is why it has remained unpolluted. And the surrational can only be imparted by God, for only He is omniscient. It is mentioned in the Koran that it was 'sent down by the Holy Spirit from the Lord with Truth' (16:102). Besides, the Koran explicitly states that if Mohammed had added or modified anything on his own, God would have ripped out his main artery (69:46). True religion is not something you can sit down and invent, and if you try to do this, the result will be at best a pseudo-religion, not a true one."

Mohammed

"Why don't we go back to Carlyle," continued the sage, "and see what he has to say. Could you kindly fetch the book from that shelf again?" The disciple did so and, at the sage's direction, began to read:

> ...A greater number of God's creatures believe in Mahomet's word at this hour than in any other word whatever. Are we to suppose that it was a miserable piece of spiritual legerdemain, this which so many creatures of the Almighty have lived by and died by? I, for my part, cannot form any such supposition.

> But of a Great Man, especially of him, I will venture to assert that it is incredible that he should have been any other than true...I should say *sincerity*, a deep, great, genuine sincerity, is the first characteristic of all men in any way heroic.

> Such a man is what we call an *original* man; he comes to us at first-hand...Really his utterances, are they not a kind of 'revelation'—what we must call such for want of some other name? It is from the heart of the world that he comes, he is a portion of the primal reality of things.

> The man's words were not false, nor his workings here below...To *kindle* the world; the world's maker had ordered it so...A silent, great soul; he was one of those who cannot *but* be in earnest: whom Nature herself has appointed to be sincere. While others walk in formulas and hearsays, contented enough to dwell there, this man could not screen himself in formulas; he was alone with his own soul and the reality of things.

> A Hero, as I repeat, has this first distinction, which, indeed, we may call first and last, the Alpha and Omega of his whole Heroism. That he looks through the shows of things into *things*.

> Communing with his own heart, in the silence of the mountains; himself silent; open to the 'small, still voices'; it was a right natural custom!

...That we must *submit* to God. That our whole strength lies in resigned submission to Him, whatsoever He do to us...Much has been said of Mahomet's propagating his Religion by the sword...Yet withal, if we take this for an argument of the truth or falsehood of a religion, there is a radical mistake in it. The sword indeed: but where will you get your sword! Every new opinion, at its starting, is precisely in a *minority of one.* In one man's head alone, there it dwells as yet. One man alone of the whole world believes it: there is one man against all men. That *he* take a sword, and try to propagate with that, will do little for him. You must first get your sword!

The student looked up. "Pardon me, sir," he said, "but why Carlyle? I mean, why are we reading Carlyle's words rather than anyone else's?"

"Because," replied the sage, "Carlyle is one of the first Europeans, perhaps the very first, to recognize the Prophet's true worth." He made an indication with his hand to read on.

...[Nature] requires of a thing only that it *be* genuine of heart: she will protect it if so; will not if not so. There is a soul of truth in all the things she ever gave harbor to.

The body of all Truth dies; and yet in all, I say, there is a soul which never dies; which in new and ever-nobler embodiment lives immortal as man himself! It is the way with Nature. The genuine essence of Truth never dies.

If a book comes from the heart, it will contrive to reach other hearts; all art and authorcraft is of small account to that. One would say the primary character of the Koran is this of its *genuineness,* of its being a *bona fide* book...

To his [Mahomet's] eyes it is forever clear that this world wholly is miraculous. He sees what, as we said once before, all great thinkers...in one way or other, have contrived to see: That this so solid-looking material world is, at bottom, in very deed, Nothing;

is a visual and tact[ile] Manifestation of God's power and presence—a shadow hung out by Him on the bosom o' the void
Infinite; nothing more.

Much has been said and written about the sensuality of Mahomet's
Religion: more than was just. [Polygamous practices], criminal
to us, which he permitted, were not of his appointment; he found
them practised, unquestioned from immemorial time in Arabia;
what he did was to curtail them, restrict them, not on one but
on many sides.

...Enjoying things which are pleasant: that is not the evil: it is the
reducing of our mortal self to slavery by them that is...It is a
calumny on men to say that they are roused to heroic action by
ease, hope of pleasure, recompense—sugar-plums of any kind,
in this world or the next! In the meanest mortal there lies something nobler...Difficulty, abnegation, martyrdom, death are the
allurements that act on the heart of man. Kindle the inner genial
life of him, you have a flame that burns up all lower
considerations...Not by flattering our appetites; no, by awakening the Heroic that slumbers in every heart, can any Religion
gain followers.

They called him Prophet, you say? Why, he stood there face to
face with them: bare, not enshrined in any mystery; visibly clouting [mending] his own cloak, cobbling his own shoes; fighting,
counselling, ordering in the midst of them; they must have seen
what kind of man he *was,* let him be *called* what you like! No
emperor with his tiaras was obeyed as this man in a cloak of his
own clouting.

...I said, the Great Man was always as lightning out of Heaven:
the rest of men waited for him like fuel, and they too would
flame.

The student looked up inquiringly and, at the sage's nod, restored the
book to its place. "Tell me more about Mohammed," he said.
The sage smiled.

"You're asking me to do the impossible," he said. "No description of Mohammed is enough to reveal him to you, and in the end that is what you really need.

"A search in libraries and bookstores," he continued, "will yield many histories of Islam and biographies of Mohammed. You will learn much concerning the historical facts surrounding his life. From these you will come away with a vague sense of dissatisfaction, for none of them are sufficient to explain the Prophet, his religion, or the phenomenal success of the two. In order *really* to understand, you should have been there; you should have *seen* the light shining in his eyes, his jet-black wavy hair, his arresting appearance, his ineffable, electrifying *presence* that would have told you immediately that here was a person who could not lie, even in jest. He was the handsomest human being who ever lived, but more important was his beauty of character and supreme moral conduct. One glance would be sufficient to anyone whose heart isn't blind that if ever there was a Prophet of God, this was it. His enemies themselves, in fact, never doubted these truths; it was only their innate stubbornness and their vested interests which they felt he challenged that prevented them from openly acknowledging the obvious. And now, today, the facts of his life have become a kind of Rorschach test for all his biographers—lacking, naturally enough, such a vision, each one tries to account for his unique success with an explanation that he or she likes best. They read their pet theory, their own favorite brainchild, into his life.

His Battles

"Take his battles, for instance. Biographers make much of his campaigns because the most facts are recorded about them and because wars are the stuff which history is made of. Yet these are of secondary importance, because they were necessary for the survival of the newborn religion and for the eradication of evil, but not essential for the original Revelation itself. Just think: the Archangel Gabriel had already come to Mohammed, God had already revealed His religion, and the Prophet and his small flock of followers had endured more than a decade of religious persecution. The Prophet had already experienced his Ascension, the highest spiritual elevation known to humanity. During all this time the Prophet tried to spread his religion peacefully. It was only when it became obvious that his enemies would not suffer him or Islam to survive that the Prophet emigrated to Medina, drew his sword, and did not sheath it again until Mecca was conquered. It was both self-defense, and an attempt to make the world safe for Islam; an attempt which succeeded against impossible odds, and which was won with a minimum of casualties on both sides. The total of dead did not exceed five hundred in all his battles put together, and in one was as low as ten.

"One historian has noted that the life of the Prophet is a tale of two cities, and such is indeed the case. The period of Revelation belonged to Mecca, the period of consolidation to Medina. If the Prophet had not combated evil from his base in Medina, Islam could not have survived. But the essence of Revelation had already been communicated to him in Mecca. The period in Medina added fresh details, without altering this essence in any way. If the idolaters had not been so implacably opposed to Mohammed, so bent on destroying him and his religion, the battles might not have taken place at all. He was not the warlord that some people make him out to be. He was a businessman, you know, and he had the highest praise for knowledge and science—more than any other prophet or religion."

His Miracles

"What about miracles?" the student asked. "All prophets have shown miracles. Did he do so too?"

"Well, we should first get one thing straight about miracles," the sage said. "Miracles are primarily the 'calling cards' of God, which tell a certain people: 'Here is a person to whom I have entrusted my instructions. Heed him, and you won't lose.' Miracles are performed *by* God *for* the people, not by a prophet himself.

"But in the end, we can't place much store by miracles, for they are specific to prophets alone. They can't be deemed a basis for widespread emulation, and are not what religion is all about. Religion is moral behavior towards every being in the universe, closeness to God, and attainment of this closeness through worship—or techniques—which God specifies. Hence, not only is it impossible for ordinary people like you and me to perform miracles or extraordinary psychic feats, but these are actually a hindrance to religion and spiritual progress, for they keep the mind focused on the wrong things.

"Now many miracles are recounted about the Prophet, which I leave you to discover in his biographies. He himself used to say that his only miracle worthy of note was the Koran—meaning its beauty, profoundness, and inviolability.

"The Prophet called the Koran his 'standing miracle'—that he, unschooled to the point of barely being able to write his name, should have authored the Koran, the masterpiece of all time of Arabic, the most evocative language in the world, is so unthinkable that its miraculous nature would be clear to all but the most obstinate. In the Prophet's case, unlettered meant unfettered—an unfettered mind, a heart unhindered by the pride that comes from too much book-learning. He was thus a conduit ready to convey undistorted the pure, pristine Truth of God."

The sage then proceeded to instruct the student about what Mohammed said, what he did, and what he was—*who* he was, based on eyewitness accounts.

His Asceticism

"The mountain and the desert," the sage continued, "are key symbols in the careers of the greatest prophets. Just as Moses had his forty days on Mount Sinai with his Lord, and Jesus spent forty days in the desert overcoming the temptations of Satan, Mohammed's prophethood was preceded by long sojourns on the Mountain of Light (Mt. Hira) in a cave facing a rocky deserted expanse, where Gabriel first announced his mission to him. He heard the rocks and trees call to him: 'Messenger of God,' which might have been attributed to a mental state, were it not for the fact that Ali, his cousin, heard them too on occasions when he accompanied him. The Prophet was at first deeply frightened by the unexpected turn his ascetic practices had taken, but was reassured by a relative of his first wife, a Christian deeply versed in the Old and New Testaments, who said: 'The Archangel has come upon him, the greatest *nomos* (the Law or *Torah*) has come to him.'"

His Morality

"What about his morality?" the student asked.
"The Prophet of God was the most generous, the most truthful and

gentlest of men. He was always immersed in meditation. His silence was longer than his speech, and he never spoke in vain. He would mention God's name at the beginning and end of his words. In talking he chose short words rich with meaning. His words were true and to the point. He never used more words, or less, than was necessary.

"He never broke anyone's feelings, nor did he belittle anyone. He did not get angry over worldly things. But when someone's rights were violated, nothing could stop his anger before the wrong was righted. However, he never got angry about or avenged a wrong directed at his own person or business. When he got angry, he would immediately give up on his anger and would conceal it. He would not laugh out loud; the most he did was smile.

"He always displayed a cheerful countenance and good disposition to those in his presence. He was very kind and forgiving. Hardness of heart, bitterness of tongue, and repulsiveness of nature did not exist in him.

"He did not argue with or shout at anyone. He did not use bad language or scold anybody. He was not a miser. What he disliked, he pretended not to see. He did not disillusion the expectant, and remained silent about what he did not like. He did not quarrel with anyone, speak too much, or busy himself with vain things.

"He left the public alone on three points: he did not criticize or blame anybody, either to their face or behind their back; he did not pry after the shames or shortcomings of anyone; and he never told anyone anything that was not good or edifying for them.

"He listened to the last person with the same attention he accorded to the first speaker. If those present found something amusing, he would join in their mirth, and if they were amazed at something, he too would express wonder. He tolerated the blunt, even harsh, words and questions directed at him by strangers, so that his Companions might follow his example. He used to say: 'When you see a needy person requesting something, help them to meet that need.'

"He did not accept praise that was not truthful. As long as a right was not violated, he would not interrupt a conversation. When it was, he would either forbid it or depart from that company.

"He brought brotherhood, compassion, virtue, and lovingkindness, and taught people the meaning and purpose of being human. He would talk gently with his Companions and joke with them. He would love and fondle children and take them in his arms. All human beings, whether slaves or free persons, rich or poor, were the same to him. He pleased everybody. He would visit the sick living on the outskirts of the city. He would greet people without waiting for them to greet him first. He said: 'Exchange greetings, so that you may come to love one another.' He always smiled at and spoke gently with people. A pleasant smile always hovered on his lips. If someone came to him while he was at Prayer, he would cut it short so as not to keep them waiting and inquire about their situation.

"He was very harmonious in his family life. He would not hurt anyone in his household, and would shower them with tenderness. Love and gentleness permeated his whole being. He took pity on those in need. Because he always tried to answer their needs, not much could be found in his household at any time. He would give to whoever asked for something. If he didn't have anything, he would borrow from others to fulfill someone's need.

"He was very humble. He ate with his servants and conversed with them. He would serve guests himself. He always spoke well of others. He was very tenderhearted towards the poor. He always considered it a duty to mend their broken hearts. He loved children. His grandchildren would clamber all over him during Prayer, and he would not say anything. Nor was his love confined to human beings; it extended to animals and indeed, to all beings. He also counseled love for flowers, plants, and trees. He promised recompense for anyone who watered a parched tree. As a poet once observed: 'He went to a school where God was the teacher. Accept the summary of words: he was human, but higher than the angels.'"

His Trustworthiness

"The Prophet was so absolutely dependable in both word and deed," the sage went on, "that he earned the title 'the Trustworthy' among his people long before he received his commission of prophethood. In fact, in his first public appearance as prophet, he stood on a hill and addressed his listeners: 'If I were to tell you that an army is behind this hill, ready to attack you, would you believe me?' 'Yes, we would, for we have never seen you lie,' they all replied, and among them were Amr (a.k.a. the

Father of Ignorance)[70] and Abdul Uzza (a.k.a. the Father of Flame)[71] who later became archenemies of the Prophet."

"Yet they still didn't believe his message?"

"Unfortunately, no. Such is the way with all prophets: Pharaoh and his henchmen didn't believe in Moses, few of his contemporaries believed in Jesus, and, naturally, not everyone believed in Mohammed.

"Later on, the Prophet was sending letters to the political leaders of his time, inviting them to join the new religion. He sent one such letter to the Eastern Roman Emperor Heraclius, who summoned one of the greatest enemies of the Prophet to discuss the matter. This man confirmed that the Prophet had never been known to lie. Heraclius then made a very wise observation: 'It is unthinkable,' he remarked, 'that a man should refrain from lying for so long and yet lie against God.' In addition, it is nothing short of amazing that the Prophet was so truthful that even his greatest enemies could not lie against him."

"That certainly *is* interesting," remarked the student.

"A saying of the Prophet enjoins truthfulness on his followers: 'Promise me regarding six points, and I promise you Paradise:

    1. When you speak, speak the truth.

    2. When you make a promise, fulfill it.

    3. When something is entrusted to you, be trustworthy.

    4. Guard your private parts.

    5. Shut your eyes to what is Forbidden.

    6. Keep your hands away from what is Forbidden.'

"Once, the Prophet saw a woman call her child: 'See what I'm going to give you,' said she. 'What are you going to give him?' he asked. 'A few dates,' she replied. 'If you weren't going to give him anything, you would have been telling a lie,' he remarked. He taught that one has to be truthful, even to a child or an animal."

The disciple said nothing, but his demeanor showed that he was impressed.

His Tolerance

"Was he a tolerant person?" he asked.

"Well, look at it this way," said the sage. "Noah placed a curse on his people that resulted in the Flood. Moses did not save Pharaoh when the Red Sea closed upon him, even though Pharaoh repented, accepted faith in God, and called for help in his last moments. Even the gentle Jesus sometimes railed against 'fools, hypocrites, serpents, generations of vipers.'

"Contrast this now with the conduct of the Prophet, who went to a town called Taif to seek help, and was insulted and driven away with sticks and stones by an angry mob. His adopted son tried to shield him, but he was nevertheless bloodied all over by stones that struck home. At that moment the Archangel Gabriel appeared to him, and said: 'If you so desire, I will lay waste to this town.' 'No,' came the Prophet's reply, 'that's not what I've been sent for.' And he took refuge in God's mercy with a prayer.

"A woman on the side of the enemy once tried to poison him, but he forgave her. The only thing he found intolerable was high treason in wartime.

"And at the Battle of Uhud, when the Prophet's followers suffered a temporary defeat, the Prophet's life was in danger, and he was hit with a rock that pierced his cheek and knocked out a tooth. Even then, he prayed to his Lord: 'Forgive my people, for they do not know.'

"Why, that's just like Jesus!" the student exclaimed.

"Of course," said the sage, "but there's more to come. The woman Hind and her prosperous husband were sworn enemies of the Prophet. When Hamza, one of the Prophet's uncles, slew her uncle and delivered the deathblow to her father in the first great battle between the Prophet and his opponents, the fiery Hind swore revenge, promising to eat Hamza's liver raw.

"Accordingly she enlisted the help of Savage, an Abyssinian slave and expert lancer, promising him his freedom and other rewards. At the next battle, Savage stalked Hamza and, seeing his opportunity, hurled his lance. Hamza fell, dead. When the battle was over, Savage went over to Hamza's body and, on Hind's instructions, ripped open his belly, cut out his liver, and brought it to Hind. She took it, bit away a piece, chewed it, swallowed a morsel in fulfillment of her vow, and spat out the rest. He then led her to the body, where she cut off his nose, ears, and other parts of his flesh, telling the women around her to mutilate other bodies."

The disciple's revulsion was evident.

"When the Prophet saw the remains of his uncle, he was angry as he had never been before. And if he had wished to avenge himself for any wrong, this barbarous act would have been it. Yet when he entered Mecca in triumph, he asked his enemies, among whom were Hind and Savage: 'What do you expect of me?' They replied that they expected mercy of him. He then spoke to them in words of forgiveness, as Joseph had done to his brothers long ago in Egypt: 'Verily, I say, as my brother Joseph said: "This day you will not be upbraided or reproached. God forgives you, and He is the Most Merciful of the merciful" (12:92). You may go, you are all free.' When he saw Savage later on, he asked him to recount the details, and when he was finished, said: 'Alas, take your face from me, don't let me look upon you again.' And with these words he set him free. It was never his way to reward evil with evil."[72]

"How did he treat people who made gross mistakes?" the student asked.

"Well," said the sage, "consider the following episode: The first mosque in Medina had no roof. One day there was a great commotion in the mosque. Everybody was in an uproar. When the Prophet emerged from his home to investigate, he discovered that an ignorant and boorish follower had urinated in the mosque. Everyone was furious, and the man was trying to defend himself on the grounds that the hot sun would soon dry away the puddle.

"At this juncture we should remember that excrement of any kind is considered foul in Islam, and that even the tiniest drop of urine must be washed away from one's clothes. A saying attributed to the Prophet states: 'Cleanliness derives from faith.' Urinating in a place reserved for God and worship is thus tantamount to sacrilege.

"Far from berating the man, however, the Prophet explained to the Companions that he didn't know any better. 'He doesn't know,' he said, 'and this indicates his need to learn. Teach him, tell him, don't shout at him. Make things easy, not difficult.' Then, according to one account, the Prophet had some water brought in. He prevented others who wanted to clean up the mess. 'This is my task,' he said. And with his own hands, he washed the mosque clean without a bad word or complaint."

"With his own hands," murmured the disciple.

"On another occasion this same man said to the Prophet: 'May God place just you and me in His Paradise, and exclude everyone else.' 'What a pity,' the Prophet observed, 'that you've confined such limitless mercy to such a small circle.'"

"How did he tolerate his enemies?"

"One of the archenemies of the Prophet—I've mentioned him already—was the powerful and wealthy 'Father of Ignorance.' Everyone feared him because of his ruthlessness. He thought the Prophet was a dangerous sorcerer. Once, he chanced upon the Prophet when he was alone at the Holy Sanctuary in Mecca, and could not resist the chance to make clear that he, at least, was not overawed. So he proceeded to insult him with all the abuse he could muster, but the Prophet never said a word, and just looked at him. When he had heaped on him all the insults he could think of, he went his way, and the Prophet sadly rose to his feet and went home."

His Compassion

"Now the story is told," continued the master, "that the Father of Ignorance, in his extreme hatred, once dug a wide manhole in a street where the Prophet often passed, filled it with filth, covered it with branches, and proceeded to wait. His idea was that the Prophet would fall into the hole, emerge covered with dirt and excrement, and thus be humiliated. When he heard shouts that the Prophet was coming, he rushed to witness the spectacle; in his excitement tripped, however, and fell into the very hole he had intended for the Prophet. When the Prophet came upon him, and saw him standing in the filth in a dazed sort of way, he understood immediately what had happened. Without a word he reached out his hand, pulled him out of the slime, cleaned him with his own hands as best he could, and gave him his cloak to cover himself until he got home, saying merely: 'Don't do it again.' 'Falling into a hole (trap) of his own making,' an expression famous in the Middle East, derives from this event.

"The Prophet and his Companions had returned to Medina after a battle with many casualties. The next day, after the morning Prayer and the funeral Prayer for their dead, the Prophet asked: 'Suppose after a battle you are walking through the battlefield, and see a wounded Companion and a wounded enemy soldier not far away. Both are in need of water, and you have some water with you. Whom would you give it to?'

"The Companions all said they would give it to their friend. Omar, however, intervened: 'God and His Messenger know best,' he said. 'What do you suggest?'

"'I would give half the water to our man and the other half to the enemy soldier,' the Prophet replied, 'no matter how much or how little water is available.' The Companions were all surprised at this answer. 'How can this be?' they asked.

"The Prophet explained: 'The situation is different under those circumstances. The other person is no longer an enemy soldier, but a wounded, thirsty man, a human being in need. It doesn't matter if he gets up and resumes fighting against us afterwards, it is incumbent on us to share the water between the two.'

"This illustrates the attribute of Compassion, which rules for all beings simply by virtue of the fact that they exist, regardless of anything else. The Prophet used to tell the story of a whore who gained Paradise because she saw a dog dying of thirst one day, fashioned a rope out of her dress, tied her shoe to it, lowered the shoe into a well, and saved the dog with the water she drew out. He also told a complementary story of a woman who went to Hell because she was cruel to her cat and starved it to death."

The disciple shook his head in amazement. "You're telling me things I've never heard before," he said. "How come I haven't heard any of this?"

"Perhaps," the sage replied gently, "because you haven't met anyone who could tell you about them."

His Mercy

"God addresses his Messenger in the Koran: 'I did not send you except as a mercy to the worlds,' and indeed the Prophet was the most merciful of men. He himself once remarked: 'I have been sent as a mercy, not as a bringer of curses.'

"During one of their encampments, a Companion brought in a fledgling he had caught. One of the parent birds came and threw itself into his hands. Men's faces were full of wonder, and the Prophet said: 'Do you wonder at this bird? You have taken its young, and it has thrown itself down in merciful tenderness to its young. Yet I swear by God, your Lord is more merciful to you than this bird is to its fledgling.' And he told the man to put back the young bird where he had found it.

"On another occasion, a snake emerged from the rocks when he was at Mina. The Companions all fell upon it, but the snake managed to escape. The Prophet, who was watching from a distance, remarked: 'You're now free of its harm, and it is free of yours.'

"A poet had strenuously rejected the new religion and had written vilifying verses against the Prophet. In return, a warrant was out for his head. But his brother persuaded him to go to the Prophet and ask forgiveness, for he would not kill anyone who came to him in repentance. The poet therefore went to the Prophet and, without revealing who he was, asked him whether he would receive the poet if he were to bring the repenting poet to the Prophet. When the Prophet said he would, he revealed who he was, and the Prophet stopped angry Companions from harming him, saying: 'He has come in repentance, and is no longer what he used to be.'

"When the Prophet's little son was dying, he was by his side. As the child breathed his last, the Prophet took him in his arms, and tears flowed from his eyes. Since he had forbidden loud wailing after the dead, people thought that all expression of grief was to be denied, and hence a Companion addressed him: 'This is what you have forbidden. When Moslems see you weeping, they too will weep.' The Prophet continued to weep, and when he could find his voice he said: 'This I don't forbid. These are the promptings of tenderness and mercy, and he who shows no mercy will receive no mercy...The eye weeps, the heart grieves, nor do we say anything that would offend the Lord.'

"A man, seeing the Prophet frolic with his little grandsons on his lap, remarked: 'I have ten children, yet I haven't ever kissed one of them.' The Prophet, who was an orphan twice over and had lost his closest kin while only a child, retorted: 'What can I do if God has removed mercy from your heart?'"

His Intelligence

"All prophets are gifted with innate genius," continued the sage, "and the Prophet was the most accomplished of them all. When he was young, the tribes of Mecca were repairing the Holy Kaaba ("Cube"),[73] but could not agree among themselves as to which tribe should have the honor of lifting the Black Stone—the cornerstone—into place. Things were getting out of hand, and they finally decided to appoint the first person entering the Holy Sanctuary as arbiter between them. This happened to be Mohammed. When the situation was explained to him, he told them to place the Black Stone in the center of a large piece of cloth. A representative of each tribe would hold the cloth on one side, and they would lift it collectively. When this was done, the future Prophet took the Black Stone and placed it in its niche himself."

"Isn't that clever," the student thought. Aloud, he said: "Was the Prophet a man of reason?"

"Certainly," said the sage. "Common sense played a great part in the Prophet's deeds and advice. Once, a Companion came in from outdoors, and the Prophet asked him what he had done with his camel. 'I entrusted it to God,' the man said, implying that he had left the camel free to wander. The Prophet disapproved. 'First tether your camel to a secure post, then trust in God,' he said. Obviously, this is meant not just for camels, but indicates the need to take precautions so that the desired results may be obtained in any enterprise."

"What a vast generalization from the simplest of examples," the student marveled. "Such an economy of words to describe a vast domain of experience."

His Love of Work

"The Prophet was extremely industrious," resumed the sage, "and when on a task he worked harder than anyone else. Such was the case, for example, when a ditch was being dug for the defense of Medina. During expeditions the Prophet would gather firewood just like anyone else, in spite of the fact that his Companions tried to prevent him from doing menial labor.

"Once, the Prophet and an entourage of Companions were going somewhere. On their way they came upon a man who was sitting on the ground, doing nothing. The Prophet passed by him without a greeting. On their way back, they passed by the same man, who by this time had picked up a stick and was idly drawing figures on the ground. This time the Prophet greeted him. The people who were with him inquired why he had not greeted the man the first time around but had done so on the second. 'The first time he wasn't doing anything,' the Prophet replied. 'The second time around, at least he was doing something.'"

His Attitude to the Poor

"The Prophet always befriended the poor, and tried to help them out as best he could. A part of one of the long colonnades in the Medina mosque was reserved for the homeless and destitute, and because of a bench reserved for them they were called 'the People of the Bench.' The Prophet spent time with the poor whenever he could, listening to their troubles and devising solutions. Whenever there was a food shortage, as there often was, he used to say: 'The food of one is enough for two, the food of two is enough for four, and the food of four is enough for eight.'"

His Resolve

"At an early stage of his career, the vested interests of Mecca tried to discourage the Prophet and buy him off. They summoned his beloved uncle, under whose protection he was, and told him: 'If it is riches your nephew is after, we will make him the richest man in Mecca. If it is power he wants, we will give him leadership. If it is women, he can take his pick. Anything, so long as he desists from this newfangled religion of his. Otherwise, we cannot guarantee his safety.'

"When his uncle told him that the rulers of Mecca had sent him a message, the Prophet was at first overjoyed, thinking that this signified their acceptance of God's religion. Imagine the letdown he suffered when he learned the truth. The worst came, however, when his uncle said: 'I cannot safeguard you unless you accept their terms.'

"The Prophet took a few moments to adjust to the blow. Then he said: 'Uncle, hear me well, and relate to them exactly what I say. If they were to put the sun in my right hand and the moon in my left, I still would not turn back from my path.' Having said this, he stepped out into the clean night air, and broke down. 'If you do not protect your religion, my Lord, what can I do?' he implored.

"And at that moment, God's mercy reached out and touched his uncle's heart. 'I cannot leave my nephew to the mercy of these cynics,' he thought. He stepped out and assured the Prophet that he would stand by him through thick or thin. And the two were reunited in tears."

His Patience

"Once his protecting uncle was dead," the sage continued after a pause, "control passed over to another uncle who was inimical—I've mentioned him, 'the Father of Flame.' The protection he gave his nephew was a sham, and the Prophet was subjected to ridicule and humiliation as never before, which he met with uncommon forbearance. On one occasion someone passing by leaned over his gate and tossed a piece of putrefying offal into his cooking-pot. On another, a man threw a sheep's uterus, filthy with blood and excrement, over his neck when he was praying in the courtyard of his house. In response, the Prophet merely picked up the object on the end of a stick and, standing at his gate, loudly inquired what kind of protection this was.

"At another time, when the Prophet was coming from the Kaaba, a man took a handful of filth and threw it in his face and over his head. When he came home, one of his daughters washed him clean, crying as she did so. 'Don't cry, dear,' he said; 'God will protect your father.'"

"What they did was terrible," said the disciple.

"It certainly was," the master replied. "The Prophet didn't fight those battles for nothing. Besides, I'm not even telling you about how his followers were persecuted."

His Temperance

"A relative once came to the Prophet, and asked permission to make himself a eunuch and spend the rest of his life as a wandering beggar. Although he was married, he had been an ascetic before the revelation of Islam.

"'Don't you have a fair example in me?' asked the Prophet. 'I associate with women, I eat meat, I fast, and I break my fast. Whoever makes himself or other men eunuchs does not belong to my people.' However, the Prophet had reason to believe that he was not fully understood, so on another occasion he asked him the same question, adding: 'You fast every day, and keep vigil every night in prayer. Don't do so. For your eyes have rights over you, and your body has its rights, and your family have their rights. So pray, and sleep, and fast, and break your fast.'

"At another time, three Companions were vying with each other. One claimed that he fasted all the time, the second that he spent the nights without sleep, and the third said that he did not approach women. When the Prophet heard this, he said: 'This is not my way. I fast on some days and eat on others, I stay awake sometimes but I sleep, too, and I am married.' And he added the rejoinder: 'Beware of excess in your religion.' Moderation was always his motto."

His Generosity

"One of the Companions had a camel which was old and weak, and he could not afford a better one. The Prophet asked him: 'Will you sell me this camel of yours?' He answered: 'I will give it to you.' 'No,' the Prophet said, 'sell it to me.' He understood from the Prophet's tone that he was expected to bargain, so they bargained until the price was raised to an ounce of gold. When he brought the camel to the Prophet, he was given a bit more than an ounce, and as he turned to go, the Prophet called him back. 'Take your camel,' he said. 'It is yours, and please keep the price you were paid for it.'

"Once, a Bedouin came and asked the Prophet to give him something. The Prophet did so. A second request was again met. Since the Prophet had nothing left to give, on the third request he promised he would give again at his first opportunity. Omar was disturbed by this, and commented: 'You shouldn't trouble yourself so much.' These words, however, displeased the Messenger of God. Sensing this, a Companion rose and said: 'Give, don't think that God will make you poor and remove His bounty from you.' 'This,' replied the Prophet, 'is what I've been ordered to do.' An unbeliever, overwhelmed by the generosity of the Prophet, once similarly remarked: 'My people, rush to enter Islam. Mohammed gives in such a manner that only a person who doesn't fear poverty and trusts in God completely can give in this way.'"

His Humility

"The Prophet used to rest on a bare straw mat. Once, a woman brought him a present, a kind of cushion that was a bit—if not much—more comfortable. When he saw it, the Prophet instructed his wife to give it back. 'If I had wished,' he said, 'God would have caused mountains of gold and silver to walk by my side; but I don't want it.' And he once addressed a man trembling in awe of him: 'My brother, do not fear me. Like you, I am a human being, whose mother broke dry bread.'

"Sometimes the Prophet would pray until morning, or stand in Prayer until his feet were all blisters. Once, he was asked: 'God has forgiven you everything. Why do you exert yourself so much?' He answered: 'Then shouldn't I be a servant of God who gives thanks?'

"On another occasion, he was warning his followers never to be sure of their fate and always to strive diligently. 'How about you?' they asked. 'For me it's the same,' he replied. They were taken aback. 'How can that be?' they asked. 'Yes,' he said, 'I am the Messenger of God, and God has vouchsafed everything to me, yet even I can't be sure what my end will be.'"

"So humble, too," the student thought to himself.

"It was not his desire to become a ruler. When circumstances forced him to act as one, he was the epitome of Plato's 'philosopher king' or Nietzsche's 'Caesar with the heart of Christ.'

"Humility and simplicity were the essence of his morality. He used to tell his Companions: 'Don't praise me excessively like Christians have done with Jesus. I am a servant of God. Just call me God's servant and messenger.'

"Once, leaning on his staff, he came upon his Companions. They all stood up immediately. He didn't like this, however, and said: 'Don't stand up for me like strangers do who wish to show respect for each other.'"

His Companions

"One great advantage Mohammed had over Jesus," the sage went on to explain, "was the impeccable nature of his Companions. Some of Jesus' disciples betrayed him or deserted him at the critical moment. Mohammed's Companions, on the other hand, formed a 'wall of flesh,' as it were, whenever their Beloved Prophet was threatened. This is indicative of Divine protection—it points to the intention of Providence to make sure that the Prophet and his message would survive. One of his enemies once remarked: 'No father loves his son as much as his Companions love Mohammed.' And one of their ambassadors remarked when he returned to Mecca: 'I have been sent as envoy to kings—to Caesar and Chosroes and the Negus[74]—and I have not seen a king whose men honor him as much as the Companions of Mohammed honor Mohammed. If he commands anything, they almost outstrip his word in fulfilling it; when he performs his ablution, they almost fight to take away its water; when he speaks, their voices are hushed in his presence; nor will they look him fully in the face, but lower their eyes in reverence for him.'

"It was his Companions, too, who bore the burden of faithfully recording the Koran and the Prophet's Way and successfully transmitting them to later generations, not only in word but in deed. It is for this reason that he remarked: 'My Companions are like the fixed stars in the night sky. Follow any one of them, and you will be rightly guided.'"

Epilogue

The seeker looked despondent. "What you've been telling me, sir," he protested, "is just too good to be true. How can anyone ever hope to emulate such an example successfully?"

The sage laughed. "Cheer up, son," he said. "The burden is light. The Prophet's religion is the easiest to perform. There's nothing in it that an average adolescent can't learn or practice. And while the Prophet's example may be unattainable, we're not all called upon to be him.

"But if you *would* aspire to approach him, to be like him, then you're talking about sainthood. And this has been eased so much nowadays that only a little sincere effort is enough to accomplish a lot.

"For example, Ibrahim Atham was a sultan, but he had to forsake all he possessed in order to become a saint. In a later age, Gilani, the great sage, remarked: 'Had he lived today, we would have made him a saint in any case. He wouldn't have had to renounce his kingdom.'

"The main point in sainthood is self-control. That's how the Prophet achieved what he did. His Companions would ask: 'Don't you have a self, an ego?' And he would answer: 'Of course I do. As a matter of fact, mine is greater and worse than any of yours. But I've made it surrender to God'—succeeded, that is, in making it a Moslem."

The student fidgeted in his seat. "I beg your pardon ever so much, sir," he said, "but can't we possibly do without the God concept? Because I think that's what this is all leading up to."

"I'm afraid we can't," was the sage's reply. "The existence of God is the central fact about the universe. That's why almost all religions have emphasized it so much. Ultimate, or Absolute, Reality had a reason for spawning relative, conditioned reality. God created the universe and man for a purpose, and unless we act in accordance with that purpose, we can never achieve lasting happiness. We will then be tossed to and fro like driftwood on the high seas.

"Furthermore, God is Compassionate and All-forgiving, but there is one thing He won't forgive: associating partners with Him.[75] If He won't stand for transgressions against His Unity, think how much worse it must be to reduce that Unity to zero in one's mind.

"Let me just quote you a passage from *The Upanishads:* 'If you think you know the truth about Brahman, know that you know little.'"

"Brahman?"

"'Truth is One, yet the sages call it by many names.'"

"There's another thing," the student said. "I still can't swallow this bit about the afterlife and Heaven and Hell."

"My boy," said the sage, "it doesn't matter whether you accept a fact or not. A fact is a fact, and will make itself known as such in its own due time. We can only inquire *why* God created Heaven and Hell. In Sufism we have a saying: 'The disciple should always be between hope and fear.' He will be attracted by hope and repelled by fear, and this will aid his spiritual ascent. Just as we can't have electric current without positive and negative poles, and as we can't have magnetism without the North and South poles, so we can't obtain spiritual evolution without the twin poles of hope and fear. There's an adage in English that summarizes things beautifully: 'We promise according to our hopes, but perform according to our fears.' In other words: no fear, no performance. On the other hand, fear without hope leads to paralysis and despair, so hope is needed, too.

It's all right to dwell on the Blissful Aspect (Beauty) of God, on Love and Compassion and Mercy, but you'll watch your step only if you bear in mind that He has a Wrathful Aspect (Majesty), too. The combination of the Blissful and the Wrathful makes for Maturity or Perfection. Fear of God leads us to obey His laws, and obeying His laws inspires love for God in our hearts. In other words, if God's commandments are obeyed, they lead to the love of God. The proper destiny of man takes him from earth and leads him to Heaven, but if one isn't careful one can easily find that one has landed in 'the other place.' So care and caution are necessary.

"An uneducated man came to the Prophet of God one day, and the Prophet assigned him a teacher who would teach him the Koran. They studied for a long time, until they came to the verses: 'He who does a particle of good shall see its recompense, and he who does a particle of evil shall see its recompense' (99:7-8). 'That's it!' the man exclaimed. "That's all the information I need.' His teacher was rather taken aback; they had much more studying to do. So they decided to take the matter to the Prophet. The man said: 'I am an illiterate man, and I don't have much time for studies. Is it okay if I act by these verses and skip the rest?' The Prophet confirmed this, and the man went his way.

"That, in a nutshell, is the reason for Heaven and Hell. And the man was a wise one indeed, for it is the quintessential wisdom of all the prophets and sages: 'Whatever you do, you do to yourself.' 'As you sow, so shall you reap,' and that is why you must 'do as you would be done by.' 'That is all you know on earth, and all you need to know,' as Keats might have put it. But beyond this first and foremost principle, there are also many other details to be known, and we could never have discovered or fathomed them if God hadn't revealed them to us through the prophets."

The student scratched his head. "I don't get it, sir," he said. "What's your angle? I mean, there are so many different versions of Islam today. Which one do you profess to?"

"My son," said the sage, "before all the interpretations of Islam; long before the twelve major dervish orders, the countless sects, the four schools of law; before Sunnism or Shiism or Sufism or anything else; before, indeed, the Prophet's death or even his Emigration to Medina, there was the pure, crystal-clear teaching of Mohammed. It is that which is important above all else, although you shouldn't deny yourself the developments of later generations. For they are the fruit of the seed that the Prophet planted; they make explicit what was latent in his teachings. It is Mohammedanism, leading a Mohammedan life, that is all-important.

Of course, in saying this I don't intend or imply a deification of Mohammed. What I have in mind is the emulation of Mohammed's example in one's daily life. Mark my words: Mohammed is not only the Prophet of Moslems, but of all humanity; and the Koran is not just the book of Islam, but of all humankind.

"What you and I are doing is," he continued, "we're taking a time tunnel back to the age of the Prophet. Or maybe"—and here he smiled enigmatically—"the Prophet is taking a time tunnel to our age."

The student sighed. "What a pity," he said, "that we can't witness Mohammed today. Those who lived in his time were the really lucky ones."

"My son," the sage replied, "allow me to let you in on a little secret. Mohammed's corporeal life has indeed passed away, and there's nothing we can do about that. But his spirit survives on another plane of existence, where it is still accessible to those who ardently desire to meet him. May God grant that you and I be lucky enough to be graced with a vision of him on that plane."

And with that remark, he ended his words.

Divine Law

Introduction

As we have seen, Holy—or Divine—Law (*sharia*) is formed from: (a) the Koran and (b) the Way of the Prophet. In his Farewell Pilgrimage speech, the Prophet said that he was leaving his followers two things to keep them on the right path: they are the Koran and the Way. As will be shown here, these are integral parts of a whole—neither is sufficient without the other.

This issue is especially important today because of the many misinterpretations of Islam we see around us. These often stem from very limited and decontextualized readings of the Koran that do not include the Prophet's example. Narrow-minded, literalist misreadings such as these can be especially dangerous and influential (since many Moslems have not read these things themselves and rely upon others to interpret them). Law then is not always Holy Law, just presented as such. These misinterpretations have affected everything from the daily lives of women and minorities to societal attitudes toward Western cultures.

The main problem is this: Islam has been misunderstood not only by the West, but in recent times, also by some people who are Moslems themselves. Now the West is surely excusable, because after all, Islam is not widespread here. What is much more difficult to justify and explain is that people who adhere to a religion should remain ignorant of it. This does have something to do with the breakdown of traditional Islamic education in many countries, but the causes cannot be that simple. And if those who profess Islam don't know it properly, who is going to explain it to those who come to it from the outside? It's bad enough when outsiders misrepresent Islam, but what are we going to do when Moslems themselves are guilty of the charge?

Traditionally, Holy Law has been regarded as the most exoteric (secular) aspect of Islam whereas Sufism has been regarded as the most esoteric (mystical) end of the spectrum. But as the Master taught in his version of contemplative Islam, we must synthesize all of these aspects of Islam to make it whole: neither the letter of the Law (*sharia*) nor its spirit (mysticism) can be complete without the other.

As my Master stressed, ethics must always precede enlightenment. So it is essential that one learn to restrain or perfect the self, following the exoteric path (the Five Pillars of Faith, and so on), prior—or parallel—to embarking upon any further spiritual journey (of the kind traditionally represented by Sufism).

Islamic Epistemology and the Foundations of Islamic Law

Prior to any discussion of epistemology, a distinction should first be made between exoteric and esoteric knowledge. Exoteric knowledge deals with the outer aspects of things, and esoteric knowledge with the inward. In Islam, there are two sources of exoteric knowledge: reason (*aql*) and transmission (*naql*). Hence, we have the rational sciences on the one hand, and the transmitted (or revelatory) sciences on the other. The first are the positive (posit-ive) sciences, such as mathematics, physics, and chemistry, which have little if anything to do with religion directly.

Transmitted—or normative—sciences are those branches of knowledge that do not lend themselves to easy discovery by reason and have to be accepted as revealed; these are the religious sciences such as Koranic exegesis, Prophetic sayings, and code of law (*fiqh*). Yet even here, there is room for reason to operate.

In Islam, reason, or intellect, is one of the greatest gifts God has given to human beings. Relying on input in the form of impressions or sense data from the external world, filtered through reason, allows humans to reach accurate conclusions regarding that world. It enables them to survive therein, and to build sciences and civilizations.

Yet there are things which we inevitably accept on hearsay. Science itself is of this nature, for no single human lifetime could suffice to repeat all the experiments of science, or rediscover from scratch the sum total of human knowledge accumulated over thousands of years. This is equally true for the religious, or spiritual, sciences. The question then arises: to what extent should reason be exercised in religious matters, and at what point should one refrain from further reasoning of this kind?

This subject was much debated in the early period of Islam. The solution that yields the greatest benefit is this: where there is an explicit injunction of the Koran, and/or a reliable precedent of the Prophet, it is useless to argue any further; that line of action should be followed. For instance, if God has commanded us to perform the five daily Prayers, mere reason cannot explain why He has done so, nor why there are five Prayers rather than, say, six. We must then take these as given, or received, and continue from there.

Where a parallel can be drawn to a Koranic or Prophetic injunction, even if an identical case cannot be found, it is fruitful to do so. Finally, if there is a unanimous consensus within the Islamic community (meaning, in practice, a consensus of the scholars) regarding a certain matter, that should be followed. As a matter of fact, what has been outlined here is none other than the four foundations of Islamic law (*fiqh,* meaning "comprehension"): the Koran, the Way, analogy, and consensus.

This is where the Four Schools of Law come in: Islam has enough flexibility to allow a certain latitude in some matters. The four founders of these schools (Shafii, Abu Hanifa, Ibn Hanbal, and Malik) were all respectful towards one another's derivations. Yet in the end the schools differ little, and the variations pertain to matters of secondary detail. The Hanifite school is perhaps the most liberal and tolerant of the four.

One can choose to follow any one of these schools, and its deductions and guidelines can be implemented. For anything further, one is free to employ one's reason with impunity, provided one is sufficiently well-versed and competent to do so.

The important thing is to maintain a fine, healthy balance between reason and transmission, thereby having the best of both worlds and avoiding destructive interference between the two.

In societies where Islam predominated, it was quite natural for people to adopt Islamic law as the legal code governing them. In individual cases, it is up to the individual to adopt a particular school for his or her personal conduct. What should never be forgotten is that the Koran and the Prophet laid down general rules only; their implementation in specific cases is a matter for individual discretion, with the schools providing religious guidance in matters of detail. The Divine Law (*sharia*) is an individual matter. In societies where the population is predominantly Islamic, people may choose to be governed by an application of Holy Law to the social sphere, in which case the right of religious minorities to be bound by their own religious laws is respected.

As for esoteric knowledge, this lies mainly in the domain of Sufism (to be explored at length in a later chapter). It, too, can be divided into two parts:

1. *Direct* or *non-dual* (*tawhidi:* unitary) knowledge: Immediate or sympathetic perception, in which the object-subject distinction is transcended or nullified in some respect. One then knows something in the same way that one knows oneself or part of oneself. Distinct categories that fall under this heading are the inspirational (*ilham*), revelatory (*wahy*), intuitive (*kashf*) varieties of knowledge, and knowledge gained through veridical dreams.

2. Information or material related to the attainment, realization, and various states of the first kind of esoteric knowledge.

Exoteric Practices: The Five Pillars of Islam

Once one has entered the Islamic religion, there are many religious observances one is required to perform—the exoteric practices. For convenience, however, these have been summarized under five headings, called the Five Pillars of Islam. But before anything else one must consider morality, which is their foundation. Attempting to practice religious precepts without perfecting one's moral conduct is like building a house on quicksand—the more one builds, the faster it disappears. As we shall see in the later section on Sufism, each of these exoteric practices has a corresponding esoteric meaning as well. Any religious or spiritual advancement can be realized only on the basis of exemplary conduct. With this proviso in mind, the Five Pillars of Islam (to be discussed at length later) are as follows:

1. *Saying the Word of Witnessing.* This provides an individual's entry into Islam, a few simple words.

2. *Performing the five daily Prayers.* These are the (pre-)Dawn, Noon, Afternoon, Evening (Dusk), and Night Prayers. Although we call them "Prayers," this does not mean that we open our hands to God and ask Him for this or that. This is in fact done, but only after the main course of the Prayer has been performed. We call this "Prayer" in English only for want of a better word. This involves worshipping God by reciting certain sections from the Koran while standing, genuflecting, straightening up again, prostrating, and sitting. This cycle is then repeated, usually in multiples of two. These Prayers are the most important of a person's activities as a Moslem.

   The five daily Prayers comprise a total of forty cycles, but only half this number is obligatory. Moreover, although there is a definite time for each Prayer, obligatory Prayers can be postponed and performed even when they are overdue—they can be performed together and done in the evenings, for instance.

   While a single cycle can be extended almost indefinitely if desired, the average time it takes is about a minute. If we add five minutes for the Ablution with water (which is a prerequisite of Prayer), we end up with less than half an hour daily for taking time out from our daily routines, to God, being alone with God in worship and devotion, and returning to normal life refreshed and replenished.

   Now for the question of language. Ideally, the recitations within Prayer should be in Arabic. This is because of the necessity to recite chapters from the Koran, which is untranslatable; recitation in any other language would be recitation of a translation, not of the Koran itself. Yet, since we translate the Koran in order to understand it, if we insist on understanding what we recite in Prayer, there is no obstacle to doing so (though strict literalists would probably disagree). God understands all languages, and the first thing He looks at is the honesty of a person's intention and the earnestness in his or her heart. He does not judge people according to their race, or language, or nationality. To Him they are all His servants. If you can, recite Prayer in Arabic. If you can't, recite it in whatever language you are able to. This applies even to the proper name of God. If you can't bring yourself to say "Allah," then say "God," or "Gott," or "Dieu," in whatever language you prefer.

3. *Fasting* during the lunar month of Ramadan. This means to abstain for a period of twenty-eight days from food, sex, and profane actions until sundown in order to nurture and raise the spirit.

4. *Paying the Alms-tax,* or "Poor's Due." The poor have a right to a portion (usually one-fortieth, or two-and-a-half percent) of our assets, their due. Islam combines the spiritual with the material, the individual with the social. Hence, wherever performance of the Prayer is mentioned in the Koran, it is almost invariably accompanied by mention of the Alms-tax, and the latter is an act comparable to the former.

5. *Making the Pilgrimage (Hajj).* Once in a lifetime, every prosperous Moslem must go to Mecca and circumambulate the Kaaba (literally "Cube").

Needless to say, there are numerous details and spiritual subtleties associated with each of these Pillars, but none of these are insuperable or difficult to learn for those of sound mind.[76]

The Six Pillars of Faith or the Moslem's Creed

The Five Pillars of Islam pertain to actions, but what are the fundamental tenets of belief? These, too, have been summarized for convenience, and constitute the Moslem's Creed:

> *I believe in God; in His Angels, His Books, and His*
> *Mesengers; in the Day of Judgment; that whatever*
> *destiny befalls us, good and ill, is from God; and in the*
> *Resurrection after Death.*

Optionally, one can add: *"in Heaven and in Hell."* This recitation is capped by repeating the Word of Witnessing. Let us now look briefly at the meaning of this creed.

1. *Belief in God* is self-explanatory: there is One God that has created all beings, that is beyond all conception and comprehension, even beyond the beyond.

2. *God's Angels* are nonphysical, sexless, conscious entities that carry out His orders, maintain the laws of the universe, praise God constantly, and communicate His messages and commandments to humanity.

3. *God's Books* have been revealed by His Angels to His Prophets and thence, to humankind. They contain knowledge of the divine that is not easily accessible to human reasoning or experimentation, but which one nevertheless needs to know and act upon. These comprise a total of One Hundred Pages, revealed to various prophets at different times, and the Four Major Books: the Torah revealed to Moses, the Psalms revealed to David, the Gospel revealed to Jesus, and the Koran revealed to Mohammed.

   According to Islamic teaching, the three earlier books each contained a part of the Koran and its teachings. However, they were not designed to last, and consequently did not survive in their original form. The Koran, on the other hand, encompasses everything in the earlier books and much more besides, and is designed to survive unchanged till the end of time.

   The Koran has concealed some matters that were more clearly expressed in the earlier books, and has made explicit other things which they mentioned only covertly. There are several reasons for this. The first is that the Koran, as mentioned above, abrogates certain aspects of earlier sacred law—for instance, the Islamic Divine Law is easier and more lenient than Jewish Law. Another reason is that some of the statements in earlier books, while true, can be easily misunderstood, and wrong action follows upon such misunderstanding. A third reason is that the Koran lays emphasis on the improvement of right action, and hence gives further details not available in earlier sources.

4. *God's Messengers* are those human beings chosen by God to convey His messages, orders, and advice to the rest of mankind. Their honesty, veracity, and truthfulness is beyond doubt; otherwise they would not have been entrusted with such a burden or responsibility. The first

prophet was also the first man, namely Adam, and the last prophet was Mohammed, to whom True Religion was revealed in its final, its most mature and complete, form.

Tradition has it that there have been 124,000 prophets, of whom twenty-eight have been named in the Koran. Since True Religion reached its peak or zenith with Mohammed, there will be no further prophets. The difference between a prophet and a messenger in the present context is that a messenger comes with new dispensation, a new version of Holy Law, whereas a prophet does not; he merely refreshes and reiterates the version of Holy Law revealed by the last messenger preceding Him. Every messenger is also a prophet, but not every prophet is a messenger according to this definition. Every prophet bringing a Book is also a messenger—Moses, for example.

5. *The Day of Judgment,* or the Last Day, is the day when all human spirits will be resurrected and gathered together after bodily death; will be judged according to their good or evil deeds during their life on earth, and will then be dispatched to their proper destination: Heaven or Hell. Hence, closely related to this are:

Resurrection after death, which will occur for the judgment of souls. "This world," said the Prophet, "is a field to be sown for the next;" and as we sow, so shall we reap. No good deed is in vain, and no evil deed is without eventual, inexorable punishment.

Heaven and Hell, which are the final destinations of human beings in the afterlife. Righteous and virtuous persons will go to Heaven, a place of blessings, but evil persons will be sent to Hell, where they will receive punishment. There are Eight Levels of Heaven and Seven Circles of Hell, according to the degree of virtue or sin a person has accumulated.

6. *Good and ill destiny from God:* Whatever befalls us is either a response from God to our actions, or a trial from God. God has preordained a good recompense for good deeds and retribution for evil ones. In addition there are certain things which we as humans cannot change, try as we might; but even here it is not an iron law that operates, for we can pray to God, who in His compassion may grant our prayers. Further,

a perceived ill may be a blessing in disguise; we only know that God is the source of all.

Fate and predestination are matters that have frequently been misunderstood, and can easily bog one down in philosophical conundrums. The best course in this regard was pointed out by the Messenger of God to a group of his Companions: don't waste time thinking or arguing too much about it. Man cannot know what is predestined by God—only God has that knowledge. But man has his orders from God, and it is his duty to carry these out, not to become entangled in paradoxes of the mind. (More about this article of faith below.)

Having summarized the Six Pillars of Faith in this way, it is next necessary to ask: what does it mean to know these? Supposing we knew them by heart, would it be of any use if we failed in right action, action inspired by these principles?

As it says in the Buddhist *Dhammapada,* "All that we are is the result of what we have thought." Our most deeply held beliefs actively shape our lives and influence our destinies.

> *Sow a thought, reap an act;*
> *Sow an act, reap a habit;*
> *Sow a habit, reap a character;*
> *Sow a character, reap a destiny.*

And therefore:

> *Sowing a thought reaps a destiny.*

So, placing the Six Pillars at the center of our faith should lead to more than mindless reenactment of the Five Pillars of Religion. Merely "going through the motions" is a bane that deadens the soul and stultifies one's faith.

The Six Pillars of Faith are a precondition for performing the Five Pillars of Islam. But this is not enough. Suppose you believe in God, that God exists and is One. Unless you recognize that He sees and hears whatever you do—that He can read your innermost thoughts—and adjust your conduct accordingly, your faith will be of no avail. It is not enough to just believe in God's angels. We should, like those angels, implement God's orders perfectly and meticulously. Our actions should be in moral conformity with angelic behavior.

It is not enough to believe in God's books, to love the Koran. We should study it to learn what it contains, and strive to carry out its instructions. Our morality should be, like the Prophet's, an image of the Koran.

Granted that we have faith in God's prophets, is this of itself sufficient, or should we not rather try to be exemplary human beings and model servants of God as they were? If we love and cherish Mohammed, are we able to follow in his footsteps, to conform to his Way?

Supposing we believe in the Judgment Day, do we arrange our actions and lives bearing it in mind, preparing for it properly, or do we go on living just the way we used to before we started believing in it?

What is good for this world is not necessarily good for the afterworld. But what is good for the next world is also good for this world. If we arrange our affairs with the other world in mind, we shall find salvation in both this life and the afterlife.

We believe that destiny, whether good or ill, is from God. But do we take the precautions necessary to ensure that we shall receive a good recompense? What percentage of the deeds required for a happy fate do we perform?

We believe in resurrection after death. What preparations have we made for that terrifying day, when there will be no escape and no place to hide? Have we taken, or are we now taking, measures to escape bewilderment and punishment?

The Pillars of Faith leave us face to face with an ethical choice. They require us to adopt, even transcend, the moral conduct of angels. They invite us to invest ourselves with the morality of God's prophets and chosen ones. A child can recite the Pillars of Faith. What is much more important—and difficult—is to live them; to complement theory with practice. To *be* Islamic.

Grading of Actions

Actions, or deeds, are graded according to the merit or sin they entail. Here, the *intention* behind a deed is as important as the deed itself. The main division is between Allowed (*halal*) actions, which gain merit (*sawab*), and illicit or Forbidden (*haram*) deeds, which are sinful (*gunah*). These are further subdivided within themselves to yield five gradings:

Obligatory or mandatory (*farz*)
Recommended (*wajib*)
Neutral (*mubah*)
Disgusting (*makruh*)
Forbidden (*haram*)

Each person will be judged in the afterlife according to the grades s/he has accumulated during his or her lifetime. One good deed and one bad deed of equal value cancel each other. Of course, God's Attribute of Justice (*adl*) requires that even the finest distinction not be missed in Judgment, so a grading over one hundred points would be closer to the truth. These are, however, the main divisions.

This grading system is very similar to that existing in our educational institutions, and suggests that the whole world is a school—a scene for our training, testing, and maturation.

On Destiny

The question of predestination has long occupied the minds of human beings. The philosophical dilemmas one can easily land oneself in have caused many to turn to atheism. Yet there is no need for this; what is necessary is to maintain a proper perspective.

People find it difficult to reconcile the horrors we see in the world with the concept of a loving God. If God is compassionate, the argument continues, how come He foreordains some to Heaven and others to Hell?

Obviously, there cannot be responsibility without freedom of choice. If God had not given humans this freedom, He in His justice would not hold them accountable. The very fact that a system of rewards and punishments exists bespeaks our freedom to choose between good and evil.

This freedom is a *sine qua non* for the fulfillment of the purpose of existence. Yet it is also a heavy burden. Most of the evils we observe in the world are a product of wrong choices made by human beings, not God. It is easier to blame one's Creator for one's own misdeeds than to shoulder responsibility and solve them. But this is to add insult to injury, and only exacerbates our eventual punishment. To say: "God created me this way. What can I do? I would have acted good if He had created me good," is the worst form of cop-out. God is not responsible for stopping the evils of this world—*we* are. For the worst of them are man-made. Furthermore, God has made us the stewards and custodians of this world, and it is our duty to take proper care of our planet.

But if God is omniscient and all-powerful, how can He punish our misdeeds? Aren't these predetermined by God, too? The Islamic response is as follows: God has donated a small portion, a fragment, of His will to each individual human being, which a person is entitled to exercise freely. This partial or fragmentary will of man can choose to comply with or oppose the total or universal will of God. If God *forced* us to make an ethical choice, only in that case would He and not us be responsible for it. And in fact, we shall be held accountable only for our free moral choices and actions, not for the situations we may find ourselves in through no fault of our own. A moral choice made under adverse circumstances, however, is of greater merit than the same choice under conditions of ease.

Note here the existence of a very fine, delicate point: the will exercised by each of us has been loaned to us by God; it is a fragment of *God's own will*. This is a very great responsibility: a human being can, under certain conditions, influence the fate of millions of human beings for good or ill. Hence, it is only normal that humans should be held accountable for its misuse. This also means that we cannot always let events follow their course. Under certain conditions, moral conduct requires us to intervene.

Prayer: The Ascension for All

God Almighty instructed Adam, the first human and first prophet, to perform the Prayer (*salat*). Before Adam, the angels had been performing it. This goes to show how important Prayer is.

Of the Five Pillars of Islam, Prayer is the highest; Prayer is the one that is repeated most often and the one that requires the greatest perseverance. In contrast, the Word of Witnessing, which is the point of entry into

Islam, need be uttered only once (although it can be, and is, repeated many times later on). The Pilgrimage is incumbent on us only once in a lifetime, and then only on those with sufficient means to fulfill it. The Alms-tax is paid only once a year, by the prosperous to the poor. The Fasting is confined to the lunar month of Ramadan. Contrast these now with the Prayer, which is performed five times daily and comprises a total of forty cycles (*raqah*), and you will see what a paramount place it has in the religion of Islam. Indeed, it is the very axis around which Islam revolves.

Why is Prayer so central to Islam? And why does it consist, as it does, of a series of repetitive bodily postures and movements in conjunction with recitation of sacred formulas, rather than simple supplication to God like ordinary prayer?

When the Prophet of God was raised to the presence of God in his Ascension (*Miraj:* "ladder"), he became closer to God than anyone before or since. And God, as a gift to the Prophet's Community of the Faithful, enjoined the five daily Prayers upon them.

A saying of the Prophet reveals the meaning of Prayer: "Prayer is the Ascension of the faithful." Another saying makes clear that "He who has no Prayer makes no Ascension." This means that a ladder ("Jacob's Ladder"), an escalator or elevator, has been instituted by God for the faithful to approach His presence, and this is none other than Prayer. If a believer performs the Prayer properly and with the care and attention it deserves, there can be no doubt that s/he will approach God.

That s/he should fail to be conscious of this is immaterial. Matters of the spirit are by and large hidden from human consciousness and senses. If the veils were to fall from the believer's eyes, s/he would actually be able to witness his or her Ascension in spiritual (as distinct from physical) space. But it is only at very advanced levels of spiritual progress that this may become possible.

Two factors can be singled out in the Prayer process: the first being the bodily postures, and the second the recited formulas. The reason for the bodily movements is as follows:

A human as a totality possesses two aspects—body and spirit. (We disregard for the time being a third factor, the self). More precisely, s/he possesses a physical body, which we all know, and a non-physical, spiritual body, of which few people are aware. During life on earth, the spiritual body is connected, engaged, or "coupled" to the physical body.

Hence, the bodily motions in Prayer are intended primarily for the *spiritual body*, not for the physical body (although they have an ameliorating influence on that as well). By moving the physical body, one actualizes the movement of the spiritual body, *which is coupled to it.* It is this motion of the spiritual body that escalates or elevates the spirit, not that of the physical body directly.

The second component of Prayer as indicated above is the recitation of certain formulas, mainly verses from the Koran. If the postures and movements are the form of Prayer, the recitations are its content. These both aid in concentration and attach "wings," as it were, to the spirit. Thus, the humble Prayer rug beneath one's feet becomes the magic carpet or "cosmic treadmill" by which the believer rises towards God.

We shall not go into the details of these formulas here, but confine ourselves to indicating the repetition of the names of the Lord. Two of the Almighty's names are repeated six times in each cycle, which makes a total of twelve. Since there are forty cycles in a day, this gives four-hundred-and-eighty repetitions.

After the bodily movement part is finished, God's names are recited in three lots of thirty-three, or ninety-nine, times in a sitting position during each of the Five Prayers. This means that the names of the Lord are invoked nearly a thousand times a day, *even counting only the bare bones of Prayer* and leaving out additional recitations. This is none other than the invocation or remembrance (*zikr*) of God. These invocations help to concentrate the attention on God and aid the believer's Ascension in spiritual (not physical!) space.

All the prophets from Adam to Mohammed, the last prophet, have been bestowed with Prayer. Bowing down to the ground (prostration) was common to all, whereas the respective Divine Laws and worship were different. But they all came with the command to Prayer, and explained its details to their respective communities.

The Koran mentions that the following prophets and communities were given the instruction of prostration: David (38:24), the Children of Israel (7:161), the Virgin Mary (18:107), and those of previous generations (19:59). Explicit mention is made of the following prophets in the

Koran as having been ordered to perform the Prayer: Moses (10:87, 20:10), Abraham (14:40), Ishmael (19:57), Loqman (31:17), Jesus (19:32), and Abraham, Isaac, and Jacob (21:73).

Since all prophets have told their faithful to perform the Prayer, how come we don't come across Prayer or some form of it in the observances of other religions? The truth is that we do, but we encounter only their remnants. Prayer is the royal road to God, but it is also hard work. At one point or other, the religious communities of the past fell by the wayside and abandoned the performance of their Prayer. This is one of the reasons why Islam had to be revealed, in order to make Prayer permanent. Yet we can still find traces of ancient versions of Prayer in some observances of the Hindus, in the prostrations of Tibetan Buddhists, in the Asanas of Yoga, and in the practices of far-eastern religious philosophies such as T'ai Chi Ch'uan in China.

Furthermore, close inspection of the Bible reveals that aspects of Prayer can be found there as well, even though it may no longer be practiced regularly. Indications of this are present both in the Old Testament and the New. Worship, prayer, and bowing down to the ground are mentioned also in the Torah, revealed to Moses (Genesis 24:52; Exodus 33:10, 34:8), in the Psalms of David (5:7, 95:6, 138:2), and the Old Testament in general (1 Kings 18:42; Nehemiah 8:6, 9:3; Daniel 6:10, 8:18, 10:9; Ezra 9:5; 2 Chronicles 7:3).

Special attention should be drawn here to 1 Kings 18:42. The form of prostration here prescribed for the prophet Elijah, so similar to the Islamic prostration, was continued within the Judaic tradition by the Merkabah ("Throne" or "Chariot") mystics between the second and tenth centuries A.D. That is why they speak of a *descent* to the Chariot, the latter term designating the posture of prostration. Drawings of postures in the ancient Judaic prayer ritual, published by Rabbi Hayim Donin, leave no doubt whatsoever that it was almost identical to Moslem Prayer. The standing, genuflection, and prostration postures are there for all to see.[77] For the various references to prostration (bowing down to the ground) in the New Testament, one may cite Matthew 26:39, Mark 14:35, and Luke 22:41 as examples.

Moslems perform the Prayer by facing Mecca (more precisely, the Cube or *Kaabah*) as the focal point (*qiblah*). It is interesting to find the same concept in the Old Testament, where people worshiped by facing the Old Temple in Jerusalem—the Temple of Solomon (Psalms 5:7, 138:2; 1 Kings 8:30,35; Daniel 6:10). As a matter of fact, Moslems initially prayed facing Jerusalem to underline their relatedness and continuity with the previous two great monotheistic faiths (Judaism and Christianity), until commanded by God to pray facing the Kaaba, thus emphasizing their distinction from the other two.

All the saints, the Friends of God, have found a path to God only in performing the Prayer. They have been able to approach the Throne of the Almighty only in this way. Hence, no one who fails to do the Prayer should lay claim to sainthood, and such a person should deceive and mislead neither him-/herself nor anyone else. (As for prayers that are simply recited, those considered most important by the Master are given in Appendix B.)

In this chapter, we have examined Holy Law and how it is comprised of two integral aspects, the Koran and the Way of the Prophet. We have also considered the exoteric practices of Islam, the Five Pillars (or actions)—with an in-depth consideration of Prayer—and the Six Pillars of Faith.

The Secret of Love at the Heart of Islam

—— ✤ ——

(As I hope this book will make clear, reducing Islam to a list of sins and "shalt nots," enforced by religious police, makes a mockery of it. Misguided approaches extant today strip Islam of everything but a skeletal and decontextualized interpretation of the code of law so that it does not reflect true Islam at all.

These actions clearly controvert the clear and unfailing messages about love that are at the heart of Islam. Holy Law is essential to Islam, but Law is at its core the directive to control the Base Self and to seek communion with God. It cannot be repeated too frequently that there is no coercion in Islam—these matters are between the individual and his or her God.

This chapter was one of the Master's favorite handouts. It connects the exoteric/legal aspect of Islam with the esoteric/mystical/Sufi concept of love, via the ethical bridge of conscience. Islam is the religion of ethics. Two keys unlock the door of the heart, enabling the fountain of love to bubble therein: Worship, which is the expression of devotion to God, and Courtesy (adab) or noble conduct towards all beings. Love and superior conduct then mutually reinforce each other in an ever-expanding spiral.

Islam reaches out towards society with Divine Law on one hand, and reaches inward towards the individual's heart with love on the other. When love informs all our relationships with others, that is real ethics, while Law is simply the codification of ethical principles in a social contract. Thus, it is seen that Law,

Conscience, and Love are intimately related, in the same way that justice, ethics, and spirituality are extensions of one another. Their underlying fundamental unity has rarely been better expressed. This is Unification (tawhid) at its highest conceptual level.)

The secret of religion is love. This is a fundamental truth. Religion is Divine Law (rights). The secret of Law is conscience. And, in a nested fashion, the secret of conscience is love.

Religion comprises these three in the same way that a fruit is composed of rind, flesh, and a core. Although the core is not apparent from the outside, it is the innermost, the active part. The heart of all religion is love. Love gives rise to conscience, to consideration, to compassion, and to tolerance.

The Law is the external covering of all this. It prevents the flesh and the core from being spoiled and destroyed. Although it may not, at first glance, appear to have much in common with its contents, in reality it is directly based on them. Just as conscience arises from love, Law in turn arises from conscience. It is merely the codification of rights already granted implicitly at the level of conscience.

The Secret That is Law

As I have already mentioned, Law is a delicate balance between rights and duties, between liberties and limitations. The duty of one person is nothing but the right of another, and the limitation of one is the freedom of another. Absolute freedom cannot exist, and if it could, then law, and hence justice, would not exist. It is as if freedom were in short supply and had to be apportioned equally. For the increase of one's freedom occurs only at the expense of another's, and if justice is not distributed equally, that is injustice. Hence we have equality before the law, and equality before human law is based on equality before God's Law, since all people are equal before God.

Because Law is based on conscience and ultimately on love, what is lawful in Islam is that which is informed by love. To put this is a little differently, the only action which is free of blame is that which is based on love, and the Divine Law is a compendium of such action or non-action.

The all-important conclusion from this is that even if you do not feel love for a creature, you will have done it no wrong if you treat it according to the prescription of Divine Law. Thus Islam answers the critical question: "How should I behave toward beings?" in the following concise way: treat them as if you loved them, in the same way as you would act if you loved them. And for our convenience, Islam outlines in its prescriptions of Holy Law what such action is.

In religion, Law means righteousness above all else. For instance, a person must not touch or covet what does not belong to him or her. When we say Law or rights, this doesn't mean only those rights pertaining to humanity. Law means to recognize the same right for all beings in the universe, whether animate or inanimate, from an atom to the sun. It is the requirement of being human and of being a Moslem to treat them in the same way. For all beings are the creatures of God. If one claims to love God, one absolutely must love His beings as well. One who does not love existence cannot be said to love God. In view of this, our own personal choices of what is good and bad, beautiful and ugly, useful and harmful, attractive and repulsive, have no place in Law. If these become involved, they precipitate the wrath of God. Here, to like or dislike is one thing, and Law is another.

The inability of human beings to truly progress arises from their failure to understand this point. One who does not abide by the Law is the greatest of sinners and has no inkling of what it means to be human. About this there should be no doubt whatsoever.

A person is free to act according to his or her disposition. One may not take an interest in any being one dislikes, finds bad, harmful, or repulsive. But if for any reason an interest or relationship is established, one must recognize their rights. This is because a human being is responsible for rights, and for rights alone. Whether one is a Moslem or a Christian is immaterial at this point. For this is where the door of happiness opens. All beings are the forms, the manifestations, of God's names. Therefore, the holy books declare God's order unanimously: "You are to think of the other as you think of yourself." For all things contain a spark from His spirit.[78]

It is due to this fact that where Law is concerned, no one can act according to his or her whim. God has forbidden this. For His command is not whim, but the very yardstick by which all things are to be measured. The human heart is His holy dwelling-place which He has reserved for Himself. S/he who breaks a heart will suffer, even if the poor person doesn't understand why.[79]

In reality, man is the representative of God and His viceregent over creation. As such, human beings are burdened with the utmost legal responsibility and obligation. A human being is responsible for all things living and nonliving, from the stone s/he steps on to the bird in the sky. This is why the People of God say: "The requirement of honesty is to consider one another," and they do not show negligence in serving this rule.

God has graced humans above all other beings and placed the others under human care. If a mishap occurs, however, this is due to us. If man becomes corrupt, everything becomes corrupt. If humans are polluted, all nature is polluted. Hence the present state of nature can stand as a mirror to our internal state. We should know that this is so and touch everything with "In the name of God" on our lips, replacing it with these same words. We should never forget whilst using something that it possesses spirit. We should treat it in the same way as we treat and care for a part of our own body. Then the Koranic statement: "You are pleased with God and He is pleased with you" (89:28) becomes reality—that is, you will be pleased with Him and He will be pleased with you. This is the answer that heals (makes whole).

The Secret That is Conscience

Law is derived from conscience. Without conscience, there would be no consideration of others and no respect for their rights. In fact, not even the existence of such rights would be recognized. Conscience requires the implicit presupposition that "the other" is, at some basic level, the same as or at least not different from the self. This leads to an unexpected conclusion, that the so-called "positive sciences" are, in fact, covertly normative. Behaviorist psychology, for example, by taking the other and his inner world as an unknown, by treating the other as a "black box" that can be judged only on the basis of exhibited behavior, reduces people to the status of automatons, quietly revoking their claim to rights. This, in turn, is nothing but lawlessness where the "other" is concerned. All rights then belong to the self, and to the other?—None. This is nothing but injustice.

This also indicates the need to be very careful with our sciences and philosophies. It is never very obvious what metaphysics lurk behind our "objective" hypotheses or conclusions—nor where they may lead. If metaphysics is an ineradicable residue underlying all science and philosophy, then it is much better that this be of a life-enhancing, rather than life-denying, nature.

Conscience is the prime mover of Law—it creates and resonates in the heart and mobilizes man. If a person does everything lawfully, in the way prescribed by Law, believing in its utter rightness and content in his or her heart about its truth—this, then, is conscience. This is the foundation of Law; another name for it is "faith." It is the "still, small voice" that comes from the depths of one's heart. It is the product of an indubitable, pure, and undefiled feeling. May God grant us all that state, which comes to us on a tide of the ocean of compassion. If someone has no faith, neither does s/he possess conscience. Lacking conscience, s/he also lacks humanity. Blessed are those who recognize Law and have a clear conscience, for God is with them.

The Secret That Is Love

Love is the real source of an individual's feelings of compassion and kindness, the sublime synthesis of his or her finest and most delicate feelings of conscience. Since the sway of conscience has purified the heart, purging it of all things, good and bad alike, God installs His throne of manifestation in that heart. Thus love of God engulfs one's being, and that person becomes pure love. Then everything loves one, and one loves everything.

And so, that person becomes invested with God's attributes and friendship, harmony and welfare, and joins His Chosen People. Henceforth, one's place in both worlds is Paradise and one's station, comfort and friendship.

This is a three-stage process: (1) Righteousness, diligent observation of the Law, enabling (2) the conscience to flower—and the full maturity of conscience is (3) love. But what happens once one becomes, as it were, an incarnation of love? Does one shed the Law and conscience as if they were autumn leaves?

On the contrary, the Law and conscience find their fullest, most mature, manifestation in a person who has become pure love. Rote Imitation becomes Realization. He or she no longer acts out of blind obedience to the letter of the Law, but in full knowledge and consciousness of why the Law prescribes or prohibits a certain thing. The clumsy, mechanical, sometimes jarring and disturbing implementation of the Divine Law gives way to a smooth, harmonious flow—the grace of love. Such people are a guiding light to all beings lucky enough to come within their sphere.

Such a person is called a saint, or a "friend of God," and has become identified with pure love. The motto of the friend of God is "I, if I be lifted up, will lift up all mankind with me." The saints are the channels or vehicles by which God's love, compassion, and mercy reach the world. Indeed in ages when there are many saints of high realization, there are fewer wars, plagues, and calamities—the world is a "closer" place to Paradise. In ages when they are few and far between, these channels of access to grace are "clogged," as it were, and the situation is reversed. Look around you and, with this measure in hand, you will be able to judge what kind of times we live in.

Eight Heavens, Seven Hells

Islam is based on eight principles. These are referred to as the eight gates of Heaven:

1. Compassion, kindness, and affection.
2. Righteousness.
3. Loyalty.
4. Generosity.
5. Patience.
6. Discretion.
7. Knowing one's poverty and weakness.
8. Giving thanks to God.

Without these, there is no peace, happiness, or Paradise in either world. Anyone who is clothed in these praiseworthy traits and has made them part of his or her constitution is a proper Moslem and worthy of the Noble Messenger of God, Mohammed. For these praiseworthy manners and characteristics are the beautiful traits and attributes of our Prophet. They have radiated from him to his family, children, and Companions, thence becoming the fundamental constituents of Islam.

And this is why Islam is not simply the recitation of the Word of Witnessing or the search for Heaven in a mosque. The firmness of God's revelatory secrets depends on these qualities; hence, so do the continuance of life, its peace and happiness. Throughout one's life one must always be based in the good, the true, and the beautiful. Only with these verities are immortality and eternity feasible.

It is for this reason that the above principles have always been a guiding light and torch in the hands of humankind and the travelers to Truth. Just as one cannot see in the dark or find one's way, neither can one reach the Lord. God says: "Be light, come to Me, attain My mystery," and desires us. Our great Prophet exemplified the meaning of this declaration in his Ascension (the *Miraj*). Without these lights of truth, in the darkness of our ignorance, how could we find the way to our Lord and be worthy of His pleasure?

Therefore, these agreeable traits and characteristics are what is valuable, whether at the stage of general Law, or of mystical schools (conscience), or of attaining Reality (love). Without them, a person cannot be worthy of his or her Lord, no matter whether one is a prophet or a madman. This is the secret of the Four Books and the Hundred Pages revealed to the various Prophets. These eight principles are the sources of life for humanity and human conscience that bestow happiness, peace, and joy.

All the virtues and merits in the world are encompassed by these traits. This is why they have been called the eight gates of Heaven. Those who possess them live in paradise even while in this world.

As for the seven circles of Hell, the following are the traits that open their gates:

1. Pride.
2. Covetousness.

3. Envy.
4. Discord.
5. Backbiting.
6. Lust.
7. Anger.

All the evil traits and manners in the world are, in turn, contained in these. No matter what or who one is or how true one may appear to be, these are the characteristics that lie close to a person's heart if he or she does not acknowledge goodness, beauty, and truth. It makes no difference if one never raises one's head from prostration. Being human and being a Moslem are both possible only by relying on Truth.[80] Islam cannot be attained by following the lead of one's caprice, by being carried away by one's ego, by exhibitionism, or by fishing for other people's praise. One will then have opened the gates of the seven Hells, pride, rebellion, and downfall.

Note, however, that there are eight Heavens as opposed to only seven Hells. This is because God Almighty has said: "My Mercy encompasses (is greater than) My Wrath." Indeed in Islam, "In the Name of God, the Compassionate, the Merciful" precedes everything. No matter how great one's sins, they are swept away in a torrent of Divine Compassion and Mercy, provided one resolves to rectify one's ways in accordance with the Law. The opportunity for absolution is always there, and never far away. For the secret of religion is love.

✠

This chapter revealed how Love is actually embedded in the spirit of the Holy Law, and how observance of the Law means trying to develop the Eight Heavens (agreeable traits) and to avoid the Seven Hells (evil traits) of Islam. The following chapter now describes the Koran and how it helps the individual seeker to "open" to or attain higher consciousness, once he or she has fully understood its more literal or exoteric aspects and is ready to access the more esoteric readings of the Koran.

The Music of the Koran
————— ⚜ —————

(This chapter reveals the beauty of the Koran and its many lay-ered meanings, from literal to mystical. It introduces the idea that the Koran can lead us to awaken to the harmony and unity that underlies the world, which in turn leads to the path of bliss—to be outlined in later chapters on Islam and Sufism.)

The Fractured Mirror

In our age, we are faced with an "atomization of consciousness:" the world, or rather our mental mirror of it, has exploded into smithereens, and the result is a ruination that belies the magnificence, the infinite interrelatedness, of the universe which is its object. In our effort to un-derstand the world, we have divided and subdivided it *ad infinitum* into disjointed categories having little or no relationship with each other. As Yeats prophetically declared at the beginning of this century, in lines well-worn precisely because they are so succinct:

> *Things fall apart; the center cannot hold;*
> *Mere anarchy is loosed upon the world.*

It is a common human failing to confuse our descriptions with that which is described. As Alan Watts used to point out, the map is not the territory; the transparent film of divisions and abstract concepts which we overlay on the "seamless web of the universe" and which constitutes our mental picture of it *is not* the universe. This is true of analytical thought, and even of language. Our fragmented picture of the world is not the world itself, and if this fragmentation has progressed to the point where our appreciation of reality is seriously impaired, we need to heal it, to make it whole again.

Un-fracturing

This project of making our worldview whole is called "Unification" (*tawhid*) in Islam. At the simplest level, of course, Unification means the recognition that "God is One." But on a deeper, subtler level, it means that the rigid compartmentalization we impose on the world is a mental construct of our own. The gridwork of latitudes and longitudes, for example, is useful for navigating our globe; but they are invisible when we look at the Earth from space, for the simple reason that they don't exist in reality. The seamless structure of the planet is echoed in the interconnectedness of the universe. Quantum physics has unwittingly taken a step toward rediscovering the "great chain of being" positing countless links, which used to be appreciated in the West; the discovery of "nonlocality" and "entanglement" in recent years has lent strength to the view that seemingly unrelated parts of the world are, in fact, connected.

Before the discovery of nonlocality, gravitation was recognized as such a connecting medium in physics, and it still retains the advantage of being effective on the everyday and macrocosmic levels, rather than only on the quantum level. In the field of ecology, Barry Commoner framed one of the basic principles of ecology as: "Everything is connected to everything else." If a fire breaks out in the Amazon forests, for example, everybody everywhere suffers, even though they might not realize it. In recent years the science of chaos has not only revealed order masquerading as apparent randomness, it has also shown that intuitively negligible quantities or perturbations can have counterintuitive consequences out of all proportion to their own scale. Sensitive dependence on initial conditions can have unforeseen consequences in seemingly unrelated locations. Thus, our sciences have reached a sophistication and sensitivity where previously unnoticed correlations, connections, and correspondences are now beginning to be recognized. Here, the poet Francis Thompson has summarized this idea beautifully:

All things by immortal power,
Near and far,
Hiddenly
To each other linked are,
That thou canst not stir a flower
Without troubling a star.

Thus, we find that our science has caught up with our art, in an unexpected vindication of Keats: "Truth is beauty, and beauty truth." This is the deeper meaning of Unification: that the three cardinal principles, truth, beauty, and goodness, are ultimately one, that they are but aspects of the One Ultimate Reality, the Ground of all being. And this is the vision that we have to recapture if we are to escape schizoid grief: that the only atom in the universe—*a-tom* in the sense of "indivisible"—is the universe itself, that it is a joyous celebration of infinite Unity and existence, rather than a hell of irreconcilable, broken fragments. *This* world which we presently inhabit is the *chaos,* the world apparently ruled by chance in which few things make sense. Our task is to transform it into *cosmos* (an ordered universe) by purifying our consciousness and integrating the world, discovering the infinite interrelatedness of phenomena with God at the helm, in the end realizing that the world is, and in fact was, a cosmos all along.

Unification

Let us recapitulate. The universe is a seamless unity, but we do not ordinarily perceive it that way. From childhood onwards, humans begin to inhabit a world of multiplicity. On this multiplicity, which is already a "given," we next superimpose the artificial abstractions and divisions of analytical thinking. In other words, whereas our objective should be to move towards unity, we move a further step towards fragmentation. This is not to deny the utility of analytical thought. But it should be counterbalanced by a *synthesis.* We should integrate what we have previously differentiated.

The following analogy may be helpful: ordinarily, we look at the world through a pair of glasses. Even if our vision is twenty-twenty, our spectacles still have smooth glass in place of lenses. Now imagine that the glass or lenses has multiple fractures, but is still held in place (say by a transparent plastic coating). When we look at the world through these glasses, we see borders, separations, reflections, even multiple images of the same object, that do not exist in reality. Analytical thought can be compared to this.

Suppose now that we take off the broken glasses. We will now be able to view the world without an obstacle. Yet we still cannot perceive the Truth, the seamless unity. As the great mystical poet William Blake said: "If the doors of perception were cleansed, everything would appear to man as it is, infinite." The fact that we do not ordinarily perceive the world in this way implies that a sensory/noetic "filtering" is taking place. Aldous Huxley took this cue from Blake to suggest in *The Doors of Perception* that the sense organs and the mind act as a "reducing valve." So how can we regain a full, complete view of reality?

Islamic Sufism suggests that this is possible by Unification. We must bear witness to the unity of God, unify the universe, and unify our selves. It further suggests that these three are connected. Picture the universe we live in as a horizontal axis. This is the universe as we perceive it in our ordinary, everyday self. But there are other levels of selfhood that are possible, which can best be pictured as ordered along a vertical axis.

Now to every state or level of the self there corresponds a different state of consciousness, which yields a different state of reality to our perception. Hence, Islamic Sufism suggests that the key to "cleansing the doors of perception" actually lies in self-purification, by which the "ladder of unification" is climbed until one perceives the clear light of Unity, of Truth, at the summit. This process begins with exoteric practices such as Prayer, so that one learns to conquer the Base Self before exploring more esoteric practices (to be discussed in the last section of this book).

The Source of Bliss

Ideally, Unitary thought transcends all dualisms and divisions. The dichotomies of matter and spirit, mind and heart, object and subject, inner and outer are thus left behind, and one passes beyond all artificial distinctions to the seamless Unity of Truth. This is not a matter of "either/or," and beyond even "both/and." To borrow a concept from quantum physics, it is "tunneling" beyond the crack between opposites that originates them, and finding oneself in a pure Unitary state. The Hindus had a name for this state that described it beautifully: *sat-chit-ananda*, Infinite Being, Consciousness, and Bliss. And the Buddhist name for it, which is equivalent to the *fana* of the Sufis, described how it can be attained: *Nirvana*, or "snuffing out" the candle—the extinguishing of all selfish desires in oneself. The result is inexpressible, but Blake made an attempt at it, though all such attempts are doomed to failure:

> *To see the world in a grain of sand,*
> *And Heaven in a wild flower;*
> *Hold infinity in the palm of your hand*
> *And eternity in an hour.*

Ultimate Reality, which is known to us by the more familiar name of "God" (the Divinity), is the source not only of all being, but of all happiness—such that even a small step towards God will lead us out of grief into a great enhancement of happiness. If human beings, therefore, turn their backs on God and start walking, they don't stand a chance; there is no power in the universe that can deliver them from despair.

Truth, Beauty, Goodness

"God is beautiful," goes a Tradition, "He loves beauty." Truth (*Haqq*), Beauty (*Jamal*), and the Good (*Birr*) are divine names and attributes of God in Islam. Hence knowledge or science, which deals with truth; aesthetics, which concerns itself with beauty; and ethics, or moral philosophy, must complement and complete each other, since they reflect different facets of the same Unity.

The ancient Greeks, despite their polytheism, came very close to this insight. In Greek thought, goodness and beauty were identical. They expressed this by a hybrid term, "good-beautiful" (*kalokagathia*) (and Keats took the above quotation identifying truth and beauty from a Grecian urn). Plato also spoke of the unity of goodness and beauty. The concept has proved remarkably persistent in Western philosophy, right down to Wittgenstein, who in his *Tractatus* speaks of ethics and aesthetics as one 7e. And while Kant wishes to distinguish between knowledge, ethics, and aesthetics, a close inspection of his three *Critiques* reveals that he considered ethics and aesthetics one in principle, and they further unite with knowledge at an apex.

Quantum physicist and Nobel Prizewinner Paul A. M. Dirac combined truth with beauty in his epigraph: "A physical law must possess mathematical beauty." "God is a mathematician of a very high order," he wrote, "and He used very advanced mathematics in constructing the universe." Dirac was able to predict the existence of antimatter by relying on considerations of symmetry, a prime ingredient of beauty (mathematical or otherwise).[81] It was on this basis that he asserted: "A theory with mathematical beauty is more likely to be correct than an ugly one that fits some experimental data."[82] Here we stand at the interface between scientific truth and artistic sensibility, where the simplicity and elegance of a scientific theory take precedence over cumbersome explanatory devices— just as Kepler's elliptical orbits disposed of the inelegant theory of epicycles. It is for this reason that the Koran declares: "You do not see any imperfection in the creation of the Compassionate. Return your gaze; do you see any fissure? Look again and again; your gaze comes back to you, dazzled and tired" (67:3-4). In other words, if at first you don't succeed in discerning this perfection, look again, revise your theories, and finally you will perceive pure magnificence.

The Music of the Koran

Pickthall, one of its interpreters, called the Koran "that inimitable symphony," and Arberry, another interpreter, recognized "the Koran's undeniable claim to rank amongst the greatest literary masterpieces of mankind." Because it is untranslatable, even the most successful interpretations fall miserably short of the breathtaking beauty of the original.

The Koran is neither prose nor poetry, but a unique combination of both. Further, the lilting sing-song in which it is recited, although unfamiliar to ears accustomed to Western music, highlights the quasi-musical nature of the Koran. Thus, it combines prose, poetry, and musicality. At this point we may well remember Carlyle:

All inmost things, we may say, are melodious; naturally utter themselves in Song. The meaning of Song goes deep. Who is there that, in logical words, can express the effect music has on us? A kind of inarticulate unfathomable speech, which leads us to the edge of the Infinite and lets us for moments gaze into that!

All deep things are Song...See deep enough, and you see musically; the heart of Nature *being* everywhere music, if you can only reach it.

Seen in this light, the recitation of the Koran is music, "a mystic unfathomable song." If the universe is the "music of the spheres," then so is the Koran, which deciphers the mysterious universe to human comprehension. It is not, however, *any* song; the intonations and cadences of the Koran are all its own.

While the Koran is cast in the form of beauty, its contents are goodness and truth. As it declares itself: "There is no doubt in this book" (2:2); "It is an advice to the whole world, to those who wish to go straight" (81:27-28); and "This is a book that discriminates between truth and falsehood" (86:13-14). It takes the various strands of wisdom of all traditions—whether ancient or modern—and, consummately completing them, weaves them together in a rich tapestry that cannot be improved upon.

When we scrutinize the key concepts of the Koran, we find that it identifies goodness with beauty. In Arabic, words deriving from the root HSN (such as *husn, ihsan,* and *hasan*) all have this dual meaning, "good-beautiful." A good deed inherently appeals to the sense of beauty in human beings. Conversely, bad is identified with ugly, and is repulsive. Why should this be so? Because human nature is inherently good, although it does have a propensity for badness as well.

Thus, the moral or ethical distinctions of the Koran are simultaneously aesthetic distinctions. The beauty intended here, however, is spiritual beauty more than physical beauty, and points to the fact that courtesy (*adab*) and sublime moral conduct, which are beauteous in themselves, lead to beauty of spirit in the person who practices them. In Koranic terms, again, "good" is that which is balanced, while "bad" or "ill" is indicative of imbalance. Justice (*adl*) is explained directly in terms of balance. Cruelty or oppression (*zulm*), squandering (*israf*), being spoiled by excessive affluence (*itraf*), and illicit sex (*fahsha*) all have the meaning of imbalance and extremism. The Koran, in short, invites us to live by the Golden Mean, and in each case it clearly outlines for us where this mean lies.

A second conclusion following from the inspection of its key concepts is the emphasis laid on "the straight path," the path that leads straight to God, Paradise, and happiness. This is the path of the righteous, of those who do "good-beautiful" deeds. But there is also a second path: the road that leads to Hell. Hence, the Koranic concept of path may be compared to a two-way highway: one leading toward God and the other, away from Him.

The Chapter of the Opening

The Koran begins with the chapter called "the Opening." The Arabic root of its name is FTH, from which also derive the words "key" (*miftah*) and "victory" (*fath*). From this constellation of words, we may understand that the Prelude of the Koran is a key which opens the doors to spiritual conquest and to victory over evil and despair. It is said that this chapter summarizes the Koran in a nutshell, and it is so important that it is recited in every Prayer cycle.

> *I take refuge in God from Satan, the accursed.*
> *In the name of God, the Compassionate, the Merciful.*
>
> *Praise be to God, the Lord of all being,*
> *The Compassionate, the Merciful,*
> *Master of the Judgment Day.*
> *You alone we worship, and you alone we ask for help.*
> *Guide us along your Straight Path,*
> *The path of those whom you have blessed,*
> *Not of those who incur your wrath, nor of those who go*
> *astray.*
>
> *Amen.*

Let us examine these sacred verses one by one, in order to appreciate their meaning more fully. The main text of the Opening Chapter is preceded by "the Naming," of which the second line is invoked more often:

"In the name of God..." The Naming precedes almost all the chapters of the Koran. The main text of the chapter is ended by saying "Amen" ("so be it").

Let us first look at the Naming:

I take refuge in God from Satan, the accursed.
In the name of God, the Compassionate, the Merciful.

The word interpreted as "accursed" above actually means "stoned" in the Arabic original, from which we understand that Satan was driven from the presence of the Lord. What God is saying here is this: "When you want to read my Divine Word, my Book, take refuge in Me from Satan, who has been banished and driven away from Divine Grace."

Taking Refuge in God is to seek asylum with Him from everything that presents a barrier to grace, wisdom, and divine light, and thus to seek to witness the Presence of God. This becomes possible by the Knowledge of God. For Satan fears only the heart of the saint. The sun of Mohammedan Truth which is born in the depths of the saint's heart burns the Devil and drives him away. When a servant sincerely seeks refuge in his Lord in this way, the Almighty replies: "Fear not. Say: 'I begin in the name of God, the Compassionate, the Merciful.'" It is suggested to start upon any task by repeating the Naming, for otherwise it may not have an end.

Three divine names are invoked in the Naming: God, Compassionate, and Merciful. There is reference here to three classes of God's servants, as explained elsewhere in the Koran (35:32):

1. Those who leave their selves in darkness,

2. Those who brake (control) their selves,

3. Those who do good works.

God is the Lord of all. Compassion is for those who control their selves, and Mercy, or a higher elevation, belongs to those who actively do good works.

We now arrive at the main text of the Opening Chapter, which is composed of seven verses (the Naming is added sometimes, to give a total of eight). The first three verses are said to be specific to God alone, the fourth verse of supplication is shared between God and humans, and the last three verses belong to the person of faith. Thus, the Opening begins on God's side and ends on the human side, which shows that humans by themselves can do nothing—Divine aid has to start with God.

Praise be to God, the Lord of all being.

All the thanks, or praise, of all beings that may originate in the form of words or deeds belong to the Lord of the universe, "the Lord of all the worlds." From this we understand that God has created more than one world, and each human being is a separate world. When a human being begins to wonder: "Who am I? Where did I come from, and where am I being led? For surely my coming and going occur outside my own volition," that person has attained the base level of being human. S/he is then faced with the proposition: "Seek your origin," and this search begins by giving thanks.

There are three kinds of thanksgiving: giving thanks in the language of human beings, in the language of the spirit, and in the language of the Lord. Giving thanks in the language of human beings is the thanks of the ordinary person. This is to thank God for His blessings. A person is to acknowledge a gift of God, and to use that gift in the proper way. Giving thanks in the language of the spirit is the thanks of the Elect. It is done with the heart. The person's condition is trained and his or her conduct is purified. Thanksgiving in the language of the Lord is the thanks of the Wise. The Folk of Love give thanks, and are enabled to the light of unveiling by it. The Folk of Knowledge give thanks, and are enabled to witness God's visage.

In short, thanksgiving is to praise the Lord, to exalt Him. This is why both the beginning and the end of life is praise. No one can know or give the praise that God is worthy of. Hence, all salvation is from God. Thanks and praise are due to God alone, who creates and saves His creatures by His Essence, Attributes, and Actions. He is the Lord of the Worlds; He trains the hearts of the Faithful with patience and sincerity, with loyalty and perseverance.

He is the Lord of the Worlds; He trains bodies by bringing gifts into existence.

He is the Lord of the Worlds; He trains souls by displaying His generosity.

The beginning of all creation is the Light of Mohammed, which is the Universal Intellect, and the world is its explication and unfolding.

The Compassionate, the Merciful.

The Compassionate (*Rahman*) creates and preserves the world, the Merciful (*Rahim*) saves it. "The Compassionate" is the name of the eternal past; "the Merciful" is the name of the eternal future. All things are brought into being and sustained by the Compassionate; God grants His special grace on a subset of existence with the Merciful.

Master of the Judgment Day.

God is the Master of "the Day of Religion," the Judgment Day. The Judgment Day is the Gathering of souls, the Last Judgment, and their Dispersal to Heaven and Hell. It is the day when the purposes and struggles of people are evaluated. It is the day when the wise gaze upon the Noble Face of their Lord, when the doers of good works find their reward, and when oppressors meet their retribution.

The small licenses we are allowed in this world are removed on that day. That day only the owner of the Station of Praise—the recipient of the decree: "My Lord will give you of His bounty, and you will be pleased"—namely, the Prophet Mohammed, will have full authority.

Next is the verse that proclaims the independence and joy of the spirit, and indicates worship and the request for help:

You alone we worship, and you alone we ask for help.

The person who recites this is saying, in effect: "Dear Lord, we beg you for every help, and we worship you with the strength you give us. Our worship is not of our own. Power and strength belong to you. You have helped us, and we have worshiped you with that help. We look to you for grace, and do not trust in our own deeds. We neither trust our works nor ask for reward; we only worship you. We wish you to grant bountifully. We have stripped ourselves of every purpose, interest, and relationship. Help us in this condition; we beg for the continuation of this state. We worship you by your command and beg for help by your leave. Everything is temporary, only you are permanent."

As this prayer implies, there are four ways to worship God: with desire, with fear, with shame, and with love. The best kind of worship is that done with love. Unification occurs through the operation of this verse, for it unites humans with God. Asking for aid can only occur when one has reconciled oneself with the presence of God's Prophet (i.e., acknowledged him as such), for no one goes unto the Lord except by him (or, if one has lived during the reign of previous prophets, by their mediation).

Guide us along your Straight Path.

The Straight Path is that which God has set down for human beings. It consists of obeying His commandments. If one follows that path, one is sure to attain bliss by the shortest possible route. So the person who prays continues: "Dear Lord, guide us to the Right Way with your aid. Give us guidance to whatever is your plan for us. We beg you to present us with the path that leads to the Summit of your Unity."

The path of those whom you have blessed.

In other words: "That path is the road of the Prophet, the Martyrs, the Righteous, and the Perfect. It is the station of knowing you, of beautiful courtesy. You have given these of your Grace."

Not of those who incur your wrath, nor of those who go astray.

That is: "We beg not to be of those who earn your wrath, who persist in error, who remain stuck in rote Imitation and cannot attain Realization, who are driven from the gate of servanthood, who are misguided, progress without deserving it, or show fake psychic feats."

Amen.

"Please accept our supplication, dear Lord."

Epilogue

What is it then that we are awakened or opened to by this chapter? The rest of the Koran—the miracle of God, the Book in which nothing is neglected (6:38) and which is a guidance and a healing (41:44). And to a proper conscious understanding of the workings of the cosmos itself: God as the Compassionate and the Most Merciful. We attain a state whereby we are healed and not separate from that healing, remembering Him who continually remembers us.

God is the healer of all wounds, the mender of all schisms of the spirit. In order to achieve Unification we must apply to Him alone, using the way He has revealed to us through the Prophet. If we do so, there can be no doubt that we will receive salvation, no matter how "lost" we may be, for "well able is He to save." The broken mirror of our minds and our psyches can be mended—but only if we remember God again.

⚘

This chapter revealed how the Koran subtly heals us, allowing us to attain bliss by becoming individually unified (our perception cleansed), able to recognize the beauty and unity that underlies the world. The following chapter now asks the question whether Islam is in need of Reformation in view of recent historical zealotry and events that have been described as "Islamic."

Should There Be A "Reformation" in Islam?

———————— ✿ ————————

(In this chapter, we will consider the question as to whether Islam as a religion might need reform, or whether it is the behavior of Moslems that stands in need of reform. The most important distinction to be made here is that between Islam and "Islamists" (for there is a great distinction). The chapter was written at a time when the Taliban, etc. were still extant; the reader is referred to the Prologue for an updated treatment. Its message is still relevant, however. Other important points to be covered in this chapter are that: the letter of Islamic Holy Law cannot be considered apart from its spirit (even though some have tried), the Way of the Prophet and the Koran must always be considered together, and repressive cruelty and terrorism have no place in Islam.)[83]

Introduction

As the twenty-first century begins, Moslems all over the world would seem to be sliding into aberrant behavior, causing concern to the world and distress to their friends. If we take the "representatives" of Islam around the world, we find that their actions are frequently at variance with the teachings they supposedly uphold. Consider the following facts (and these are but a few examples):

- The Taliban in Afghanistan forbids girls from going to school (1997).

Mohammed, the Prophet of God, said: "It is incumbent on every Moslem man and every Moslem woman to seek and learn knowledge." (Where is one to learn knowledge/science, except at school? And where is the religion whose educational institutions were once legendary?)

- Iran's Khomeini passes a death sentence on writer Salman Rushdie (1989). (The *fatwa* was recently withdrawn, but it was in effect for years, causing Rushdie to live in hiding.)

When Mohammed conquered Mecca, he forgave all his greatest enemies at the peak of his power and allowed them to go scot-free.

- Middle-Eastern guerrillas engage in terrorist activities, causing the concept of "terrorism" to become associated with the name of Islam (the 1970s and '80s).

The victims of terrorism are almost always innocent people. In Islam, human beings are personally responsible for their own words and deeds, but the Koran says: "No soul bears the burden of another." Therefore, to kill an innocent human being in retaliation for the errors of others is a flagrant violation of this principle.

- Various purportedly "Islamic" (actually "Islamist") regimes attempt—or give the impression of attempting—to enforce Islam by repression and cruelty.

It cannot be stated any more clearly: this is absolutely wrong and cannot be called "Islamic." The Prophet said: "A society where cruelty and oppression are present cannot survive."

In an age of increasing violence, is this how Moslems hope to set an example for emulation by other people? Or do they themselves thereby become compliant victims of the same trend? Not only do such actions put off those who might otherwise be inclined to view Islam in a favorable light, but they constitute grave offenses against the religion, inviting the wrath of God. The crime is thus compounded. To make things clearer, Islam doesn't need reform, the behavior of Moslems does. The only consolation is that the perpetrators of such acts do not represent the vast "silent majority" of Moslems who peacefully go about their business and worship every day. Only news unusual enough to attract attention has the sales potential to get reported in the news media—and these are "worst case" characteristics.

All this—and more—suggests that Islam and these kinds of Islamist "Moslems" have become two different things. It does no good to attempt to hide this fact, or to find excuses, such as that Moslems in our day are operating under a siege mentality engendered by a two-hundred-year offensive of Western civilization.[84] The reasons may be many and varied, deriving both from within Moslems and without. These are, of course, important in themselves. But what is even more important is to recognize that *such "Moslems" have, by and large, lost their ability to be regarded as representatives of Islam.*

Fundamentalists are fundamentally confused: they seem to be unaware of the highest principles (ethical, spiritual, and human) that the Prophet Mohammed represents. Since Islam is strictly monotheistic, the fear of covert polytheism (also called "associating partners with God") has led to the devaluation and conscious evasion of anything other than God and the Koran—including, in the case of Arabia, even the example of the Prophet himself.[85] But the Koran cannot be lived without the human example who embodies it.

Any uninformed outsider observing the behavior of such present-day "Moslems" would conclude—and would be justified in concluding—that Islam is an oppressive, bloodthirsty, intolerant, fanatical religion. So we are led to the sad conclusion that neither outsiders nor these "Moslems" themselves any longer know *what Islam really is.*

If this is the case, then we must, Moslems and non-Moslems alike, first disabuse ourselves of our ignorance concerning Islam. We must ask: Is the behavior we associate with "Moslems" commensurate with the principles of Islam? Can "Moslems," in all fairness, claim that they faithfully represent their religion? And which stands in need of reform: "Moslems," Islam, or both?

Let us consider the words of a prominent Moslem of the past, Abu Darda. When asked: "What is good for human beings?" he replied: "Good does not consist in much property or many children. It lies in *the increase of one's knowledge, one's modesty, and one's gentleness.* Good consists in vying with human beings in the service of God and in serving one's religion. If you do good, give thanks to God; if you do bad, repent to Him." (Emphasis added.) One look at these words is enough to convince us that there is a great discrepancy between them and the actions listed above. Obviously, "something is rotten in the kingdom," but what? Who, or what, needs to be changed?

Religion is a social institution of primary importance. As times and societies change, it is natural to expect changes in their institutions as well. Thus the question arises as to whether the religion of Islam can be changed to adapt to changing circumstances, and if so, how. Many people think that the wide-reaching changes in society resulting from scientific and technological advances, especially in the twentieth century, call for a reform or revision in established religions. In this connection, it is suggested that Islam should undergo a "Reformation" similar to that which occurred in Christianity in the sixteenth century. The intention of this chapter is to investigate the question of "Reform in Islam."

The Koran

For something to need reform, it must first be deformed. There has, however, been no distortion in the basic principles of Islam. This is especially true of the Koran, the source of those principles, which has remained unaltered for fourteen centuries. *Not one word has been changed,* as anyone can verify by checking the latest copies against the earliest ones. What has not happened, though, is a renewal of the understanding of Islam in keeping with contemporary realities. The perennial principles of faith, worship, and ethics need to be refreshed in each age using a contemporary idiom that will keep them ever young and fertile. What is necessary is not to reform, but to rephrase—not to change the principles, but render them comprehensible to our age. Meanwhile, there are Moslems who give the impression of being mired in the Middle Ages, and that impression is then generalized to the community as a whole.

As the last scripture revealed to humankind, the Koran distills the essence of earlier religious texts, including the Old and New Testaments—a fact that cannot be appreciated without actually reading it. In presenting this final, timeless Revelation to humanity, it was God's intention not to leave any loose ends. He also wished to bequeath to humanity a religion that would, from that point onwards, suffice to meet all its religious needs. Accordingly He revealed the Koran, which is preserved in the form it was intended and is the most well-preserved book in history.

The Koran contains everything that God wished to convey to humanity for the rest of time. For those who can decipher it, it contains everything of importance that humanity needs for salvation. It is a book free of contradictions.[86] This is why there have been no heterodoxies or heresies within Islam proper—in fact, it is not only an orthodoxy but, as such commentators as Hans Küng and Malise Ruthven have noted, also an "orthopraxy" (right action or practice).

At the same time, it should be recognized that the Koran, being the last and most sophisticated of holy texts, is not always an easy text to understand. Side by side with simple statements, it contains expressions which make it more akin to a textbook in advanced calculus than a primary-school book. That it can be easily read in Arabic or another language obscures its difficulties, and gives the deceptive appearance of simplicity. Also, various religious observances are mentioned only briefly therein. With the Book, therefore, there also had to be the Man—the Prophet—who would both convey the Revelation, and would, in word and deed, exemplify the kind of human being (*homo religiosus* and, beyond that, *homo perfectus*) desired by God. Left standing alone, the more difficult parts of the Koran would have lent themselves to a variety of interpretations. (They still do, but not to the point of engendering schisms.) As mentioned earlier, the exemplar of the Prophet was necessary to show how the Koran should be lived out in real life. And indeed, when asked about the morality of the Prophet, his wife Aisha replied: "His morality was the Koran." In addressing the Prophet, God adds the rejoinder in the Koran: "Verily you are upon a mighty morality."

The Prophet of God

When pronouncing on religious matters, Mohammed never spoke on his own. Hence, the scholars of Islam have distinguished between "Revelation that is recited"—written Revelation, meaning the Koran—and "Revelation that is not recited," or the pronouncements and actions of the Prophet. The two complete and complement each other. The extensive body of knowledge covering the sayings and actions of the Prophet, as well as those of his close followers, the saints, delivers the Koran from being interpreted by everyone in his or her own way, which could lead to individualism, anarchy, and even nihilism.

As a prophet, Mohammed provided the knowledge needed by human beings to shape their course through life. When the Prophet's example is followed, every Moslem knows how to live correctly, how best to meet each situation, what action is suited to which occasion.

In his daily life, Mohammed took great pains to instruct people how to live. He explained the relations between man and wife, between employer and employee, how to preserve health, how to educate children, how to make a living, how to prevent poverty and suffering, how to wage war even though war itself is undesirable,[87] and how to restore peace at the earliest opportunity. Mohammed gave much practical information, and his spiritual advice was clear and perennial enough to be applied in any age—including our day.

Such a person, who would act as a role model for humanity in the future, had perforce to live in the very thick of life. He not only had to establish and defend the new Revelation, but in addition had to live as an ordinary person among other people—eating, drinking, marrying, having children and grandchildren, fighting wars of self-defense, engaging in commerce, acting as a leader, and so on. In doing all these, he had to demonstrate to his followers and to future generations how, exactly, a pious person should behave, or is expected to behave by God, under these widely varying conditions. This truly gargantuan task could be entrusted by God only to a person capable of bearing such a tremendous weight and carrying out the mission successfully.

Most of all, anyone should be able to imitate such a person, and this imitation should end in salvation and liberation. Following his example should lead to success and happiness both in this world and the next. To withdraw from the world is neither desirable, nor possible; that kind of solution just wouldn't work. A role model for humanity has to be someone who is acquainted with worldly life, who wholeheartedly accepts life on earth. Only a person who has survived to an old age, who has lived and experienced the world, who has married,[88] and had a profession, could be a model of how to live for the vast majority of human beings.

Here we come to the crux of the matter. How can such a life be reconciled with spirituality, sanctity, and true piety? Is such a thing even possible?

Can a human being both live a secular life, and yet still achieve true sainthood? The answer given by the life of Mohammed to all these questions is a resounding *Yes*. Islam stands as proof that the saintly life does not require that one become a hermit, an ascetic, or a recluse. Human beings do many other things besides walking about, talking wisely, and doing nothing at all.

Such a person as Mohammed, then, can be a model, a solution, and an answer. In other words, true spirituality does not require a life dedicated entirely to the spirit, to the exclusion of the physical world and daily life. To be "in the world, but not of it" is the motto of the Moslem saint, or Sufi. This is not to say that such a life would be easy. But it was *made easy* by God for humanity, as exemplified in the life of Mohammed. Spiritual life wedded to material life makes for the well-rounded human being whose entire range of potentials is actualized. The Prophet was such an exemplar, with an optimum blend of the secular and the spiritual.

In a religion intended for all human beings, we should be careful to distinguish between what is universal and what is merely local. As I mentioned earlier, the fact that the Prophet spoke and prayed in Arabic doesn't mean we have to do so, too. Just because he lived in a naturally polygamous society doesn't mean that every man has to take several wives. That the Prophet rode on a camel need no more detain us from driving a car than the fact that Jesus rode on an ass. If Mohammed had lived in this day and age, we may be sure that he would have worn a suit and tie and used the amenities of modern technology.[89]

Once such quirks of local custom, culture, geography, and history are weeded out, we are left with a template, a program, of how the pious human being should behave. For example, the Prophet *did* mend his own clothing, eat with his servants, and play with his children and grandchildren, and these actions are to be emulated. Mohammed, who lived in a comparatively recent age, is the first and only prophet for whom definite historical data are available. When we examine the Prophet's life in detail, we find that its hallmark is *courtesy towards, and compassion for, all beings.* He was the quintessential gentleman, even toward his enemies. He was always kind and considerate to his wives. Even when he became the uncontested leader of the fledgling Islamic community, he combined "sageliness within and kingliness without"—he was, to use Nietzsche's words, "Caesar with the heart of Christ."

Here, then, we have a person whom we can, without reservation, commend as a model of beautiful conduct to anyone. The reason we have dwelt on the Prophet at such length is because this aspect of his importance is so frequently neglected in discussions on Islam. Moslems and non-Moslems alike, in focusing on the primary importance of the Koran as the word of God, too often overlook the fact that it was the Prophet who interpreted the Koran for human use—for practical implementation—by his words and actions, and that we would not know where to start understanding the Koran otherwise. Indeed, the image in the West of Islam as harsh and unforgiving is due to the fact that many of its adherents fail to live up to his example. The all-pervasive lovingkindness of the Prophet all too often fails to find expression in the brittle behavior of would-be followers.

Now these twin pillars—the Koran and the Prophet's Way—render a church unnecessary in Islam.[90] As we have seen, Islam is a churchless faith. Everything is clearly and definitely defined. Hence, there is no church, clergy, theocracy, or religious bureaucracy bent on self-perpetuation.[91] There is no need for a teaching authority, and although scholars, saints, and Sufis carry out religious instruction, they do not constitute a social or religious class apart from the laity. Since there are no Sacraments, neither is there any need for a sacramental agent. Between a human being and God stands nothing. Everyone knows what to do, and does not need a separate agency or external authority to mediate with God. One worships, confesses, and repents to God oneself. The individual's relationship with God is a sacred and private matter that brooks no intervention. We might, in fact, call this the democratization of faith, or the emancipation of humankind.

This does not mean that Islam neglects the social realm. The Almstax, the Pilgrimage, congregational prayers, religious holidays, charity, and so on are all matters of social import. It is only that an entrenched religious institution is not required as intermediary between God and humanity. Where there is no church, the separation of church and state likewise poses no problem.[92]

The Koran tells us that true Moslems are a "middle people"—or, if you like, "people of the Middle Way"—and, as such, are an example to everyone. In what follows we shall take a look at Islam's stand on major themes of concern to humanity. As we shall see, its principles are general enough to encompass every human situation. The quotations interspersed here are mostly from the Koran and the Prophet's Traditions.

Reason

The basis of any religion is revelation and its transmission. Revelation is also the source of all laws of nature and of science. Hence, revelation and reason—as described by religion—cannot be opposed to each other, but are partners. The Prophet himself has stated: "He who has no reason has no religion, either." In Islam, reason and revelation (or transmission) cannot conflict with each other. This is true right from the ground level of daily life, all the way up to the loftiest heights of spirituality and mysticism. If there is an apparent contradiction between the two, either reason is in error, or revelation has been improperly understood. The Koran and the Prophet's Way form an internally self-consistent, noncontradictory body of doctrine. As I will reiterate throughout this book, no institution is needed to pronounce orthodoxy in Islam.

There are no "mysteries" in Islam. Since there is no Original Sin, neither are there Sacraments to cure one's spiritual ills or achieve immortality; worship and good works take care of everything. Thus, the need for a religious institution that administers sacraments is obviated. The individual soul is not sacrificed to collectivism, and it becomes possible to obtain an individual religious experience of God.

Every principle of Islam is in accordance with reason and logic. This entirely rational attitude, however, does not lead to the loss of mysticism or access to the higher reaches of the human personality. Instead, it leads to a rational and reasonable approach at every step of our spiritual ascent. No one is driven to make a choice between faith and reason, or to a decision that will torment his or her conscience.

Islam satisfies both the emotions and the intellect. The human spirit is addressed, but the appeal is to reason, which is highly valued. Islam does not consist *only* of reason, however, for it would then be a rational philosophy and nothing more. As a result, a positive faith and an enlightened intellect are prized as guards against fanaticism. "Strip yourself of bigotry and selfishness, leave aside bias and egotism, then love God," is Islam's advice. It also claims that "It is not enough to know, it is necessary to think," and calls us to "see that which is"—to recognize Reality.

Knowledge and Science

Among religions, Islam places the greatest premium on knowledge and science. It tells us that: "Ignorance leads to bad morals, and bad morals lead to destruction." Implicit in this is the recognition that knowledge saves, sooner or later. The great emphasis on knowledge in Islamic culture is underscored by the Prophet's admonition for everyone (men and women) to learn: "Desiring and learning knowledge/science is mandatory upon every Moslem man and woman."

The very first word of revelation to the Prophet was: "Read" (96:1), as was the second. Even the single Prophetic precept, "Learn knowledge from cradle to the grave," would be enough to secure the education of humankind.

Islam proclaims that no matter from which nation scientific advances originate, they are the common property of all humanity. There is no opposition between religion and science in Islam. The more one progresses in science and knowledge, the more one is able to appreciate the handiwork of God displayed throughout the universe, and the greater one's admiration becomes for the infinitely superior Intelligence and wisdom pervading the cosmos. At the height of Islamic civilization, a person who did not know astronomy (the workings of the universe) and anatomy (the workings of the human body) was regarded as lacking in the Knowledge of God. In other words, one who does not comprehend the workings of the world cannot understand God well enough, either. The Prophet declared, "The science of sciences is, first: the science of bodies [physics and physiology], and next: the science of religions [spiritual science]." Knowledge of one to the exclusion of the other would be one-sided, and therefore deficient.

Faith

The only unforgiveable error in Islam is to worship finite creatures (other humans, idols, and so on). Divine Grace can forgive all other sins. Islam is entirely free of this mistake, and replaces it with the faith in One God. "One" here means That Which There is No Other, the One without a Second, the All-Encompassing. God is an illimitable Living Presence, not an abstraction or an idol. He loves human beings, His servants, but His retribution can be wrathful, too. It is a mark of wisdom never to consider oneself exempt from such retribution.

The word for faithlessness or infidelity is "concealment" in Islam. This means that since God is the ultimate Reality, those who lack faith are only concealing the truth—from themselves even more than from others. Concealment is based on two principles: the ridicule of exaltation (making fun of faith and those who love and worship God), and the exaltation of ridicule (elevating such mockery above all other things). Hence, it is not worthy of further comment here.

A person of faith finds solace, not in causing injury to others, but in healing injuries. For Islam defines life not as warfare, but as a sharing and mutual aid. The outcome of discord and strife is division, while the result of mutual aid is embracing one another.

Neither will a faithful person tolerate cruelty and injustice. The faithful Moslem says: "There is One who knows me better than I know myself," and even: "I am not, He is." He tries to live like a perfect human being, and avoids opposing and attacking the rights of others. Far from doing such things, he won't even touch a lost article he finds on the road.

Faithlessness and Despair

Whenever mankind has lived in faith, the world has been a peaceful place. When faith is corrupted and religion degenerates, then come the times when every crime and every kind of ill pervade society.

Lack of faith in God leads to desperation on both the individual and social levels.

A person of piety believes that the success or failure of one's endeavors depends on a superior regulatory power. Because s/he believes in eternal life, the failures s/he meets with in this life do not discourage him or her. Thanks to faith, s/he never falls into despair—such faith precludes hopelessness. In a heart full of faith in the omnipresence of Reality, not a trace can be found of despair.

However, the heart lacking faith is the playground of doubts. It falls prey to one doubt after another, never experiencing the bliss of certainty. It is plagued by distress and uncertainties.

Faith in eternity is essential if people are to accept the essence of morality. A person convinced that the universe is nothing but a coincidence, that s/he is evolved from the animals, that the afterlife and eternity are mere fairy tales, will never think about paying his or her debts to society and humanity, for s/he will say: "Life and fulfillment consist in my ability to satisfy the desires and drives of my self." Only the belief in an ultimate Judgment can restrain human beings from committing the worst they are capable of. Without faith, there is no basis for preferring altruism over egotism or self-sacrifice over self-promotion. In its absence, the greatest geniuses, the best economists, the most powerful security brokers will be powerless to curb the ego's desires or the resulting cries of despair. Civilizations built upon the passions of the Base Self will be torn apart by those same passions.

While Islam tries to prevent this on the one hand, it also advises us to heal wounds mutually by administering to one another, rather than injuring others and increasing the present ills and sorrows of society. Since this will eliminate despair, it will also put an end to suicide and insanity, and peace and contentment will reign.

Faith, Evidence, and Good Works

Islam advises us that faith should rest, not on empty claims, but on firm evidence: accept nothing without proof that convinces your reason. If something is absurd or a logical impossibility, don't believe it.

Faith rooted in proof is something new in the history of religions. The Koran tells us that God Himself will demand unbelievers to "produce their evidence" for their claims on Judgment Day. If their evidence doesn't hold water, too bad—but also, too late. The Prophet also warned against blindly following what is unknown. "Accept nothing which you do not know to be true. And don't claim knowledge in things you are ignorant of, for you will be held to account." People of true faith are considered to possess uncommon discernment in Islam: "Be wary of the discernment of the faithful, for he sees by the light of God."

The adherents of this religion are called, not to be concerned about death, but to regret only the meaning that slips through their fingers, the irretrievable spiritual happiness that escapes them. They are called upon to "consider the Artist, not just the painting."

Faith in Action

Faith is hidden in the heart; only God can know of it. But if such abstract faith were enough, God would have spared us the trouble of religious rules requiring worship and right action. To declare that religion is a matter for conscience without harvesting its concrete fruits would be a vacuous claim and a waste of time. "Faith without works is naught," and if the works are there, one may be reasonably assured of God's grace—though this shouldn't lead to self-congratulation, vanity, or pride, which could yield terrible results. Surrender to God becomes explicit in surrender to His commands and prohibitions. Hence, faith must be fortified with deeds; theory should be complemented by practice.

Attitude to Nonbelievers

What of those who, in spite of everything, refuse to believe? "You are only a warner," God advises Mohammed in the Koran, "Tell them: 'To you, your religion; to me, mine.'" This means that unbelievers should be left alone, not converted by force. The use of violence in observing Islam is prohibited by the Koran itself: "There is no compulsion in [the Islamic] religion" (2:256).

Faith then is a matter for individual conscience. Hence, freedom of religion is guaranteed right from its very inception. Even those who do not belong to "the People of the Book" (possessing holy texts of earlier revelation, such as Jews and Christians) cannot be compelled to obey the rules of the Koran.

Ethics and Morality

Islam is above all the religion of morality. As the Prophet remarked: "I was sent only in order to complete morality." The essence of this religion is to become adorned with all praiseworthy morals, and to shed all blameworthy traits. It is thanks to this fact that Islam was able to win the hearts of those who came into contact with it. Contrary to theories of "conquest by the sword," it was never imposed upon people by coercion.

Islam tells us that: "An immoral society cannot survive," and also: "The imitation of evil is suicide." Love, morality, measure, and proper balance are the cornerstones of this religion. Islam encourages us to strive constantly to transcend ourselves. The Prophet informs us that we must always work hard to improve our lot (material and spiritual): "Whoever is at the same level—materially and spiritually—for two consecutive days has been deceived, and whoever is worse off today than he was yesterday has suffered a loss." Again: "Even if you receive news that Doomsday is imminent, don't refrain from planting a sapling." The good Moslem is defined as "the person who does others no harm, by hand or by word," and is called to "leave those alone who leave you alone." One is also encouraged to seek the counsel of others, since in heeding others the false sense of self is demolished.

Freedom and Duty

According to Islam, the freedom desired by humankind is bounded by morality, where morality consists of respect for one's duties. The lowest level of duty is justice towards others and control towards one's self. Its highest level is generosity to others, and restraint of the self.

Islam defines as "free" only the person who knows his or her self, who can control his or her passions and sorrows. Hence, freedom is possible only by knowing the tricks of the Base Self, and by refusing to obey it. That person is "free" who knows his or her self, and is not the prisoner of his or her passions or the offences given by others. The devil, the personified external principle of evil, has no great power unless he finds an ally in the Base Self, in which case the evil becomes internalized and the ego becomes an instrument of the devil.

One must always be careful to grant the Base Self its rights, but to deny it Forbidden pleasures. Every pleasure is not a sin. Anything agreeable is not necessarily immoral. Morality is not self-torture or doing unpleasant things, though these may be necessary under certain conditions. As long as Illicit Gain and Illicit Sex are avoided, one will not have much trouble confining the Base Self. But the Base Self should not be permitted self-satisfaction.

Islam's claim is that only by preserving freedoms can human potentials flower, and that it offers freedom tempered by justice. True freedom, then, is Islam itself. It is the staff of life; it encourages valiant deeds, and forbids vile desires.

It may be asked: from where do humans receive a sense of freedom? Does matter give us the desire for it? And if matter does not possess will, how can it lend us freedom? In Islam, the spiritual world is frequently referred to as "the World of Meaning," because it is this which infuses sense and order into matter. In other words, *no account of the universe that leaves out meaning (the spiritual world) can be considered complete.* Humans cannot receive will or freedom from insensate, meaningless existence. Ultimately, we receive freedom as a gift from God. Since freedom is nowhere to be found in the universe of matter, it is obviously given us by God. In that case, one who denies God is depriving oneself of freedom, for one can never discover the hidden Source of will and freedom within.

Ecological and Social Catastrophe

The reason that we are faced with global crises, psychic and social disintegration, violence, and dissatisfaction in the midst of plenty and at the peak of civilization, is that we have tried to quench our thirst by material means alone. But a human being is not just a material creature. As long as his or her spiritual dimension is overlooked, entire oceans of matter will not suffice to sate the spiritual hunger gnawing inside. Yet, under the mistaken impression that the problem is one of quantity, humans crave more and ever more, straining the resources of our planet that can feed everyone but, being finite, cannot satisfy a craving that is infinite. Only God, eternal life, and the assurance of personal survival after death can fill this gaping void in a person. And the priorities of God and the spirit are different from the drive towards material excess. The Koran advises us to consider the ruins strewn across the earth of civilizations that were, in certain respects, superior to ours. Their remains stand as mute testimony to the fact that as long as *all* human needs are not met by a fine-tuned adjustment, humankind will be like a TV set out of kilter, and sooner or later self-destruct. Unless our civilization rises to this challenge, it will be only one in a long series, or—given the magnitude of its capacity for destruction—perhaps the last.

Peace

Who can deny that humanity is in need of peace? Why does it prove so elusive? How come minds capable of devising ways to dive to the bottom of the sea, probe the farthest reaches of space, and cause mass destruction in an instant, fail miserably when it comes to creating peace? Only a religion that satisfies the whole spectrum of human possibilities can do this, but nobody is knocking at its door.

The very name "Islam" is derived from "peace." The peace of heart granted by this religion is such that all the material treasures of the world mean less than a mosquito's wing to the spiritually mature. Ideally, the Moslem is a person at peace with God, with himself, with fellow human beings, with nature, and with the cosmos.

Unfortunately, there are those who would capitalize on the peaceful intentions of others. Although Islam counsels peace, it does not advise flight when the only answer is combat. "If you want peace, prepare for war," the old adage goes. When provoked in the extreme or defending themselves, Islam advises that human beings have no recourse but to engage in battle.

The Arabic word *jihad,* which is usually mistranslated as "holy war," actually means "struggle" in the way of God: struggle with one's possessions and oneself, i.e., against one's Base Self. The age of conquests is now closed, for weapons of mass destruction will cause the decimation of innocents and threaten the very existence of the human race. My Master was of the opinion that henceforth, one should fight with the pen, not with the sword. He thus indirectly implied that verses dealing with war in the Koran are now "deactivated," and can only be interpreted in terms of struggle as described above. Today, real valor resides in the ability to conquer people's hearts—with the pen and with sublime truths, not with weapons, massacres, or bloodshed.

Luxury and Ecology

Islam counsels a streamlined life, free of troubles, pretensions, and excess baggage. This saves us from wasting time on unnecessary things, and leads to a peaceful and comfortable life. Religion directs us to a balanced living and to right livelihood. Just as it prohibits laziness and insufficient work, it also cautions against doing work harmful to others.

No matter how much work it involves, an ostentatious and luxurious life cannot be maintained solely on the work of one person. A lifestyle that ceaselessly excites the appetites of the Base Self must in some way or other involve the exploitation of others, because a single person's earnings would be insufficient to satisfy these appetites. Excessive profits may also exact a cost on the environment and on future generations. As a result, religion tells us, cries of despair will never cease in society. Wealth is allowed, but not at the expense of others.

The concept of luxury differs according to the society we live in. In the developed countries of our day, for example, having a telephone and a car are not luxuries but necessities. It is only when wealth is squandered in excess of the current social norm that it becomes a waste of valuable resources. Moreover, Islam advises us to use resources sparingly even when we are in possession of an apparently inexhaustible supply—to use only so much water as we need, for instance, even when we are standing beside an ocean. This is not only a recognition of the finite nature of our planet, vast though it may be, but also a recognition of the natural rights of our fellow humans.

Charity and Equality

Those with magnanimity in their nature, feeling compassion for all beings, are invariably impressed by the Alms-tax, one of the Five Pillars of Islam (described earlier in this book). Although the injunction to perform the Prayer occurs thirty-two times in the Koran, and the Pilgrimage and Fasting are each mentioned only once, the commandment to "give" and to "share," to help the downtrodden, is repeated seventy-two times. To raise the fallen by charity is worship of the highest order. While parsimony is sinful, the Koran advises us to be balanced, not excessive, in our handouts; our charity should not lead to destitution for ourselves. Otherwise, the count of the charitable will be decreased, and the number of those needing charity increased, by at least one the next time around.

Before God, rich and poor are one. Human beings are absolutely equal; a slave can—and in early Islamic history, did—become a commander, and even a king, and bloodline does not confer privilege.

But in Islam, charity means much more than donations to the needy. According to the Prophet, "Any good deed is charity," and "Any good word is charity." For example, it is charity for a creditor to postpone payment for a debtor who is unable to pay up, and as the Prophet said, "To treat your wife kindly is also charity; to remove a stone from a path which could cause a person to trip and fall is also charity; to greet or smile at someone you meet along the road is also charity." Any act of giving, ultimately of one's very self, is hallowed.

Of Vice and Virtue

Islam holds that like gold and silver, there are virtues of perennial value and lasting worth. Courtesy, in particular, is so highly valued that its presence is equal to the fulfillment of half the religion (see Appendix A for sayings on courtesy).

Islamic morality requires that one should submit to God out of one's own free will, avoid anything that runs counter to reason and logic, and uphold the family of humankind. It calls upon us to abide with truth at all costs. It tells us to conquer evil with good rather than surrendering to it, and shows the easy ways of doing this. Personal responsibility is fundamental; there are no scapegoats. Every human being, having reached puberty and of sound mind, is responsible for him- or herself and no one else: "No soul bears the load of another," states the Koran.

This religion counsels patience against anger, gentleness in the face of ignorance, and forgiveness towards evil. "Be patient, forbearing, and take refuge in God so that you may attain salvation," the Prophet advised. Patience and forbearance do not mean passive abandon, but an active struggle against the Base Self, which the Prophet defined as "the Greatest Battle." As for salvation, all this takes is an honest resolve and earnest intention—nothing could be simpler.

Whoever surveys creation with the eye of wisdom tries not to see anything ugly, because any perceived ugliness is a mask, a shell, for beauty within beauty. The wise person remembers that: "There are no thorns in Reality. If you find one, it is your self." S/he recognizes the same light shining from every corner in the universe, from behind every facade, and meets anger with patience, ignorance with gentleness, and ill will with friendship.

In Islam, one is invited to self-criticism, to call oneself to account, before one criticizes anyone else, and before one is called to account at the Last Judgment. One must examine one's conscience in an objective, matter-of-fact way, without excessive self-blame or guilt, and rectify one's future conduct accordingly.

Hypocrisy, jealousy, and lying are among the worst evils. Eliminate these, and the Almighty will spread Heaven beneath your feet. Bigotry is condemned, because this religion is opposed to the weakness, ignorance, and imitation of evil that are the basis of fanaticism. It is only in relation to God that weakness is proper. The Prophet is reported to have said, "He who knows his self knows his Lord"—i.e., whoever knows that he is weak and inconsequential before his Lord of infinite power will efface himself, and when that is done, the attributes of the Lord are manifested. In other words, knowledge of one's self leads to the Knowledge of God, or Gnosis.[93]

Gnosis

Islam proclaims Gnosis (God-knowledge) as the reason for creation. Sufism and mysticism are built into the religion and—barring extreme manifestations—are an integral part of it. Ultimately, Gnosis leads to the overflow of happiness. It is the cause of peace with one's conscience. It is the legacy of Islam, and the essence of being human.

Gnosis represents the pinnacle of knowledge for humans, because God is the loftiest Being capable of being known. God desires us to "contemplate His loftiness." All pleasures other than the pleasure of knowing God are temporary. The purpose in this life is to reach God, and Gnosis is closeness to God or certainty of God. To this end, in addition to the external world, man's inner (spiritual) states must be studied. A constellation of sacred images helps to organize unconscious psychic contents in the most beneficial way. At the same time, idolatry is avoided by the exclusion of icons and the emphasis on worship of only One God. Islam is radically iconoclastic; the veneration of saints takes the form of deep respect only, not worship.

The stations of wisdom begin with the realization that the universe as macrocosmos is mirrored in the human being, the microcosmos. Two sayings from Sufic Islam are "whatever is in the universe exists in man" and "the cosmos is a big man, man is a small universe." The essence of existence is hidden in us. Man is the essence of the universe, as the Heart is the essence of the human body. This Heart, the essence of essences, is the House of the Lord, the place God looks upon. S/he who comes to

122 . Tˮ Sǫ & Iǫ&&

the last station of wisdom, the highest level of selfhood, becomes a sage, a Perfect Human.

The human, according to Islam, is the bearer of God's trust. For this reason, the honor of humans cannot be desecrated. The Koran tells us that the human being is the deputy of God on earth—the viceregent of God's Attributes, and the steward of the heavens and the earth, of all existence. As it is said, "There are so many signs, so many truths to draw lessons from in the earth and the heavens, yet [some people] pass them all by."

Knowledge of God starts with faith in God, with the belief that there is something to be known to begin with: God, who is present with His Being (before the Beginning and after the End), encompassing through His Attributes, known via His Names, manifest in His Actions, and apparent through His works. Faith is attendant upon Gnosis, which, as the true purpose of existence, is superior to worship and obeying God's commandments. Unless Knowledge of God is aimed at, nothing much will come from the rote repetition of worship and obedience to God out of habit, although these are in themselves sufficient to secure salvation in the afterlife. Faith is then only the prelude to experience.

This religion defines the liberation of every person as the harmonious development of his or her potentials. It is every person's duty to foster this development, to "tend his or her own garden." We sow in this life in order that we may reap both in this life and in the next. One who sows ignorance cannot reap the fruit of Gnosis, of wisdom. As it is said, "Humanity exists, not for consumption, but for honest work and earnings, and for elevation," and "True exaltation is not possible as long as virtue is not preferred over self-interest."

Repayment of Evil

As discussed earlier in the section on "Peace," Islam counsels us that we have the right to demand just retribution for an evil. It allows us to "repay enmity to the same extent." The admonition to "turn the other cheek" is not recommended, because this is just not realistic. At the same time, however, Islam advises us that whoever possesses a higher morality should repay evil with good: "The punishment for a wrong is repayment in proportion and kind. But whoever chooses the path of forgiveness and goodness, his reward lies with God, who will repay this in a way befitting with His Majesty. God does not love oppressors." "If you forgive, you will have acted as befits the God-fearing," and "Cling to mercy, enjoin the good, and turn away from ignorance." In a Tradition of the Prophet, we are told that those who forgive people will *enter Paradise directly, without Judgment or retribution.*

There is a story about the thoroughbred horse of a prominent Moslem that was stolen as he was Praying. "I saw the thief," he remarked, "but I was engaged in something vastly more important, so I couldn't interrupt it." When his friends began to curse the thief, he stopped them: "Nobody has wronged me, that fellow has wronged himself. Isn't his self-wronging enough for him, that you and I should wrong him too?" Such nobility of soul will find an echo only in those who share it. Those doomed to a shadow play in a house of mirrors will simply laugh the whole affair off.

The next two examples are not just stories, they're history. The murderer of Ali, the Fourth Caliph, struck him in the neck with a poisoned sword. As his friends captured the fiend and began to manhandle him, Ali, in pain, warded them off, warning them to beware of doing wrong in their efforts to avenge him.

During the Battle of the Ditch, the same Ali had bested his opponent and was about to strike his last blow, when the man spat in his face. Ali immediately rose to his feet, and told him to get up. The enemy was astonished. "Why are you releasing me?" he asked. "When you spat in my face," replied Ali, "my Base Self (ego) became furious. If I had struck you at that point, it would have been for my Base Self, not for the sake of God. Our struggle is only for the objective purpose of defending God's religion. Now we must fight again." This anecdote illustrates the strict conditions under which retribution is allowed.

Gentleness

Islam counsels us to be gentle as far as possible. In the Koran, it is related that God sent Moses and Aaron to Pharaoh, advising them to "speak gently" with him. God knew, of course, that Pharaoh would not accept Moses' message, yet He advised them to treat even this arch-foe of

God with gentleness. This means that gentleness and gentle(wo)manly conduct should be our guiding light in all our dealings.

Cleanliness

The Prophet said, "Cleanliness (not just material but also spiritual cleanliness) derives from faith (Godliness)," a sentiment echoed in other religions and cultures. Not only is bodily cleanness necessary, but sins are defined as spiritual dirt in need of cleansing in accordance with the precepts of the Koran (which distinguish right from wrong and discriminate between good and bad). For instance, doing good with the ulterior motive of obtaining a favor is considered to be a "dirty" act.

Prohibitions

Anything capable of inflicting harm, not merely on others but on the tiniest creature, is branded "forbidden" in Islam. Whatever harms your body, your religion, and your good manners is prohibited. Together with all other things detrimental to the wellbeing of anyone—to one's body, religion, and courtesy—Islam has forbidden gambling, alcohol, and fornication.

This chapter explained that it is not Islam but Moslems who are in need of reform, illustrating that properly interpreted and followed, Islam is consistent with compassionate, rational, and democratic principles rooted in the highly ethical and caring life of each individual practitioner. The next chapter will ask whether Islam and democracy are compatible, given the many non-democratic Moslem nations in the world today.

Islam and Democracy

———————— ✣ ————————

(As we have seen, Islam is a religion, not a political system or a political ideology. But because it is a holistic religion, neither does it exclude politics altogether. Being the religion of all humanity for the rest of time, Islam could not be tied down to any specific polity, since down through history its adherents would live under a variety of political forms, one of which is democracy. Although it does not advocate this or that specific regime, investigation of the Islamic religion reveals that it is libertarian and egalitarian and that it supports social justice. Democracy comes closest to advocating and realizing these principles among the political systems of our day.

Certain basic concepts are common to the three great monotheistic religions. Unlikely as it may appear in the wake of recent events, democracy may actually find its strongest ally in Islam. Western countries famous for their democratic traditions are able to realize democracy to the extent that they possess—however unknowingly—elements of Mohammedan ethics. And the apparent present dead ends and difficulties of democracy can only be resolved by a higher, Islamic, morality. From this point of view, the Koran is democracy personified—as this section intends to demonstrate.)

Introduction

The intention of this chapter is to investigate the connections and relationships between Islam and democracy. As I have described earlier, recent times have seen a profusion of views being aired labeling Islam as "totalitarian" or "totalistic." The existence of few democracies[94] among the fifty-seven Islamic nations in the world is advanced as proof in support of this thesis. It has therefore become a necessity to analyze the extent to which Islam is compatible with democracy.

It should first and foremost be indicated that the lack of democracy in many Islamic countries is due, not to Islam, but to other factors. First of all, this lack is related to security and anarchy. No government can give in to anarchy or allow it to be victorious. Second, the political regimes in Islamic countries have as little to do with Islam as the military junta in Burma (Myanmar) has to do with Buddhism, or Hitler's Germany had to do with Christianity. Although the great majority of Islamic nations today are police states under occupation by their own armies, the reason for this is not religion, and certainly not Islam. Rather, it is the result of various internal and (more often) external factors of a social, political, and economic nature, such as a colonial past, oil, money, and power politics. It would be unjust to put the blame which is their due on Islam. Turkey is, so far, fortunate in being independent enough of these factors to be able to preserve its democracy whilst remaining an Islamic country.

But our purpose here is not to present an analysis of the conditions that render democracy unfeasible in Islamic nations. Rather, we intend to investigate how favorable and proximate Islam itself is to democracy. And we wish to take this research deeper than has been done hitherto.

Those who claim that Islam lacks a democratic structure sometimes point out that the history of Islam is strewn with sultanates, empires, and kingdoms, not with democracies. But, in the contemporary world, democracy has a history of only about two hundred years. The democratic nations of Europe were, until recently, kingdoms themselves, and some are still ruled by constitutional monarchies. As for the dictatorships of the recent past, to which the term "totalitarian" is eminently more applicable, some of these converted to democracy in 1945, while others have done so only recently. In history, on the other hand, democracy has been seen in no land and religion with the exception of ancient

Greece and, perhaps, Switzerland. This may be attributed to the general progress of humanity with time. What is important is this: Is the religion of Islam a help or a hindrance to the advance of humankind toward democracy? So many vacuous arguments have seen daylight without touching upon what is essential in this matter that the present investigation has become a pressing need.

Islam and Theocracy

The favorite example of those who find Islam and democracy to be mutually exclusive is the regime founded by Ayatollah Khomeini in Iran. It must at once be pointed out that an exceptional interpretation of Islam, not shared by nine-tenths of the world's Moslems, dominates Iran. The failure of the Iranian regime's efforts to spread its brand of revolution is clear evidence that the political ideas that lie at its roots have not met with general acceptance in the Islamic world, and is nowadays meeting increased resistance even from the people of Iran.

Certain Shiite writers have explicitly stated that what they want is an "absolute theocracy." But the saying of Mohammed, the Prophet of Islam, to the effect that "There is no clergy in religion," has closed the doors on the hegemony and rule of a priest class right from the very start. This was a sign of the Prophet's wisdom and foresight, for a clergy, although it claims to act in the name of God, is made up of ordinary human beings with human failings. If these become, in addition, politically empowered in a theocracy, the least of the results will be mismanagement on a grand scale, as has become increasingly obvious in Iran since 1999. An organized Church of the form in Christianity or Buddhism does not exist in Islam—it is a *churchless faith*. If it had, it would have emerged during the Prophet's lifetime or the immediately succeeding period of the Four Caliphs at the latest, not in Iran in 1979 A.D.

To read the Koranic verse: "Judgment belongs only to God" (6:57) as: "Sovereignty belongs only to God," and thus extrapolate to politics, would also produce theocratic tendencies. For what is intended here is the absolute sovereignty of the Lord over the entire universe. We cannot carry this over to the sphere of politics, because in politics the sovereigns are rulers, who are only human. If we attempt to apply this verse to politics, the situation will arise where certain people claiming to speak in the name of God (i.e., a clerical class) lay claim to rulership. But this is precluded by the Prophetic saying cited above. We thus see that neither the history of Islam, nor the present state of Islamic countries, and certainly not the example of Iran, can shed light on the relationship between Islam and democracy.

Council

In the Koran, verses dealing with *shura* (translated as both council or counsel) occur in two places. The first of these is: "Counsel among yourselves in your tasks" (3:159), and the second is: "They carry out their tasks by counseling [or: councils] among themselves" (42:38). It should also be pointed out that the second verse is important enough to justify naming the chapter it occurs in as "Council."

The meaning of *shura* is "assembly, gathering, consultation." *Mashwarah* (consultation, council) and *mushawir* (consultant) are derived from the same Arabic root. Thus, it has been emphasized that consultation is a good thing in the most general sense. This is illustrated by the Prophet's life, who always consulted his compatriots before reaching a decision. Applying this to the political sphere, the rule of parliament and public vote and, more generally, democracy, is implicitly approved by Islam. The greatest council and counsel are nationwide elections in which the entire community participates. In the history of Islam, of course, "council" has seldom meant polling the people. The first Caliphs were, for example, chosen by "consultative committees" composed of a few members. In later times, rulers availed themselves of councils formed by specialists. This is an approach that survives today in democratic countries in the form of various commissions, reducing the possibility of error in the decision of a single person reached on the basis of incomplete knowledge.

Holy Law

People have laws in order to regulate social affairs: i.e., relationships between individuals. If human beings were angels, there would be no need for laws, because everybody would act in an ideal fashion anyway. Since this is not the case, however, we have, not simply law, but law *enforcement.*

There are two considerations in framing laws. The first is punishment, for those who have broken a specific law, since a crime cannot be allowed to pass unnoticed, and the victim has a right to justice by which the crime, if not undone, can at least be redressed. But equally, and perhaps more importantly, laws exist for prevention and deterrence—in order to discourage people from committing undesired acts in the first place.

Some of the rulings of the Holy Law which have attracted attention in the West need to be viewed in this light. Certain Koranic injunctions may appear to be unduly severe when judged by modern standards, yet it should be remembered that they are there for deterrence, not merely punishment. Prevention is intended much more than implementation, as a proper reading in the due context will reveal. The following well-known saying harbors a profound truth that is relevant here: *An ounce of prevention is worth a pound of cure.*

Many of the accusations that Islam is undemocratic and totalitarian follow from the misperception that it introduces strictures leaving very little scope for free activity in almost all fields of life. The mistake here stems from a misunderstanding of the basic concepts involved.

It is important to note that the word *sharia,* or "Holy Law," is used in our day in two different senses. The first of these is the religious principles to be observed by a Moslem, such as performing the Prayer, abstinence from alcohol, and so on. All this rests on an individual's decision in any case, so no one else can interfere. The second meaning in which the word is used is Islamic jurisprudence, or *fiqh.* Within this scope it is expected to regulate social relationships. Those who uphold the Holy Law usually mean the first sense, whereas those who deride it usually mean the second, so that although both groups use the same word, the senses in which they intend it almost never coincide.

Holy Law in the sense of religious jurisprudence is, first of all, a legal system. This means that it concerns itself with whatever activities or fields of life *any* system of laws would address. In other words, the Holy Law deals with exactly those areas which any legal code has to. On this basis, then, the Holy Law is neither more nor less totalitarian than any Law in any country.

What distinguishes Holy Law from other codes is that it is based, as far as is possible, on the orders of God (the Koran) and the example of the Prophet (the Way). But these can, by themselves, constitute only a foundation for a legal code. It is estimated that the verses in the Koran dealing with legal matters number between two hundred and four hundred (the estimate varies according to the specialist and the assumptions and definitions s/he works from). Even the simplest society cannot be ruled by so few injunctions; in modern, complex societies, thousands of regulations are required. For this reason, the rules of the Holy Law have in every age been framed by Islamic legislators. The Koran and the Way only describe the broad outlines. The details are left to the legists. Not only is there no obstacle to deriving specific principles suitable to a certain time and place from general, universal ones, there is also a necessity. For a choice that is appropriate in one situation may not be so in another.

It is also true, on the other hand, that not everything can be changed. Regulations may change with time, but there are rules that don't. If we compare religious Law to a tree, the verses of the Koran are its roots, authentic Traditions (of the Prophet) are its trunk, the Four Schools of Law are its main branches, and sundry regulations are its leaves. This tree can always sprout new branches and leaves, but to attack its roots and its trunk is tantamount to slaughtering it. Otherwise, permission has already been given in the Koran for deriving (*istinbat*) new rules (4:83).

Even in seemingly ironclad situations, legists and jurists traditionally enjoyed considerable latitude in interpreting scripture. A similar situation exists in Christianity. For example, Jesus said, "You shall not steal" (Matthew 19:18), and "If your hand or your foot causes you to sin, cut them off"[95] (Matthew 18:8, Mark 9:43, 45). In this particular respect, what the Bible says is not much different from the Koran. This is coming from the greatest authority for a Christian, yet how many Christians have actually cut off their hands? This is because the verse can lend itself to different interpretations. As Joseph Schacht, the well-known Western authority on Islamic law, has pointed out, the sanctions of the Koran "are essentially moral and only incidentally penal."[96] In the Koran, the verse that prescribes cutting off a hand for stealing (5:38) is immediately followed by: "But if the thief repents after the crime and amends his or her conduct, God turns to them in forgiveness" (5:39). This has allowed the exercise of lenience throughout the history of traditional Islam.

Some Koranic injunctions that appear more objectionable today were not always applied with indiscriminate brutality. Justice demands fair and balanced retribution. To inflict the same punishment for a small offence as for a great one without discrimination would make a mockery of justice—which, in Islam, is one of God's Attributes. The "cutting off of hands" belongs to a legal category known as "limit punishments" (*jaza al-hadd*). This means that this is the *maximum* penalty that can be administered for theft—any greater punishment cannot be inflicted. For example, the penalty for theft cannot be death. It does not mean that every boy who steals an apple has to have his hand cut off. This leaves implementers of Holy Law with a wide spectrum of choices before reaching that limiting wall. Here, they are entirely in accord with the Prophet's saying that guards against an unjust verdict: "Ward off the limits (*hudud*) by means of ambiguities" surrounding a case.

We see then that the Holy Law does not differ from other codes as far as being made by human intervention is concerned, and that it covers the same ground as they do. As for its unchanging parts: do not all codes possess certain fundamental assumptions, which remain inviolate and invariant as a particular legislation unfolds? (On how our laws, democracy, and human rights are derived from religion, see Appendix D.) The famous mathematician Leopold Kronecker once remarked of mathematics that "God created number; the rest is man's work." Regarding Islamic Law, we may similarly say that God revealed the Koran, the rest is the work of human hands.

According to Malise Ruthven, who has done in-depth research on the subject, only six hundred of the more than six thousand verses in the Koran have to do with legal responsibilities. Most of these, in turn, deal with religious obligations like Ritual Prayer, Fasting, and Pilgrimage. The number of verses dealing directly with legal matters is only about eighty, and most of these, again, are concerned with women, marriage, and inheritance.

Dr. Ruthven, having subjected Islamic Law to a thorough-going investigation, states in his book *Islam in the World:*

> Whereas Christianity inherited a body of secular law developed under the pagan Romans, Islam developed a system of religious law more or less independently of the political sphere...Far from being integrated (as many Muslims claim), the political and religious institutions remained distinct.[97]

As Ruthven explains, Islamic and state institutions grew side by side but remained separate:

> Society existed more or less independently of the state, a feature which is still evident in the Muslim world of today.[98]

> [T]he *fiqh* is less a system of law, with a developed apparatus of procedure and enforcement, than a process of socialization and acculturation...In time...observance of the Divine Law becomes a social factor functioning more or less independently of the state...the caliphs took over and adapted much of the criminal, commercial, and constitutional law of their Byzantine and Sassanid predecessors...The *qadis* (Shari'a judges) had no power to enforce legal decisions on the rulers. The rulers, while formally committed to upholding the Shari'a, were rarely prepared to submit to the decisions of the *qadis*...if such decisions...went against their interests.[99]

> Thus, while in the realm of personal or family matters the Shari'a could be implemented on the basis of doctrines elaborated by the *faqihs* [exponents of *fiqh*], in [almost all other matters] power of decision remained with the rulers, who governed by decree and settled disputes through their own *mazalim* (complaints) courts. Thus state institutions grew up parallel to Islamic ones, leading to a *de facto* separation of the religious and secular spheres....[100]

Ruthven also draws attention to the fact that the "divine right" of kings, prevalent in the West, has no place in Islam. In the face of this right to rule, which can be traced to the Christian Church, it was necessary to develop the concept of the "natural rights" of the individual, and Western politics and law reached its present state from such origins. In Islam, on the other hand, there never was such a problem to begin with.

All this proves that the Holy Law has seen a restricted application in Islamic societies and was buttressed by many external factors. This is the result of situations met with in real life. For this reason, it would be totally incorrect to view the Holy Law as a seamless monolith that governs society down to the tiniest detail and oppresses it with an iron fist.

Far from being the state's instrument of repression, the Holy Law is an institution that has been adopted and developed by civil society independently of, and sometimes even in opposition to, the state.

As for the enforcement of the Holy Law by some present-day police states in a bitterly cruel way, this stems from their desire to render themselves partially palatable by appearing "Islamic" in the eyes of their subject peoples. Their coercion and cruelty has nothing to do with the Holy Law, which has been applied leniently throughout most of Islam's fourteen centuries, but is due to their individual constitutions and legal codes. These are not the Holy Law itself, but barbarian interpretations and monstrous caricatures thereof. When one looks at the so-called "Islamic" present-day police states, indiscriminately chopping off hands right and left, one has to remember that hand severance was unheard of in the Ottoman Empire, extending over twenty million square kilometers and millions of people, in all six hundred years of its rule. Claims to the contrary notwithstanding, it can be flatly stated that no Islamic state exists in the world today. Islam itself is by no means responsible for aberrations such as cruelty, mass murder, terrorism, suicide bombings, and so on.

Islam and Terrorism

Even the thought of terrorism is anathema to Islam, the very name of which is derived from the Arabic root for "peace." "Islamic terrorism" is as plausible—to borrow Leszek Kolakowski's term—as "fried snowballs." The very name of Islam has stood for justice for more than fourteen centuries. And nothing can be more unjust than the premeditated slaughter of innocent civilians for grievances caused by other parties, which is what terrorism is all about. A fair trial and due procedure of law is what Islam requires in all cases.

There is a widespread attempt in the media to create an image where terrorism is associated with Islam. Against this, one can only protest that this is not what Islam stands for, and that far from condoning terrorist acts, Islam's most severe punishments are in fact reserved for those who foment discord and strife. Anyone in Islamic countries who is unfortunate, angry, or misguided enough to resort to terrorist acts should be made aware of this fact. (On this point, see the more detailed treatment in the Prologue.)

Islam and Slavery

Those who consider Islam to be inherently undemocratic might conceivably wish to mount an argument on the basis of Islam's historical relationship to slavery.

As we define it, a slave is a person who has no rights—the slave's master can use him or her as s/he desires. In world history, slavery has emerged from the problem of what to do with prisoners of war.

It is true that historically, Islam made no direct attempt to abolish slavery. But it did take steps to improve the lot of slaves and to abolish slavery eventually. For example, freeing a slave was prescribed as an atonement for many sins and ill treatment of slaves was prohibited. In the Farewell Sermon of the Prophet, delivered during his Farewell Pilgrimage and considered by many to be the first "Declaration of Human Rights," the Prophet advocates kind treatment: "As for slaves: give them the same food that you eat and clothe them as you yourself dress. If they make a mistake you cannot forgive, separate from them. They, too, are God's servants and do not deserve ill treatment."

Throughout the fourteen centuries of Islam, slaves have even become commanders and rulers in Islamic countries and sometimes have enjoyed more authority than free people. The legalizing precedent has again been given in the Farewell Sermon: "If a crippled black slave becomes your ruler, obey him and follow him so long as he governs you in accordance with the Koran."

Slavery is a social disease that worldwide has proven astonishingly difficult to eradicate—there are still an estimated twenty-seven-million slaves in the world.[101] This is the reason why Islam did not attempt to abolish slavery openly from the start. Slavery is not an institution that was introduced by Islam. Having found slavery already in existence, however, Islam took measures to abolish it within time, since it was impossible to do so immediately by sudden decree.

But we cannot oppose Islam or brand it as undemocratic for failing to abolish slavery, because by such reasoning we would have to include the city-state of Athens in the past and the United States of America, now considered the prototypes of democracy. As Alexis de Tocqueville points out:

> In Athens...there were only twenty thousand citizens in a popu-
> lation of over three hundred and fifty thousand. All the rest were
> slaves....
>
> Athens, then, with her universal suffrage, was no more than
> an aristocratic republic in which all the nobles had an equal right
> to government.[102]

Mother words Athens, the "cradle of democracy," was actually a society based on slavery. As for the United States, it is famous for having
enslaved millions of black Africans, and has been able to extricate itself in
the nineteenth century only by the device of a very bloody civil war. It
cannot be claimed even today that the problem of racism has been ad-
equately resolved in the United States. In our age, when South Africa has
only recently won its struggle against apartheid, Islam cannot be called to
account for not having abolished slavery fourteen hundred years ago.

In fact, it is only thanks to the development of machines which can
perform human drudgery that slavery has been pushed into the background in modern society. Slavery, and even manual work, has diminished to the extent that slaves and workers have been replaced by machines.
It is the machine, rather than significant moral advancement, that has
contributed to the eradication of slavery.

Take away the mechanical infrastructure of industry, and it would not
be surprising at all to observe, even today, the reemergence of slavery.
Nor is such a prospect as remote as it sounds. With the depletion of oil
and other fossil fuels, on which our civilization depends so much even as
it is in the process of squandering them, it is not hard to imagine vast
tracts of machinery that would become useless and abandoned in the
future. We should thank the fruits of scientific progress and technological civilization for the present-day absence of slavery, and be more concerned about our own future when it may be reinstituted if global
precautions are not put into place.

Islam and Racism

When properly interpreted, Islam is certainly not racist.[103] It has, in
fact, denounced racism fourteen centuries ago to an extent unmatched

even by contemporary Western societies, and thus demolished the notion: "he and I are different," which serves as one of the basic tenets of slavery. Here, again, it will suffice to quote a sentence from the Farewell Sermon: "Just as no Arab has any superiority to any non-Arab and vice versa, blacks have no superiority to whites, nor whites to blacks."

"God," says the Koran, "commands you to judge with justice when you judge among human beings" (4:58). "Among human beings" here covers both Moslems and non-Moslems. Islam, therefore, desires that all human beings be treated equally regardless of color, religion, language, race and social, economic, or political status. It advocates the equality of all before the law, and violations in practice cannot invalidate this principle.

Is Islam Itself Totalitarian?

The answer to this question is, of course, No, even though there are many repressive regimes associated with it in our minds. A totalitarian regime is not merely one of bloodstained oppression—it is one that gives all the rights to the state, and no liberties to the individual:

1. It attempts to restructure a whole society according to a certain ideology or system of beliefs, and aims to control even the thoughts of individuals.

2. It liquidates all individuals who do not belong to, are opposed to, or are at variance with it.

If we evaluate Islam in the light of these two distinguishing characteristics, we find that it is impossible to identify Islam with totalitarianism.

1. One of the major distinctions between Islam and other religions is its principle: "There can be no compulsion in religion." This principle is guaranteed by its place in the Koran (2:256) and cannot be violated. Islam can only use the way of gentle persuasion, and appeals to the intellect and comprehension of those it addresses. That force cannot yield desirable results is a well-known fact in Islam.

Renunciation of the use of force also applies to Moslems. It is up to the individual Moslem to decide how faithfully s/he will abide by religious rules. If a Moslem insists on not performing the Prayer, for example, s/he does only him- or herself harm. S/he may be gently reminded, but cannot be coerced. It is only when the rights of another are infringed that the Holy Law—like, indeed, all laws—comes into question. What is said here applies, of course, to places and situations where the Holy Law is properly in effect, which is to say almost nowhere in the world today.

2. There have always been people who would not be persuaded by Islam. The true nature of a system or regime emerges in how it deals with the dissidents and minorities under its rule. Islam has passed this test with flying colors until the present age, when increasingly inane things have begun to be perpetrated in its name. Every right has been granted and respect shown to people belonging to other religions. A minor proof of this is the gratitude and celebration of the Jews, five hundred years after they escaped from the tortures of the Inquisition into the arms of the Ottoman Empire in 1492.

Indeed, as mentioned earlier, there have been periods in history when the Ottoman Empire was the sole superpower in the world. If the Ottomans had pursued a policy of Islamization or extermination in those days, there would have been no religion other than Islam in the world today.

In Islam, everyone is the servant of God. A person who has properly understood Islam knows that to dominate and coerce another is to elevate oneself to the status of a god, a most unacceptable form of behavior. The rules of law—not the commands of individuals—are the basis in Islam, and the requirements of Law are carried out, for no society can function without the proper application of law. As evidenced by the Ottoman code of laws, even the Sultans were bound by the law and subject to it.

Wherever there has been arbitrary rule, this has not occurred because of Islam but in spite of it. On the other hand, Islamic law permits the coexistence of other legal systems alongside it, as is seen, for example, in the last period of the Ottomans. All of which leads us to another point: some people are currently in search of a religion, or "metareligion," that accepts all religions and tolerates them. Islam is an ideal candidate: it accepts all religions "of the Book" that have gone before it, venerates their prophets, and views them with tolerance. Hence, the metareligion eagerly sought by some already exists, and goes by the name of "Islam."

The Views of a Specialist

It may be useful, at this point, to refer to the views of an expert, a Western non-Moslem who has not refrained from criticizing Islam on other counts. Bernard Lewis is such an orientalist and historian of Islam. In his notable study, *The Political Language of Islam* (1988), he brought a wide perspective to the subject, making it unmistakably clear that Islam is neither theocratic nor dictatorial: as he succinctly states it, "Islam is clearly not...a theocracy....There is even less foundation for the portrayal of Islamic government as a system in which the ruler is an all-powerful despot and the subject his helpless slave, entirely at his mercy. This picture is false in both theory and practice."[104] In Islam, the ruler—even a caliph—has no power of religious legislation, but finds it ready for him in the form of religious law in those matters which fall within its domain. "The ruler's duty is to defend and uphold, to maintain and enforce, the law, by which he himself is bound no less than the humblest of his subjects."[105] In this sense, Islam upholds the rule of law.[106]

On the occasion of the publication of his book, the respected French periodical, *Le Nouvel Observateur*, conducted an interview with Professor Lewis. His words there are even more enlightening:

> When we in the West attempt to separate good government from bad government and despotism from democracy, we immediately take freedom as a measure. The Moslems, however, take justice. When we say "freedom," we think of the subject, and mean and indicate his rights before the government. Traditional Islam means the same thing when it says "justice." But it places the burden on the ruler's shoulders. What is for us a right belonging to the subjects is, for it, a duty belonging to the sovereign. In general terms, Islam emerges as a system of duties rather than of rights. Of course, justice is not the same thing as freedom. But it can lead to the same results.

What I am saying is that Islam does not conflict with democracy; it even shows the way leading to the latter.

In other words, Islam places on the ruler as a legal duty the recognition of rights won by people in the West only after long struggle. Although historical practice has been at variance with this, that is not the fault of Islam. Democracy can survive only when it is secured by laws, just as Islam requires.

Separation of Powers

This line of inquiry leads us naturally to the issue of religion and state (not "church and state" since, as I have mentioned more than once, there is no church in Islam). In contemporary democracies, the principle of "separation of powers" has been introduced as a counterbalance against the possibility that power could become concentrated in a few hands. These three estates are the executive, the legislative, and the judiciary.

A similar separation is also found in Islam. Long before Montesquieu introduced the separation of powers in the West, the Caliph Haroun al-Rasheed applied it by separating the judiciary and appointing Abu Yousseff as its head. In classical Islam, executive power was in the hands of the caliph or sultan. Legislation belonged to the *ulama*, or "learned doctors"—over whom presided, in the case of the Ottomans, the "Sheikh of Islam." As for the judiciary, it was in the hands of the *qadis*, or "judges," represented by a chief judge. Although the principle of "separation of powers" is not explicitly stated, the practice conforms to or is close to it. For example, a sultan could not easily fire the Sheikh of Islam, yet the latter had the power to depose a sultan. Thus, historically, the caliphate (now obsolete) did not have the kind of power now being proposed by some of its present-day advocates.

Women's Rights

Before leaving this discussion of Holy Law, it will be well to touch very briefly on the subject of women's rights (to be discussed at greater length in the next chapter). Suffice it to say here that contrary to widespread opinion in the West, women have enjoyed more rights in Islamic than in some Western countries up to—and sometimes into—the twentieth century. As the prestigious British journal, *The Economist*, notes, "The Koran is better about women than is generally realized...the two [man and woman] were born equal, 'from a single soul'."[107] Any legal differences between male and female stem not from inequality, but from biological differences, for the two were created biologically complementary to each other. To judge them by the same rules would be to infringe the God-given rights of either the one or the other. Again, historical malpractice can be used to condemn those who have perpetrated it, but certainly not Islam itself. Let the same source have the final word: "...at bottom such things do not happen to Muslim women because of what either the Koran or the Prophet said....They happen because of the preexisting habits of the people among whom Islam first took root...." (Blaming matters on the scholars of Islam neglects the fact that they too were members of these same societies, thus either sharing the same mindset as their fellow countrymen or else being forced to take that mindset into consideration, and so this explanation reduces to that given in the quotation.) This discussion about women is an important issue worthy of in-depth treatment, and will be resumed later on.

Religion: A Necessity for Democracy?

We now come to the question: is religion, in general, a desirable thing for democracy, or is it an undesirable one? The two volumes of *Democracy in America*, written by the famous lawyer and thinker Alexis de Tocqueville and published consecutively in 1835 and 1840, constitute a peak that has yet to be matched concerning democracy and its practice in America.

Here is how Tocqueville evaluates the relationship between democracy and religion: "In the United States it is not only mores that are controlled by religion [Christianity], but its sway extends even over reason."[108] After pointing out that religion introduces certain moral/ethical principles and various restrictions, Tocqueville continues: "So the human spirit never sees an unlimited field before itself; however bold it is, from time to time it feels that it must halt before insurmountable barriers... Thus, while the law allows the American people to do everything, there are things which religion prevents them from doing and forbids them to dare."[109]

Here, Tocqueville criticizes those who attack religion in the name of freedom:

> Despotism may be able to do without faith, but freedom cannot. Religion is much more needed in the republic they advocate than in the monarchy they attack, and in democratic republics most of all. How can society escape destruction if, when political ties are relaxed, moral ties are not tightened?[110]

Saying: "Religion having lost its sway over men's souls, the clearest line dividing good from ill has been obliterated; everything in the moral world seems uncertain,"[111] Tocqueville points out that the loss of religion will lead to the loss of freedom.[112]

Atheism Means Cruelty and Tyranny

But Tocqueville was not the only genius living in the nineteenth century to perceive certain truths. Two other men of genius were able to foresee the social catastrophes of the twentieth century: the Russian novelist Fyodor Dostoyevsky and the German philosopher, Friedrich Nietzsche. But why was Tocqueville right? Because, in the final analysis, God is the source of all ethics. It is God who commands human beings: "Do this, this is right," or: "Don't do that, that is wrong." But that is not all. God is also the sole enforcer of ethics. For God has also said: "If you do this, I will reward you; if you do that, I will punish you." Where there is no belief in God, fear of God also evaporates. Thus, both the definition (or delimitation) of ethics *and* its sanction are removed. This means that if belief in God ceases to exist, so does the basis of ethics and morality, and humanity is set adrift on a sea of moral relativity. And once morality is out of the way, humans lose all their human attributes, becoming an animal and even a monster. With the removal of ethics from society, not only does the crime rate begin to climb, but the nature of crime itself becomes increasingly savage. In short, once a person has taken leave of God, humanity takes leave of that person.

One of those to perceive this most clearly was Dostoyevsky. Better than any sociologist or political scientist, Dostoyevsky points to a polarization that occurs in society once people are shorn of faith, leaving two kinds of creatures. One of these is the man-god (or despot), and the other is the herd (or slaves).

In *The Devils*, Kirilov says: "If there is no God, then I am God." Having lost faith, a person can find no being superior to him or her when s/he surveys the universe. (This is only to be expected, since God has created humans as the highest of all creatures.) As a result, a person's lower, base self—or, in Sufic terminology, his or her egotistical "Impelling[113] Self"—declares itself god. But this is exactly what Nimrod did when he told Abraham: "I give life and make to die," or Pharaoh when he told his people: "I am indeed your truest Lord" (79:24). As for the pharaohs of the twentieth century, they have done things from which even a Nimrod or Pharaoh might have recoiled in horror.

Once someone loses faith in God, the "deified human" or "strong man" takes the place that rightfully belongs to God. (This is called *Tagut* in the Koran, which means the deified human who lays claim to Lordship.) The Base Self becomes the usurper of God's office. Might alone any longer makes right. Shorn of all values, having repudiated God and religion, morality and compassion, the man-god loves—is even obsessed with—only two things: power and sex. It is inevitable that all human and humane qualities must disappear from the man-god, who is a creature of his ego and hence, of Satan. Where faith in God does not exist, humans, too, cease to do so.

But Dostoyevsky also anticipated Nietzsche (by at least a decade), who is the author of such propositions as: "God is dead, we have killed Him." (Since God is immortal, of course, what had actually died was people's faith in Him.) Nietzsche, in turn, foresaw the emergence of the "superman." For the superman, human qualities were things to be ashamed of. Nietzsche said he was "cruel" and "beyond good and evil," which placed him in the territory of absolute evil, since he had already transcended morality. (It can be seen that Nietzsche's superman possesses qualities diametrically opposed to those of the Perfect Human in Islamic Sufism. On the other hand, Nietzsche was perhaps the first to prophesy the coming dangers of the totalitarian state or "monster state."[114])

Another of Dostoyevsky's characters expresses this as follows: "If God does not exist, everything is permitted." The tyrannies of the past century have amply demonstrated, by their bloodcurdling cruelties, just what these "permitted" things are. For this reason, it is necessary to study the history of the twentieth century with the utmost care. Dostoyevsky's greatest discovery, the "Grand Inquisitor," is another example of Nietzsche's superman, and highlights another fact: if coercion and torture coexist in a place with religion, there the faith of God has departed from hearts, and remains an empty claim mindlessly mouthed in words devoid of content.

The second of Dostoyevsky's social classes is the herd, composed of slaves. If humans do not have an immortal soul, if there is no reward and punishment, if anyone can get away with anything, then it becomes permissible to subject them to every manner of indignity and insult. Unfortunately, the past century has done nothing but justify Dostoyevsky's and Nietzsche's prototypes of herd and superman. If there is no morality, there can be no justice. As long as morality exists, right makes might. Whoever is right is powerful, and justice rules. But once morality is gone, might makes right, and justice disappears along with ethics.

The conclusion, then, is that where there is no faith in God, neither can morality exist. Where there is no morality, everything is permitted. Where there is no morality, there is no human—there are only the superhuman few and the subhuman, even the subanimal, herd. In short, where religion and faith in God do not exist, not only do the most horrifying nightmares come true, but they also all befall us, every single one of them.

The Tyranny of the Majority and Human Rights

Tocqueville, who inspected democracy under a magnifying glass, claims that it can lead to a "tyranny of the majority." Although he does not himself give any examples, we know that the Greek democracies of Antiquity operated in this way. A "theory of human rights" emerged in the seventeenth century in the West, led by Thomas Hobbes and, especially, John Locke. This notion found expression in the unwritten assumptions of the British Constitution and in the provisions of the American Bill of Rights.

In the conception of democracy which followed, the principle of majority rule is a necessary condition for democracy (the "rule of the people"), but not a sufficient one. The will of the majority enjoys legitimacy only if it is an expression of "freely given consent." Secondly and more importantly, certain inviolable rights and freedoms are defined that are granted to everyone. Majorities can do everything except deprive minorities of their rights and freedoms, such as speech, press, assembly, and so on. Minorities, in turn, must abide by the rules and procedures of democratic organization. (Certain institutions are also necessary, such as an impartial and independent judiciary, a free but responsible press, and a military under civilian control.)

Democratic government is one in which the minority, or its representatives, can peacefully become the majority or its representatives. Again, democracy is, as Karl Popper pointed out, the only practical and peaceful method that has been found by which the people can oust an unwanted government from power. This does not mean that democracy is paradise. There, too, there are problems and headaches. In Winston Churchill's words, "Democracy is the worst possible form of government—except for all those other forms that have been tried."

Actually, forms of government can be reduced to three: tyranny, where society obeys one person (monarchies and dictatorships); democracy, where government is in the service of the people; and anarchy, which is an absence or void of government and, as Sidney Hook rightly observed, "is the rule of a thousand tyrants." It is because anarchy can be even worse than despotism that the Koran remarks: "Obey those in authority among you" (4:59).[115]

What do we find when we look at Islam in terms of minority rights and liberties? When the Prophet of God migrated to Medina, he prepared a document with the Medinans that is the first written constitution in the world. In this "Constitution of Medina," the concept of religious community is defined as a political union that encompasses the whole people. This includes the Jews and even the polytheists and idolaters. Every group, according to the Medina Constitution, is autonomous in the fields of religion and law. All parties signed this social contract of their own free will. The Medina Constitution, as a legal document, leaves all groups free to practice their religion and lead their lives, except for the unavoidable regulations needed in mutual life. Those who do not accept Islam are not bound by its rules.

One of the articles of this document explicitly states: "The Jews...shall possess equal rights with us." Thus, "equality" and "rights" found expression in Islam a thousand years before they began to be articulated in the modern democracies of the West. The Prophet also signed a similar document with the Christians of Najran.

It can be seen that in spirit, the Medina Constitution is pluralist, libertarian, respectful of the law, and of minority rights. The definition of community given therein corresponds to the concept of "people" in democracies. That Moslems should be in the majority, therefore, does not give them the right to force their views upon minorities. This is prevented by the precedent and example of the Prophet of Islam himself. And indeed, Islamic history corroborates this in terms of respect for minorities.

It may be appropriate at this point to dwell upon two major deficiencies of democracy:

1. Democracies have not always been able to judge correctly where to draw the line on freedoms. For example, American democracy has caused a great increase in the crime rate by allowing its citizens the right to bear arms. And in general, children have become rebellious towards their parents, license and impertinence being confused with freedom.

2. One-party ("monist") democracy of the kind extant in Japan has been looked down upon, and the multi-party ("pluralist") kind has been preferred. Yet here, too, a drawback presents itself, for different parties have not shrunk from pitting—for example—brother against brother or husband against wife for the ulterior cause of coming to power. (Furthermore, the views of different parties have not always been very different.) That the struggle for power should create enmities within society is a problem associated with multi-party democracy, and it is not yet clear how it is to be satisfactorily resolved within the democratic system.

Organization of the Islamic Community

Some scholars[116] view Islam as the most democratic religion in the world today because it does not possess a priestly hierarchy like Christianity, and because its central doctrinal authority is unstructured.

The organization of the religious community has taken on different shapes in different religions. In Catholicism, for instance, the Christian community is constellated in the form of a government—it is a well-known fact that the leaders of the early Church took the Roman Empire's political institutions as their model. The Emperor of this government is the Pope, its senators are the Cardinals, and its governors are the Bishops.

The formation of the Moslem community, on the other hand, has evolved not in the shape of a government, but in the form of a university. This is why the central religious organization has been called *madrasa* (school) in Islam, whereas it is called *ecclesia* (Church) in Christianity. There is no clerical class or spiritual hegemony in Islam; there are only *mudarrises* (teachers or professors).

Islam is based on the principles of freedom, reason, and the intellect. The teachers do not force truth on anyone without convincing them by rational proofs. There is no compulsion in Islam. It is essential to believe and have faith rationally.

The scholars in the schools have solemnly vowed to guide the whole of society to the truth, and have dedicated themselves to its salvation. The activities of the schools are geared to the entire society. The "spiritual schools" (*tariqas*), on the other hand, give a more specialized training for those with spiritual aspirations. Because such people are the exception rather than the rule, however, Sunnite Islam is composed of a union of schools, not an association of dervish "convents" (*taqqas*).

The whole of Islamdom has lived as one great university. With the Ottomans, the Sheikh of Islam was the director of this university. As for the leaders of the law schools and the sheikhs of the spiritual schools, these are the equivalent of scholars with doctrines. As can be seen from all this, the religion of Islam is based on the authority of science or knowledge, not on an administrative authority. (This shows how far from the mark some repressive "Islamic" regimes are when they try to exalt the state and keep their populace from reading or attending universities.)

Why are Human Beings Equal?

Up to this point, we have seen that religion is a necessity, even a *sine qua non*, for democracy, that atheism leads to sociopolitical disaster, and that Islam as a religion accommodates democracy. Normally, this would be the point to bid the reader farewell. The really significant part, however, still remains to be said. From this point of view, what has been said above is merely a prelude to or infrastructure for what follows.

Democracy is based on the equality of all citizens. Where the equality of human beings and their votes do not hold, there democracy cannot be said to exist.

Many things have been said about equality throughout history. Rather than add to or reiterate these arguments, it is better to state the end result and continue from there. Since we find human beings to be grossly unequal and different in nature rather than equal, right down to their fingerprints, what is meant by "equality" is *equality before the law*. This is the sense in which the term is used in the French Declaration of Human Rights of 1789, which championed the formula: "Liberty, equality, fraternity." In earlier times, the Greeks expressed equality before the law by a single word, *isonomia*.

Now this brings us to the basic question that needs to be asked: why are human beings equal at all, whether before the law or not? Why is the basic assertion of oppression, racism, and slavery, "I am superior to you," invalid? From what root do all the social and political ideas lying at the base of democracy derive their strength?

The Universal Declaration of Human Rights

The first article of the Universal Declaration of Human Rights,[117] which was adopted by the United Nations in 1948 and lies at the basis of such legal documents as the Helsinki Final Accords, is as follows:

"1. All human beings are born free and equal in dignity and rights."
The Declaration continues with the generalizations "everyone" and "no one," which go on to the end:

"3. Everyone has the right to life, liberty, and the security of person."

"4. No one shall be held in slavery or servitude," and so on.

In fact, it is erroneous even to call these generalizations, for they are universally applicable without exception. In the Preamble of the Declaration, mention is made of "the equal and inalienable rights of all members of the human family," and of "faith in fundamental human rights, in the dignity and worth of the human person, and in the equal rights of men and women."

But what has "faith" got to do with it? This is an unexpected term. What is the word "faith" doing in a universal legal declaration? And since faith is obviously involved in some way, could this have anything to do with religion, the traditional repository of faith?

Declaration of the Rights of Man and the Citizen

The United Nations Universal Declaration is based on the French Declaration of the Rights of Man and the Citizen of 1789; many of its articles have been taken with little or no change from that source. Here is the first article of the French Declaration:

"1. Men are born and remain free and equal in rights."

The preamble of this declaration states: "the natural, inalienable, and sacred rights of man." Everyone knows that people possess certain inalienable, inviolable, and untransferable rights. But in what context does the word "sacred" occur?

The Declaration of Independence

The French Declaration was inspired by the Virginia Bill of Rights. This in turn finds its root in the American Declaration of Independence of 1776. The very first sentence of the main text of the Declaration of Independence reads:

> We hold these truths to be self-evident, that all men are created equal, that they are endowed by their Creator with certain unalienable Rights, that among these are Life, Liberty, and the pursuit of Happiness.

Now it is not by any means self-evident that all men are created equal. We have grown accustomed to accepting this *a priori* without questioning it. But if you ask a racist, for example, s/he will think that the notion: "I am superior to him/her"[118] is equally, if not more, self-evident. S/he may even say: "Are you blind? What can be more obvious than the difference in our skin colors?" To put it in more general terms, how are we to explain to a discriminator that all human beings are equal, are even one, beyond superficial differences such as size, weight, color, and so on? What is to be our foundation?

But mention is also made here of a "Creator." The American Declaration of Independence gives expression not merely to "faith" and the "sacred," but states that there is a Creator, that human beings have been brought into existence by Him, and that their rights have been given to them *by their Creator.*

It can be seen that as one probes deeper into the past, things become both clearer and more interesting. The final recourse of human rights in the Declaration of Independence is the Creator. Words have taken a long and winding route, finally ending up in the domain of religion.

Can support be found, then, for equality in terms of basic rights and freedoms in religions? Robert A. Dahl, one of the leading exponents of democratic theory in our day and Professor Emeritus at Yale University, puts it this way:

> Yet democracy might, like Plato's republic, be little more than a philosophical fantasy were it not for the persistent and widespread influence of the belief that human beings are intrinsically equal in a fundamental way—or at any rate some substantial group of human beings are. Historically, the idea of intrinsic equality gained much of its strength, particularly in Europe and the English-speaking countries, from the common doctrine of Judaism and Christianity (shared also by Islam) that we are equally God's children [or servants]. Indeed it was exactly on this belief that Locke grounded his assertion of the natural equality of all persons in a state of nature.[119]

Democracy in Polytheistic Societies

Although they developed the first examples of democracy because of their high regard for man, the Greek democracies proved unsuccessful in the end. First of all, these were slave societies, i.e., there was a distinction between free citizens and those deprived of political rights (slaves). Second, election results were viewed almost as a military victory, and the vanquished were reduced to the status of, if not slaves, at least second-class citizens. This resulted in a tripartite class structure within society, which led to bloody rebellions and frequently the emergence of a tyrant. Because minority rights were disregarded, these were not democracies in the modern sense of the word. Such problems had a great bearing on Plato's criticisms of democracy.

We here bear witness to the coexistence of inequality and polytheism (associationism). It was Tocqueville, again, who first drew attention to this fact. Almost a century and a half before the Shiite sociologist Ali Shariati spoke of a "sociology of associationism," Tocqueville was saying: "...when men are isolated from one another by great differences, they easily discover as many divinities as there are nations, castes, classes, and families, and they find a thousand private roads to go to heaven." On the other hand: "Men who are alike and on the same level in this world easily conceive the idea of a single God who imposes the same laws on each man and grants him future happiness at the same price. The conception of the unity of mankind ever brings them back to the idea of the unity of the Creator..."[120] Note that this can also work in the opposite direction: polytheism can lead to discrimination and inequality between human beings. The notion: "Your god is different from my god" is a basic pretext for thinking that a person is different from us, and even for not considering them human at all. (Incomprehensibly, this accusation has from time to time been leveled by Christians at Moslems, in spite of the fact that both religions believe in one God.) In such a case, human rights cannot be applied to everyone. One of the important reasons, then, why modern democracies have succeeded where those in Antiquity failed, is that the latter were polytheistic while the former are monotheistic. For Europe and America are firmly based in the Judeo-Christian tradition.

Humans in the Bible

We can now begin to discuss the implications of Gilbert Keith Chesterton's remark: "There is no basis for democracy except in a dogma about the divine origin of Man."[121] Right at the beginning of the Old Testament, the following statement is repeated three times: "God created Man (Adam) in His own image" (*Genesis*, 1:26-7). This is an expression of equality. As historian Paul Johnson has observed,[122] it is not simply Adam or the human race that has been created in the image of God; each individual human being has been created in His image. (Note that we are not here trying to unravel the true meaning of the statement: we are not interested in what "God's image" means, for example, but are investigating the possible outcomes of this statement.)

In this sense, all people are equal, because they all have been created in the same image, the same form. "All Israelites," says Johnson, "are equal before God, and therefore equal before his law."[123]

We find here the first application of equality, which is the basic principle of democracy: "As men are all equally made in God's image, they have equal rights in any fundamental sense. It is no accident that slavery among the Jews disappeared during the Second Commonwealth..."[124] Jesus, who came after Moses, tried to have everyone love and respect one another with the principle of love that he brought.

Judaism is the religion of rules. Christianity is the religion of love. Islam, with its unique synthesis of rules and love, is the full bloom and culmination of religion. Again, Judaism deals more with the material world, Christianity with the spiritual world. Islam, which combines materiality with spirituality, stands at the summit of religious thought and experience, offering us the best of both worlds.

On the other hand, Jews believe that they are the "Chosen People of God," that they are "a nation of priests," and that God intends to guide humanity through them. They see themselves—if this is the right expression—as the "clergy" or "Church" of humankind, and consider themselves the elite of the human race.

In Christianity, as everyone knows, the Faithful are divided into the Church or priestly class (clergy) and the ordinary believers (laity). In Christianity the true chosen of humanity is the Church, or the community of priests. The Church has the authority to speak in the name of God and to excommunicate. It thus possesses absolute authority over a person's afterlife (and, in ages when religious faith was strong, also over his or her life in this world). According to Christian belief, "outside the Church there is no salvation." Because of fundamental differences in viewpoint, various denominations have developed in Christianity, each with its own Church.

On the other hand, there is no clerical class and no Church in Islam: we have already had occasion to remark that it is a churchless faith. In Islam, all human beings are equal before God. As is pointed out in the Farewell Sermon, "Superiority lies only in fearing God and in doing good deeds."

Matter and Spirit

But this is not all. It is written in the sacred books that man was created from dust, or earth, or clay. The fact that they are created from the same matter in addition to the same image might be seen as a second reason for equality between human beings. But if human beings are only clay, i.e. matter, we are in effect nothing more than robots, machines. And all materialist philosophies have, in fact, treated the human as mud because they do not allow any other dimension to his or her existence. Even if they do not say so in theory, this has always been the case in practice. The twentieth century has proved this beyond doubt, if nothing else.

Even if the image of the human being made of clay is holy, therefore, this is not enough to protect human rights. The formula is incomplete; or rather, it is half. What has been said for matter must also be said for spirit, thus complementing and completing the formula. And this completion has been performed by Islam.

Humans in Islam

The principle of the Torah given above recurs in Islam in two Traditions of the Prophet: 1. "God created man in His own image," and 2. "God created man in the image of the Compassionate." The Compassionate is one of the attributes of God. Since the Essence of God cannot have a form, it is plausible that man should be created in accordance with one of God's attributes.

Both Judaism and Christianity accept that the human has a spirit. Not much information can be found, however, in their sacred books regarding this spirit. How God gave life to the first human is described in the Torah as follows: "The Lord God formed man [Adam] from the dust of the ground, and breathed into his nostrils the breath of life" (*Genesis*, 2:7).

There is nothing more here than that human beings were given life. It is stated that the first human has been given life, just like plants and animals. There is nothing that distinguishes humans from them. Similarly, in another book of the Old Testament (of which the Torah comprises only the first five books), it is stated that upon death: "The breath returns to the Lord who gave it" (*Ecclesiastes*, 12:7), which is synonymous with the Koranic verses to the effect: "We come from God, and we shall return to Him."

These statements save human beings from the status of a dead lump of clay and raise them to the level of animals and plants, but do not take them any further. Each human is a living being, and God gives him/her life or takes it back. In Sufic terms, this has brought the discussion to the level of the Animal Spirit, but not the Human Spirit.

The Human Being is Holy in Islam

In his words quoted above, Chesterton indicated that the origin of humanity was divine, and he could find only this when he sought a basis for democracy. For Chesterton, as a Christian, the meaning of this divine origin is that God created Adam and Eve and that all human beings descended from them. If we do not accept that humanity has descended from a common ancestor, we can find no basis for declaring the fraternity of humankind. Suppose, for example, that humanity had two ancestors, which did not in turn have a common progenitor. In such a case, humanity would continue forever as two separate races or classes. (This is one of the dangers inherent in Darwinian theories of evolution.) This means that the principle of "liberty, equality, fraternity," which is the motto of the French Revolution and all democracies, can be invested with meaning and validity only on the condition that we accept descent from a single ancestor (of divine origin), namely Adam.

But even this is not enough. Let us repeat our question: Why are all human beings equal? Why do we believe that every human being possesses great worth? (Because for this, even having descended from Adam is not a sufficient condition.) Why do we believe that human beings have certain rights? Why is it necessary to respect a human being, and not treat him/her as mere mud in spite of the fact that that is his or her material origin?

The answer given by Islam is as follows:

1. "We breathed into man (Adam) of Our Spirit."

This verse is repeated in three places in the Koran (15:29, 32:9, 38:72). The spirit that vitalizes Man is *God's Own Spirit* which He has breathed into the human. This is why God has ordered the angels to bow to the ground (prostrate themselves) before Adam (2:34). There is therefore a spark, a breath of God's Spirit, in every person. The Human Spirit derives directly from the Spirit of God, *and this is why all human beings are sacred.* And because each human being has this spirit, *human beings are equal in holiness.* It is important to note, however, that most emphatically, definitely, and certainly, *human beings are not God.* Rather, they bear within themselves a spark that is sacred, a trust that is divine.

The second great foundation of democracy—the proposition that there is more good than bad in human beings, that this good surfaces if the will of the people is allowed free expression[125]—now follows as a matter of course. For according to Islam, human nature is originally good—in light of the above considerations, it cannot be otherwise. This is why "the voice of the people is the voice of God" (*vox populi, vox Dei*).

It can be seen that equality in form has been transcended here, and equality in spirit has been reached. Not only image (form) but also essence (content) has found its place. In other words, it is not possible to discriminate between people not only in terms of matter and form, but also of spirit and content. This is why the Koran states: "Killing another [unjustly] is like killing the whole of humanity, and saving a human being is like saving all mankind. We have indicated this in their Book to the Children of Israel" (5:32). Or, as it is expressed in Judaism,

> *He who saves one man*
> *Saves the world entire.*

This precept is found in the Talmud (Sanhedrin, *Seder: Nezikin*/Order: Damages, 4,5). The way in which you treat one human being, therefore, is the equivalent of treating all humankind in that way.

2. "God has created you of a single soul (self)."

This verse, in turn, recurs four times in the Koran (4:1, 6:98, 7:189, 39:6). Interpreted from the Sufic (esoteric) point of view, this means that all human beings are one. If interpreted exoterically, in the sense that all men derive from Adam, it means that all human beings are brothers and sisters. And as a matter of fact, the Prophet implicitly alludes to human brotherhood in his Farewell Sermon: "Human beings, you are all descended from one father. You are all the Children of Adam." It is stated elsewhere in the same sermon that: "A Moslem is the brother of another Moslem, and so all Moslems are brethren, one of another." The only difference between the brother-and-sisterhood of humanity and that of Moslems is that the former is articulated covertly and the latter, overtly. And the only reason for this covert expression is that a non-Moslem, because s/he may be unaware of this fraternity, may tend to act in ways that do not take it into account.

We therefore see that human beings are divine, and in spite of all differences in external appearance, *their essence is the same. That is why* they are equals of each other, that is why they have equal rights, why liberty is their right, and why they are brethren. Here is where the foundation of democracy has been laid. Indeed, another of the Prophet's Traditions states: "All humans are equal, like the teeth of a comb." Note that this saying is all-inclusive—for instance, it includes women as well.

The West, where democracy saw the light of day, realized that such was the state of affairs. But this truth was not expressed with such blinding clarity in our traditions and holy books. The most that could be achieved was to say, with Chesterton, that humankind was descended from Adam. On the other hand, the flight from the negative aspects of Christianity became an escape from religion in general, and precluded in-depth study of the situation. Thus, as we have seen, the true source of democracy, equality, freedom, and fraternity lies in these explicit verses of the Koran.

Ethics and the Democratic Personality

Since this is the case, then, how should human beings behave towards each other? The answer is precisely in accordance with the morality that God has prescribed for us. This constitutes the final gift of religions—and especially, of Islam—to humanity.

Democracy is not just about the "separation of powers." It is not simply a multi-party regime, or general elections, or equality of vote. At the same time and much more importantly, it means respect for human rights, for the rights of others (and even for the rights of an animal, of a stone). In line with Voltaire's famous dictum, it is to limit one's own liberties with one's own will at the point where the rights of others begin. It means the free flowering of each individual within restrictions common to all, and to become as useful as possible to oneself, to society, and to humankind. And this is what religions have all prescribed. This is the ethics of democracy. The abovementioned may be the form of democracy; this is its spirit. Where the core does not exist, purely formal democracy is reduced to an empty shell, and is bound to perish sooner or later. Where this spirit is, on the other hand, life never ceases to be bearable, and democracy can easily be built up even if the formal requirements are not met. Democracy cannot exist without a morality of democracy.

After the Second World War, Theodor W. Adorno, et al. of the Frankfurt School published a study on "the Authoritarian Personality." In this vein, it is possible to theorize a "democratic personality structure," and this can be achieved only with the morality of the Koran. Because Islamic ethics, which is based on the Koran, is the very essence of democratic morality. Respect for the rights of others and remaining within the limits of one's rights (even in the case of a ruler) has never been emphasized in any religion as much as in Islam.

Conclusion

The following prayer (distributed by my Master) is none other than the prayer of democratic ethics, of the democratic personality. To the extent that these ideals are approximated, both our lives and the lives of those around us are enriched, enlightened, and infused with value and meaning. An oasis appears in the middle of the desert. If everyone adopts this morality, peace, contentment, and happiness will belong to everyone. And that is when the true flower of democracy will reach full bloom.

> *Dear God, grant that we may sow peace wherever we go. Let us be reconcilers and unifiers, not sowers of dissent. Allow us to disseminate love where there is hate, forgiveness where there is injury, faith where there is doubt, hope where there is despair, light where there is darkness, and joy where there is sorrow. Grant that we may become in mercy like the sun, in generosity like the rain, in humility like the earth, in hiding the shames of others like the night; and in bestowing favors on everyone without discrimination, like all four.*

These ideas associated with democracy take us one step further, for it now becomes possible to view democracy not as an end in itself, but as a means to something greater. Contemporary democracy provides the institutions, the basis, conducive to the best development of the human personality. It is here that Islam can provide a guiding light, for the aim of Islamic Sufism is precisely to cultivate development of the Self to stages where higher forms of thinking, ethics, and behavior are possible.

Lewis Mumford, that astute social critic and one of the most incisive minds of the twentieth century, recognized that the transformation of social institutions without the re-education of human beings would not be sufficient to establish a happier society. "In rejecting a twofold change, inner and outer," he said, the proponents of lasting, significant social change "overlooked the organic connection between personality and community, between the individual and the collective form. They sought to transform the institutions of society...and create a high order of social existence without bothering to develop and discipline *a higher type of self.*"[126]

Although not well acquainted with certain aspects of Islam, Mumford nevertheless clearly understood that social and spiritual improvement complement each other. While Islam is quite down-to-earth, nonutopian, and immediately practicable, it should be recognized that it opens the door to "self-actualization"—to use psychologist Abraham Maslow's term in a deeper, Sufic, context—and the consequent betterment of society is quite feasible. Not only that, but Sufism also describes the various levels of Self with great precision, and outlines the process of self-actualization step by step.[127] Thus, Islam doesn't lead us simply to democracy as a political form, but also to its fulfillment.

But what if democracy does not take its inspiration from Islam—what then?

1. A multitude of parties will sow enmity between brother and sister, father and son, and will prevent the oneness of humankind for the sake of negligible differences.

2. The triad of government, businessmen, and banks will unite for illegitimate profits.

3. Politicians, the media (press, radio, TV, computer networks), and the merchants of passion will fan the fires of illicit sex.

4. Behavior in accordance with the Four Holy Books (the Torah, the Psalms, the Gospel, and the Koran) will disappear.

To say this is nothing more than to repeat Tocqueville's observation that when political ties are relaxed, moral ties must be strengthened if society is to escape destruction. For the concept of liberty in democratic societies is not based on the distinction between the "prohibited" and the "permitted" (what is legitimate and illegitimate in terms of divine sanction), and some people think that democracy means freedom without limits. Unlimited freedom, however, is not democracy but anarchy. And, furthermore, the "forbidden/allowed" (shalt not/shalt) distinction within religions has been instituted, not because God wants to make life difficult for everyone, but because humankind will be sucked into the maelstrom of its own destruction if it does not abide by these rules. And this is precisely what will happen, unless democracy takes its further inspiration from Islam.

✺

In this chapter we have seen that Islam, as a religion, is eminently suitable for democratic rule, even though only a few Moslem countries presently have democratic governments. The basis of democracy, the assertion that all human beings are equal, can be derived directly from the Koran, and is also justified by it. What remains is for Moslems to develop their own native theories of democracy, should they wish to do so. The present chapter has also reviewed the idea that Islam's lack of a church hierarchy (which can lead to theocracy) makes it highly democratic, that the history of Islamic civilization (especially the Ottoman Empire) is one of great tolerance, and that democracy is itself a new form of government that has rarely been realized historically anywhere in the world.

The next chapter will consider the issue of women's status in Islam, taking into consideration the history of women in Islam, especially the Prophet's example, as well as the contemporary failings of absolutist Islamic groups that have mistreated women.

Women in Islam

(This chapter will consider the issue of women and Islam, taking into consideration the history of how women have been treated in Islam—beginning with the Prophet's own dealings with women—in order to clarify some of the misunderstandings in the West and elsewhere about women's status in Moslem countries. It will also provide a critique of the failings of Islamic groups that have allowed and encouraged violence against and the social repression of women in direct contradiction of the Prophet's teachings. This is one of the main areas where ignorance about true Islam manifests itself, even among its adherents.)

Men are one half of an apple; women are the other half.

—Mohammed

Introduction

According to Islam, the Way of God, the mode in which God has chosen to manifest Himself, is revealed to us through the workings of nature. And these workings are often displayed in the form of complementary opposites. Day and night, light and dark, high and low, long and short, and positive and negative are just a few examples. In Chinese philosophy the multitude of opposites was summarized in the polarity of *yin* and *yang*, the first symbolizing the dark, passive, and "female" aspect and the second, the light, active, and "male" aspect of things. It is even said that the universe comes into being through opposites, for a thing cannot be manifested without its opposite. Light, for example, can only be distinguished against a background of darkness, and so on. This reciprocity extends from the macrocosmos down to the microcosmos, where quantum physicist Niels Bohr has shown that the wave and particle models of nature consummate each other in his famous Principle of Complementarity.

It is noteworthy that polarity in nature does not always imply symmetry in every respect. For example, the proton and the electron—the building blocks of the universe—are complementary in charge, yet the proton is almost two thousand times as massive as the electron. A similar disproportion exists between the female ovum and the male sperm, the latter being minute in comparison with the former. Where sexual reproduction is concerned, nature abounds in examples of asymmetry in size, as evidenced in the queen bee and smaller male bees, or the large female black widow spider and her small male counterpart.

When we come to human beings, we find that man and woman are almost identical to one another except for certain biological differences. It makes no sense to speak about sex in the case of the soul itself; the self is unitary and asexual. Yet the biological differences are there, and they are too deeply rooted and obvious to be dismissed, e.g., a male cannot bear or breast-feed a child no matter how hard he tries.

Rather than trying to accomplish the impossible and eradicate biological differences, then, what we should do is to take men and women as they are and give them their rights. The biological, psychological, and social needs of a woman are different from those of a man.[128] If these needs are not taken into account, we would be violating the rights of one side or the other.

Islam has laid down the rights of both man and woman without disregarding the differences peculiar to each. Care should be taken, however, to avoid entangling what is specifically Islamic with other, extraneous influences. If we wish to learn the truth, we need to research the matter more thoroughly.

The history of Islam is, by and large, the history of the failure of so-called "Islamic" nations to live up to the high ideals of Islam, as much as it is of their success. Islamic societies have, it is true, tried to remain faithful to the injunctions of the Koran and the noble example of the Prophet. But it is also obvious that in this they have not been entirely successful. This is why calls for a "return to the roots" are sounded so frequently, but historical inertias that lie deep seem to preclude any easy change.

What is necessary, then, is to look at *what Islam in fact says*. Ideals are always difficult to translate into practice, but the shortcoming here lies with all-too-human failings, not with the ideals themselves. The Koran and the example of the Prophet should be read with proper understanding, but most important of all, they must be read. Many Moslems themselves have not read the Koran or the Traditions at all.

When we look at Islam's perceived lore concerning women today, what we see is actually the result of several intertwined factors, especially:

1. Authentic Islamic doctrine regarding women, which is itself frequently misread. Superimposed on this are:

2. Various local, social, and cultural influences,

3. Political factors, and

4. Environmental factors.

The Prophet's Example

Once we attempt to unearth the specifically Islamic element underneath these various influences on the teachings about women, we find that the only thing to do is to go back to the original example, that of the Prophet himself. We have to supplement the written Koran with the concrete example of the "Speaking Koran" (the Prophet), who constitutes the only true role model for Moslems.

The Prophet was the archetypal family man, doing household chores, even mending his own clothes and shoes when necessary. That is the model, not only for Moslems but for all men, that Islam aspires to. And it is not just a model, but a challenge for us all.

"The best among you," remarked the Prophet, "are those who treat women well." One of his wives, in a heated discussion, once struck the

Prophet with her hand. Her mother saw this and chided her, saying: "Daughter, what are you doing? Do you realize who this is?" The Messenger of God, however, intervened and said: "No, no, don't say anything to her. My blessed wives are all like this. Don't say anything against any of them."

On another occasion, he and another wife were having a heated discussion. At one point, she began yelling at him. When her father, who had overheard, raised the subject with her, she replied simply that all the Prophet's wives enjoyed similar liberties with him.

It cannot be emphasized enough that among all his wives, *the Prophet never, ever struck any of his wives or children, not even once.* He never raised his voice against them, nor said a bad word, even when they quarreled with him.

"I have been made," said the Prophet, "to love three things in your world: women, perfume, and Prayer, the light of my eyes." This Tradition not only highlights the spiritual nature of the Prophet; it also draws attention to the intrinsic sweetness of the three items, and in associating women with Prayer, draws attention to the sacred nature of women and of marriage, which is the only approved way for relations between the sexes.

Common Fallacies Regarding the Status of Women

We have already noted that the Koran has frequently been read improperly, and without reference to the Prophet's example. This is especially true of the verses dealing with the status of women. What has happened is that meanings have been read into them which actually are not there. An attempt will be made here to demonstrate this by discussing a few examples: the most common fallacies.

Fallacy 1: Men are the masters and women are their slaves

The Koran reads: "… men are the overseers of women" (4:34), that is, men are the supporters and protectors of women and children. It must be understood that this was revealed in a patriarchal society where women had practically no rights at all, so that it is protective of women and women's rights. Barring outright slander, there is no way that one can extrapolate from this to a master/slave relationship. To make things clearer, the Prophet said in his Farewell Sermon: "Treat your women well. You have no right to oppress them." And he also said: "The best among you are the best to their wives," and: "The believers of the most perfect faith are those who exhibit the best moral conduct and are kindest to their families."

Fallacy 2: Men are superior to women

The verse so interpreted reads: "... men have a degree over women" (2:228). Although it is true that *on the average,* men have a slight edge over women in terms of physical strength, needless to say, this excludes a broad range of exceptions, and is true only in a statistical sense.[129] The same verse notes that "some are better than others," but does not assign gender to this latter expression. Indeed, as we all know, there are untold numbers of women who are superior to men in knowledge, in work, even in physical strength.

Fallacy 3: Men are permitted to beat women

The verse used to excuse the physical abuse of women is: "Admonish [or: reason with] women whom you fear may be rebellious. [If this is not enough] depart from their beds. [If this doesn't work either] slap them. If they then obey you, don't search for a way against them" (4:34).

The word "slap" above derives from the Arabic root DRB and is usually translated as "beat." Now it so happens that words derived from the same DRB root occur fifty-eight times in the Koran, and nowhere else is it used (or translated) in this sense. Of the many other meanings assigned to it, a few are: to set out (on the road), to shroud (in darkness), to strike (an example), to mint (a coin), to publish (a book), to cover (concerning ladies' dresses), to dispatch, to throw, to raise (something set down), and so on.

It can thus be seen that "beat" is by no means the obvious translation of such a word. Assuming, however, that there is a grain of truth in the interpreters' view, it has been rendered here by "slap," for as we shall see below, the sayings of the Prophet, as well as his example which we saw above, strongly militate against the use of violence where women are concerned.

Even if we accept this translation, men are told to strike *rebellious women*—lightly, according to Koranic commentators—only as a last resort. What could be the nature of the rebellion that would justify such a measure? On an occasion in which the Prophet spoke of "disciplining without bruises or injuries," and also in the Farewell Sermon, this is linked with adultery. For as the verse says, the measure is used not when a woman *is actually* "rebellious," but when one *merely fears* it. And this can be justified only on the grounds of infidelity. Otherwise, anything could be made a pretext for violence, which is surely not what is intended by the verse. To prevent adultery, if one can, before it happens—this seems to be the only justification for the measure. For adultery is the one sure way to wreck a marriage, and if the latter can be saved in this manner, we have a rationale for the action.

Indeed, the Tradition itself speaks of overt fornication, i.e., if a man actually witnesses his wife with another man, he is entitled to "discipline" her; yet even here the recommendation of Islam is to divorce her peacefully rather than to engage in violence. Of course, there can be no question of remaining together after such an event has been witnessed. Of all permitted things under heaven, the most detestable in God's sight is divorce, yet there are occasions where it is unavoidable.

Over and against this we have to set the following sayings of the Prophet: "Those who beat their wives are not good men," "I myself will be the claimant on Judgment Day against the man who beats his wife," and "Could any of you beat his wife as he might a slave, and then lie with her in the evening?" Reliable collections contain Traditions of the Prophet to the effect that he forbade the beating of *any* woman, saying: "Never beat God's handmaidens." All this goes to show that the Koranic sanction can be invoked, if at all, only under the most exceptional of circumstances. It also demonstrates one of the central theses of this book: leave out the Prophet, and God only knows what you will end up with.

Fallacy 4: One man equals two women

The Koranic verse reads: "... the male receives two shares of the inheritance, the female one share" (4:11,176), but this is qualified by the decree: "Men support women from their means" (4:34). Thus, the upkeep of the sister(s) are incumbent on the brother(s). The reverse is not true, even if a sister earns her living and a brother does not. Further, this is only one of the injunctions regulating inheritance, and hence one among a host of legal cases.

Fallacy 5: One male witness equals two female witnesses

When taken out of context, the Koranic verse indeed reads: "...two male witnesses, or one male and two female witnesses, so that one of them can remind the other" (2:282). When read in its proper context, however, it becomes clear that this applies only to a certain subset of commercial law—namely, in cases of commercial liability with a maturity period, and Letters of Credit. (In France, women were not allowed to sign checks until 1962.)

Historical, Social, and Cultural Influences on Islam

When a religion emerges into a society, it never finds a blank slate before it. No matter what the society, it has customs, mores, and traditions that antedate the introduction of that religion, and which color its response to the latter. This basic fact of sociology and anthropology is also observed in the case of Islam. Islam itself is universal, but the response of every culture to Islam will be conditioned by its own peculiar characteristics. For this reason, it is necessary to know the cultural history of the Middle East, not to mention the other areas where Islam has spread.

The people of the Middle East where Islam originated belonged to a male-dominant culture. The period before Islam, referred to as "the Age of Ignorance," was replete with the ill treatment of females. A woman was considered a vehicle for sexual satisfaction and little else—lacking, in many cases, even the legal protection of a marital arrangement. Little girls were disposed of by burying them alive. Very few women had the means to become prominent and powerful members of society. Women could be gambled on and given away in bets; they could be inherited like a household object.

Against this backdrop, Islam introduced almost every right that women enjoyed in the twentieth century. The right of women in France to exercise property rights independently of their husbands was granted only at the beginning of the twentieth century. In Italy, the right to divorce had to wait until the last third of the twentieth century. God's instruction to the Prophet to accept the allegiance of women (60:12) has been interpreted by Moslems as the right to vote; in the U.S., women could not vote until 1920. Today, at the end of the twentieth century, universal suffrage still does not exist in Switzerland. In Germany, a woman could not hold a bank account until 1958, in France until 1965. The true emancipation of women in Europe is the matter of a scant fifty years.

Now it may come as something of a surprise that women were granted all these rights, explicitly or implicitly, not today, not yesterday, but *one thousand four hundred years ago* with the emergence of Islam. Mohammed, the Messenger of God, effected the elevation of womankind, not in an age of emancipation, but at a time when woman did not count for anything at all. He put an end to female infanticide. Above all, Islam introduced the treatment of woman as a *person;* much later, in the Middle Ages, Europeans would be debating whether a woman has a soul and should be considered human or not. The greatness of this achievement has to be measured not against what humanity has accomplished today after millennia of struggle, but in its own historical context. Moreover, as we shall see below, women still lack those very same rights given by Mohammed even in this day.

Certain measures which may at first glance look like restrictions actually worked to the woman's benefit. It may be difficult for us, living as we do at the pinnacle of civilization, to assess what a giant leap this was in comparison with what preceded it. For example, in transactions dealing with commercial debt having a maturity period, a second female witness might be called in, but this relieved the first from the burden of having to face singly the responsibility of remembering complicated numerical details. A woman might receive less of a share in inheritance, but this was balanced by the fact that the male heir was responsible for supporting her. Thus, in many cases, she lost a pittance but gained lifelong security in return. Giving her an equal share might have resulted in male protest and the removal of this privilege altogether. Moreover, this happens to be only a particular case in Islamic law—there are many other cases where she receives a greater or even an equal share. Further, a woman didn't have to take care of anyone else and was totally free to dispense with her money as she liked. She didn't (and doesn't) have to spend a penny for her livelihood even if she had wealth of her own; her husband had (and has) to take care of her. She doesn't have to breast-feed the baby or do household chores if she doesn't want to; the husband has to find a foster-mother in one case, and a servant in the other. She cannot be married off by her parents to a man she doesn't want—as long as one abides by Islam, that is.

We can see that regulations which at first appear to be detrimental to women were actually meant, and worked, for their benefit as protective measures ("positive discrimination" of the kind now being discarded by women in the West). In the early days of Islam, furthermore, women were accorded much more freedom than was forthcoming later on— they could accompany their menfolk in war, act as nurses, engage in commerce and trade, and so on. Karen Armstrong, the author of an important biography about Mohammed, merely tells the truth when she observes: "Women were not crushed by Islam, as people tend to imagine in the West."[130]

As time passed, however, old social habits—atavisms from the Age of Ignorance—began to reassert themselves. Also, as Islam spread to other lands and other cultures, it was forced to assimilate the mores and norms of *those* regions as well. Some of these, the religion could tame; there was too much sociocultural resistance against taming others. What justification can be found within Islam, for example, for the clitoridectomies performed in North Africa? None whatsoever. The result was that, over the course of the centuries, elements foreign to Islam with its protection of women became blended into the mixture. The interaction of Islam with each new culture of course led to altogether different results.

Take, for example, the case of the veil. The veil existed in the Middle East prior to Islam, e.g., the Virgin Mary is depicted wearing a veil in the early churches. Apparently, it first began as a measure to ensure protection from the male tendency to exploit and molest women. Therefore, legislation for covering was not intended to oppress women, but rather to counter the lack of self-control of men with respect to women (as we know, sexual harassment, to say nothing of rape, is a worldwide problem even in our day).

The Prophet's wives and women were enjoined in the Koran (24:30-31) to cover themselves in a general sense as an aspect of modesty. Originally, only the Prophet's wives were required to veil themselves; this was their exclusive privilege. In time, the veil became a status symbol and fashionable among other women as well. As Armstrong remarks, "Islamic culture was strongly egalitarian and it seemed incongruous that the Prophet's wives should be distinguished and honored in this way. Thus many of the Muslim women who first took the veil saw it as a symbol of power and influence, not as a badge of male oppression."[131] It was only later on that the veil became a sign of female seclusion in a patriarchal society, and was transformed from an emblem of superiority into its exact opposite.

There is also another dimension to this. For example, the headscarf is worn by Catholic nuns, and in their case it is revered as a sign of holiness. There is no reason why Islamic usage of the headscarf should not be accorded similar respect.

The sayings, or "Traditions," of the Prophet have also undergone a process of "socialization" or "acculturation." It is known that spurious Traditions were invented at various times, and in a culture with a certain attitude towards women these inventions would tend to be correspondingly biased. However, collectors of Traditions have made painstaking efforts to separate spurious Traditions from authentic ones. Since the Prophet himself indicated that false Traditions would be invented in his name, one should be very careful in handling sayings that go against the general tendency of Islam, which can be summarized as respect for women, within an overall spirit of tolerance, compassion, and mercy.

Political Factors

Without doubt, rulers exert an influence over the societies they rule. This influence extends to the laws of a society, and the religious law of Islam—the Holy Law, which is comprised of Koranic rulings, the sayings and example of the Prophet, derivations based on analogy, and the consensus of scholars—has not been exempt from it. Rulers have found it expedient to reinterpret religious law according to their own lights.

Take the case of Saudi Arabia, where the restrictions on women are more severe than in other Islamic countries (they cannot drive a car, for instance). Saudi law also requires that anyone bringing narcotics into the country be decapitated, and the Saudis claim that this practice is firmly based on the Holy Law. (Recall at this point that the Saudis are mostly

Wahhabis who go for the strictest interpretation.) Yet there are other Islamic lands where this is not the case, for the simple reason that narcotics as such didn't exist at the time when Islam was revealed. How then could the Holy Law have ruled beheading as punishment for a narcotic offense? It is not the attempt to draw analogies from precedents that is at error here, but rather that rulers have passed laws of their own and called these "the Holy Law." Besides, every severe Koranic ruling is followed by a verse that absolves the repentant, emphasizes God's Compassion and Mercy, and exhorts human beings to emulate these qualities. This is a clear case where Islam is used as a front to cover up other intentions, which are mainly aimed at keeping a specific society under political control. And women, too, have received an unequal share in this process.

Geographical Factors

When you throw a stone into a still pond, you are bound to get ripples. At least some of the repercussions in the Middle East appear to be caused by comparatively recent developments.

Without engaging in any value judgments, I would like to draw attention to an objective fact which has too often been overlooked: namely, that the presence of Israel has modified response patterns in the Middle East. This seems to be a part of Middle-Eastern reactions to the more general ascendancy of the West. People's attitudes appear to be modulated by "the Western challenge," and the result has been reinforcement and retrenchment within an overall defensive stance. Just as liberties are curtailed under extraordinary circumstances, Middle-Eastern nations, intimidated by continual encroachments against what they regard as their geographical and cultural territory, have overreacted with puritanism, and women's status has been adversely affected as a result.

About Polygamy

It is important to recognize that during the Prophet's life, polygamy was not only socially accepted, it was a mark of distinction in ancient society. According to the Bible, for example, David had a harem (2 *Samuel* 5.13), Abraham, Jacob (*Genesis* 32.22), and Elkanah (1 *Samuel* 1.2) each had two wives, and Esau had several (*Genesis* 28.9). Solomon had seven hundred wives as well as three hundred concubines (1 *Kings* 11.3). At this time, a man of high standing was *expected* to take many wives.

Another reason for polygamy is that wars deplete the male portion of the population, and there are fewer husbands to go around. This is not merely a problem of the past. In early 1996, Buryat women—who live in the vicinity of Lake Baikal—were campaigning for polygamy, saying that their people were on the verge of extinction and that they considered it better to be the second or third wife of a good man than the only wife of a drunkard, or otherwise unfit mate.

It should be remembered that the Old Testament sanctions unlimited polygamy, the only requirement being that: "If [a man] takes another wife to himself, he shall not diminish the food, clothing, or marital rights of the first wife [or wives]" (*Exodus* 21.10).

In spite of the existence of polygamy, the Prophet of God was strictly monogamous with his first wife, Khadija. He was twenty-five and she forty when they married; he remained faithful to her for more than a quarter-century. As she grew older, Khadija suggested to the Prophet that he take a second wife, but he always laughed off such suggestions. After her death, with the spread of Islam, he had to take several wives for various political, diplomatic, or protective reasons, though among them his true love was only one, Aisha, whom he betrothed when she was still very young. (This practice is cross-culturally common: for example, in Medieval Europe as well, it was customary for nine- or ten-year old girls to marry. Fruit ripens more quickly in that hot climate, and Aisha was a particularly early bloomer. Their marriage was consummated later, when she was older.) In Mohammed's defense, Professor Laura Veccia Vaglieri remarks,

> during those years of his life when by nature the sexual urge is strongest, although he lived in a society like that of the Arabs, where the institution of marriage was almost non-existent, where polygamy was the rule, and where divorce was very easy indeed, he was married to one woman alone, Khadija, who was much older than himself, [and] for twenty-five years he was her faithful, loving husband. Only when she died and when he was already more than fifty years old did he marry again and more than once. Each of these marriages had a social and political reason,

for he wanted through the women he married to honour pious women, or to establish marriage relations with other clans and tribes for the purpose of opening the way for the propagation of Islam. With the sole exception of Aisha, [Mohammed] married women who were neither virgins, nor young, nor beautiful. Was this sensuality?[132]

In his work *Studies in a Mosque*, Stanley Lane-Poole gives a fair-minded assessment that also happens to be true:

> The simple austerity of his life, to the very last, his hard mat for sleeping on, his plain food, his self-imposed menial work, point him as an ascetic rather than a voluptuary in most senses of the word...A great deal too much has been said about his wives....Be it remembered that, within his unlimited power, he need not have restricted himself to a number insignificant compared with the harems of some of his successors...that all of them save one were widows...Several of these marriages must have been entered into from the feeling that those women whose husbands had fallen in battle for the faith, and who had been left unprotected, had a claim upon the generosity of him who prompted the fight. Other marriages were contracted from motives of policy, in order to conciliate the heads of rival factions.[133]

The important thing is that the Prophet was *legally married* to all his wives, even to slave girls with whom he was presented. In Islam, not multiple marriages but illicit sex—pre- or extramarital fornication and adultery—is immoral. Islam limited the number of female consorts to four (but recommended one), and this with the proviso that all were brought under the protective umbrella of legal marriage. On the other hand, the right for a woman to divorce a man was granted from the start: when Umaima wished to divorce the Prophet she did so, receiving gifts during the split.

Given that this was a society with a tradition of allowing an unlimited number of wives, polygamy could not be eradicated immediately. The Koran, however, curtailed this number and said: "You can take up to four wives, but *only if* you can treat them all equally" (4:3), adding the rejoinder:

"You cannot treat them all equally" (4:129). Thus, the Koran recognizes polygamy but paves the way for monogamy.

As far as sexual satisfaction is concerned, one spouse is enough. Yet there have always been sexually overactive men in all societies who could not control their egotistical drives and who have had carnal relationships with more than one woman. Rather than leave such types to wallow in the sin of fornication and adultery, and in order to secure legal marital rights for their consorts, the Koran did not ban polygamy entirely. The verses quoted above, however, indicate where its true preference lies.

If the Koran allows a man with several wives (polygyny), why not a woman with several husbands (polyandry)? This is one of the cases where asymmetry in nature asserts itself. If a man has several wives, the parents of any offspring are immediately identified. The father is known, the mother is known, and hence it is immediately obvious who is responsible for a child.[134] If, however, a woman has sexual relations with more than one man, the mother is known but the father is not. Therefore, it is not certain who will take responsibility for the child other than its mother—in the end, no one might. But this is practically the same situation as that found in prostitution, and social rights cannot be properly established for women and children under polyandry.

Views of Western Orientalists

The West has had a long-standing interest in the Islamic religion, and has studied it at great length. Scholars who specialize in this field are known as orientalists. Of course, there have been biased persons among them; but there have been fair ones too, and even in the case of the most biased, professional integrity has at times caused them to acknowledge the truth. Let us now see what a series of Western orientalists and historians have to say concerning the treatment of women in Islam:

Sir Hamilton A.R. Gibb: "That [Mohammed's] reforms enhanced the status of women in general by contrast with the anarchy of pre-Islamic Arabia is universally admitted. ...critics have tended to overlook the almost unfailing patience which he displayed even under provocation and the gentleness with which he attended to the griefs of all sorts of women and comforted them, even at times to the extent of revising his legislation."

Alfred Guillaume: "…it is laid down that wives are to be treated with kindness and strict impartiality; if a man cannot treat all alike he should keep to one. The husband pays the woman a dowry at the time of marriage, and the money or property so allotted remains her own."

Stanley Lane-Poole: No great lawmaker has ever made such significant changes as Mohammed did on the subject of women. Rulings concerning women have been outlined in the Koran in great detail. This is the point at which Mohammed's greatest reforms have occurred. Although these reforms may appear insignificant to a European, they are actually tremendous. The restriction placed on polygamy, the recommendation of monogamy, the introduction of degrees of prohibition in place of the appalling collectivism and intermixing of Arab marriages, the limitations on divorce, the duty of a husband to take care of his ex-wife for a certain period even after they are divorced, the severe rulings to ensure her livelihood, the introduction of the novelty that women are legal heirs—even if at half the rate of men—so that children may be properly looked after, and the ability of a widow to receive her dead husband's inheritance—all these constitute a programme of far-reaching reforms.

Will Durant: Mohammed put an end to female infanticide. In court cases and financial matters, he made woman the equal of man. A woman can enter every legal profession; she can keep her earnings for herself; she can inherit money and property, and use her fortune as she desires. Mohammed removed the Arab custom by which women passed from father to son as part of the inheritance.

Laura Veccia Vaglieri: Even though woman has risen to a high social status in Europe, she has not, at least until recently, attained in many countries the independence and liberty enjoyed by a Moslem woman in the face of the law. In reality, the woman in Islam possesses the right to share in inheritance, even if to an extent less than her brothers; the right to marry according to her own choice and not to tolerate the ill treatment of a brutish husband; but further, the rights to receive dowry payment from her husband, to have her needs met by her husband even if she is rich, and to be absolutely independent in the disposal of her inherited property.

Gaudefroy-Demombynes: The rulings of the Koran, which are amazingly in favor of woman, provide her, even if theoretically, with a status better than [nineteenth century] European laws allowed. The Islamic woman has the right to a separate fortune in financial matters. She owns her share, her property received through donation or inheritance, and her labor's dues to the end of her life. Although it is difficult for her to make practical use of these rights, her sustenance, shelter, and other requirements are guaranteed in accordance with her standing.

Clement Huart: It is the duty of the husband to take care of his wife. He does not have the right to force her to work in a job that conflicts with her social standing, or to work at all in return for pay.

As these testimonies of well-known historians and orientalists demonstrate, the discoveries of Western research in this field have not yet become common knowledge. Although many Islamist groups severely curtail women's rights, their actions cannot be justified.

Family Life

"We created you [both man and woman] from a single soul" (4:1), says the Koran. This verse points to the basically unitary and nonpolar nature of the soul, or self; it is asexual, and man and woman are not merely equal, but identical in this respect. As far as the Koran is concerned, the only inequality worthy of note is that based on closeness to God, which has nothing to do with maleness or femaleness, wealth or poverty, race, nationality, or prominence: "Surely the noblest among you in the sight of God is the most Godfearing of you" (49:13). Another way to read this verse would be: "The only superiority in God's sight consists in preserving oneself from evil."

"There is no monkery in Islam," said the Prophet. This and the fact that he was married indicate that spirituality and raising a family are not mutually contradictory or exclusive of each other. Spirituality does not require celibacy. An ordinary householder can enjoy sex and raise children without forfeiting true spirituality. In other words, spirituality and family life can and should be combined. Men and women, says the Koran, are garments of one another: "They are a garment for you and you are a garment to them" (2:187). It also says that God "has created spouses for you among yourselves so that you may dwell in tranquility with them, and He has planted love and mercy between you. In that are signs for people who reflect" (30:21).

Men and women are often mentioned in the same breath in the Koran, emphasizing their equality in all but a very few respects. Here, for instance, is a beautiful verse from the Koran (33:35), in Arthur J. Arberry's superb interpretation:[135]

> *Men and women who have surrendered* [i.e., are Moslems],
> *believing men and women,*
> *obedient men and women,*
> *truthful men and women,*
> *enduring men and women,*
> *humble men and women,*
> *men and women who give in charity,*
> *men who fast and women who fast,*
> *men and women who guard their private parts,*
> *men and women who remember God oft—*
> *for them God has prepared forgiveness*
> *and a mighty wage.*

Islam's egalitarianism is brought out in another saying of the Prophet: "It is mandatory for every male and female Moslem to learn knowledge (science) and to research." The Koranic verse: "Men shall receive the fruits of their labor, and women shall receive the fruits of their labor" (4:32) not only guarantees the labor rights of women on an equal par with men, but also causes Islamic law to recognize personal responsibility for actions, irrespective of sex. When the Koranic teachings are plumbed for their deeper meaning, one finds that the Koran is trying to protect a third thing rather than either a man or a woman alone, and this is the family.

"Paradise," said the Prophet, "lies under the feet of mothers." This means not only that they are superior even to Paradise, but that one can earn a place in Heaven only by pleasing one's mother. Islam has only the highest praise for mothers; the task of raising a family is regarded as almost sacred. Parents and children are regarded as signs of God's mercy and magnificence.

In Islam, not individuals as such but the family is the basic unit of society; if the former are atoms, the family is the molecule that provides continuity and stability. Most of all, man and woman are co-workers with God in the production of new human beings. The creation of a new human is not a task to be taken lightly. It requires a minimum of twenty years of careful nurture in a warm, loving family environment; otherwise the task can easily end in an abomination which can jeopardize not merely the family, but society itself. Therefore, having and raising children is a matter of the utmost gravity. "Free sex" (or sex outside of marriage) devalues children, and thus humanity.

When sex, which is nature's way of reproducing the species, is divorced from its true intent and made to serve human pleasure *exclusively*, that is when things begin to go wrong. Hence, it is illicit sex—adultery, fornication, and the like—that Islam is against. Since it has no conception of original sin, sex in itself (within marriage) is not a defiling act, nor is womankind held responsible for the fall of humans as in the story of Adam and Eve, and hence is not viewed as despicable. Women are considered holy in Islam.

In ecology, nature responds to violations of its balance by trying to eliminate the cause. In the field of forbidden sexual relationships, venereal disease is nature's way of kicking back. Again, the only way to protect oneself is to engage in a healthy marital relationship—which is all that Islam is advocating.

Islam is not alone in condemning extramarital sex. Sages of every time and clime have recognized the necessity of marriage for a balanced, clean, and healthy life. When, for example, Theano, the wife of Pythagoras and also his spiritual successor, was asked how much time is necessary for a woman to become pure after engaging in a sexual act with a man, she replied: "If it is with her husband, she *is* pure immediately; if it is with another, she *never* is pure." Of course, this holds true for the man as well.

Women in Islam have an important role in the education of society. They are not simply the instructors of their children, nor teachers in primary school, but guides that train people at every age. The first precedent for this was the Prophet's wife Aisha, followed by his other wives, who gave instruction to everyone in religious matters.

Love and the Sufis

According to the findings of modern psychiatry, the story of sexual perversion is essentially the story of sex without love. Hence, it goes without saying that love is the most important thing in a relationship between man and woman. As Édouard Schuré pointed out, "it is love which justifies marriage." And marriage, in turn, sanctifies love.

Romantic love first entered Europe in the Middle Ages through the troubadours and minstrels, who in turn were inspired by the Moslem Moors, Saracens, and the Sufis of Andalusia. Idries Shah has convincingly shown in *The Sufis* (1964) that the latter gave the gift of romantic love to the West. As mystics, the Sufis have always been more liberal-minded than the literalists, and this holds true also in the case of women.

The Sufis regard love between the sexes as a mode of something higher, as a station on the way to divine love. They believe that love of another person may lead one to the more refined love of God. For the Sufis, in fact, sexual love is metaphorical; in deeply loving another, we love the very essence of that person, which is none other than the Divine Mystery, from which derives the Sufic claim that true love is a human's love for God. Thus, in the deepest, most fulfilling love, men and women discover the divine in each other.

Hence, family life at its best will lead to the blossoming of God's love in the hearts of both man and woman, and their happiness will be incomparably enhanced. Then they will give thanks for themselves and for all creation, and because they are the sentient spokespersons for that creation, they will truly be "God's viceregents on earth" of which the Koran speaks: they will become vehicles of God's Compassion and Mercy.

One of the outstanding Sufis who valued women highly was Ibn Arabi, also known as "the Greatest Sheikh." Ibn Arabi always adhered to the letter of the Koran, so it is unthinkable that he should have strayed beyond the bounds of Koranic doctrine.

Because the creative action (of reproduction) takes place inside women's bodies, says Ibn Arabi, they are closer to the Creator than men. "In some respects," he says, "woman is superior to man, and is his equal in most other cases" (*Futuhat*). He subscribes to the association between a male heaven and a female earth as a poetic metaphor, which was also prevalent in ancient cultures. He also indicates that in all matters concerning women, one female witness is worth two fair male witnesses.

Ibn Arabi is of the opinion that the differences between men and women are few and negligible. These differences give priority sometimes to one side and sometimes to the other, balancing each other out when taken all together. Deficiencies in both men and women with respect to each other are compensated by surpluses in other areas. Thus a balance is struck between the sexes, and the meaning of the Prophetic Tradition: "Men are half of an apple, women the other half" becomes manifest. Ibn Arabi also notes, again correctly in terms of the Arabic, that the Prophet's words: "You are all shepherds and responsible for your flock" applies to men and women alike.

"In the name of God, the Compassionate, the Merciful," begins the Koran. Both the attributes of Compassion and Mercy in Arabic derive, as Ibn Arabi points out, from the root RHM. The significance of this derivation is especially brought out in the case of the Merciful (*rahim*)—it also means "the female womb," which encompasses, protects, and nurtures the baby within. The Merciful is etymologically derived from the Compassionate (*rahman*), and points to a higher concentration of grace. Indeed, all that exists is brought into being and nourished by the attribute of Compassion, whereas the gift of Paradise—the attribute of Mercy—is reserved for the faithful as a special dispensation from God. Believers thus benefit from both Divine Names, one universally extensive and the other intensive. Women are the honored, if unwitting, bearers of a Divine Name. And it is a cosmic divine mystery that the universe and Paradise are brought into existence and sustained by Compassion and Mercy respectively, both feminine attributes.

Ibn Arabi indicates, furthermore, that women are not necessarily ruled out when men are mentioned, for women may possess attributes that we customarily associate with men. Gender references in a language are not always gender-specific. In English, too, bravery—to take an example—is a characteristic normally associated with masculinity. But can we thereby claim that there are no women who are brave, that Joan of Arc, for instance, was not brave?[136] Likewise, the female gender in speech does not necessarily exclude men, for there are men who share attributes we ordinarily link with femininity.

Contemporary Societies

Esmé Wynne-Tyson has put our modern predicament in a nutshell, arguing that involvement in the world should not lead to the loss of women's essential qualities:

> It is quite certain that if woman continues to regard unceasing materialistic labour as a proof of progress, she will not only be unable to share [increased] leisure but will have no time to civilize—even when she is capable of it—either her husband or children. Moreover, by such blind acquiescence to the plans of our modern Pharaohs to turn the world into a large State-termitary, she is rapidly losing her soul, or divinity... : her sense of spirituality, her natural response to beauty, her innate womanliness most perfectly expressed in selfless maternal love.[137]

Women have been oppressed in almost all societies. In some societies they have been regarded as wicked or socially inferior for hundreds of years, and today they are reacting against this. What is right in their cause should be acknowledged, without, however, going to the extreme of—in Hobbes' words—"the war of all against all." For in the end, men and women have to live together. Can we separate them, with a nation composed entirely of men on the one hand and a nation of women on the other? We cannot.

In our age, with all its liberties and sexual revolutions, women are still looked upon as sex objects. In fact, the rhetoric of sexual liberation has been used to give women a false sense of freedom, and they have been conned into thinking that family ties and marriage are chains. As a result, men have become free to take their fill of women without any of the responsibilities imposed on men by family life. Women are reduced to objects, to be cast off after men have satisfied their sexual pleasures. This is nothing but a reemergence of the Age of Ignorance—to such an extent, in fact, that female infanticide is still practiced today in China, as it was in pre-Islamic times in Arabia. Further, as women have gained their economic independence they have felt more at liberty to terminate a marital relationship, as if economic support were all there is to marriage. The result is the increase of single-parent families. The delicate connective tissue—a home, a father and mother—without which a human being cannot be nurtured properly is being sundered. Karen Armstrong has drawn attention to the fact that our "view of women and the relations between the sexes is confused. We preach equality and liberation, but at the same time exploit and degrade women in advertising, pornography, and much popular entertainment..."[138]

From the extreme of belittling and vilifying woman for centuries, we have today fallen into the opposite extreme of unlimited sexual freedom. Beneath all the rhetoric masquerading as rights and liberties, however, there still lurks the same cynical disregard for the well-being of women. For example, Sweden is a country that has moved earliest and farthest in the direction of sexual freedom. Here, Hans Nestius, National Chairman for Swedish Sex Information, summarizes the results as follows:

> The laws that existed against pornography in the past represented hypocrisy, narrow-mindedness, and the oppression of sexual life. We wanted to open the door a bit and let some air and light come in. We hoped that sex would cease to be something mysterious. We expected that freedom would at first create a wave of pornography, but that in time, the initial interest would be lost and everything would return to normal. But after a decade had passed, it was clear that events had progressed contrary to expectations. Today the pornography market has become much richer than what it used to be. Furthermore, rape and prostitution have increased along with deviant relationships. Another development has been the intensive and extensive rise of alcoholism.[139]

Today as never before, female nakedness is used for the advertisement of products and universally abused by the media. Organized crime has progressively escalated what is known as the "white-slave trade." In our supposedly emancipated civilization, women and the display of their bodies have become a commercial commodity. This has to be recognized for what it is: a crime against humanity. Illicit sex, the prostitution even of little girls, has become a large-scale industry. The hypocrisy of this situation is obvious: the sexual exploitation of the female is depicted as freedom, leading to her acquiescence in a plot that enslaves her to the most degrading existence.

The point is that the degradation of women is the degradation of humanity—of men and children as well. Women should be restored to their rightful stature, and supplied with their God-given rights—rights recognized by Islam fourteen centuries ago.

Conclusion

Finally, we have to consider whether, or to what extent, women's present status is part of a much deeper problem. Is their predicament the disease itself, or only one of its symptoms? The last few centuries have witnessed the progressive "desacralization" of humanity—the withering away of the Sacred, the disenchantment of the world, its "ungottierung" or "un-Godification" as expressed in German.

Yet if the divine exists within human beings, they are, by this very act, turning their backs on their center, their source. When the connection between the heart and the mind is severed, the heart ceases to inform the actions of the mind. It is replaced by the ego—the egotistical self (*nafs*), as the Sufis call it—which then commandeers the mind to fulfill its every whim. Hence, what we observe today are the results of the ego unleashed: global exploitation, the dehumanization of humanity, viewing each other (and hence, women) as objects rather than God's subjects; the devastation of nature; mass culture and commodity markets exploiting the basest in human desires, the reduction of human beings to their lowest common denominator as "consumers," and nothing more.

It is precisely here that Islam vouchsafes a fuller meaning for humanity. It reiterates the truth, first expressed by Jesus, that "man does not live by bread alone," that humans were meant for higher things. Now that we have reached the zenith of material affluence, it calls on us to complement these riches with *spiritual* wealth, in order that the full meaning of "civilization" may be realized.

The essence of Islamic law is *protection*. And the Moslem, as defined by the Prophet, is "a person whose hands, sexuality, and tongue do not harm others." The aim of this protection is for people to become fully human—both by being safe from the injury of others, and by not injuring them—and thus to realize God's purpose in creating human beings on earth.

Our problems can be traced to the lack of the feminine principle of Mercy, the life principle, the ability for Compassion, the protector of life unto death. God's manifestation of this principle needs to come into the world now, and to be realized in each human heart. The ideal relationship between the sexes is one in which one woman and one man are committed to each other, and in which that commitment is tested as true by life. Both support and protect each other in such a blessed relationship, and are both the teachers and students of one another.

Islam can help us by reminding us that marriage is the proper environment for this togetherness. Its instructions to both man and woman are simple: "Don't oppress your spouse, don't hurt your spouse's feelings." Islam's counsel is always mutual tenderness, gentleness, and concern. "Live with them in kindness," enjoins the Koran; "even if you dislike them, perhaps you dislike something in which God has placed much good" (4:19).

The family is the basic unit for social and spiritual development, the theater for clean relations and service and spiritual progress. In Islam, spirituality is not a separate "discipline" at odds with having a spouse and children. Marriage is the proper format for the sacred task of raising a family: one of the clearest signs of God's mercy and magnificence is revealed in the actual difficulty and selflessness of this act, if endured.

But further, Islam also invites us to rediscover the wellsprings of sacredness within ourselves—to apply brakes on the ego run rampant, to replace the hegemony of egotism over the mind with cooperation between mind and heart; to *stop harming others* by treating them as puppets of our egos, and to become full human beings.

This also points to the inability of most "Islamic" nations to truly live up to the wealth of their own tradition. Perhaps we all have something to learn from Islam—some of us by examining it anew, some of us by rediscovering its still-untapped resources, and some of us by coming to it for the first time.

❧

This chapter reviewed the ways in which Western media have mischaracterized the relationship between Islam and women, especially historically, and it also provided an important critique of the many misuses and misinterpretations of Islamic Law (by extremist groups) with respect to women. Religion (in this case, Islam) is just one of the components that constitute a culture, and if other cultural elements predominate, the rules of religion may not be sufficient to correct them.

In the next section, we will shift our attention to the esoteric (or mystical) aspects of Islam, paying particular attention to the path traditionally considered the Sufic path.

PART II

❧

The Esoteric Path: Sufism

Introduction to Sufism

Although there is a great deal of interest about *jihad, sharia,* democracy, and women's rights in the West these days when it comes to Islam, I can testify that these are nonproblems for the average Moslem, who is too busy trying to survive in daily life. Hence, some of the preceding material was brought up only to lay certain widespread misconceptions to rest. With that out of the way, we finally arrive at what I *really* want to write about, which is the spiritual/esoteric/mystical dimension of Islam. And I am not alone in considering this matter important, for this is also the concern of the widespread Moslem masses, who are able to withstand the vicissitudes of life through the strength and nourishment they draw from Islamic spirituality—Sufism, for short. Some have called this "folk Islam" to distinguish it from the "legalistic" Islam of intellectual elites, but it deals with issues so sublime, and simultaneously so wondrous, that many of its adherents are themselves intellectuals or well-educated.[140] So we may say that *this* is the true Islam, rather than anything that might be advocated by fanatics or madmen (by which I intend both the angry and the insane).

As we have seen, the history of Islam shows that it is a religion of tolerance—Islam itself is not in need of reform, Moslems are. At its best, according to the Master, Islam concerns itself with politics only to the extent that it seeks to build a virtuous society: ethics should be the basis of politics, as indeed of all human conduct. The core meaning of *jihad* is thus "to struggle or make war against the Base Self," learning to rein in our desires. True Islam, then, consists of both the exoteric and the esoteric path, a combination rarely seen in practice. In a flash, we are transported

189

back to the days of the Prophet, when the esoteric had not yet been segregated from the exoteric and given a separate name, when the two constituted a seamless whole. As one of the early Sufis remarked, "Formerly, Sufism was a reality without a name."

The way to accomplish this combination is to follow Sufic principles without omitting the well-known observances, because although Islam is highly rational, it considers the mystical path (historically associated with Sufism) an integral aspect of the religion. More explicitly, in Islam rationality and mysticism are not mutually exclusive.[141] The philosophy of Ibn Arabi, a Sufi, still commands respect among today's intellectuals. Because the exoteric path is in full view, it tends to be considered the whole of Islam (even by many Moslems). But as great as its emphasis on knowledge is, Islamic culture has always valued wisdom—the mystical/contemplative/spiritual component—more highly. Both the heart and mind are integral to this path and when they are properly balanced, the misinterpretations of militant extremism and related branches can be seen for the false paths they are. The goal of the Islamic path (shared with many other religions) is direct connection with God and in this sense, Love is the core of Islam. The world-famous poetry of Rumi, of Saadi and Hafiz (both of Shiraz), are but a drop in the ocean of love that is Islamic spirituality.

In this section, I will elaborate upon the Sufic path (which I first introduced in my book, *The Station of No Station*). As I mentioned earlier, Sufis are properly followers of the Middle Way (combining the inner and outer path) and as such, represent the path of true Islam. (One should be wary of pseudo "Sufis" who dismiss or disregard the exoteric path of external rules and behavior.) The outer pilgrimage to Mecca, for example, prefigures the inner journey to the heart. As the Grand Saint Abdulqader Gilani says, "Gnosis is attained by uncovering the dark veil of the Base Self from the mirror of the heart, and by purifying the heart." (Gilani, *The Mystery of Mysteries.*)

The mystical portion of Islam must always be preceded or accompanied by study and implementation of the Koran and the Way—they form the strong foundation and establish the self-control and moral character needed to contain the more mystical theories and practices described here. Salutary moral conduct is an absolute prerequisite to further spiritual growth. Although Islam is rooted in the direct connection between the believer and God, the tie between master and disciple becomes more important in these mystical stages of Islam. The master is the experienced mountain climber who guides the seeker in avoiding pitfalls on the climb to the Summit of Unification, so it is quite essential to have a capable teacher during that climb.

The Spiritual Journey

The Spiritual Journey is the journey of a disciple or aspirant (*murid*) to God, Who is the Truth or Absolute Reality. The person who has embarked on this journey (*thuluq*) is called the Wayfarer or Seeker (*thaliq*).

For the person wishing to make this journey, the first and by far the most important prerequisite is a guide. Hence, the first thing to be done is to find a wise and mature Teacher or Master (*murshid:* Enlightener). To start off on this journey without a guide is like climbing a strange mountain at night without a light. One cannot see where s/he is going or where to step. There is no telling where a poisonous snake might bite him or her or where s/he will be attacked by a predatory beast. An unbridgeable chasm will yawn under him or her at the least expected moment. Without help, it is almost impossible to survive such a journey intact.

The wise teacher, on the other hand, has already performed the journey and survived. Further, he has seen and is thoroughly familiar with all the pitfalls and dangers of the route. He guides his disciple along the path with ease, and sees to it that s/he reaches the Summit of Unification safe and sound.

If you ask: "Where, in this day and age, is such a person to be found?" the fact is that although rare, such people exist in every age. Needless to say, fake gurus abound. As Niyazi Misri said, "Don't follow every teacher, he will lead your path astray." But it cannot be denied that true masters also exist, as I myself discovered in my own Master's presence.

The Goal: Becoming a Perfect Human

It may be appropriate at the outset to give some indication of what the goal of the journey is. In brief, it is nothing less than the total transformation or transfiguration of the human personality. To put this as simply as possible, there is another, hidden "you" that inheres in you. This other "you," the real "you," is wonderful, beautiful, and adorable, and the objective is to bring it out into the open, to realize it, to transfer it from the potential to the actual. Anyone in whom this inner "you" is born (has emerged) is called "twice-born." The metamorphosis of a cat-erpillar—through a chrysalis—into a butterfly is an apt metaphor here. In this process, the master is midwife to the disciple's rebirth.

"Know thyself," said Socrates, and this was also the inscription at the entrance to the Temple at Delphi. The Aristotelian injunction, "Realize yourself," and the Humanist injunction, "Perfect yourself," were but dif-ferent expressions of the same idea.

Suppose we ask: what is the highest achievement of which a human is capable? Obviously, the highest achievement for a scientist is to be like Newton or Einstein—at least, to win the Nobel Prize. The highest achieve-ment for an artist is to become as famous as, say, a Picasso or a Michelangelo. For a writer, it is to be mentioned in the same breath as a Goethe or Tolstoy, and so on.

We next ask: what is the greatest achievement that *person as a human being* is capable of? What is the full realization, the perfection, of our potential as a human being?

According to the Sufis, it is to become a Perfect Human, a Friend of God, saint, or sage. In English, Universal Human or Unitary Human appear to be equally appropriate terms. Furthermore, this is a stage that lies even beyond genius; if the greatest names of science, art, literature, philosophy, statesmanship, and so on, are mountain peaks in compari-son with the rest of humanity, the sage is an even higher mountain peak than them. (This excludes the prophets, since prophethood ended with Mohammed. Sainthood is the only option now available to humans.)

The Socratic dictum "Know thyself" finds its culmination in the Pro-phetic Saying: "He who knows himself knows his Lord." Moreover, in the Koranic statement: "I created human beings only so that they should worship Me" (51:56), "worship" has been interpreted by the saints as "knowledge" (Gnosis), since the worship of God leads to knowledge of God. And there is no greater experience or achievement for a human being than to know—not superficially or theoretically, but *truly* to know—his or her Lord, to be a "God-realized" person. In such a person, a new, altruistic personality has congealed and crystallized, like a lily or lotus emerging from a muddy pond, or butter out of milk.

Indeed, those who have successfully completed the journey are re-ferred to as "the Transformed" (*abdal*, pl. *budala*). The term is derived from the Arabic *badal*, which affords some further insight into what is involved. The latter, meaning "price," indicates that these persons have cultivated a nonegotistical personality, and have given everything for the sake of God and His Prophet: they have "paid the price." What they receive in return for this payment are God and His Prophet themselves, meaning that they have become clothed in the divine attributes of God, have become invested with a Godly morality, and have achieved a Mo-hammedan (i.e., perfect) purity, morality, spirituality, and personality. This is why they are also called "Perfect Humans" (*insan al-kamil*).

Sufism:
The Case of the Cryptic Wineglass
——————— ❧ ———————

(The seeker in Islam, one who has entered a more mystical path, is attempting to transform the self through love, to become what is called the Perfect Human. The reward of this path is a vision that is indescribable, though the Latin American writer Jorge Luis Borges attempted it in his short story "The Aleph." This transformative vision of love—a state called "Attainment," among other things, by the Sufis—is made possible by opening one's heart, controlling one's Base Self, and losing one's ego.)

Aleph and the Transfinite

Jorge Luis Borges, the Latin American writer whose work foreshadowed the coming of the World Wide Web and the pocket computer in *The Book of Sands*, and whose interest in Sufism, Cabalism, metaphysics, and mysticism, has been the subject of more than one study, also wrote a gripping tale of uncanny power, "The Aleph," which describes a state the Sufi seeker may attain.

In this story, "Borges" (the first-person narrator) is first alerted to the existence of the Aleph through Carlos Argentino, whose house has a cellar containing one. "An Aleph," writes Borges by way of introduction, "is one of the points in space containing all points...the place where, without any possible confusion, all places in the world are found, seen from every angle."

195

The incredulous narrator is led by the cranky Argentino down the stairs, and told to fix his gaze on the nineteenth step. He has a moment's hesitation where he suspects treachery and fears for his life. "Then," he writes,

> I saw the Aleph.

> In that gigantic instant I saw millions of delightful and atrocious acts; none astonished me more than the fact that all of them together occupied the same point, without superposition and without transparency....The Aleph's diameter must have been about two or three centimeters, but Cosmic Space was within it, without diminution of size. Each object was infinite objects, for I clearly saw it from all points in the universe.

Here, Borges embarks on a listing of the multifarious things he saw; to my knowledge, the only thing to compare with it in all of modern literature is the vision in Hermann Hesse's *Siddhartha*. "[I] cried," writes Borges, "because my eyes had seen that conjectural and secret object whose name men usurp but which no man has gazed on: the inconceivable universe. I felt infinite veneration, infinite compassion."[142]

This, of course, is not the first time this overwhelming concept has been described. One is reminded of the gypsy madam's crystal ball, and Borges himself mentions the mirror of Alexander, the mirror of Merlin, "the septuple goblet of Kai Josru." By this route we are led back into Persian mythology, and to the crystal wineglass of Jem (or Jemshid).

According to legend, Jem was the inventor of wine, and his wineglass was capable of displaying to view all eternity and infinity at once. According to a variant form, the goblet is made of a mixture of seven metals. It is known as *jaam-i jem* (rhymes with "john-a gem," substituting an "m" for the "n"). Let us trace the story of the wineglass through Fariduddin Attar, the Sufi poet, who deals with it in *The Book of the Divine*.

According to Attar, the Persian king Kai Khosru somehow came into possession of Jem's Wineglass, and was watching the secrets of the seven climes, and the courses of the seven stars (note the repetition of the number seven). "There was nothing, whether good or bad," continues Attar, "that remained hidden from him. He wanted to see the Cup of Jem, to watch the entire universe in it." And so he did, but by and by he came to a curious realization: although he could see everything in the universe through the goblet, he could not see *the goblet itself* therein. As he was pondering this mystery, an inscription appeared in the goblet. It said:

"How can you see us in us? We have passed away entirely from ourselves. Whatever you see, is not us. You can see everything through us, but it is impossible to see us in between."

Reading these words, the king understands that his kingdom itself is naught, and renounces his crown and his throne. He enters a cave with the goblet. There, he draws Jem's Wineglass to his bosom, takes refuge in the Fortress of Nonbeing, dons the Cloak of Invisibility and is lost forever from human cognition.

Such is the story. Now for the interpretation from a Sufic perspective: "Know," says the great Persian Sufi poet Sanai in his *Food for Seekers,* "know that the cup of Jem is your heart. If you want to see the cosmos, it is possible to see all things in that heart. The eye of the head sees bodies composed of the elements; only the Eye of the Heart can see what is hidden. First open the Eye of your Heart, watch everything afterwards."

The Wineglass, then, is a symbol for the heart of the Islamic mystic, the Sufi. As René Guénon has shown, the cave is also a metaphor of the heart. Hence, we should search for the Aleph, not on the nineteenth step of a cellar staircase, but in our own hearts. Nevertheless, the staircase, implying spiritual elevation or "Ascension," has its own significance. In classical Islamic cosmology, the number of worlds created by God is eighteen (or eighteen thousand, a thousand subuniverses to each universe); nineteen points beyond them all, and was considered a sacred number in the ancient Near East. The sevenfold nature of the goblet derives from the fact that only after the spiritual journey through the Seven Stages of Selfhood is finished does the heart "become" the Wineglass—that is, it displays the entire universe to view.

For this to happen, however, the Sufi must first experience the transformation, or transmutation, of the self (the crude, raw self) to Self: he or she must be lost to this world. Not only must the world be unable to find him, but *he himself must be unable to find himself* (or her herself), having found God. One cannot find God without losing one's self, one's individual selfhood. "Jane Smith" cannot find God without first dissolving and losing Jane Smith (the Fortress of Nonbeing). Hence, when Jane Smith rests in Witnessing (Observation), she beholds God's infinite beauty; she experiences the incredible fullness—effulgence—of God. In that moment, she is invisible, she is nowhere to be found, she cannot be seen—which is the actual meaning of the Cloak of Invisibility.

The greatest obstacle to the clear perception of God is your own individuality (or ego). Get rid of it, and you will see what was always already there to begin with! Moreover, when you look into your heart, you will see the universe and everything that is in it—which, of course, is easier said than done.

So why don't we see anything, let alone the universe, when we look into our hearts? It is because our hearts have become clouded over with concerns other than God. Think of a glass full of murky water. It is impossible to see anything in it. Or if the glass itself has become opaque, one cannot see whether there is any liquid in it or not. But if you purify your heart—of everything other than God, that is—it will become crystal clear, and will contain the divine water of life. Then, like a crystal ball, it will reveal what is on the other side. Because God's unmanifest Essence cannot be seen in the observable universe, it is through His Attributes— which manifest themselves as the cosmos—that He becomes known.

But why a wineglass, exactly? Because "wine," in Sufism—but especially in Persian Sufism—is the symbol of divine love, the love of God. This love is heady; it makes your head spin. Like ordinary wine, it makes you drunk, but it is worlds apart from ordinary wine. It is wine divine; it is the ambrosia of God, to which nothing can be compared.[143] Hence, ordinary wine can only be a simile for it, and an immeasurably inadequate one at that. The wineglass, in that case, is a metaphor for the pure heart full of the love of God.

Human Beings and God

Human plans for ourselves and God's plans for us are two different things. We wish to make the best of our time in this fleeting world, to have a good time before our hour strikes. God, too, wishes for us to use our time wisely, productively—but humans and God differ in how this is to be done. Humans, knowing little, not knowing where we have come from nor where we are going, try to act in accordance with their own limited preconceptions. God, knowing why He created the universe, knowing why and to what purpose He created us, has an infinitely better knowledge of what we should do, and why. It is in our own best self-interest to heed the counsel of God. We are fortunate indeed that God, the Lord of the Worlds, should have bothered at all to guide humanity every now and then. We are even luckier to possess a foolproof method revealed by God leading to felicity. Not heeding it is tantamount to self-condemnation. Life is short, and we shall not have this opportunity forever. It is better to act wisely now than to make the wrong choice and regret it in the end.

Seeking the Wineglass is not for the timid, the lazy, or the faint of heart. Just as not everyone can become an Einstein or Mozart, neither can everyone become a saint or a Friend of God. Nevertheless, even a small step in the right direction helps. Even if you cannot achieve total liberation, you have taken one step closer to salvation.

Here we encounter a problem. Historically, the path of the solitary saint has been quite different and much more exacting than that of the ordinary person, resulting in extreme asceticism, monkery, and monastic retreat. Nevertheless, it stands to reason that there must exist a path that leads to the desired endpoint. In other words, the path should be the same, and the difference should be one of degree, not of direction. If you and I set out to climb a mountain, and you make it to the top, I should be able to get there too if only I follow in your footsteps—but I may not be resourceful or diligent enough to do so. Yet I should still end up higher than I was before.

This is what the methods of Islam address. Islam is, by and large, for the ordinary person, yet the ordinary person, if s/he really applies him- or herself to it, can become a mystic or saint merely by practicing its methods with greater intensity (but not necessarily greater quantity—a healthy balance is all-important). The path itself is not different. Paradise is a way station on the road that leads to God, it does not lie at the end of a different road. Hence, however much you invest your energy, so shall you reap.

At the same time, it should be realized that "effortless Enlightenment" and "instant Nirvana" are not viable options. Even if it may be easier today, those who wish to conquer Mt. Everest should be prepared to expend an effort at least comparable to that of Hillary and Tenzing. And even then, it is only by the grace of God that one finally reaches the top.

Courtesy, the Golden Thread Between Exoteric and Esoteric

Perhaps because Islam has had a bad press lately, there is a tendency to dissociate Sufism from Islam, and to treat it as an entirely separate entity. Some works on Sufism, for example, scarcely make any reference to Islam. Unfortunately, this is misleading. Islam as a religion does not deserve the derisive treatment it receives in the media, especially since it is at one with the media in condemning wrong action, even if such action comes from its own adherents. As I said earlier, where terrorism (unjust murder of innocents) begins, Islam ends.

As also mentioned earlier, Islam comprises an exoteric and an esoteric aspect. The exoteric aspect, composed of exterior rules and regulations, a code of moral conduct and psychophysical practices, is called the Divine Law (*sharia*).[144] The esoteric side, which deals with the interiority, the spiritual aspect of human life, is called Sufism. Properly, *Islam is the Law plus Sufism,* the exoteric plus the esoteric. However, because its esotericism is accessed with difficulty while its exotericism is in full display, there is a tendency to equate Islam with the exoteric Law alone, a terminological error.

In fact, the Law and Sufism—or exoteric Islam and Sufism—are related to each other as body and soul are related. Without Sufism, the Law alone would be a lifeless corpse. Without the Law, Sufism would be a disembodied spirit—a ghost. It is the combination of both that transforms them into a living, breathing entity.

It is well-known that those who have faith and do good works will be rewarded in the afterlife, and unbelievers who do ill will be punished. But this is not all. A golden thread that leads beyond this simple Heaven-Hell dualism is woven into the very fabric of the Koran. This thread is for the Elect, for those who are not satisfied with mere gardens of Paradise and aspire to greater things. Although all human beings will be subject to judgment, the Elect can, by individual struggle, attain nobler goals.

But it must be added at once: how best may we serve the deeper meaning of the Koran? By being as faithful as possible to its exoteric meaning. For the literal meaning is the shell, the wrapping, that protects the soft kernel inside. The two are related to each other as form and content are related; both are indispensable.

Therefore, one cannot have Sufism without the Law. The Divine Law provides the foundation upon which rises the superstructure of Sufism. Pull out the base from underneath, and the whole edifice would collapse. The moral and ethical principles, the external observations, are essential if any true spiritual progress is to be achieved. If, for example, the spiritual development of a person disregards the rights of others, if it throws moral conduct to the winds, the result will be a journey into narcissism, a horizontal inflation of the ego rather than a vertical elevation of the Self. The Italian Professor of Turcology, Anna Masala, who has spent many years in association with Sufis, is quite unequivocal in viewing the Law as a prerequisite of true spirituality. As she says of the desire to study the more mystical aspects of Islam, "One must first learn and understand Islam, and then make the transition to Sufism."

In particular, the fact that the concept of original sin does not exist has profound implications for Islam. (Even though Adam and Eve were relocated from heaven to earth, thus initiating the great adventure of humanity, this did not result in an irrevocable genetic pathology visited upon their progeny for the rest of time.[145]) Because of this, there is no need for a Savior, or the train of associated concepts that follows in its wake: the sacrificial death of the Savior, salvation of the community through this supreme act of sacrifice, sacraments such as the Eucharist, or a priesthood with the authority to administer such sacraments. As one study notes about Islam: "Those who lead prayers, preach sermons, and interpret the law do so by virtue of their superior religious knowledge and scholarship rather than because of any special powers or prerogatives conferred by ordination."[146]

In a saying attributed to him, the Prophet of God declared: "Ignorance is the mother of all evils." In the Islamic view, the fundamental problem of the human condition is ignorance rather than sin. Human beings are viewed as essentially good but, because of ignorance, easily prone to error. It is this weakness that Islam sets out to remedy, by fortifying us with knowledge.

The most important thing in Sufism is not visions or spiritual experiences or an elated state of mind. The most important thing is salutary moral conduct, which is honed to a degree of refinement where it surpasses pure and simple ethical behavior, and becomes what the Sufis call Courtesy, or gracious conduct (*adab*) (as mentioned earlier—see Appendix A). This is the epitome of gentle(wo)manly behavior towards all creatures, to act with consideration toward everything, nobility of soul; to extend tolerance and compassion to all God's creatures out of our love for Him. No spiritual experience, no matter how lofty or impressive, can substitute for courteous conduct, for it is this conduct which certifies the experience's authenticity. And it is only when it is severely tested that it becomes clear whether this courtesy is permanent, or whether it bleaches at the first wash. It is easy to be magnanimous when one is in a happy mood, but it becomes extremely difficult to maintain this attitude when faced with hardships. Thus, self- and spiritual development is grounded in moral conduct from the very first step.

This is one of the reasons why alcohol is prohibited in Islam. The Arabic original word for wine is *hamr*, which, however, has the meaning of "dulling one's senses and consciousness." In other words, not just wine or alcohol but anything that pulls a veil over one's attention, one's awareness (such as narcotics), falls into this category. The main result of dulled mental acumen is the failure to discriminate between right and wrong, and hence to avoid unethical conduct while drunk. One is then open to the hazard of flagrantly violating all moral inhibitions and regretting the outcome. Sufism aims at reaching a higher consciousness, not a lower one.

"Contact" Between Human and Divine

Although we live in a society that has neglected the spiritual dimension of knowledge, the inner, spiritual, side of human beings just *will not* be repressed. The more we try to drive it out, the more insistently it keeps coming back to us. This is not just because it is an integral part of our existence, but rather because it is our fundamental reason for being in this universe, on this planet. According to the Koran, God created us only that we should worship Him, and a relative of the Prophet —as well as Sufis ever since—interpreted this to mean that we should know Him, since God has no need for our worship and worship only serves to bring us closer to Him.

Take, for example, the case of Carl Sagan, the great astrophysicist who passed away in 1996. Many of us were exposed to our first serious treatment of the possibility of extraterrestrial life through a work he co-authored with I. M. Shklovskii, *Intelligent Life In The Universe* (1966). Also a peerless popularizer of science, Sagan could never bring himself to a faith in God; he died an agnostic. Yet *Contact* (1985), his only novel, deals with the perennial concerns and condition of humankind under the guise of being a story about extraterrestrials.

The movie *Contact* (1997), filmed by Robert Zemeckis and dedicated "for Carl," is replete with bleed-throughs that make eminent sense when viewed from a spiritual standpoint. The movie opens with the earth seen from space. We are treated to an Ascension (Arabic *miraj*) that moves out through the solar system, beyond the rings of Saturn, goes out to loci of star formation shot by the Hubble Space Telescope, out to myriads of galaxies revealed through the Hubble Deep Field study, and ends with "Let there be Light."

It then cuts to the childhood of Ellie Arroway, who is searching for her dead mother over the airwaves of ham radio. Then her father dies of a heart attack, and contacting outer space becomes an obsession for her. She grows up to become a radio astronomer, an agnostic like Sagan himself, who will not believe anything unsupported by scientific evidence. Angels (beings from inner space) are out; aliens (beings from outer space) are in.

Dr. Arroway's research is sponsored by Hadden, a reclusive magnate, formerly an engineer, who does not live on earth (he resides either on a private jet or, later on, in the space station *Mir*). Finally, she intercepts a radio transmission from Vega, a star twenty-seven light-years from earth. Once the code is deciphered, it turns out that the extraterrestrials are sending the plans for a transporter.

To summarize the story, Arroway represents humanity. The transporter is a contraption made of rotating rings, somewhat like the Bohr model of the atom, and a spherical metal capsule housing Arroway is supposed to fall into its center. Inside the capsule is only a seat. The metal hatch seals on her, and she is isolated from the rest of the world. A vibration begins building up; the bottom of the capsule becomes transparent at times. Then she is hurled through a system of "Einstein-Rosen wormholes," but when the armchair breaks off and hits the ceiling she is left in pitch dark and the capsule becomes her tomb.

She then moves to the top, which becomes transparent and reveals a galaxy in all its splendor. Through its reflection in her eyeball we move to a scene where she is descending onto a planet, to a beautiful coast with palm trees, exactly the scene she painted when she was a child. An apparition of her father tells her that the extraterrestrials have selected this mode of communicating with her to make her feel at home. She clocks eighteen hours.

Then the capsule falls into the sea. It has fallen straight through the contraption! As far as those outside are concerned, nothing at all extraordinary has happened. In fact, the experiment might be considered a big failure.

And now Arroway—in an instance of supreme irony (or is it divine justice?)—who once did not believe in claims unsupported by evidence, is *herself* unable to convince others of her experience. The only shred of evidence that speaks in her favor is eighteen hours of recorded static on the monitors.

All this is well and good, and as plausible a scenario of extraterrestrial contact as could be expected. But we can also interpret this from the time-honored (mystical) point of view. Hadden the magnate (hairless and reminiscent of a Buddhist monk) is our heroine's guru, who contacts her from other planes of existence. Her entombment in the capsule is a flashback to the initiation ceremonies of Hermeticism, a precursor of Sufism.[147] The mechanical vibration she experiences is possibly a side effect of an Out-of-Body Experience (OBE). The wormholes are instances of the "space bending (or folding)" (*tayy al-makan*) reported by Sufis.[148] She is left in utter darkness, experiences an "Unveiling," and her spirit (the "inner Arroway") is transported to a place resembling Heaven. Here she meets a being in the guise of her father—in religious traditions, it is well-known that angels can assume human form, perhaps for precisely the same reason as do the hypothesized aliens. She returns to the ordinary world, and is unable to convince anyone else of her experience.

Look at the spiritual traditions of the entire world, and everywhere, for as far back as the mind's eye can see, you will find similar experiences reported in a similar way by human beings from totally different cultural backgrounds. It is not for nothing that more than one critic has remarked the religious overtones of *Contact*. The difference is that today, we transpose the experience into the physical realm. This, however, does not detract from its importance, for it is crying out loud to make us stand up and take notice of it. No matter how much humans deny their spiritual side, it will keep knocking at the door, whether one is an agnostic or an atheist or a free-thinker. All we have to do is sit up and understand the message.

Dare we press the analogy a bit further? The message from outer space is a message from "the Supreme Extraterrestrial;" the incomprehensible alien cipher is the Koran. Once decoded properly, the Koran bears the plans (God's instructions to human beings) for a transporter that will "beam us up" straight to Unity.

Some Contemporary Western Parallels

Both *Contact* and *2001: A Space Odyssey* were produced from a nontheistic, if not overtly atheistic, viewpoint, describing purely physical events or a physical evolution; yet the concerns they give voice to are the perennial concerns of religion, despite the fact that nothing could have been further from the conscious intentions of their creators. What is happening is that the latter are taking valid religious and transcendental metaphors, projecting these onto the physical plane, then conceiving the realization of these shadows. Now these flatland projections may themselves represent valid goals. But they are not the original goals, and they cannot lead to the grander experience.

In the last two centuries, the highest aspirations of our Western culture have coincided with the highest aspirations of the Sufis. The difference is that, because it refuses to acknowledge God, our culture is trapped in a dead end, whereas the Sufis are not—their recognition of God opens up avenues of self-transformation that are otherwise denied.

This brings us, furthermore, to a crucial insight of Sufism: the love of God and the love of others (indeed, of all creation, of which human beings are the acme) are not inimical to each other, but must go hand in hand. Not only that, but denying one leads, in the end, to the inevitable negation of the other: "Love restricted is love denied." *This* is what lies at the root of our failure—we have tried to reach enlightenment without God, or else we have denied the possibility of human perfection (due to the doctrine of original sin). The first leads to the fate of Icarus: his wings of wax are melted by the sun, and he plunges to his doom. As for the second case, one cannot even rise off the ground.

In short, God is both Within and Without. If you do not believe in God, you are not going to search for Him within. And while it's not guaranteed that you will find God if you seek Him, you are definitely *never* going to find Him if you don't search for Him. (As one famous Sufi put it: "Not all who seek God find Him, but those who find Him are only those who seek.") And supposing you don't seek Him—which is quite natural, since this is not everyone's calling—lack of faith in God will cause you to be careless with His Prohibitions, about which God is very particular, leaving you open to error and unprotected by Right Action against negative recompense.

Law, School, Gnosis, Reality

The edifice of Sufism can be compared to a three-story building. The ground floor, the entry level, is the Divine Law (*sharia*). The second floor is the mystical schools and their practices (*tariqa*). The top floor is Gnosis—i.e., learning about God or the knowledge of God (*marifa*), at which point we climb onto the flat roof of the building. This is the takeoff point for the Ascension (*miraj*), for the last lap of the spiritual journey to Ultimate Reality. Hence, the roof and what lies beyond is called "Reality" (*haqiqa*).

We can also conceive of these four levels as primary school, secondary school, high school, and university. Just as there can be no higher education without primary school, there can be no esoteric success without the divine (and moral) law.

The Sufi view of God is that God is both Within and Without; He is the Inward as well as the Outward. Note that there is room here both for the human subject and the divine subject. The human "I" is not God, but somewhere within, deep below the layers of the subconscious, the divine subject exists. The human subject, the individual's consciousness, is a raft floating on an ocean; the entire depth of that ocean separates a person from the Ground of all Being.

On the other hand, if God were purely Inward, that would limit the Illimitable to a single or multiple location; the divine would exist within a human or humans, and nowhere else. This is why God is also the Outward—He pervades the universe and what is beyond. Nevertheless, the place for a human being to discover God is within him- or herself. In the external world, one can discover not God Himself, but only His signs; in the inner world, too, His signs veil God from us. We can draw near God, and God may reveal as many of His signs to us as He pleases; but a human can never become God. When God chooses to reveal His more intimate signs, neither humans nor mountains can survive that blast. This is the story of Moses as related in the Koran (7:143). When Moses pleaded with God on Mount Sinai: "Reveal Yourself," God said: "You cannot see Me. But I shall manifest Myself to the mountain, and if the mountain survives, then you can see Me." Whereupon God manifested Himself, and the mountain shattered. When he came to, Moses begged God's forgiveness, and said: "I am the first of the believers."

Deconstructing the Base Self

Deconstruction has become a byword of postmodern discourse. In recent times, our thinkers have "deconstructed" everything from language to history. Welcome, then, to the ultimate event in Sufism: the deconstruction of the self.[149] By deconstructing the self, I mean that the bad habits of the Base Self need to be willfully deconstructed if we expect to find the polished jewel (also sought by medieval alchemists under the metaphor of "gold"), the Pure Self within, which is at present lying under a mountain of rubbish. Once all traces of the Base Self are deactivated, the Pure or Perfect Self shines forth. In between are discrete stages of selfhood, all with their distinctive characteristics.

Although the stages of self-development have received attention from psychologists in recent years, it is only the mystical thinkers—Ken Wilber among them—who have recognized that there are stages beyond the normal, well-adjusted adult personality. The Sufis have traditionally enumerated seven discrete stages: 1. the Compelling Self (what we have been calling the "Base Self" all along), 2. the Incriminating Self (which blames itself), 3. the Inspired Self (which has begun to receive partial inspirations from the Divine), 4. the Peaceful Self (which has finally arrived at a point where spiritual development is irreversibly secured), 5. the Pleased Self (pleased with his or her Lord), 6. the Pleasing Self (which is pleasing to God), and 7. the Purified or Perfected Self (which is the final stage).

Each stage is distinguished by its own characteristics, which an authentic teacher can monitor in a disciple. (As mentioned earlier, such a journey should never even be contemplated, let alone attempted, without a true teacher. It is said that "When the disciple is ready, the teacher will appear." Until you find one, stick to the normal Prohibitions, Permissions, and practices—the Five Pillars—of Islam.)

If you wish, you can compare the elevation through these stages to climbing a skyscraper.[150] At the base level, you are in the ordinary, everyday world. As you progress upwards, the restrictions on your view fall away, and you can see a farther horizon at each stage of your ascent. When, finally, you arrive at the top, you take in the magnificent beauty of the entire landscape, and are engulfed in spellbound rapture.

Sufism and Gurdjieff

A great deal of information about Sufism has reached the West at various times, some along quite unexpected avenues. George I. Gurdjieff was one of those who acted as a long-unrecognized conveyor of such information, but he was reluctant to reveal his sources.

John G. Bennett devoted most of his life to tracking down the sources of Gurdjieff's wisdom. By the time he wrote *Gurdjieff: Making a New World* (1973), he had identified these as the Masters of Wisdom of Central Asia, the Khwajagan Order that initiated the Naqshbandi branch of the Sufis. Based on information gleaned from the Sufi Master Hasan Shushud of Istanbul, Bennett wrote his last book, *The Masters of Wisdom* (1977). In this book, published posthumously (he died in 1974), he definitively identified the Sufis as Gurdjieff's source—or at least, the source of the essential core of Gurdjieff's multifaceted teachings. To support Bennett's case would require a separate study in itself, so I shall be content to indicate just one of the dead giveaways which demonstrate Gurdjieff's debt to Sufism.

Some time around 1915, Gurdjieff identified three "ways to immortality," these he described as the way of the fakir, the way of the monk, and the way of the yogi. To summarize, the fakir worked on the physical body, the monk chose the path of religious faith and love, and the yogi worked with the mind and knowledge (Gurdjieff must have had the *Raja* and *Jnana* modes of Yoga in mind). All three, Gurdjieff added, required retirement from the world and renunciation of worldly life. This requirement would leave the ordinary person in a hopeless situation in terms of spiritual development, were it not for the fact that a "fourth way" existed. This way, he added, did not require seclusion, but could be practiced under the usual conditions of life, work, and social involvement, without having to go into the hills or the desert.[151] Mysteriously, he described the essence of this way as follows: "what substances he needs for his aims...*can be introduced into the organism from without if it is known how to do it.*"[152]

What could this cryptic method be? Gurdjieff leaves few clues as to its nature. We are left in the dark, until we learn from Annemarie Schimmel of the Sufic technique of *rabita,* wherein a "tie" or "connection" is established between master and disciple,[153] enabling the transfer—or download—of spiritual power or *baraka* into the disciple's heart. Establishing "contact" is mentioned as *rabitu* in the Koran (3:200), but almost never interpreted—due to lack of knowledge—in the sense described here. (Schimmel also gives an alternate technical term, *tawajjuh,* i.e., concentration of the disciple upon the master and/or vice versa.) This is a trademark of the Sufi tradition and something very specific[154]—not to be confused with the ordinary teacher/student tie, which, of course, occurs in many traditions. As we have seen, Sufism does not counsel becoming a recluse; it advises us to be *in* the world but not *of* the world, to remain aloof from the ebb and flow of daily life.

This single example should suffice to show that Gurdjieff was deeply indebted to the Sufis for his information, but he was so reticent in divulging his sources that it took John Bennett most of his life to track down and identify the roots.

Paranormal Powers and Other Distractions Along the Path

Having first been led to religion and mysticism partly via the scientific study of the paranormal, I can testify that this is not the best route to approach the subject. There are two reasons for this. The first is that paranormal phenomena cannot be demonstrated conclusively, at any rate to the satisfaction of hard-boiled critics. Every paranormal event is subjected to the difficult test: "extraordinary claims demand extraordinary evidence," and to my knowledge there has not been a single survivor to date. Nor can there be. For, whereas the total amount of evidence that can be produced for a particular event is necessarily finite, one can always consider this insufficient and demand more. The limit of the latter process tends to infinity, so that some people will never be convinced of the authenticity of paranormal events, no matter what. Additionally, in our day, stage magic and technological fixes enable us to fake such feats with comparative ease. For readers of this skeptical persuasion, there is nothing more to be said in this respect.

Second, for readers who do attach credence to such phenomena, it should be said that even if they are true, paranormal events are still not the avenue of choice for a proper approach to Sufism. It is much better approached through a levelheaded attitude that emphasizes morality, good manners, and serving one's fellow human beings.

It is accepted as a matter of course, for example, that psychic phenomena may be experienced with increasing frequency by the Seeker during progress on the Path. (The powers that manifest themselves in this way are called *karama* by the Sufis and *siddhi*s in Yoga.) Far from attaching importance to these, however, the disciple is advised to ignore them, since they are only signposts on the road leading to an immeasurably greater and grander goal. Under no circumstances should they be confused with the destination. They may be considered as data reflecting the level of attainment a person has reached, and nothing more. They are mere byproducts of a largely involuntary nature, spontaneous spin-offs, and rarely under conscious control by the individual. For this reason, many saints have regarded such uncontrolled manifestations of extraordinary powers as positively shameful. They can also engender a false sense of ego and power in a person, leading to the loss of whatever ground had been previously gained.

The way to travel this course is through meekness and humility, through healthy morals, salutary conduct, self-effacement, and being socially useful to others (helping all beings, in fact). Aggrandizement of the ego through the display of so-called "powers," or being fascinated or obsessed by them, is a hindrance that can not only retard progress, but even nullify it entirely.

Moderate Intake of Food

In order to progress on the Path, one should apply the techniques discussed elsewhere in this book—mainly, the Five Pillars of Islam, among which Formal Prayer has the highest priority. However, these cannot be complete without another ingredient of prime importance: hunger. It is not just fasting we are talking about here, but light food intake (ditto for drink) at normal times as well (not to mention short hours of sleep). This does not mean an extreme diet that exhausts the body and causes more harm than good, but eating and drinking sparingly.

Science supports this admonition to eat sparingly. In recent years, experiments on rodents have shown not only that their life span is improved by almost a third through low food ingestion, but that the risk of cancer is also significantly reduced.[155] These, however, are only the physical effects easiest to observe.

The discoveries of modern science have their correlates in the spiritual realm and can be viewed as metaphors for spiritual events. This is the true meaning of "hidden science" (*ilm ladunni*), and we here reach an understanding where all knowledge or science—physical and spiritual—is one. This is a higher form of knowledge that has manifestations or shadows—projections—in both the physical and spiritual worlds.

Black holes, supernovae, the metamorphosis of insects, these and other discoveries all have their precise correlates in the Knowledge of the Self. One such example, relevant here, is the method that led to the recent resounding success in cloning experiments.[156]

To recall that method briefly, cells were starved of nutrients until they entered a latent, quiescent state. It is well-known that, although each cell in an organism contains the entire genetic blueprint, i.e., all the DNA-coded information to reconstruct any part—or even the whole—of the organism, it loses the ability to do so once these cells are differentiated to form a hand, a toe, or a liver. Only specific genes are now activated, and all the others are switched off. The great discovery of the Scottish group was to dedifferentiate the cells and render them capable of such universal expression once more—a result previously considered impossible—and *this they achieved through undernourishment.*

What is more, John Cairns, in his directed mutation experiments, took bacteria lacking the genes to digest lactose, and starved them on no food at all for several days. These then entered a transmutable state, and when he placed them in a solution with lactose as the only nutrient, they were able to develop genes that would digest lactose. We may surmise that under nutritional stress, random behavior is suspended, ordinary laws of probability cease to apply, and another level of determinism begins to operate.[157] Now this is the exact physical counterpart of a spiritual phenomenon. For all the prophets, sages, and mystics, from time immemorial, have used hyponutrition to corner, control, and overcome the Base Self; to return to their origin, their essence. Not for nothing did the Prophet remark: "Hunger is the food of God."[158] The human spiritual entity, once it is brought to a state of quiescence through hunger, *becomes,* like DNA, *capable of universal expression.* Then the cosmos can flower in one's heart, and then one can watch the galaxies as they unfold through oneself. As Shakespeare so eloquently described this state, one

> *Finds tongues in trees, books in the running brooks,*
> *Sermons in stones, and good in everything.*[159]

Formal Prayer alone, important as it is, is not sufficient to secure this result. In order to attain a state of "Unveiling," hunger—sparse food intake—is a must.

Fusion: The Unitive Vision

While "Unveiling" is the removal of a person's ordinary sensory limitations, enabling the perception of higher realities, there is a further stage in which one experiences "Union" or "Unification" with all things. And so we come back to Borges, and to the astounding Cup of Jem. We have seen the role of Jem as a mythical hero. There is another meaning of the word *jem,* however, which is important to Sufis and for which reason they have employed it in wordplay. *Jem* means "fusion, integration, union," in the same way that all points in the universe are unified in the Aleph. The Aleph was the mathematical symbol chosen by mathematician Georg Cantor for his transfinite numbers, a fact which was also not lost on Borges. Its corresponding letter in Arabic is the *alif,* which is very similar to our numeral one. That unity and infinity should be united in the same symbol and its correlates is itself significant. The purified heart displays the Aleph, meaning that God takes His seat in the pure heart, that His manifestations—which comprise the universe—are reflected in the heart of the Sufi sage.

Just as there is a place within us, within our hearts, that allows totality to be seen, so there is a place within our minds, our intellects, from which vantage point we can see truth, goodness, and beauty as One. This means that there is a mental state—a state of consciousness, if you will—where science, ethics, and art are integrated, where they are seen to be different facets of the same overall Reality. Just think—not only a synthesis of mathematics, physics, and biology; not only of music and painting and sculpture; not only of love, compassion, and charity—*but a synthesis of all of these with all the rest.*

What I intend by this is not necessarily a superhuman state of mind. It also means that we can appreciate the beauty sculpted into a DNA molecule, the beauty in the music of waves slowly lapping against the shore at night, in the magnificence of a sunset accompanied by wisps of cloud, in the sleek "aero"dynamics of a dolphin. We can also perceive the beauty of an act of charity, of nonpossessive love, of self-sacrificing compassion. And in the beauty of planetary orbits we can discern precise mathematical shapes, or be surprised by fractal order arising out of what seemed for eons to be random chaos. And perhaps we can discern, in all of these, facets of the self-expression, the infinitely varied unfolding, of the One—unity in diversity in unity.[160]

This is why Sufism is not just a science, but a *superscience.* This if anything, I submit, is worthy of being called a Grand Unified Theory (GUT), a Theory of Everything (TOE). Philosophers, astronomers, physicists, biologists, and artists all have parts of the big picture. Such an all-comprehensive view cannot be encompassed by one field of science alone (or even several), but it can be attained by the Total or Perfect Human

Being. In this book, I have been trying to suggest that: 1) such a state exists, and 2) that it is possible for a human being to achieve it. It exists, not in some far-off ancient civilization or mystery school, but today. Here. Now. For you. (Provided, of course, you're interested.)

This is such a state that all imagination pales and falls to the ground in the attempt to come to terms with it. Moreover, it is the only game there is: the struggle for human self-realization to a degree surpassing the dreams of Maslow and the rest of the psychologists. This, moreover, is not my own personal invention, but a perennial wisdom attested to by all the mystics, saints, and prophets of history—although perhaps their point of view was not expressed in quite this way.

And the portal, the entrance, the doorway to this is faith in God, the one and only, the Alpha and the Omega, and the Outward and the Inward. As the Chinese proverb has it, "The journey of a thousand miles begins with one step." Anyone who plays The Only Game There Is becomes eligible to progress and receive a reward, no matter how feeble his or her efforts. As for those who think that the universe is devoid of meaning, "a tale...full of sound and fury, signifying nothing," leave them to their idle play, for they will be—by their own choice they *destine* themselves to be—the losers.

From Hermeticism to Sufism

————————— ✣ —————————

(Just as there is only one religion yet various manifestations of it throughout history, the same is true for esoteric schools. The Master suggested that Hermeticism was the Sufism of its time, and many of its ceremonies are similar to what the Sufi seeker experiences in real-life situations. To give us a flavor of Sufism, he used an excerpt from Edouard Schuré's The Great Initiates *(1889), an imaginative recreation of what these Hermetic rites may have been like. It was a text to which the Master often referred. In this section, you will recognize the mention of "Opening," the term for that moment when the veil of ignorance falls away and the adept is filled with love of truth. This is the state of preparedness the true adept finds with proper guidance.)*

When information doubles, knowledge halves and
wisdom quarters.
—ROBERT THEOBALD

The Knowledge Society, the Contemporary West

With the widespread use of computers in all fields of life, social observers have begun to speak of the emergence of an "information society." John Naisbitt, for example, predicted a shift from industrial society to information society, and management guru Peter F. Drucker claimed that we were now moving from capitalist society to a "knowledge soci-ety."[161]

Ever since the advent of the scientific revolution, knowledge has been highly valued in the West. But this new, knowledge-based society differs from its predecessors in the fact that knowledge now becomes a prime mover driving the economy. Industrial society no longer answers eco-nomic, technological, and social needs. Knowledge has become the fourth production factor after labor, ground, and capital; it is now an economic asset.

Key to this development is the use of information technologies (IT), basically meaning the Information Highway, comprised of the Internet and the World Wide Web. With its global reach via satellite communica-tions, fiber optics, and the like, the Web integrates the entire world, making knowledge available to anyone with access to a computer. In a knowledge-based information society, the Web is fast evolving into an essential component of business, leisure, and culture. The turn of the millennium is marked by the emergence of this knowledge society.

Another significant aspect of the knowledge-based society is that it signals lifelong learning for everyone. Education cannot stop, because new information is ceaselessly being produced. This also entails a hith-erto unparalleled degree of integration between the universities and in-dustrial companies, from which, perhaps, an entirely new entity will emerge.

It will also entail a crucial shift in the way that we view information and knowledge per se. The very abundance of information necessarily forces us to try to distinguish between the two. As the ease with which we can access information increases, so does the difficulty in simply deal-ing with it, in learning how to *use* it. We have to actively choose, as we become inundated with information, between the useful and the super-fluous. Thus the vertical axis of *understanding* becomes even more cru-cial for postmodern people. (We might profitably ask ourselves what knowledge itself is, but the answer to that will emerge shortly.)

Islamic Civilization, the Other Knowledge Society

At this point, we may do well to remember another turn of the millenium, and another knowledge society. Just as the year 2000 marks the knowledge society of globalized Western civilization, the year 1000 A.D. (with a margin of ± two hundred years) marked the knowledge society of Islamic civilization, mentioned in earlier chapters. At that time, it was the universities of the Islamic world that attracted attention, and scientific developments occurred almost wholly in Islamic lands. The scientific knowledge, discoveries, and inventions stemming from Islamic regions astounded the court of Charlemagne and later generations in Europe.[162] Just at the point where the West conceived an appreciation for physical science (*circa* 1600), however, the world of Islam lost interest, and handed the torch over to the West. But the grounds for that appreciation had already been laid earlier. Cultural historian William Irwin Thompson expresses it this way: "In the culture of Europe, the father is Islam and the mother is Dark Age Europe—the child is the Renaissance which then moves to America and the New World."[163]

Besides the West, medieval Islamic civilization is the only other society (discounting uncertain possibilities such as Atlantis) to have been infatuated with knowledge in the most general sense. In his *Knowledge Triumphant,* eminent scholar Franz Rosenthal made an in-depth study of this infatuation, starting with the Arabic word for knowledge:

> Arabic *'ilm* is fairly well rendered by our "knowledge." However, "knowledge" falls short of expressing all the factual and emotional contents of *'ilm.* For *'ilm* is one of those concepts that have dominated Islam and given Muslim civilization its distinctive shape and complexion. In fact, there is no other concept that has been operative as a determinant of Muslim civilization in all its aspects to the same extent as *'ilm.* This holds good even for the most powerful among the terms of Muslim religious life such as, for instance, *tawhîd* "recognition of the oneness of God," *ad-dîn* "the true religion," and many others that are used constantly and emphatically. None of them equals *'ilm* in depth of meaning and wide incidence of use. There is no branch of Muslim intellectual life, of Muslim religious and political life, and of the daily life of the average Muslim that remained untouched by the all-pervasive attitude toward "knowledge" as something of supreme value for Muslim being. *'Ilm* is Islam...[164]

The word *ilm* occurs about seven-hundred-and-fifty times in the Koran, which represents nearly one percent of a seventy-eight-thousand-word text. Rosenthal demonstrates how knowledge was identified with spiritual food, with light, and even with life itself. Books were regarded as the best friends a person could have. As he says, "For medieval Muslim civilization...the glorification of knowledge...extended to all phases of life and educational activity and to all classes of the population."[165]

As described by Rosenthal, the Islamic view of education was identical with our postmodern views of lifelong learning: "Education had to be a continuous process throughout the lifetime of the individual. Both the vastness of knowledge and the natural dynamics of the process of learning required that it never stopped."[166] Those with knowledge comprised a meritocracy: "In Islam...knowledge acquired tremendous significance for an individual's social standing..."[167] Rosenthal deftly summarizes the Islamic stance regarding this most exalted of human pursuits in the following words: "Nothing is more sterile than uncommunicated knowledge.[168] Nothing is more significant for society at large than the small groupings of teachers and students. Nothing, in short, has greater basic value for society than knowledge." His conclusion is that "in Islam, the concept of knowledge enjoyed an importance unparalleled in other civilizations."[169]

It is interesting to compare the contemporary knowledge society with the one of a thousand years ago. Science and technology have, of course, progressed immensely since then. Yet, as Rosenthal observes: "If two different civilizations were to hold the same value judgments on matters of central concern to them, they probably would not be really different."[170]

In the Koran and the Traditions of the Prophet, "knowledge" is used in the most general sense, without differentiation between knowledge of the physical world and religious (i.e., moral and spiritual) knowledge. The claim voiced by some that only religious knowledge is intended must be refuted in the most emphatic terms. This is why Islam was able to achieve deep inroads into physical science in the medieval period. Yet the term can easily be misread, as Rosenthal observes, to denote purely religious knowledge,[171] and more specifically, that deriving from the Prophet. This, perhaps, explains the subsequent Islamic disaffection from studies of the external world (what we would call "scientific research" today). "For the Sufi," writes Rosenthal, "the knowledge of God was the only knowledge deserving of the name..."[172] This is quite understandable, and designates theirs as a more specialized sense of knowledge—though there have been exceptional Sufis, such as Ibrahim Hakki of Erzurum, who were well-versed in both the physical and the spiritual sciences of their day. (See Appendix C for a poem by Ibrahim Hakki.) For those who viewed physical science as the study of God's custom (*sunnah Allah*), as the way God chose to manifest Himself (or His will) in the external world, there was never a problem—they could, like physicist Stephen Hawking, consider that they were obtaining direct insight into the workings of "the mind of God." To others, the study of the external world represented a distraction from deeper things. One is tempted to observe that maintaining a balance between extremes is one of the most difficult things for human beings to achieve, despite the fact that the Koran summons its adherents, as "middle people," to the Middle Way.

We, unfortunately, are likewise not exempt from that failing, for our phenomenal success in science and technology has blinded us to the need for a moral and spiritual science that complements our achievements in the physical realm. Vaclav Havel puts it this way: "Contemporary global civilization...is in essence a deeply atheistic one. Indeed, it is the first atheistic civilization in the history of humankind."[173]

We, too, have failed. We, too, have been unable to strike a proper balance. We have erred against the side of morality and spirituality. Our civilization, which prides itself on being the best-informed in history, is yet lacking in moral and spiritual knowledge. Even when we possess such knowledge, we delegate it to the same place as fortune-telling and soothsaying, and fail to act on it. But knowledge without action is practically the same thing as no knowledge at all—which was also a failing of Islamic civilization. A parallel trend is that there is a great interest in spiritual growth, but because this need is not satisfied through normal outlets, the way is opened for all kinds of irrationality to rush in.

It is high time we disabused ourselves of this deplorable ignorance. We have to realize that Reason (or the Enlightenment of the West) is by no means inimical to Spirit (or the Enlightenment of the East). Far from being so, the world of the spirit has its own laws, which, while they might be different from the laws of the physical world, are equally universal. But the fruits of true knowledge of the spiritual path are only available to those who walk this path, who know the meaning of knowledge and action.

Comparative-religion specialist Mircea Eliade and many others have lamented the singularity of Western civilization in its almost total neglect of spiritual matters. Of all the peoples the earth has seen, we are alone in our ignorance—or even outright denial—of the transcendent. For most of humankind, knowledge always meant spiritual as well as material, esoteric as well as exoteric, knowledge, though again it has not always been easy to maintain a healthy balance between the two. We can trace this all the way back into the misty depths of time, to an age when the ancient Egyptians also honored knowledge.

Knowledge in Egyptian Civilization: Thoth, Archetype of Wisdom

For the ancient Egyptians, Thoth (a Greek corruption from the Egyptian name, Tahuti) was the archetype[174] of knowledge and wisdom. He was also the inventor of writing, and was credited with having taught men how to write. Thoth was often depicted as a man with the head of an ibis bird, and carried a pen and scrolls upon which he recorded things. His wife was *Maat,* which means "Truth" and "Justice." Thoth also invented numbers, making him the first mathematician; he measured time, making him the first experimental physicist; and he was also the inventor of medicine, or the first doctor. The lore of plants also belonged to him, so he was a botanist—as did that of minerals, making him a mineralogist. The Jewish people were to associate him with Enoch, Moslems with the prophet Idris.

In ancient Greece, Euhemerus advanced the idea that the "gods" were originally exceptional human beings, who later became elevated by others to divine status. Given the fact that similar events have happened even in our age, there is nothing to prevent us from accepting this view, provided it is not extended to Absolute Reality itself. Originally, Thoth could well have been the first outstanding patron of the arts and sciences, of learning and knowledge, or the human inventor of writing.

It can be seen, then, that Thoth's studies prefigured physical science. It is of the greatest significance, however, that his knowledge was not confined to that of the external world alone. On the contrary, as Joscelyn Godwin has written: "In Egyptian myth, Thoth is described variously as the spirit and intelligence of the Creator; god of learning and of healing; judge of celestial disputes and secretary of the gods; weigher of the souls of the dead."[175] It was widely believed that he invented the magical and hermetic arts. In the popular imagination, he was associated with magic spells and astrology.

In particular, Thoth presided over the judgment of the soul in the after-death state. According to the *Egyptian Book of the Dead* ("The Book of Coming Forth by Day"), the soul of the deceased had to pass through a series of "halls" (stages). The soul engaged in the famous "negative confession," in which it denied that it had perpetrated any evils during worldly life. Finally, it reached the scene of the great judgment.

There, the heart of the deceased would be weighed against the feather of *Maat,* of truth and justice, and if the soul passed this test, it would be ready for the fields of bounty and the banquet table of Osiris. The heavy-hearted souls, laden with sins which are "excreta of the heart," would be devoured by serpents or chimerical monsters. It was Thoth who supervised this ceremony in the afterworld, carefully taking note of the weighing process. In the *Book of the Dead,* Chapters 101–124 give the prayers necessary for the deceased to gain knowledge of the Secret Books of Thoth. These prayers enabled the soul to pass the seven "Degrees of Light" and enter the kingdom of Osiris, the "god" of death and resurrection who sires his son, the Horus-child.[176]

Of course, as soon as we bring in the spiritual knowledge of Thoth, the whole complex of Egyptian Mysteries and mythology is called to mind, but the subject is too vast to fit into the confines of this chapter. Once again, I must suppress an urge to write at length about the spiritual journey as revealed through the mysterious pictures bequeathed us by the ancient Egyptians. Nevertheless, we should bear in mind that they did have their Mystery rites, and these in turn influenced the Greeks at a later date. Solon, Thales, Pythagoras, Plato, and others were all to tread the path to Egypt. Pythagoras in particular was initiated by the Egyptian priests in all the sacred ceremonies, and remained there some twenty years.

Hermes

Hermes, fleet-footed messenger (conveyor of information or knowledge) to the Greek gods, was likewise involved in the post-death journey of the soul: he guided souls to Hades. With the conquests of Alexander the Great, the Egyptian gods quickly became disseminated throughout the Hellenistic world, and would soon be copied or combined with their classical counterparts. In this process, Thoth became associated with Hermes (although Daedalus might have been a better choice), under the name "Thrice-Greatest Hermes" (*Hermes Trismegistus*). The celestial journey attributed to Hermes parallels, in some ways, the ancient Egyptian journey of the soul. The Greek philosophical mind, savoring a divine cosmic order, found great appeal in the combination of material and spiritual knowledge that this philosopher king, Hermes-Thoth, represented.

The *Corpus Hermeticum*

The main writings of Hermeticism that have come down to us date from the first to the third centuries A.D. Called the *Corpus Hermeticum* and written in Hellenistic Egypt, they are a collection of writings by several unknown authors. While they are not entirely consistent with each other, the fact they *do* agree upon many things shows that there was a coherent Hermetic doctrine, however unformed. The most famous among these writings is the "Divine Pymander" or *Poimandres* (Greek *Poimen Anthropos*, "the Shepherd of Men"). In what follows, I have boiled the *Corpus Hermeticum* down to its essentials without attempting to be exhaustive.[177] This will serve as a basis for later comparison between Sufism and Hermeticism.

God

According to the Hermetic *Corpus,* God is the source of all things (3.1): "There is someone who is the Maker and the Lord of all these things" (5.4).He is the author of all things, the One and Only (4.1, 8).

One, then, is God (11.11). God does not stand in need of anything. Nothing is superior to Him (6.1). All things depend on Him (9.9). God is Light (1.6), the father (Creator) of all. He is Mind and Light and Life (1.12). He is the Eternal (8.2). God is All-powerful, holy, better than all praise (1.31). God should be conceived, not as space, but as energy that can contain all space (2.6). God is not Mind, or Spirit, or Light, but their common Cause (2.14). The names: Good,[178] and Father, belong to Him and no one else (2.14, 6.1, 3). The Good is he who gives all things and receives nothing. God, then, gives all things and receives nothing (2.16). The other name of God is Father, because He is the That-which-makes-all (i.e., the Creator) (2.17).

God, being unmanifest, is changeless. Becoming belongs to what is manifest (5.1). (Yet at the same time,) nothing is more manifest than He, for He has made all things in order that through them all, you may see Him (11.22). Neither is He inactive, since all things would then lack activity, for all are full of God (11.5). He ever is at work. For if He separated Himself from His creation, all things would then collapse, and all must die. God is the One Life, and He makes and supports them all (11.14). He is "our Lord and Father, the One-and-Only One" (5.2). "He is Himself, both things that are and things that are not" (5.9, 12.23). He who makes all things, is in them all (Immanence) (11.6, 12.21). But equally, all are in God, He contains them all (Transcendence) (11.18). He surrounds all and permeates all (12.20). Nothing is like Him, That which has no like, and is Alone and One (11.5). "No ear can hear Him, nor can eye see Him, nor tongue speak of Him, but [only] mind and heart" (7.2). "God's essence is the Beautiful; the Beautiful is further also Good" (6.4). If you seek God, you seek the Beautiful whose Beauty is beyond compare. The Path that leads to the Beautiful is One—Devotion joined with Gnosis (6.5). If you would contemplate God, behold the ordering of the *kosmos* (Greek "order"), and see the orderly behavior of its ordering (12.21).

Human Beings

What follows is a list of statements about human beings. The world was made for man, man was made for God (1.26).[179] God brought forth man, whom He loved, and who, having the Image of his Father, is beautiful (1.12). Man is mortal in body and immortal in essence (1.15). The Soul is deathless (8.1). Body's sleep (which may also mean death) becomes soul's awakening (1.30). Pious and merciful people, loving God and invoking His name, win His love (1.22). The wicked are punished by fire, their torment and darkness increases (1.23). People have given themselves to drunkenness, sleep, and ignorance of God (1.27). Some people devote themselves to the pleasures of the body, but others know this is not what they are here for (4.5). Passions and irrational desires are great ills, And God has set up Mind (a function of Thoth) to play the part of judge and executioner over these (12.4).

The Straight Path

Of the path, it is said: "The greatest bad there is, is not to know God's Good; but to be able to know [Good], and will, and hope, is a Straight Way, the Good's own [Path], both leading there and easy." If you set foot on this path, it will meet you everywhere (11.21). There is only one way to worship God, and that is: not to be bad (i.e., to be good) (12.23).

The Base Self

Although the concept of the Base Self is as yet undeveloped in the *Corpus,* we can still find traces of it. Here are some examples: To travel on the way to Truth, to make the journey to the Good, the Soul must first war against its own self (1.8–9). The one hastens to the Good, desiring liberty. The other is neighbor to Evil, and loves bondage and slavery (1.10). But you must first tear off from yourself the web of ignorance, the ground of bad, the robber in your house who hates you and bears enmity towards you (7.2). This hateful cloak you wear keeps you from gazing above. It schemes against you and throttles you. It has blocked up the senses and crammed them full of loathsome lust, so that you may not hear the things you should hear, nor see the things you should see[180] (7.3). Belly-lust is a great ill, the error that leads the band of all other ills and turns us away from Good (6.3). He who expends his love upon his body through a love that leads astray, stays in darkness and in death (1.19).

Gnosis

What follows is a list of statements about Gnosis ("God-knowledge"). Gnosis is possible for human beings (11.20). He who has faith can ascend to God (4.4). There is something called the "Eye of the Heart" (7.1) (its meaning is not explained). Rebirth is to pass into a body that can never die, yet this can occur while still in the (physical) body (10.6, 13.3).

The part of father is to make. So it is the most pious thing in this world to have a child,[181] and the soul of a person who has no child is condemned and pitiable (2.17). The natural body perceived by sense is mortal, but death cannot touch the birth of the essence (13.14). The soul, in its ascent through the seven heavenly spheres,[182] leaves behind a negative trait at every stage, finally achieving the eighth stage of those who praise God ceaselessly (the company of the Blessed) (1.25-26). This is the way of Birth in God (13.6). The way to achieve this is to withdraw into yourself, to shut the doors of the senses, to rid yourself of twelve tormentors (sins), and adorn yourself with ten virtues (13.7). This is the manner of Rebirth, of Birth in God: driving out the twelve sins and replacing them with the ten virtues. This is the way of purification. The result is bliss (13.10). When the Gnosis of God arrives, ignorance is cast out and joy comes (13.8)."Error flees, and truth is with us" (13.9). He who knows himself, reaches Good and goes to God (1.19, 21). You become a knower of thyself and our common Father (13.22).

Before continuing, I should like to draw special attention to 4.4, which brings on the obverse corollary that: "He who has no faith cannot ascend to God." *This is why faith is necessary.* Only if you believe: 1. that God exists, 2. that one can ascend to God, and 3. that this is a worthwhile enterprise, will you trouble yourself enough to *perform the experiment*— just as a scientist, unless s/he has faith that his or her experiment is going to yield fruitful results, will not perform the experiment. The ascent to God means following His directions, which will lead us out of the realm of hells, into the realm of paradises, and beyond them all—if we are able—to the Paradise of the Essence. This spiritual ascension is such that all other human experiences pale into insignificance when compared to it. Faith, then, is necessary in order to expend the effort required for the climb to God, during which process one continually improves one's destiny.

To be released from hell is great. To enter heaven is even better. But the grandest of all is the Paradise of the Essence, to which nothing at all can be compared. There are no adequate terms for describing it. I can only point to it by saying that if one were to experience this for only a few minutes, it would be worth more than a blissful lifetime. This is why the ascent to God is so valuable, and why mystics in general and Sufis in particular place it above all else.

Later Developments of Hermeticism

Hermeticism was also associated with alchemy, in which the true adept concentrated on forging a "radiant body," instead of (or at least, in concert with) attempting to transform physical lead into gold. After the Roman Empire, Hermeticism was to inspire much of the Western esoteric tradition. It influenced the Cabalists, the students of magic, the Rosicrucians, and the Freemasons. In these traditions, the effects of the Hermetic tradition can readily be seen. For example, here is a quotation from a Masonic text: "The purpose of Masonry is to train a human being so that he will reconstruct, through the body of change and death which he now has, a perfect physical body which shall not be subject to death. The plan is to build this deathless body, called by modern masons Solomon's Temple, out of material in the physical body, which is called the ruins of Solomon's Temple."[183] This is, of course, what is also meant by the "diamond body of the Buddha," or the "most sacred body" (*wujud al-aqdas*) of the Sufis. (One important flaw in the last quote is that the immortal body is not a physical body, but rather the attempt is made to forge it while one is still in the physical body. Otherwise, even Methuselah, allegedly the longest-lived human, is credited with having lived only nine-hundred-and-sixty-nine years. So physical immortality is not what it's all about. What Masons need to do is to study the works of famous Sufis, such as Yusuf Hamadani, Abdulqader Gilani, and Ahmed Yasavi, after which these subtle points will become much clearer.)

The Final Revelation

Because the exoteric aspect—the external practice—of Islam is in full view, people are easily misled into believing that this is all there is to it and that there is nothing more. My hope is that this chapter will leave the reader better informed in this respect. Hence, what I now propose to do is to compare the compression from the body of Hermetic writings presented above with statements from the Koran, from the sayings of the Prophet, and from the great sages who follow in his wake.

A word of caution is called for at this point. The parallels between the Koran and the *Corpus Hermeticum* or any other text should not lead us to suppose the earlier texts somehow "influenced" the composition of the Koran. The similarity between religious texts throughout history betrays the existence of a primordial wisdom tradition and a unity of revelation from Adam onwards.[184] According to Islam, all religions preceding it are also Islam—the Islam of their times, in having preached "submission to God" (which is one of the meanings of "Islam").

Suppose a person looks out a window and says: "I see the sun." Then s/he departs. After a while, another person comes in, looks out the window, and also says: "I see the sun, it is there." This does not mean that the second person was in any way influenced or instructed by the first, it means that both gave testimony to the same reality independently of each other. The observation of the second person corroborated the first. This is independent observation and verification: what unites them is the truth to which they both testify.

When, for example, St. Paul says: "No eye has seen, nor ear heard, nor the human heart conceived, what God has prepared for those who love Him" (1 Corinthians 2:9), and when the Koran states: "No soul knows what delights of the eye have been prepared for them secretly, as a reward for what they used to do" (32:17), this does not mean that the Prophet, who was in any case unlettered, somehow read the New Testament—or heard it recited—and fell under its influence. Rather, it means that Gabriel inspired Paul as the Holy Spirit in the first case and revealed the verse to the Prophet in the second. In both cases, the source of the information is the same: God and His "messenger." (The Greek word *aggelos,* from which "angel" is derived, means "messenger.")

In the Islamic view, an evolution of religions has occurred throughout history, culminating in the perfect and final religion. At each successive stage, God revealed more information to human beings, which is equivalent to saying that they discovered deeper and more profound secrets of the spiritual realm. In the theory of evolution, higher life forms may have evolved from lower organisms, but this does not mean that the higher are reducible to the lower. The higher organisms are incredibly more complex, and no study of the lower is going to inform you about the higher. (Humans were created independently, as their creation was analogous to the creation of the universe.) Evolution is, therefore, a progress and not a regress, an ascent and not a descent. Rivers flow out to the ocean, but no river can contain the ocean.

Moreover, this evolution is purposeful, goal-oriented. God could afford to wait—a billion years is but a fleeting moment in Eternity. Besides, He is equidistant to all points in the space-time continuum. God guided the evolution of the universe, of the stars and planets, of life on earth at every step of the way. Through eons of preparation, God always had humans in mind. First came unicellular organisms, then plants and animals. In all this, God was preparing the way for humans, *decorating the earth for them.* God loved human beings so much that He gave them this beautiful world, this wondrous universe, and then He went further and gave even Himself.

Quantum physicist Werner Heisenberg once observed that the passage of time may be attributable, not to the push of the past, but to the pull of the future. Time was striving towards a goal. As with less evolved organisms in the case of biology, the incomplete revelations were, in the case of religion, inching toward completion. With the revelation of the Koran to Mohammed, all previous religions, philosophies, and mystical paths found their culmination and fulfillment.

Hence, we cannot suppose that the Koran could have been "derived" from any of the earlier texts. According to the Islamic conception, they represent earlier versions of Revelation, while the Koran represents its pinnacle. Nevertheless, their thematic unity reveals the existence of a single, primordial wisdom running like a golden thread through history. Given this premise, every religion or religious philosophy may be regarded as a proper subset.

Correspondences

Before discussing Hermes, it might be useful to examine a parallel with Thoth. We have already seen how the soul of the deceased is judged in the scene of *psychostasis,* or weighing of the soul. In Islamic eschatology, too, the soul of the deceased is judged. His or her sins are put on one pan of the scales, and merits on the other. If one's merits outweigh one's sins, one wins Paradise; if vice versa, one has earned punishment. Although the details are different, the basics do not diverge substantially from the ancient Egyptian conception to the Islamic one.

Moreover, almost all traditions have agreed on the existence of post-mortem justice, reward, and retribution in one form or another.

We shall now embark on a point-by-point comparison between the Hermetic *Corpus* and esoteric Islam. First, however, let us examine a line from the Secret Hymn of the Hermetists:

> *Let us all give praise to Him, sublime above the Heav-*
> *ens, Lord of every nature. I give Thee thanks, O God*
> (13.17-18).

We next go to the Koran, and open the first line of the first chapter on the first page, where we read:

> *Praise be to God, the Lord of the Worlds* (1:1).

The Arabic word *hamd* encompasses the meanings of both "praise" and "thanksgiving." This means that the Secret Hymn of the Hermetic adepts has found expression in the very first verse of the first chapter of the Holy Book of Islam, the chapter of the "Opening," which is recited by all Moslems during each cycle of every Formal Prayer. In other words, what earlier belonged only to the very few has now become the common praise of all.

Let us now proceed to our comparison. The numbers in parentheses are chapter and verse numbers from the Koran. Traditions of the Prophet are marked by a "T," and sources for quotations from the sages are given in footnotes.

God

What follows is a list of statements about God. God is the Creator of all things (2:29, 117, 6:73). He creates and sustains all (7:54, 11:6-7, 13:16). It is He who created all nature (25:61-62). "Your God is One God; there is no God but He" (2:163). "God is One; He is the *Samad*" (112:1-2). In Arabic, *Samad* means "That which is in need of nothing, but which all things stand in need of." In other words, the Hermetic writings in this respect and the Unity Chapter of the Koran dovetail with each other. The same holds for the so-called Light Verse: "God is the Light of the heavens and the earth…Light upon Light" (24:35). He is Life, the Living (2:255, 3:2, 40:65). He is the Eternal, the Everlasting (2:255, 20:111). God is All-powerful (2:284, 6:17), the Holy, worthy of all praise (31:26). All things in the heavens and the earth praise Him (59:24). His abode is nonspace: "There is no space for Me. I am the space of space."[185] God is the Sustainer of all (51:58): He gives, and receives nothing in return. The senses of "the Good" in Greek thought, self-sufficient and self-caused, find their echo in the Koran: God is the Self-sufficient (6:133), the Self-subsisting (3:2). All good is from God (16:53). The sense of Father as That-which-makes-all is given by "the Originator of the heavens and the earth" (6:101, 42:11). "You will not find any change in the Way of God" (35:43). "Whichever way you turn, there is the Face of God" (2:115). "Nothing covers the face of Truth/ Nothing is more manifest than Truth/But to the eyeless He is hidden."[186] God is both the Manifest and the Hidden, the Outward and the Inward (rendered in the Koran by *Zahir* and *Batin*). "Every instant He is upon some task" (55:29). "There is no god but One God" (5:73).

God is both within everything and without. He (4:127) and His knowledge (6:80, 20:98) encompass all things. God's attributes are of two kinds: those of Similarity with other things (*tashbih*: Association, akin to Immanence), and attributes of Incomparability (*tanzih*: Dissociation, akin to Transcendence). Both are needed, and only when both are present can Unification (*tawhid*) be complete.[187] "Nothing is like Him" (42:11). "Eyes cannot attain to Him" (6:103).

"God is Beautiful, He loves beauty" (T). The path that leads to Him is observance of His Law (*sharia*) joined with Gnosis (*marifah*). "With the Law, God Almighty desires us to order our external world, and with Knowledge, He wishes us to arrange our internal world. From the combination of these two, Truth is born."[188]

The Koran constantly invites human beings to contemplate nature, which is a place of beauty and wonder. God created all things, and ordered them in measured proportions (25:2). "We shall show them our signs on the horizons (in the external world) and in their selves (man's inner world)" (41:53). God orders all things (6:95-99). The wisdom of the Creator is apparent in the book of the universe, the secrets of which are explained in the book of the Koran.

Human Beings

What follows is a list of statements about human beings. "The cosmos I created for man, and man I created for myself."[189] "We created man in the most beautiful stature" (95:4). "God created man in His own image" (T). "The Compassionate created man in His own image" (T).

"Every soul shall taste of death" (3:185, 29:57). Who dies once does not die again: "After the first death, they never taste death again" (44:56). "Human beings are asleep. When they die, they awake" (T). God accepts their best deeds from the Good, and ignores their misdeeds (29:7, 46:16). "Only by the invocation of God do hearts find solace" (13:28). Pious men and adepts invoke (*zikr*) God's names: "They love Him and He loves them" (5:54). Many in the world will lead you astray from God's path, but God does not love evil-doers, and they will be chastised in the afterlife. Whatever you do, you do to yourself: "If you do good, you do it to yourself, and if you do bad, you do it to yourself" (17:7). Because: "Whoever does an atom's-weight of good will see its recompense, and whoever does an atom's weight of evil will see its recompense" (99:7-8).

The Straight Path

Here, the path is described: "Guide us along Your Straight Path, the path of those whom You favor" (1:5-6). "If my servant comes to me walking, I will go to him running."[190] God recognizes all good (4:147); no good deed is wasted. So remain in the Straight Path (6:153, etc.) as you have been commanded to (42:15).

The Base Self

What follows is a list of sayings about the Base Self. This "self always compels to evil (*nafs al-ammara*)" (12:53). "The greatest war is the war against the self" (T). The Base Self is one of the most important teachings of the Sufis, and is mentioned in almost every book on the subject. The Base Self is the prime obstacle separating us from God, and is our mortal enemy. This self has to be purified if we wish to get anywhere, to do something with our lives. Illicit lusts and passions (sexual and pecuniary) are the prime weapons of the Base Self, whose only intent is to lead us astray from God's path.[191]

Gnosis

Of Gnosis, it is said that the result of purification is spiritual Ascension. In the Koran, one of the titles of God is "Lord of the Ascensions" (70:3). "Gnosis is attained by uncovering the dark veil of the Base Self from the mirror of the heart, and by purifying the heart."[192] This process opens "the Eye of the Heart," which is a psychospiritual organ of perception with the capacity for "visual" cognition: "The Heart (fouad) did not deny what it saw" (53:11). This also implies that hearts can be blind (22:46).

"To have a child" has two meanings: exoteric and esoteric. Exoterically, the Prophet said: "Get married, and multiply. I shall take pride in the numbers of my community" (T). But there is also an esoteric meaning. God will create you in new forms after death (56:60-61): "Towards the end of the spiritual journey (a journey that is made while still in the physical body), a different kind of spirit is formed. This spirit is subtler than all other spirits, and is called 'the Child of Meaning' or 'the Child of the Heart.'"[193] This is Rebirth, and anyone who has achieved this is called "Twice-born."

The Sufis have traditionally identified seven levels in the process of the self's purification, corresponding to the "seven heavens" (17:44). There are seven cardinal sins, and eight paradises that one enters as these sins are left behind. Passing through all by shedding one's negative traits at every stage, one joins the "Friends of God" (5:55) (the company of the Blessed). For this, one must cleanse oneself from sins and adorn oneself with virtues. Additionally, one must engage in "meditation" (tafakkur), which is concentration on God alone, to the exclusion of everything-other-than-God from the senses.

In order to attain Gnosis, one has to purify oneself, as shown by the following quotations: "God loves those who purify themselves" (9:108); "He desires to purify you" (5:6). Whoever purifies himself does it only for his own good (35:18). "Those who struggle in Our cause, surely we shall guide them in our ways" (29:69) to Truth. The reward of the self-purified is eternal Paradise (20:76). If the goal of human existence is to find happiness, the Friends of God are the ones who have found it. "No fear is upon them, neither shall they sorrow" (10:62). "Truth has come, and falsehood has vanished away. Surely falsehood is ever certain to vanish" (17:81). Hence, one must seek ways to draw near to God (5:35): "He who knows himself knows his Lord" (T).

Assessment

This comparison shows, I hope, the essential harmony between Hermeticism and the Koran, and again demonstrates a prime assertion of Islam: the transcendent unity of all religions. "Thirty spokes," says Lao Tzu in the *Tao Te Ching*, "are made one by a hub," and although they may differ at the perimeter of the wheel, the essence of all religions is one. At this point we should need a metareligion—except that we happen to have one already: Islam.

It is not to be supposed that the Koran and the teachings deriving from it are confined to what has been presented above. I have merely extracted from Islamic Sufism its "Hermetic subset," as it were.

It can readily be seen that the Koran suggests new terms for "Good" and "Father," due to the possibility of misinterpretation evoked by these names. Similarly, a Sufic technical term, "the Eye of the Heart," is also found in Hermeticism, but it is left unexplained. This point, too, becomes much clearer in the light of Koranic teachings. The Hermetic writings are relatively clear and simple, but any impression of directness would be deceptive, because only in the summarized version given above do certain points stand out.

But this is not all. Even the humblest Moslem has been blessed with forms of worship no Hermetic adept was ever schooled in, such as the Formal Prayer, the Alms-tax, and the Pilgrimage to Mecca. Even if s/he fasted and performed something akin to Invocation, the Hermeticist lacked the Formal Prayer, which is "the Ascension of the Faithful" (T). Thus, what was earlier the privilege of the very few has become the birthright of the many. Perhaps we might call this "the democratization of religion and of opportunities for spiritual growth."

234 ᴊᴇ THE SECRET OF ISLAM

Hermetic Initiation

Very little has come down to us regarding the Mysteries, whether Greek or Egyptian. Aspirants were sworn to strictest secrecy, and we can only surmise that the secret was well kept. From time to time, an oblique reference survives, but it is impossible for anyone who does not know the whole picture to make much of it. Nevertheless, this has not prevented people from trying to penetrate the darkness. Edouard Schuré, in his classic study of *The Great Initiates,* tried to reassemble the various pieces of the puzzle. In this he was more successful than he himself may have realized. My teacher, Master Kayhan, made use of Schuré's imaginative account describing the initiation ceremonies of Hermeticism, because he saw in it many close parallels to the spiritual journey of the Sufi.

To summarize the highlights of these ceremonies, which are actually "rites of passage," a disciple or aspirant arriving at an Egyptian temple is first subjected to an "entrance exam." The test occurs on the grounds of the temple and in its underground crypts. First, the disciple has to spend a week performing menial chores. When the trials begin, he must pass through a fearsome corridor lined with statues having the bodies of humans and the heads of animals, such as a hawk's, a lion's, or a jackal's. Then he is shut away into a dark tunnel, where the timid may easily be discouraged or even die of fright. Having passed this test, he is instructed in an arcane alphabet and its symbolic meanings. It begins to dawn on him that there is more to existence than meets the eye.

Next, the disciple has to pass through what appears to be a red-hot furnace. The hierophant (high priest or guide) soothes his fear, saying that he himself once passed through the fire as if it had been a bed of roses. Then he has to pass through water, experiencing the danger of being drowned. Finally, he experiences the most difficult trial of all, the trial by lust.

The following brief description of Hermeticism as pictured by Schuré will provide an introduction to Sufism and asceticism. This is where the seven levels of the Self were first elaborated, and for this reason it is of great spiritual and historical significance.

As we have seen, the religion of Hermeticism has played a very important role in the history of humankind. In no other religion have there been such mysterious ceremonies accompanied by such painstaking scientific investigations. Egypt was once a center for humanity's contemplative activities, revealing that several religions owe a debt to Hermeticism.

As mentioned earlier, the man who was known as "Thoth" (or Tot) in Egyptian and "Hermes" in Greek was first recognized as a prophet and later, revered as a god. He has also been identified with Idris (and is known as Enoch to the Jews). Although no holy book was revealed to him, his influence has been very far-reaching.

The ceremonies of Hermeticism are not to be found in any other religion. With Hermes (Thoth), the religious beliefs of the Egyptians turned to "Unity." In other words, they started believing in One God at a late stage, as is evident from the *Corpus*. According to their religious beliefs, before the creation of the earth, the spirit of everything was whirling in a sea, a vacuum. The Spirit of God acted upon this vacuum and created everything. He created the earth and the heavens, but was not Himself created. His body was everlasting and all-inclusive of the universe. The universe was but a small indication of the greatness of God Almighty, who was ever-present and overseeing.

According to the beliefs of the Egyptians, God was one, but manifested Himself in various personalities. God was called by different names in everything.[194] Their greatest god was Osiris, and his wife was Isis. The ancient Egyptians also used to believe in resurrection after death. Spirits were judged in the presence of Osiris. The actions of human beings on earth would be weighed on the scales of justice, and they would be punished in accordance with their sins. The evil would be tormented by scorpions and snakes, while good souls would lead a happy life at the table of Osiris. This historical information demonstrates that the comparative investigation of religions is a very instructive and fruitful endeavor, especially as we begin to study Sufism.

The Initiation Ceremonies of Hermeticism

As mentioned in brief earlier, aspirants wishing to join the Hermetic religion would go to the famous temples at Thebes or Memphis. The high priest, or hierophant, would meet the aspirant in the huge and magnificent temple. The priest would take him[195] to his room and ask who he was, where he came from, and where he had studied. He would size up the aspirant's intelligence and aptitude. If he had the capacity to comprehend advanced knowledge, he would keep him there. Otherwise, he would be sent away.

The priest then took the youth and conducted him through the inner courts and a corridor carved in stone, open to the sky, and bordered with sphinxes. At the end of the passage, there was a small temple which served as an entrance to the underground crypts. The door was disguised by a life-size statue of Isis. The goddess, sitting in a position of meditation and contemplation, held a closed book in her lap. Her face was covered by a veil, and beneath the statue was the inscription: "No mortal has lifted my veil."

The hierophant said to the youth: "This is the door to the hidden sanctuary. Look at these two columns. The red one symbolizes the ascent of the spirit into the light of Osiris. The black one signifies the imprisonment of the soul in the body. Whoever approaches our science and teaching risks his life. Madness or death await the weak and the wicked. Only the strong and the good find life and immortality. Many reckless ones have entered this door, and have not come out alive. This is such an abyss that only the fearless can emerge from it again. Therefore, consider carefully the dangers you will face. If you do not trust yourself, give up the quest, for once this door is closed behind you, it will not be opened."

The aspirant, after listening to these words in fear, would summon all his courage, and once he said: "I accept your terms," the priest would lead him to the outer court and commend him to the temple servants. The aspirant would be kept in the temple for one week; he would be requested to perform the lowliest chores, would listen to hymns, and be forbidden to talk about worldly affairs. He would complete his weekly seclusion here.

When the evening of ordeals arrived, two assistants led the candidate to the door of the secret sanctuary. The aspirant was now at the beginning of an ordeal full of mysteries. They entered a dark, dismal corridor without any visible exit, lined on both sides with human-bodied and animal-headed statues, and the statues of lions, bulls, hawks, and snakes seen dimly in the torchlight. The requirement was to go through the passage without uttering a single word. At the end of this sinister passage were a mummy and a human skeleton.

The two assistants pointed to a hole in the wall in front of the novice. This was the entrance to a corridor so low that it was impossible to pass through without crawling. One of the assistants said to the youth: "If you want you may turn back from here, because the door is not yet closed. You may return now. But if you continue, you cannot turn back." Once the youth replied: "I will continue," he was handed a small torch, and the door of the sanctuary was quickly shut behind him with a loud bang.

Trial by Death

The youth knelt down to crawl into the passage. Hardly had he eased through when he heard a voice coming from the end of the tunnel. This voice would say: "Fools who covet knowledge and power perish here!"

Due to a strange acoustical phenomenon, the sentence was echoed *seven times*. Nevertheless, he had to move forward. After a while the corridor widened, but now began to incline downward more sharply. Finally, the youth would come across a hole, into which an iron ladder disappeared. He climbed down this ladder. At the lowest rung, his frightened gaze looked downward into a terrifying abyss. Return was impossible, and beneath him a black, bottomless pit yawned. In order to save his life he looked around, and finally noticed a small crevice on his right. There was a staircase here by which he could escape. Right away, he climbed up the spiraling stairs carved into stone, and eventually came across a bronze grating. This led to a hallway supported by huge columns in the shape of draped female figures. Two rows of symbolic frescoes could be seen on the wall. All these symbols had a hidden meaning. There were eleven frescoes on either side of the hallway, and the lights in the hands of the beautiful column-statues illuminated these pictures.

A magus, the guardian of the sacred symbols, opened the bars and welcomed him with a smile. He said: "You have passed the first test successfully. Congratulations," and then, taking him across the hall, explained the sacred meanings. Under each of these pictures were a letter and a number. There were twenty-two symbols that represented the first twenty-two Mysteries. They constituted the alphabet of secret science. These letters were the keys to the secrets of the universe bestowed by

God Almighty. Employed by the right will, they became the source of all wisdom and power.

Every letter and number corresponded to a triadic law, having repercussions in the *divine world,* the *intellectual world,* and the *physical world.* For example the letter A, which corresponded to the number one, represented, in the divine world: Absolute Being from which all beings emanate; in the intellectual world: the unity, origin, and synthesis of numbers; and in the physical world: humans, the leaders of all beings, with their capacity to attain infinity. The arcanum of "A", which symbolized attainment of the Godhead, was represented by a magus dressed in the attire of Osiris, with a scepter in his hand and wearing a white robe and gold crown. The white robe stood for purity, the scepter for authority, and the gold crown for enlightenment by the light of Heaven.

The guardian of the symbols led the novice along, explaining the arcana one by one. Concerning the crown, he remarked: "Free will, which is joined to God in order to manifest truth and effect justice, participates in divine power even while in this world. This is an everlasting reward to spirits." The neophyte listened to these explanations with surprise, and the first glimmers of understanding began to take shape in his mind.

Trials by Fire and Water

The magus now opened another door, leading to a long, narrow corridor, at the end of which a red-hot furnace could be spied. The novice had to pass through it. He trembled with fear, whereupon the priest said: "My son, death frightens only weak minds. I myself once crossed this fire like a bed of roses." With that, the gate of the hall of secrets closed behind the newcomer. Approaching the fire, he perceived that it was but a visual illusion created by artifices, and quickly passed through a narrow path in the middle.

His third test was to go through a pool of stagnant black water, lit by the flames of the fire already left behind. The ordeals had by this time left him trembling and exhausted.

Next is the centerpiece of the trial period, and the prime reason behind the Master's endorsement of Schuré's account, the whole point of his introducing us to Hermeticism at all. This is the trial in which the aspirant's self-control is tested by a lovely woman. If he succumbs to her charms, he loses his chance of any spiritual progress forever.

Trial by Passion

Two assistants led him to a dim grotto where a soft couch could be seen in the flickering light of a bronze lamp. Here he was stripped and bathed, perfumed with exquisite essences, dressed in fine linen, and told to rest and wait for the hierophant.

Weak with fatigue, the novice stretched on the bed and fell asleep. Soon, tones of lascivious music reached his ears. The sounds of a harp and a flute enwrapped his soul, arousing passionate feelings in him. While he was in this semiconscious state, a woman approached.

This woman of breathtaking beauty, wearing a dress of transparent dark-red gauze and a necklace, held a cup crowned with roses in her left hand. The youth trembled at the sight of this woman with shining eyes and lips of fire. Why was she here? There was no one else in the grotto other than the two of them. The woman was reaching out to him, making plain that they should lie on the bed together, and murmuring in a husky voice: "Are you afraid of me, noble stranger? I come to you with the reward of the victorious as a present. I bring you the cup of happiness by which you may forget your troubles. Come, let us make love and spend hours of delight together." So saying, she sat on his bed and touched him to arouse his passion.

If the young man fell for this seductress, if he accepted her embraces, she would make him drink from the cup. After the wild satisfaction of his desire, his head began to swim and his throat to burn. Soon he was in a deep sleep, brought on by the medicated wine he had drunk.

The temptress would then vanish. When he awoke, he saw the hierophant standing over him with a stern face. The priest said: "You were successful in your first trials. You overcame death, fire, and water, but could not conquer your self. You, who sought the heights of mind and knowledge, could not resist the first temptation of the senses and fell into the abyss of matter. He who is a slave to his passions lives in darkness. You preferred darkness to light, so stay there henceforth. You have saved your life, but lost your freedom. From now on, you will be a slave of this temple. If you try to escape, you will die."

If, on the other hand, the aspirant turned down the temptress, he would have succeeded in this last trial as well. Then, twelve priests bearing torches escorted him into the hall of Isis. Magi, standing in a semicircle, awaited him. In the splendidly lighted hall, a colossal statue of Isis held a gold rose at her breast and wore a crown of seven rays. Her son Horus was in her arms. (Symbolized by a hawk, Horus was among the first deities of the Egyptians.)

The hierophant, clothed in velvet, swore the newcomer to silence and submission. Then he greeted him as a brother and a future initiate. What the youth had experienced up to this point was the entrance examination and ceremony.

Training

Now began long years of study and apprenticeship. He was assigned a cell to live in, and was given instruction by teachers. He could stroll in the halls and courtyards of the temple, as large as a city. He studied hiero-glyphics inscribed on the columns, as well as the history of humankind, minerology, botany, medicine, architecture, and sacred music.

The temple was, for all practical purposes, a university. Only the most intelligent students were accepted, and given sophisticated training. Many of the positive sciences saw daylight here: physics, chemistry, geometry, and astronomy were quite advanced. The laws of natural phenomena also were discovered in this environment.

Hermeticism was more a center for meditation than religion; the existence and Unity of God was known via this education. The young people here were researchers as well as students. They were all meditators and thinkers. To them, the advance of science was grounded in the birth of truth in the human spirit, and thus the latter had to be creative. But this was possible only after long and arduous effort. Their teachers did not help them in anything, for one had to discover truth by one's own efforts. They were amazed at this, but in time learned the reasons.

Absolute obedience was required, but nothing was revealed beyond certain limits. Their questions were met by the stolid reply, "Work and wait." Many students fell prey to suspicions; they regretted that they had ever come, and regarded their teachers as impostors or magicians. But with the passage of time, as their spiritual intuition flowered, they began to understand the Unseen and the Mysteries. Only then would the disciple begin to fathom the meaning of the temple.

Humanity has achieved its present level of civilization through labors of this sort. These sciences are the common heritage of humankind. No nation can lay exclusive claim to them. Human intelligence has flourished in every age. And this has started not with the material world, but with religious beliefs, with the search for the mysteries of the spiritual world, and with efforts to attain Unity.

At these temples, the young disciple tried to decipher the meaning of the hieroglyphs. In time, the invisible and impalpable truth slowly began to dawn in his heart. Sometimes he asked one of the magi: "Will I be able someday to smell the rose of Isis, to see the light of Osiris?" to which the reply was: "That depends not on us, but on you. Truth cannot be given. Either one finds it in oneself, or one does not. We cannot force you; you must become an adept yourself. Do not rush the blossoming of the divine flower. If it is destined to come, it will in its own good time. Your duty is to work and pray."

And so the disciple returned to his studies. Many years went by as he meditated and tried to discover truth. If he was a true disciple, he surrendered wholly to God and dedicated himself to truth.

The Conquest, or Opening

If he studied long and hard for many years, one day, the disciple found the hierophant standing beside him. The master said:

"My son, the time is coming when truth will be revealed to you. For you have already descended to the depths of your heart and there found the life divine. By the purity of your heart, by your love of truth, and your self-denial, you have earned that right and proven your worthiness. But no one can see Osiris' light without dying and being resurrected first. We shall take you to the crypt. Don't be afraid, for you are one of us already."

At dusk the priests, bearing torches, took the adept into the underground or "initiation" crypt, and stopped in front of an open sarcophagus made of marble. "No man escapes death," said the hierophant, "and every soul, having died, is destined to resurrection. Lie down in this coffin, and wait for the light to dawn upon you."

The initiate lay down in the sarcophagus, and the priests departed in silence. A funeral chant could be heard, coming from afar. The coldness of the tomb, the darkness, the silence, and the sadness of the chant all acted upon him. He felt he was dying.

Of all the secret practices of the ancients, this is the best-attested one: the one for which we have the most evidence. Albert Champdor, for instance, elaborates:

> Priests performed complex and secret initiatory rites in dark and spare crypts, virtually tombs, beneath the temple floors. They…removed all light from the vault. Locked in the blackness and isolated from all living things, the initiates to be came close to the death that delivers, exalts, and purifies. Their long vigil in the secret room of the sanctuary cracked slightly the formidable mystery of resurrection. The trial symbolically separated the soul from the body.…Those who returned from the depths of these spiritual and physical abysses in the pits of the mastaba burial chambers, were initiates.[196]

The student experienced dissolution in the darkness; for all practical purposes, he was indeed dying. Eventually he saw a far distant, shining point, coming closer and growing larger until it became a five-pointed star whose rays included all the colors of the rainbow. The star grew into a sun, which disappeared and gave way to a bud that blossomed into a beautiful flower. This was the mystical rose of Isis, the rose of wisdom. Soon it, too, vanished into a formless white cloud. The cloud, after assuming various forms, condensed in the shape of a human being. This was a veiled, smiling woman, a manifestation of Isis holding a scroll of papyrus in her hand. She slowly approached the tomb and said:

"I am your invisible sister, your divine soul. This is the book of your life. Its written pages contain your past life. In its blank pages, your future life will be written. Now you know who I am. I shall come whenever you call me."

Yet this, too, was a veil, an obstacle in the way, to be transcended perhaps now, perhaps in the future. Then, the adept would be raised into the light of Osiris, and be merged into the ineffable Essence of the universe of which it is impossible to speak.

The disciple felt the love of wisdom flood his heart. Falling into a deep sleep, he found the hierophant and magi leaning over him when he awoke. The high priest gave him a glass of sherbet, and said: "You are resurrected. Come celebrate with us, and tell us about your journey in the light of Osiris."

After this, his instruction by the high priest continued at a more advanced level. Having dined together, the master took the new initiate to the observatory of the temple, and instructed him in the mysteries of Hermes. He related to him the Vision of Hermes, never written on any papyrus but always orally transmitted. He told the initiate about the Ascent of Hermes, how he saw the Seven Heavens, and even the Almighty Himself. All these activities in the name of religion improved human intelligence and provided the foundation of modern science. The development of science and technology owes a great deal to these ecstatic activities of Antiquity.

Sufic Interpretation

Such, in brief, is a synopsis of Hermetic initiation. But what has all this got to do with Sufism? In what follows, I shall bring together and summarize the various explanations the Master gave, except for a longer digression (my own) on the sexual trial, because the importance the Master attaches to this event calls for a more detailed treatment.

According to the Master, then, the phenomena described in the Hermetic ceremony all arise and are manifested during the spiritual journey (*thuluq*) of the Sufi, but not within the confines or crypts of a temple. Instead, they are manifested in conditions of real life and during meditation (*tafakkur*).

In the beginning, the Seeker is frightened while passing through the corridor full of animal-headed, human-bodied statues. Although we have become accustomed to viewing these as the "gods" of the Egyptians, they are all "keepers of the gate" or "guardians of the way." Their collective message is: "You cannot pass!" All this inspires the fear of death, and is intended to scare the disciple.

Such figures (called "demonic beings" in the West and "wrathful deities" in the East) all emerge during the initial stages of meditation. As one is purified, they take on the countenance of beauty (and are replaced by "angelic beings" or "blissful deities," respectively). These are actually forms within oneself, reflections of the beauty coefficient of one's soul.

The symbolic alphabet has its Sufic counterpart in the *Abjad* letters in Arabic,[197] the purpose of which is to attain Truth.

The trials by fire and water are all included in Sufism. These represent difficulties: they are not actual fire or water, but the difficulties of life. It becomes easy to cross those difficulties if one has reached the stage of the Contented Self (*nafs al-mutmainnah*).

On the Trial by Lust

Note that the trial by lust bears the whole force of the Master's emphasis. It must be stated that this is not just a matter of concern for the disciple of Hermeticism or Sufism—it is one of great importance for us all. In a pamphlet on the subject, the Master has declared: "O student of the path, illicit lust has been forbidden to you. Beware: you will be cast out of the university altogether unless you can successfully complete this trial." To him, illicit sex represents the total negation of human potentials and possibilities—not only for the adept, but for everybody. Human beings are meant to discover the mysteries of the universe, rather than falling victim to their wayward passions and their base instincts.

Our approach toward sex is characterized by extremity. It either becomes a thing of absolute good or of unmitigated evil. But surely science has taught us to recognize different shadings, to distinguish between subtle yet important differences? Chemical substances, which are deadly poisons at certain doses, are, at different doses, used as medicine to save lives. Conversely, overindulgence can cause something that is normally harmless to become fatal.

Such is the case with sex. Sex can be part of our salvation or the cause of our ruin. More correctly, our lifestyles will determine our salvation or our ruin, and this includes our sexual habits too. The important point here is that we must achieve *balance* in every aspect of our lives. There is a middle way between excessive celibacy and total promiscuity, and mankind has not, in thousands of years, been able to devise a better solution for this than marriage, which God ordained from the very beginning.

When a married couple bring themselves to a deep participation, a total involvement in each other, within a relationship formed of emotional caring and commitment, sexuality becomes an experience bordering on the divine. And within the limits of legally approved marriage, God has pronounced His blessings on the experience He has ordained for the propagation of the human race: "Be fruitful and multiply." In such peace and security, spirituality may also blossom.

Marriage also provides the support that we need in the struggle against our lower natures. It is only within a secure relationship that the individual can achieve self-mastery and self-control, the weapons one needs to use against that tyrant, one's Base Self. It should not be forgotten that we are at our most vulnerable against our *own* selves.

The road to a person's ruin, on the other hand, is paved with excess: sexual promiscuity associated entirely with pleasure, divorced from any other considerations at all. People indulging in it take their own transient desires as their guiding principle, ostensibly released from any consequences for their actions, moral or spiritual. Sex can become the strongest weapon of the Base Self. And this is the pivot around which self-mastery and self-control rotate. One is reminded of the statement of the Buddha, who said that if there had been a second equally powerful drive to conquer, he would not have been able to achieve Enlightenment.

The consequences of promiscuous sexual encounters glare at us from every corner of the globe. To satisfy men's unfettered desires, in many parts of the world women are forced, often at an early age, to become "sex slaves"—selling their bodies to earn a living. The so-called "free sex" movement, ostensibly advocating freedom, has done nothing but exacerbate this "sexploitation" of woman. And where women and children are sacrificed, the whole of humanity pays the price. In this lamentable situation, not only is a person enslaved to his or her lower self, but women and children are victimized by that self: abused by the people who exploit them and the desires they are forced to service. And the offspring of these relationships—what do they experience of "freedom"? Characterized as they are by pain, by regret and recriminations, extramarital relationships have always been complex and debilitating—they do nothing but sap our physical and spiritual resources, both at the individual and the societal level.

This is why all monotheistic religions have denounced extramarital sex (rather than sex per se), and have tried to foster healthy marital relationships. The purpose of marriage is not to put women under the subjugation of men, but to prevent them from carrying the brunt of male selfishness—to secure their rights and their children's rights. Doing so provides the ground for a healthy individual and therefore a healthy society. It is because God loves humans so much that He has insisted on banning behavior which is sure to lead to suffering. Humans might be able to put up with such degradation themselves, but God will not suffer His finest creation to be abased in this way.

Psychologically, illicit sex is damaging to those involved. Sociologically, it is damaging to society. But there is yet a further type of damage that needs to be considered most carefully—the spiritual. All sacred texts are united in their love of purity and cleanliness. But we need to ask ourselves: "Why?" It is because the spirit, by its very nature, is subtle and pure. It is also very delicate. It needs "light" and "water" to survive in the healthiest of conditions. Consequently, it needs to be protected, to be nurtured. In all kinds of illicit sex, however, the aura or etheric envelope covering men and women alike becomes punctured. Like a plastic pitcher with a hole at the bottom, it becomes incapable of retaining divine light. The cocoon of the subtle body is ruptured like a pierced eggshell, precluding spiritual metamorphosis.

This is the deeper significance of God's ban on illicit sex. This is why the *Corpus Hermeticum* states that a love which leads astray keeps one in darkness and death (1.19). This is why the Trial by Lust in the Hermetic ceremonies is the decisive test determining whether one will attain liberation or remain a slave of one's Base Self. And this, again, is why in Sufism, legitimate (marital) sex is considered, together with lawful gain and Formal Prayer, a precondition to the Friendship of God.

Against this backdrop, we can now see that the role of the moral Law is to create and preserve the infrastructure necessary for spiritual progress. Remove it, and you cannot have progress: you are denying yourself access to the Path. This is the meaning of the Trial by Passion—it is a spiritual barrier, and the moral barrier is there because the two are inseparable. Without morality, there is no spirituality. Thus, in the Divine Law, anything that helps spiritual advancement has been called "good," and anything that hinders it has been called "bad." It is not for nothing that God forbids or allows certain things.

The whole point of knowledge (*ilm*), to return to the subject that opened this chapter, is that it takes human beings—or more correctly, it allows them to take themselves—from what is bad to what is good: it improves one's life. Knowledge, as knowledge, needs to be translated into right action; action characterized by both material *and* spiritual gain. Only such action will allow us to realize our true potential as human beings, taking us from the schoolhouse to the university.

Graduation

Let us now return to the exact parallels between the Hermetic ceremony and the Sufic journey. Seclusion and the drawing in of the senses are an essential part of the spiritual death-rebirth process. Underground vaults, rooms, or cellars have been traditionally used for this purpose. Many Sufi sages, such as Hadji Bektash, Rumi, Yunus Emre, Hadji Bayram, and Eshrefoghlu, have experienced Unveiling (*kashf*) underground. In the poetic words of Rumi: "I was raw, I was cooked, I burned." Whilst we are preoccupied with the world and its treasures, we are denied spiritual growth simply because our focus needs to become more refined, more purified, less dominated by the outer and more by the inner. To use another metaphor, we need to journey from the garden to the house and then to the most secret rooms in that house.

The star that appears during the journey occurs also in Sufism, and has been incorporated into the higher stages of Freemasonry, that is, the Masons have accepted this star. The ripening mystic rose or blooming flower are also experienced at this stage in Sufism. The pretty woman who appears and says: "I am your soul" is your spirit. From here on, all human beings are your brothers and sisters. Passions of illicit lust do not arise in you. This woman has a double-edged aspect, for although she represents a great achievement, she is at the same time a final "obstacle" (*hitan*), because she still possesses form. In other words, one still hasn't broken loose from the world of forms and appearances—finitude—to attain the Formless, the Infinite.

The sherbet offered to the disciple is actually given in the "imaginal world" (*alam al-mithal*), and has an orange-lemon color. Once you drink it, nothing is left of the Base Self (*nafs al-ammara*). There is also an imaginal meal, where food is brought to the triumphant adept for him to dine.

At that point, the third and final university begins. One becomes a Perfect Human (Turkish/Persian pronunciation *insan-e kiamil*). Although one doesn't see the Face of God, one does hear His voice and can—like Moses—converse with Him.

Conclusion

We have come a long way from the knowledge society of Islamic civilization, but we have not forgotten it. Knowledge of the physical world, we possess in abundance already. What we lack is authentic spiritual knowledge—both in theory and in practice. The day we recover the vision of Thoth, of Hermes, will be a grand day for humanity. In that vision, physical knowledge and moral/spiritual knowledge are united, and—as Einstein always desired—complement each other.

Up to now, a superficial perspective that only focuses on the surface of things has cramped our vision. And science too has become compartmentalized, too specialized, since it is only interested in the *material* realm. So has religion. We have to withdraw to a distance from which the earth can be seen, in astrophysicist Carl Sagan's words, as a "pale blue dot." Then, all our quibblings over detail will fade from view, and we will be left with the grandeur of the universe and with what the Sufis call a "Unitary" vision, a recognition that all things are one.

The communication protocols on which the Internet, that globe-girdling computer network, is based, took their cue from the Open Systems Interconnection model. In this model, there are seven layers: the physical, data link, network, transport, session, presentation, and application layers. We can think of this in terms of a seven-layered cake. The physical layer deals with how data signals are transmitted: the production and transmission of streams of electrons (or photons). It is oblivious to even the *kind* of information that is transmitted. We rise from the physical level through various levels of abstraction, until we reach the application layer, at which stage information transfer is occurring in its most sophisticated form.

In a similar way, our adherence to a strictly materialistic reading of the universe—the "what knocks you on the head is real" kind of materialism—

is causing us to ignore all the other layers of information in the universe. Everything except atoms and photons, electrons and protons, neutrinos and neutrons, is passing us by. We go through life imagining a mute, silent universe, and then, suddenly, the darkness closes in around us. We fail to see the signified behind all these signs. If this isn't a waste of human potential, a total negation of human possibilities, I don't know what is. Because all around us, at this very moment, information transfer of the subtlest kind is going on at the most sophisticated levels. At this very moment, if nothing else, TV and radio waves from a thousand stations are passing around us and through you. *Show me just one of them!* And these are only the coarsest harbingers of what is actually going on. Some day our sciences, I believe, will progress enough to understand this.

Researchers studying the lowly leech, for example, found that when they touched a leech at an angle b away from the point on the skin that causes a neuron to fire most rapidly, the corresponding neuron fired at a rate proportional to the cosine of b. The leech's nervous system thus computes, with mathematical precision, the coordinates of the point where its skin is touched, and is able to perform even more complicated trigonometric calculations. The ability to do this sort of calculation is built into the neurons themselves.[198] In other words, we now know that mathematical information—beyond any simple signal transfer—is being processed in a highly sophisticated manner in this "primitive organism." The neural system then uses this information to bend away from the stimulus. (As an aside: if the leech can do this with its forty neurons, what might we be able to do with our billions of neurons, were they to be in tune?)

Since the leech itself did not design this ability into its neurons, who did? Any engineer can tell you: there are so many ways a design can go wrong that only the greatest conscious effort will prevent it from doing so. If you leave things to chance, you will *never* get it right. No engineer, no inventor, ever designed anything by randomly flipping coins. And since when did random evolution learn trigonometry? To attribute mathematical order of this kind to chance is to disregard the laws of probability, which set the limits for what chance can or cannot do. The only way to get around this is to confuse the definitions of order and randomness. The laws of probability tell us that it is almost impossible for chance to achieve order of this kind.

Meanwhile, we live in an ocean of information, and that astounding things are happening all around us all the time in the most unexpected places. As the Koran puts it: "Look, then look again. Your gaze will return to you, dazzled and amazed" (67:4). But where information (non-random data) is, there must also be Intelligence, and this Intelligence predates humans or their discovery of that information.

It is interesting that Hermeticism and Islam were the only wisdom traditions to find equal worth in physical and spiritual knowledge, which they viewed as complementary. In both, the divine order evident in the cosmos and within humans reflected the omniscience of God.

Our comparison between the selected Hermetic writings and Koran-based teachings has revealed an almost one-to-one correspondence. We have seen, further, how the Hermetic initiation ceremonies are vindicated and corroborated by living Sufic practice. In other words, both the theory and the practice of Hermeticism are validated in contemporary society by the (true) followers of Mohammed. The fact, moreover, that the two wisdom traditions are in substantial agreement despite great variations in time, locality, and the persons involved, *demonstrates that there exists an objective science of spiritual transformation.* The conclusion, then, is inescapable: Although it is itself now extinct, the Hermetic tradition lives on in Islam, in Sufism.

✴

In this chapter, we have seen how the wisdom traditions of Hermeticism and Islam are similar through a close textual comparison of their writings and an analysis of other correspondences such as the initiation ceremony. In the next chapter, we will survey the various Sufi techniques of transmitting knowledge and how they categorize the stages experienced in this journey.

The Spiritual Journey of the Sufi
―――――――― ✳ ――――――――

(In this chapter, we will explore Sufi methods of teaching and study some of the rules, methods, and principles they employ. The spiritual journey has been charted carefully by Sufi masters and precise terms have been applied to the various stages an adept may pass through.

Although there are many spiritual schools or mystical orders in Sufism, the main orders, founded by the principal saints, are twelve in number, the rest being offshoots from these twelve major orders. And while the various orders exhibit diverse characteristics and peculiarities, they all operate within the boundaries of the same spiritual science, under the auspices of the Word of Witnessing and the Word of Unification.

The following outline of the Sufic disciple's spiritual journey is based mainly on the practices of the Naqshbandi Order, my Master's order, which, like all the orders, was named after its founding saint, Master Bahauddin Naqshband. However, anyone who studies this journey in detail will understand the meaning and content of all the spiritual schools.)

Exoteric/Esoteric

As mentioned earlier in the chapter on Holy Law, every true religion has two components: an outward (exoteric, *zahiri*) and an inward (esoteric, *batini*) aspect. The exoteric aspect is more concerned with external behavior and forms of worship, with social and corporeal conduct. The esoteric, on the other hand, deals with the inner world of humans, with our spiritual, mystical, and psychological dimension.

Now it is important to realize that if religion is a coin, then its exoteric and esoteric aspects are two sides of the same coin, comparable to the body and spirit of a human being. One cannot survive without the other. A religion reduced to exotericism is like a corpse—it has become pure, rigid formalism. And a religion that relies on esotericism alone is a mere wraith, a ghost that cannot animate its body. If a religion, on the other hand, combines both the exoteric and the esoteric, then we can say that we are truly in the presence of a living religion, a religion with the power to invigorate, to bestow life and felicity.

In terms of this criterion, one can order religions within a spectrum ranging from exoteric to esoteric. Most will be found to lie somewhere between the two extremes. The two religious philosophies of China, Confucianism and Taoism, are notable for the fact that they lie at the ends of this spectrum: the former is almost entirely formal, while the latter is almost wholly inward. (This, of course, does not diminish the many great truths and values embodied by either.) The two thus complement each other.

Ideally, a religion should strike a balance between the inner and the outer. It should be able to meet both the external requirements and the internal needs of humankind. Moreover, *form should match content.* The external laws, customs, methods, and so on of a religion should be in conformity with its inner practices. For this, there are two requirements: that the religion should be a revealed religion, and that it should have weathered time in its pristine condition.

Only God, the Creator of human beings, knows best what is good for them. No scientist or philosopher can know this, for the simple reason that the sum total of the possibilities and potentials of humans remain obscure to even the best minds. This is why a religion should be revealed by God. Moreover, only God can make the proper coupling between internal and external and maintain their perfect balance.

Further, it is also necessary that such a religion as practiced in our day should be a faithful copy of its original: metaphorically speaking, its clear stream should not have become polluted, corrupted, or shifted from its course. This brings us back to the requirement that form should be coupled to its proper content. When we peel a banana, we do not expect to find a slice of watermelon inside. God has created every exoteric formalism in association with its proper esoteric essence, and the divorce of the two—for instance, trying to live the inner aspect of a religion without regard for its external prerequisites—or substituting one kind of interior for another while retaining the same exterior, will not lead to results that are desirable.

Religions are organic, not mechanical things. You cannot break them down and recombine them as you like. If you lop off the head of a cat, the wings of a rooster, the body of a lion, and the tail of a peacock and attempt to put them together, the result will be a chimera, and a dead one at that. This is why syncretism in religion often spells trouble. To sum up, the external, exoteric aspect of Islam is known as the Holy Law, and its spiritual, esoteric aspect is called Sufism; these two must be combined.

Spiritual Schools

For every kind of knowledge there is a school. Anyone wishing to obtain higher education after primary and secondary school will go on to college or university; to medical school, law school, or polytechnic institute in order to become a doctor, lawyer, or engineer.

The difficulty, however, is that state-based systems of education everywhere prepare people only for the material world, for worldly success. They inculcate the basic knowledge necessary for surviving in this world, and endow people with a profession. But they do not recognize or answer the inner needs of human beings, nor do they assist their psychic/spiritual/psychological development. Even religious instruction is oriented more towards external conduct, regulations, and principles—all exoteric matters. The inner life of human beings is neglected.

But we neglect that inner life at our peril. The inner lives and outer lives of human beings are intimately connected—if the first is out of order, the second can't be healthy, either. If nothing else, the self-destruction of Europe in two world wars should give us pause to think and reflect: we should recognize that negative subconscious contents and accretions can result in explosive discharges that are as totally unexpected as they are universally destructive. The outer world shapes the inner world of humans; but conversely, the inner world of the individual also has an influence on the outer and social world. Without appropriate spiritual training, pacifying the soul, and satisfying its inner cravings, that influence can only be negative.

In our day, the need for such moral/spiritual instruction has taken on an added urgency. Humankind's scientific and technological advancement has far outstripped its moral progress. Somehow, man's spiritual maturity must be brought to the same level as our technical prowess—if nothing else, in order to control the latter and channel it to constructive ends—*and the need for this is much more urgent in a scientifically advanced society than it was in ages and civilizations that led a more pastoral existence.* This is not only because of technology's incredibly magnified capacities for destruction, but because, having solved its economic problem and rid itself of material want, the way lies wide open for humanity's unfettered spiritual improvement. The Chinese symbol for crisis is composed of two parts, one signifying danger and the other, opportunity. The dangers inherent in our present civilization are great, yet the opportunities are equally great.

Since, therefore, human beings do not live in the external world alone—since each one possesses an inner world in addition to the outer, which they all share—and since training this inner world is not only possible, but absolutely necessary, there have to be certain esoteric, or spiritual, schools in order to provide this education. And so there are. If they did not exist they would have to be invented, in order to meet this unsatisfied need of human beings.

These are the schools of the "Mohammedan University." Each one follows a different path, but they are all united in the end result. They are, as it were, the educational units of an "Invisible College." Whoever attains moral, spiritual, and psychological growth advances in these schools.

There is an important reason why these schools are not formal and official, like other schools. In this case, institutionalization yields results at odds with the intended goal. The official university is predominantly a matter of rigid form and structure. What is intended here, however, is exactly the opposite—the purpose is to pass from form to content, from external appearance to inner meaning. Spiritual education and progress is not something to be achieved formally, by bureaucracy and red tape. But the human tendency to organize and to create institutions is so strong that examples can be found in history where even these schools, with their extremely fluid and informal structure, have become ossified and consequently less able to fulfill their purpose.

The Perfect Master for the Esoteric Path

Although there are no formal schools for learning Sufism, the master-disciple relationship is a time-honored method of teaching. As Michael Polanyi has pointed out,[199] it holds no less true in science than it does in mysticism. Indeed, it is the accepted form of instruction in all branches of science and art.

Although mature spiritual masters have many distinguishing properties that set them apart from other people, the main ones are as follows:

1. They follow God's Commandments and the Way of the Prophet meticulously.

2. Your worries and anxieties are dissipated in their presence, giving way to contentment and affection.

3. You do not wish to leave their presence. Your enthusiasm and affection increases with every pearl of wisdom they utter.

4. All persons young and old, of high or lowly standing—even heads of state—feel obliged to offer them their respects and receive their blessings.

(Note that extrasensory powers or acumen are not counted among the above. Such capabilities may or may not be manifest in a master, but these cannot be taken as basis for proper instruction. A student who approaches a true teacher with the sole purpose of mastering such powers will be rejected, and rightly so, for these are merely possible and mostly undesirable by-products, not the goal, of the journey.)

Walt Whitman was speaking for the perfect master when he said: "I and mine do not convince by arguments; we convince by our presence." What the Koran says can be read in the master's movements and face. All the actions, behavior, and disposition of a person having these characteristics are consistent with the model of the Prophet. It is necessary to submit with a sincere submission to whomever possesses these traits without hypocrisy or exhibitionism. Once the aspirant has ascertained that this is a true master, s/he should be like a "dead person in the hands of the one washing the body" with such a master, obeying every instruction. In fact, even admonishments and punishments should be regarded as a blessing.

Actually, perfect masters are the most loving and affectionate of human beings. Especially those who are ardent for God and His love find them to be kinder and more compassionate than their own parents. To the wayfarers who visit them, they first teach the science of religion. They resolve difficulties in accordance with the Way (*sunnah*) of the Prophet. They clear away doubts, rectifying and fortifying faith. Then they give instruction in matters of cleanliness and performance of the Prayer (Arabic *salat*, Persian *namaz*). Because, as emphasized earlier in this book, *nothing is possible without Prayer.* They also explain submission, contentment, trust in God, and the importance of pleasing God.

Another characteristic of mature masters is to cover up shames. They never reveal the shames, errors, and misdeeds of people, and always conceal them from others. They know how to keep a secret. They are never angry with anyone and never utter a word that will hurt somebody. Their anger and severity are reserved only for situations which devotion to God require.

Such a perfect human always chooses the middle course in eating and drinking, in sleep, speech, and dealing with people. Applying the principle: "The median of everything is the best" in both habits and worship, such a person avoids the extremes of too much and too little, following a path midway between the two. This intermediate form of conduct is specific only to saints and perfect humans of the highest standing. Indeed, our Prophet has remarked: "Moderate conduct is the most beautiful of acts and the most admired of charming traits." There can be no doubt that a mature person endowed with this "Golden Mean" is the worthiest to instruct and advise others, and best suited to this task.

The Gifted Disciple

In the spiritual journey, not only the master but the disciple, too, must possess certain qualities. Receiving is as important as giving; if a student cannot receive instruction, the efforts of even the best teacher will be foiled. In addition, appropriate preparation is as necessary here as in the case of an ordinary journey.

The distinguishing characteristic of a gifted disciple is this: he or she is constantly at war with his or her self. (What follows applies to male and female alike—the third-person male gender is used only for brevity.) He torments and tortures this enemy with hunger, thirst, and speechlessness. He endures various difficulties and resists the inclinations of his self, grasps it with a powerful grip, and succeeds in subduing it. The gifted disciple is a self-surmounter; he is always striving to climb beyond his present level of selfhood.

It goes without saying that at this time the disciple or seeker has already mastered the exoteric path—the Five Pillars (Words of Witnessing, Formal Prayer, fasting, giving alms, and making the *hajj* to Mecca at least once in a lifetime) and the various other requirements of the exoteric path. Each of these outward actions has a corresponding inner action that leads the seeker eventually to the Flowering of the Perfect Human, the ultimate goal (or Golden Fleece) of the Islamic-Sufic journey.

The sole desire of the talented disciple is to purge his self of all undesirable and condemned characteristics. For he knows that his self is his own greatest enemy and that it is the source of the most dangerous spiritual illnesses. And for this reason, he strives his utmost to free himself from the effects of his ego.

Why is this characteristic required in a disciple? Because if he is content and satisfied with the level of self he happens to be in, there will be no motivation left for further progress to higher stages. Self-satisfaction is the nemesis of self-transcendence, and freezes progress.

Bahauddin Naqshband, the founder of the school known by his name, says:

"I have two legacies for travelers on this path. The first is: no matter what stage the traveler attains, no matter how far he progresses, he cannot achieve salvation and liberation unless he regards his self as a hundred times worse than the self of Pharaoh.[200] And the second is: no matter what stage he reaches, the traveler cannot be saved and will be ruined unless he considers himself a novice, who has as yet taken only the first step on the road."

If someone hurts him, the talented disciple does not curse or swear in return. Instead, he finds fault with his self, and says: "If my self were not bad, God would not allow these servants of His to pester me like this." If someone complains of him to his master, he tells his master that not they, but he, is to blame, and that the fault is his.

Such a traveler, then, who can conquer the self, can hold it in his palm, and who blames only his self for all errors, is gifted and worthy to enter this path. If he exhibits certain errors and imperfections from time to time, these may be excused, and do not constitute a permanent obstacle to entering the True Path. For when he observes bad behavior in himself, he criticizes his self. He does not exchange bad words with anyone, nor does he swear at them. He blames his self for every mistake and never sides with it. The true disciple does not allow himself feelings of superiority.

But if the traveler is happy with his self; if he fails to struggle against it; if self-love and pride overcome him; if he cannot vanquish it by remaining hungry, thirsty, and sleepless when necessary; if he places the blame on those who beat or swear at him; if he takes offense, becomes their enemy, and tries to exact revenge; if he sides with his self, seeking its ease and comfort—this disciple does not have the talent to embark on the journey, and cannot even sniff the aroma of the path of the saints.

The basis of the road of those close to God is to be displeased with one's self and to be its enemy—to "Struggle" (*mujahada*) against the self and thereby join the ranks of those who achieve "Observation" (*mushahada*). If the traveler does not build his spiritual career on this foundation, he will be building on quicksand, and sooner or later it will fall down like a house of cards. Because someone who does not know his enemy cannot find his friend.

We should pause here to clarify the meaning of "Struggle" and "Observation," and the relationship between the two. Struggle is also called the Great Work, effort, or labor against the self and its selfishness. As selfishness is defeated, one rises to progressively higher levels of the self. Now the degrees of observation (or perception) available to these different levels are not the same. The five outer (physical) senses are common to all human beings; they correspond to the Base Self, and determine our perception of what is called the "observable universe." There is, however, an "Invisible (*ghayb*) World" in addition to the visible world. As we know, there are things that are invisible or unobservable to the unaided senses, such as radio waves, even in the visible world. When we say Invisible World, however, we mean primarily the Spiritual World, susceptible to perception by the five inner (spiritual) senses, which are the counterparts of the five external senses (inner sight, inner hearing, and so on). Naturally, since these inner senses ordinarily lie dormant, people are not aware of their existence. As one attains higher levels of the self, these senses are awakened, and what is normally invisible becomes observable. This is what is meant by Observation, which comprises various categories such as Revelation (*wahy*), Unveiling (*kashf*), and Intuition or intuitive perception (emergence into consciousness). The highest stage of Observation is the Vision of God, but this sight is possible only in the most refined states of self-purification.

On this journey, three rules of conduct are essential for the traveler:

1. No matter what level of maturity the disciple attains by the grace of God or the aid of his master, he must try to increase his humility, self-effacement, and nothingness. If he is able to do so, he should consider this, too, to be a grace of God and give thanks to Him. He should never fall into self-assertion. The servant should remain firmly established in poverty, weakness, and nothingness, which characterize the station of servanthood. He should not reach out for power, majesty, and self-sufficiency, which are the attributes of God, until God strips that person of human attributes and grants him subsistence through His Essence. Deviation from self-denial and self-renunciation on this road is unbecoming in a disciple. Whoever desires to be freed of mortality will abide by this.

2. When a state, behavior, or anything else that displeases the master manifests itself in the disciple as an ordinary human failing, he should not lose heart and cease to visit or serve that master in the belief that all is lost, and that he is of no use anymore. Utmost attention should be paid to this point.

3. When the master orders something, it should be carried out happily and with gladness of heart to the best of one's abilities. These three issues are of the greatest necessity for the disciple.

General Rules

On the road to Truth, there are many things to be learned and many methods to be applied. We shall only dwell on certain general rules here, and shall select the Way of the Naqshbandi (Naqshi for short) as an example. It has been said that "the end of all roads is the beginning of the Naqshbandi road." It is the shortest path of closeness to God.

One of the finer points inherent in this saying is that with the Naqshis, the master shows the disciple the goal of the journey at the very outset, so that the disciple can then concentrate his efforts with full consciousness on the achievement of the goal. The Prophet taught the science of wisdom and presence privately to Abu Bakr (the first Caliph), but did not divulge it to the general public, not even to the other caliphs. There are three principles on this path: eating sparingly, sleeping sparingly, and talking sparingly.

Eating little leads to short sleep, short sleep leads to talking little, and talking little is a great aid in invoking God within one's heart at every instant. Hence, the main thing is to eat sparingly.

Eating little also has a second benefit. Satiety leads to pride, and pride leads to anger. Thus, eating little also holds these two in check.

Actually, it is enough for those entering this path to observe moderation in food, drink, sleep, and speech. There are three conditions for this:

1. To put away all worldly thoughts, images, and memories from the mind.

2. Never to forget God, always invoking (remembering) Him in one's heart.

3. Always to be in Vigil (wakeful watching) of, or Communion with, God (*muraqaba*), to bear God in mind.

The spiritual prerequisite of this path is the love of God and longing for Him. If this worry, this concern has entered a heart, this should be regarded as the greatest gift, and one should ceaselessly strive to increase it without losing it.

The Invocation (*zikr:* literally, "remembrance") of God in one's heart is the shortest road that leads to God, and the key to the inconceivable world of Unity, which also protects one against troubles and calamities. The gain of those entering this path is always to be in God's Presence. When that Presence takes root in the heart, it is called Observation (*mushahada*). When Presence becomes Stabilized (*tamkin*), i.e., when it becomes permanent and free from Variation (*talwin*), the goal is achieved. God is known at every moment, one is always with Him, and is never heedless of Him at any instant.

What follows are three methods the Naqshis have to achieve this state:

Method 1: The Word of Unity

The invocation (*zikr*) of the phrase: "No deity but God" (*la ilaha illAllah*). The invoker repeats this "Word of Unity" with a peaceful heart. In the case of the Naqshis, the repetition is performed not aloud, but silently, from the heart. (The Prophet taught the silent invocation to Abu Bakr, the first Caliph, and the vocal invocation to Ali, the fourth Caliph.) In pronouncing the negation: "(There is) no deity," one considers all things and all beings as nothing, and in pronouncing the affirmation: "but God," one contemplates the eternal existence of God. During the repetition of this sacred word, the tongue is folded back and its bottom is pressed upon the palate. The wayfarer holds his breath for reasonable periods of time, and repeats the invocation with such intensity that its effect is spread to all parts of the body. In everything the disciple does, s/he does not fail to repeat it under any circumstances. This repetition is not weakened or relaxed even when speaking, eating, or during sleep. When one notices that this state is waning, one summons one's attention and again concentrates, and finally the invocation settles and becomes permanent.

Method 2: The Invocation of God

The invocation of "God" (*Allah*). The invoker turns to God with his or her heart and invokes His majestic name. In repeating, one should consider God as being present at every point in the universe. He should repeat the invocation with such vigor that he passes away from himself, and arrives at such a rank that this state is ever present in the heart—it becomes a property of one's heart, which is filled with that light, and one experiences great pleasure. Whatever the states of the heart may be, these should remain in the heart. The secrets that are revealed to it should not be divulged to the public, and one should not step beyond the bounds of the Divine Law (the principles of Islam).

If the invoker does not fail to think of God for even an instant, if he invokes God's name even in his sleep and does not stand aloof from Him, his sleep as well as his wakefulness will be the presence of God; he will quickly achieve "spiritual poverty" and "extinction."[201] Depending on the aptitude of the aspirant and the grace of God, the period in question can be anywhere from an instant to a lifetime.

Method 3: Spiritual Connection with the Master

The third method, Connection (*rabita*), is the way of binding the heart. The wonderful conversations of a perfect master pave the way to divine communion. By the power and virtue (*baraka*) of those discussions, the light of spirituality and inner meaning flows into the aspirant's heart. If this meaning is diminished, the disciple must again avail himself of the master's discussions, until he can hold the master's image in his imagination even when they are separated. The disciple drives all other thoughts and memories from his heart, leaving only the form and memories of the master.

There is no closer way than this. If the enlightened face of that master—perhaps the middle of his eyebrows—does not leave the disciple's mind for even a second, if he is not heedless of it while sitting, standing, or eating, if he can always bear it in mind—and this is quite difficult to achieve for the disciple—the wayfarer reaches such a rank in the end that the image of the perfect master takes root in his heart, and he can imagine it at every instant without difficulty.

But if courtesy (good manners) is violated, this path of illumination can be interrupted in the disciple. It is then very difficult to reestablish "the Tie" and communication. To find the conversation and teachings of an exalted and valuable master is a great boon in this day and age.

The Eleven Principles

We cannot, in a treatment such as this, leave the "Eleven Words" of the Naqshbandis unmentioned. The first eight of these were established by Master Abdulhaliq Gujduwani, and the last three were added by Sheikh Naqshband. They are as follows:

1. *Invocation (Yad Kard or zikr).* Basically, this is to invoke the Word of Unity while holding one's breath (*habs dam*) for a suitable period of time. Retaining the breath during a certain number of invocations prevents the attention from wavering and the mind from wandering.

2. *Knots (Baz Gasht).* This refers to short prayers that punctuate Invocation (see above). When the number of invocations during breath retention is finished and one is exhaling, one repeats a formula such as: "My Lord, You are my goal and my desire is to please You." This prevents one's thoughts from straying, and the invoker is delivered from recollections and baseless thoughts that might flood his heart.

3. *Wakefulness (Nigah Dasht).* This refers to cognizance of, and combat against, mental distractions. One must fight off various thoughts and images that assail the mind, and the heart and attention should remain centered on God. This is very difficult and requires great effort. Breath control is the most important aid in achieving it.

4. *Recollection (Yad Dasht).* This means always to remain attentive of God. Everything except God should be removed from the heart and mind, and concentration should be centered on Him.

5. *Watching one's breath (Hosh Dar Dam).* Every breath of the Seeker should be inhaled and exhaled with wakefulness and awareness. Breathing should be controlled, and one must be fully conscious of one's inhalations and exhalations. Master Shahabuddin Suhrawardi has clarified the reason as follows: "He who does not control his breath cannot control his self, and he who cannot control his self belongs to the company of the ruined."

6. *Journey to the homeland (Safar Dar Watan).* This is the spiritual journey back to God, from whence the traveler (and indeed, everything

else) came. The voyage from bad and disgusting behavior to salutary conduct.

7. *Watching one's step (Nazar Bar Qadam).* The Seeker should always keep his eyes on his feet. If the disciple looks around indiscriminately, his attention will stray; what he sees will be impressed on his heart, and confusion will result. Also, in a metaphorical sense, he should always be aware of where he is going, and never lose sight of the journey's goal.

8. *Solitude in company (Halwat Dar Anjuman).* The Seeker must be *in* the world, but not *of* the world; to be with people (or God's creation) externally, but to remain with Truth (God) internally. The aim is to concentrate on preserving one's spiritual state as if one were alone, even in the presence of others.

9. *Pause of time (Wuquf Zamani).* The Seeker should pause from time to time for self-examination and self-criticism. One should give thanks for one's good conduct and repent for what is bad in oneself.

10. *Pause of numbers (Wuquf Adadi).* Another aim is to take care that the required number of invocations have been completed during breath retention. One begins with a single invocation (say, of the Word of Unity) and gradually raises this to twenty-one. For example, one inhales, repeats the formula three times, then exhales. If a certain result has not been obtained even though twenty-one repetitions have been reached, it may be necessary to repeat the cycle.

11. *Pause of the heart (Wuquf qalbi).* Here, the Seeker tries to imagine that the true name of God is inscribed in his or her heart, and aims to train the mind until this visualization becomes permanent.

As we have seen, these eleven rules are mostly concerned with the concentration of attention, and with breath retention and breath control.

Chart of the Spiritual Journey

On the road to Truth, to Absolute Reality, the traveler is always in a different state at each step of the way. It is useful to tabulate these in order to gain an overall view. The contents of this chart, shown in Table 1, will be briefly described. The points that we need to bear in mind are:

1. The chart is not precise, but serves to give a general idea only.

2. Various sources give this table in different and sometimes conflicting ways. The classification of Ibrahim Hakki of Erzurum, a great saint, is followed here, but other sources have also been consulted.

3. The journey of each traveler diplays individual peculiarities. Perhaps for this reason, masters do not indulge in detailed explanations about the chart of spiritual progress. It should be remembered that the chart is only a convenient device for comprehension, rather than a rigorous exposition of details.

Worlds

In the Sufic conception, the observable universe, the physical world of coarse matter, is only the lowest of existential realms. Beyond it are domains that do not lend themselves to physical measurement for the simple reason that they are nonphysical (or prephysical, "pre-" being here used in an ontological rather than necessarily temporal sense). The number of worlds, including the physical, are basically four. And no one has expressed this fourfoldness with greater poetic beauty than William Blake:[202]

> Now I a fourfold vision see,
> And a fourfold vision is given to me;
> 'Tis fourfold in my supreme delight
> And threefold in soft Beulah's night
> And twofold Always. May God us keep
> From single vision and Newton's sleep.

"Single vision" is the vision that sees only the world of gross matter, that denies reality to any other level of existence, including God, who is Absolute Reality. Thus, a relative, partial vision of reality negates total, Absolute Reality on the basis of nothing except its own bias and incompleteness, which is the very epitome of irrationality.

Yet the founders of modern science never intended it this way. To exclude every reality other than what is capable of knocking one on the head is a betrayal and travesty of their original conception. To be sure, they confined their investigations to the realm of sensory experience; and behind every law of nature they saw the Divine Lawmaker, without whom all would be chaos, if indeed it could exist at all (which it could not). Newton believed in One God: as he said, "This being governs all things...as Lord over all; and on account of his dominion he is wont to be called Lord God Pantocrator, or Universal Ruler" (*Principia*). His research into alchemy points to the interest of this great scientist in the transformation of the soul, for which the transformation of base metal into gold is merely a metaphor.

Kepler combined in himself love of the One God with scientific devotion to the discovery of His harmony as evidenced in nature (specifically, the elliptical motions of the planets)—he was the most salutary example of the fusion of science and religion in a scientist.

Descartes, too, believed in God. As quantum physicist Werner Heisenberg once noted of him, he trisected totality into God, man and universe, and the division between man and universe he formulated in the dualism between mind or consciousness (*res cogitans*) without extension, and matter or extension (*res extensa*) without consciousness. Copernicus rightly believed that scientific knowledge could only lead to evil in the hands of the spiritually impure. The metaphysical assumptions of these great thinkers may have finally led to our present conception of a soulless, Godless, mathematical, and mechanical universe, but this was never their initial conscious aim.

Hence, what we have to do is to "re-vision" the whole scientific enterprise, to go back to the founders of modern science; not necessarily to revise, but to take a fresh look, to examine our knowledge and assumptions in a new light. When we do so, we shall discover that there is nothing in our science to rule out or contradict the existence of other existential domains, since that knowledge was never intended to describe anything other than the physical world in the first place. If I decide to confine my attention to a study of the objects in my room, without even bothering to look out the window, this does not mean that nothing exists beyond my room.

The Sufis, then, believe in the existence of the material world, but allow also for the existence of other planes of reality (*alam*, plural *awalim*). This is not a question of reducing the material world to the spiritual or ideal (note that "spiritual" and "ideal" are not identical) world, or vice versa; not a question of "either/or," but of "both/and."

These "other worlds"—or, if you wish, "parallel universes"—have each been referred to by more than one name by the Sufis. As in Blake's Four-fold Vision, there are four realms in the simpler, basic classification: Human, Angelic, Majestic, and Divine (respectively *Nasut, Malakut, Jabarut,* and *Lahut*). These are to be conceived as hierarchical rather than equal in rank.

The Human World is, quite simply, the world of human beings, the world we witness and perceive with our five senses—the physical, material, or observable universe. For this reason, it is also called the World of Witnessing (i.e., the world that we witness), the Base (lowly) World, or the World of: Elements (after the classical four elements), Births, Creation and Dissipation, the Visible, Fear, Heavens, Spheres, Stars and Bodies. It is often called the Kingdom (*mulk*).

The Angelic World is the world of dominion, where God is the recognized absolute ruler. For this reason, it is also called the World of Command. It is the Unseen (*ghayb*) world of angels and spirits.

In our chart, the Angelic World occupies two adjacent cells, the Interworld and the World of Spirits:

a) *The Interworld* is the "isthmus" or intermediate world, the World of Imagination, accessible in twilight states of consciousness (between sleep and wakefulness). Its basis is the Imaginal World (*alam al-mithal*) or World of Symbols (Archetypes), which is superior to it.

b) *The World of Spirits* is superior to the Interworld, and is also known as the World of Meanings or the Dreamworld. It is the locus of awe.

The Majestic World is the World of Power. It is also known as the World of Realities. This is also the stage where the Mohammedan Reality manifests itself, and the disciple is filled with Mohammedan Light.

The Divine World is the World of Divinity, and is, like the Angelic and Majestic Worlds, an Unseen, Unobservable, or Invisible world—in fact, it is the Unseen of the Unseen of the Unseen, or U^3. The divine principles are framed at this level, the World of Loftiness. It is the World of the (Infinite) Cloud (*ama*), to which the Prophet referred when he was asked: "Where was God before He created the universe?" He answered: "My Lord was in point of a cloud without top or bottom." (That is, He was present at every point of an infinite—homogeneous and isotropic—cloud of white light.) In Sufism, it refers to the level of Absolute Unity and Eternity. Although it appears in only one cell, it actually encompasses the last three cells of our chart.

Sometimes, the Self or Identity of God is differentiated from this Divine World and assigned a separate status. This is then called *Hahut* (from *huwiya:* "He-ness," Identity, or Divine Ipseity) and the five realms that thus result are called the "Five Presences" (*hazrat hamsah*). In this case, when one wishes to refer to the fourfold scheme, *Lahut* and *Hahut* together are called the World of Glory (*Izzah*).

The Essence (*zat*) of God in relation to Himself is called Absolute Unity (*Ahadiyah*), and corresponds to *Hahut*. (This is the unknowable Hidden God, the *deus absconditus,* and it is forbidden to speculate about the nature of God's Self or Essence.) In relation to His Creation, it is called Oneness (*Wahidiyah*), and corresponds to *Lahut.* The latter is associated with the Most Sacred Body (*wujud al-aqdas*).

Return to Witnessing. Here, the return begins from the Unseen to the Human (Witnessed) World. This, however, is not a return to an earlier state, but a proceeding, a going forth.

Unity in Diversity, Diversity in Unity. The Divine World is experienced in the states of Extinction (*fana*) and Subsistence (*baqa*). Unity in Diversity is the final stage.

Present at the Creation

Creation begins with God. In the beginning—and this is an ontological, not a temporal, beginning, since time does not yet exist and hence it makes no sense to speak in temporal terms—God was a hidden Being who had not yet manifested Himself. This is the stage of Absolute Invisibility, Absolute or Unconditioned (nondelimited) Unity, the World of the Absolute, the Singular Existent, or Mother of the Book (the book of the universe). Since space and time do not yet exist, this is totally nonspatial and nontemporal; it is non-space and non-time. Rather, it may be called "the spacetime of spacetime," since the entire spacetime continuum takes shape within it. (In terms of Unity versus Multiplicity, we can compare this stage to a priceless, perfect jewel possessing absolute symmetry, and which is single, whole, and one in every imaginable way.)

When God desired to be known, He manifested His being in the remaining three worlds:

First, in the World of Divine Power—the First Conditioning or Limitation, the First Manifestation, Primordial Substance, Mohammedan Light or Mohammedan Reality. (At this stage, the jewel is still whole, but the possibility of differentiation and multiplicity has arisen, and micro-cracks or fractures in the symmetry have appeared.)

Next, in the Angelic World—the Second Conditioning or Limitation, the Second Manifestation, also known as the Isthmus or "Lote-tree of the Boundary." (Our jewel is still whole, but fissures now crisscross its surface.)

And finally, in the Kingdom, or world of human beings. This is the Third Conditioning or Limitation. (At this stage, the jewel has exploded, bursting and shattering into smithereens and giving rise to the infinite multiplicity of the observable universe—yet this Multiplicity is still One, although this fact is not evident to our senses. For the fragmentation of the jewel is illusory. It is only to our fragmented consciousness that it appears shattered. In reality, even at this instant, it remains in its pristine unity.)

We can now see that the journey of the seeker is back to the Source, and that he traverses the ontological stages of Creation in the reverse order. He travels from Multiplicity to Unity, and in the end discovers the true meaning of religion, the mystery of God, and the secret of being human.

Abdulqader Gilani, the Great Helper and diver into the bottomless Ocean of Unity, explains:

"All conduct, states, and limits between the Human and Angelic Worlds belong to the Divine Law (*sharia*). Those between the Angelic and Majestic Worlds belong to the spiritual schools or Orders (*tariqah:* Paths). And those between the Majestic and Divine Worlds belong to Truth or Reality (*haqiqah*)."

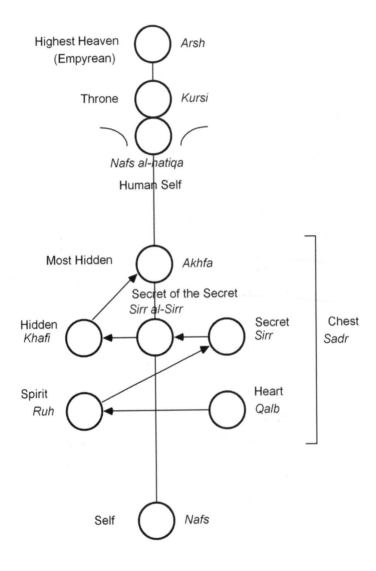

FIGURE 1. The Ten Subtleties (*lataif*).

The final stage, Knowledge of God (*marifah:* Gnosis), corresponds to the Divine World, or Absolute, Undifferentiated Unity, where knowledge of everything else (Multiplicity) is unlearned (this is the "Cloud of Unknowing").

States

The seeker's state at the beginning of the journey is characterized by an *inclination to lust* and pleasure. He follows the lead of his selfish and lustful desires. The master's instruction and training, however, soon result in the emergence of *affection* and enthusiasm. This is not sexual affection, but the pure and unsullied attraction to Truth. This affection increases and is finally transformed into *love.* Nothing is possible without love. Love is what delivers results. It gives rise to *attainment* and, when perfect faith has crystallized in the heart, to *fulfillment.*

The seeker then loses himself utterly (*fana:* Extinction or Annihilation). Only God is left, which is why this state is also called Extinction in God (*fana fi-Allah*). After this point is reached, certain divine mysteries are revealed to the seeker, who consequently is thrown into a state of *wonder.* Finally comes the state of Survival, Continuation, or Subsistence (*baqa*), whereby the traveler is given a renewed existence by and through God (*baqa bi-Allah*).

Locations

In order to understand locations, we first have to learn about Subtleties (*lataif,* sing. *latifah*) or psychic centers. We have already seen that human beings possess a spirit. This spirit is coupled to the physical body in the form of a *spiritual body.* Now this spiritual body possesses a *psychic anatomy* or structure, just as the material body has a physical anatomy. When Sufis speak of the Heart, for example, what they have in mind is not the physical lump of flesh that pumps blood throughout the body. They refer, rather, to the heart of the spiritual body, which is associated with the spiritual body and animates the physical body as long as a human being is alive.

In the same way, there are other psychic centers within the spiritual body akin to the Heart center, and it is to these that the term "Subtleties" applies. These psychic centers are variously referred to as the Five

Subtleties, the Seven Subtleties, or the Ten Subtleties. All ten Subtleties are shown in Figure 1.[203]

The five basic subtleties are located in the chest (*Sadr*). These are: the Heart (*Qalb*), the Spirit (*Ruh*), the Secret (*Sirr*), the Hidden (*Khafi*), and the Most Hidden (*Akhfa* or *Ikhfa*).

In order to obtain the seven subtleties, the Self (*Nafs*) is added to the beginning of this list, and the Human Self (*Nafs al-natiqa*, or Speaking/Reasoning Self) is added to the end. Sometimes the Self (*Nafs*) is omitted, and the Total (*Kull*) is added to give the seven subtleties.

An intermediate stage called the Secret of the Secret (*Sirr al-Sirr*, or S^2), and two further centers beyond the Human Self—the Throne (*Kursi*), and the Highest Heaven or Empyrean (*Arsh*)—complete the list of ten subtleties. Occasionally a further center, the Total (*Kull*) or the Universal Intellect (*Aql al-Kull*), is inserted between the Human Self and the Throne. (This may be considered a subcenter of the Throne.)

Further information concerning these subtleties is outlined below. (Note that all measured distances are approximate, and that the colors and locations of the centers are sometimes listed differently.)

The Self: This is the center of the animal (animating) self, and corresponds to the *Hara,* or Life Center, of the Japanese. It is located within the body an inch below the navel or belly button.

The Heart: Also called *Fouad,* this does not actually coincide with the physical heart (which is more centrally placed), but is located an inch below the left nipple. It is associated with the color red and the prophet Adam, "whom God purified."

The Spirit: Its location is an inch below the right nipple. Color: yellow. Prophet: Noah, "whom God saved."

The Secret: Location: an inch above the left nipple. Color: white. Prophet: Moses, "who talked with God."

S^2: Location: center of the chest (between Secret and Hidden). Color: black. Prophet: Jesus, "the Mystery of God."

The Hidden: Location: an inch above the right nipple. Color: green. Prophet: Mohammed, "the Beloved of God."

The Most Hidden: Location: top of sternum (just below the neckline). Colorless. In some charts this is called the Axis of the Secret (*Mustawa al-Sirr*).

The Human Self: Location: between the two eyebrows. According to some Sufis, this is the station of *Qaaba Qawsayn,* "the distance—or meeting—of two bows/arcs" (eyebrows) (53:9). Color: ocher.

The Total and/or *the Throne:* Location: center of the forehead. This is where, at a certain stage of development, the famous "third eye" opens. (Please note, however, that the third eye has nothing to do with physical anatomy, such as the pineal gland, as Descartes claimed.)

*The Highest Heaven (Empyrean):*Located at the crown or topmost point of the head. Corresponds to the *Sahasrara Chakra* (the "thousand-petaled lotus") in Yoga. (These correlations with other traditions are mentioned not because the Sufic conception was taken from these as sources, but in order to highlight the fact that the corresponding realities have also been recognized in other traditions, since truth is one.) This is where divine light—called "the most sacred effusion" (*fayz al-aqdas*) by the Sufis—appears, initially in the form of a star. This location also corresponds to the juncture of the cranial bones, and in some traditions has been considered the entry point of the soul into the body (the bones are not joined in the newborn baby, but close later on).

Now that we have formed some idea about the subtleties, how does one utilize this "tree of life"? Basically, the procedure is to activate the psychic centers in ascending order. One starts by concentrating on the chest area (*Sadr*) as a whole. (Note that its color, blue, is also the color of a healthy psychic aura.) One then concentrates on the Heart subtlety, and so on in accordance with the direction of arrows in FIGURE 1. Each center is awakened by concentrating the invocation appropriate to that stage in that center. For instance, looking at Table 1, *Allah* is the invocation proper to the Heart center. Once an invocation becomes fixed or permanent in its center, and light of a color specific to that center (as well as certain other signs) becomes manifest, the center is considered to be "conquered" or "opened." One then passes on to concentrating invocation in the next higher center.

Warning: Note once again that one must not try to awaken any center without the permission of a qualified master. This is very dangerous. Do not try to "teach yourself," and don't experiment. Without proper guidance, you're liable to get lost in God knows what sector of inner space.

God has stated in a Sacred Tradition: "Know that there is a [physical] Heart in each body. There is a *Fouad* [spiritual Heart] in each Heart. There is a Secret in each spiritual Heart. There is a Hidden in each Secret, and there is a Most Hidden in each Hidden. I am in that Most Hidden."

This "withinness" should not be compared or confused with physical contiguity. It has no quality and quantity, and is different from whatever may occur to the mind.

Supports

The entire comport of the seeker from the beginning right through to the end should lie within the Divine Law, that is, the prescriptions and restrictions of Islam. At no stage should adherence to the Sacred Law be abandoned, for it is the basis, the foundation, of all.

Upon his works in accordance with the Holy Law, the aspirant next builds the knowledge and practices of the spiritual schools. New restrictions are added upon those of the Divine Law. One passes from License, where some things are allowed by Holy Law, to Restraint, or further limitation (compression) of the self. This is followed by Knowledge, which is the Knowledge of God, i.e., being informed about God. This information and these practices lead the seeker to Truth. After this he can attain Sainthood, or the Friendship of God. His next support is the Essence of Divine Law. He does not remain ignorant of the reasons for the Divine Law, and acts out its requirements in full knowledge and consciousness of their reason for being. Finally, his support becomes the Universal Essence.

Lights

Lights with colors distinguish one subtlety from another. This color is blue in the beginning. The Heart center glows with a reddish light when it is activated. The color of the Spirit center is yellow, and so on.

Names

Names define the invocation to be performed by the seeker at a certain stage. A specific name of God is invoked at each stage, and the aspirant passes from one to another as he progresses.

Perceptions

Perceptions refer to various levels through which a wayfarer passes. They are activated only at the last three stages of selfhood. We may distinguish here between perceptions of Unification (*tawhid*) and those of Fusion (*jam*).

Unification of Deeds/Verbs—of Attributes/Adjectives—of Essence

The universe has often been compared to a great book by the wise. "The book of the universe," said Galileo, "is written in the language of mathematics." One of God's ninety-nine Beautiful Names, the Counter (or Reckoner: *Muhsi*), bears testimony to the fact that God indeed created in numerical measure and proportion. Wherever we look in the observable universe, we witness the mathematical beauty that the Great Artist (*Sani*) has built into it.

So Galileo was right—but his understanding was, nevertheless, incomplete. Our modern science, which is quantitative through and through, gives us only a one-dimensional picture of the universe: that projected upon the Real-Number Line. Numbers can tell us a lot, but they can't tell us everything. It is as if scientists had opened the book of the universe, encountered letters, words, and sentences on each page, then proceeded to measure the dimensions of characters, their groupings into words, their frequency and regularity of occurence, and so on. This is a very telling metaphor, for in physics and chemistry the "alphabet" of the universe is composed of the ninety-two naturally-occuring elements, in biology of twenty-two amino acids, and so forth.

But because of its exclusive preoccupation with quantity, modern science has neglected to actually *read* the Grand Book of the Universe—to *read* and to *understand* it. Our measurements performed on it are unsurpassed, yet our understanding of it is still insufficient. The secrets it harbors remain as locked as ever, and it is these we need to decipher.

Now the Sufis, too, have viewed the universe as a book to be read. In Arabic, *fiil* refers both to an action and, linguistically, to a verb; *sifat* refers both to an attribute and to an adjective, *ism* both to a name and a noun. Taking their cue from this, the Sufis have represented the Book of the Universe as being composed of verbs, which are God's actions; adjectives, which are His attributes; and nouns, which are His names. In their conception, the Essence of God gives rise to the Divine Names and

Attributes, from each of which derive myriads of Divine Actions, and the universe is scene to the vast and continual interplay between these elements. Hence to return to the Source, one has to unify, first, the actions to reach the level of God's Names and Attributes, and then to unify these in turn to reach the unity of the Essence. This, in the Sufic view, is how pure, changeless, infinite Being becomes conditioned or transformed into continual yet finite Becoming: through the endless interplay of Names, Attributes, and Actions.

We may compare this process to the differentiation of pure white light into a rainbow of colors when it passes through a prism, and in this analogy the prism would be comparable to the "Immutable Entities" or "Permanent Archetypes" (*ayan al-thabita*), as the Sufis have termed it. From every Name and Attribute that has thus been differentiated, myriads of actions are spawned. Thus, everything in the universe is an intersection or locus of specific Divine Names, Attributes, and Actions. One must reverse this process in order to reach the Source, which is the Essence of God. The unification of Actions leads to their origin in a Divine Name or Attribute, and unification of the latter yields the pure white light of the Essence, which is then seen to stand behind all the countless manifestations occuring in the universe.

Fusion (F⁰), the Presence of Fusion (F¹), Fusion of Fusion (F²), Unity of Fusion (F³)

The various states of Fusion are achieved only by the rarest individuals who have attained the heights of Sufic mysticism. They are best understood in terms of Annihilation and Subsistence (in God). A possible interpretation of the relationship between the stages of Unification and those of Fusion is given in FIGURE 2.

It is difficult to decribe these states because, unfortunately, these terms have little meaning for those who have not experienced these states. As Rumi, the great mystic, said: "*Be* me, and you will know." I shall try to decribe them, but please keep in mind the difficulty of expressing them.

Manifestation

These next states are manifestations of Actions, Names/Attributes, and Essence in the manifestation of Actions: An action amongst the Actions of God is born and manifested in the heart of a servant. An aspect of the Divine Power flowing through all things becomes manifest in that person. That servant thus perceives that God is the cause of all motion and change. Only the "possessor of this station" (the person who has reached the permanence of this state) knows and understands this.

In the manifestation of Names: God causes a name from among His Beautiful Names to be born in the heart of a servant. This person is so overwhelmed by the divine effulgence that engulfs him through the power and lights of this name that if that Divine Name were to be called upon at that instant, he would answer.

In the manifestation of Attributes: The Lord manifests one of His Attributes in the heart of his servant. All human attributes disappear from him, and God appears in his heart in the guise of that Attribute. For instance, if God appears to him in the Attribute of Hearing, that person hears and understands the voices and sounds of all beings, whether animate or inanimate.

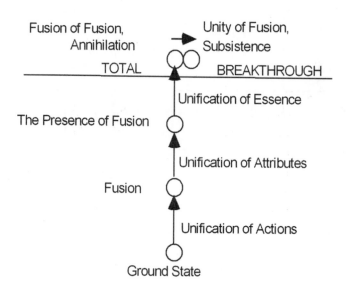

FIGURE 2. State Transition Diagram of the Spiritual Journey

STATION OF SELF (nafs)	IMPELLING (Carnal or Base Self) (ammara) (12:53)	CRITICAL (Self-Reproaching) (lawwama) (75:2)	INSPIRED (mulhimma) (91:8)
JOURNEY (thuluq)	To God (il-Allah)	Toward God (li-llah)	Upon God (al-Allah)
WORLD (Realm) (alam)	Witnessing (shahada) HUMAN (NASUT)	Interworld (Isthmus) (barzah) ANGELIC	Spirits (arwah) (MALAKUT)
STATE (hal)	Tendency to Lust (shahwah)	Affection (muhabbah)	Love (ashq)
ABODE (Subtlety) (latifa)	Chest (sadr)	Heart (qalb, fouad)	Spirit (ruh)
ARRIVAL (Support) (warid)	Revealed Law (sharia)	Path (Schools) (tariqa)	Gnosis (Knowledge) (marifa)
LIGHT (nur)	Blue	Red	Yellow
NAME (Invocation) (ism)	No god but God (la ilaha illAllah)	God (Allah)	He (Hu)
LEVEL (tabaqa)	Aspirant (talib)	Seeker (murid)	Wayfarer (thaliq)
STATION (maqam)	Repentance (tawba)	Avoiding prohibitions (wara)	Asceticism (zuhd)

TABLE 1. Chart of the Spiritual Journey

SERENE (Tranquil) *(mutmainna)* (89:27)	PLEASED (God-Satisfied) *(radhiya)* (89:28)	PLEASING (God-Satisfying) *(mardhiya)* (89:28)	PERFECTED, PURIFIED or SANCTIFIED[1] *(kamila, zakiya* or *safiya)*
With God *(ma-Allah)*	In God *(fi-llah)*	From God *(ani-llah)*	By God *(bi-llah)*
POWER (JABARUT)	*DIVINE (LAHUT)*	Return to Witnessing *(shahada)* *(LAHUT)*	Unity in diversity, diversity in unity *(LAHUT)*
Attainment *(wuslah)*	Extinction *(fana)*	Wonder *(hayrah)*	Subsistence *(baqa)*
Secret *(sirr)*	Secret of the Secret *(sirr as-sirr)*	Hidden *(khafi)*	Most Hidden *(akhfa)*
Truth *(haqiqa)*	Sainthood *(wilaya)*	Essence of Revealed Law *(zat ash- sharia)*	Universal Essence *(zat al-kull)*
White	Black	Green	Colorless
the Truth *(Haqq)*	the Living *(Hayy)*	the Everlasting *(Qayyum)*	the Overwhelming *(Qahhar)*
Voyager *(sair)*	Flier *(tair)*	Attainer *(wasil)*	Pole *(qutb)*
Poverty *(faqr)*	Patience *(sabr)*	Pleasure *(ridha)*	Trust in God *(tawaqqul)*

[1] Sometimes counted separately to give a total of nine.

The manifestation of the Essence: To achieve this state is to be very close to God. By dint of worship, the wayfarer has become adorned with humility, spiritual poverty, and consciousness of his own weakness. He knows God through his self and attributes, and knows this self through the Attributes of God. Because the self of this Perfect Human has found lowliness and nothingness, the mirror of servanthood stands face to face with the Mirror of the Divine, and whatever is visible in one is reflected in the other. On this basis the Lord has declared: "The heavens and the earth cannot contain me, yet the heart of my faithful servant does."

All these details and techniques, however, will be of no avail if the aspirant does not pay attention to two crucial points: *abstention from illicit gain, and from illicit sex.* For all the icy baths of the Brahmins, the sleepless nights of the Buddhist and Christian ascetics, the self-inflicted tortures of the Hindu fakirs, the seclusion of Sufi dervishes in mountain caves or dungeon-like cellars—these all served only one end: the control of the Self. And yet, self-control is actually predicated on these two critical points alone: Forbidden passion and pecuniary interest. Protect yourself from these, and the way to sainthood will remain open. Otherwise, not only will all your efforts come to naught, but the gates of fire will welcome you. Here, it is necessary to watch one's eyes, one's ears, one's tongue, and one's mind. If at any time you observe a tendency in these toward Forbidden earnings or passions, then the Work—the Struggle—has not been completed.

Provided the two points above are fulfilled, meditation (*tafakkur*) and invocation connecting the heart with the mind—more precisely, the Heart Center with the Center of the Human Self—will lead to progress on the path, never neglecting the other requirements, beginning with Prayer.

Above and beyond all these details lies the progress of the seeker through the levels of selfhood. The treatment of these levels is important enough to merit a chapter in its own right.

The Flowering of the Perfect Human

————————— ✫ —————————

(This final chapter leads us through the various stages of selfhood, the "stations of wisdom" on the way to the flowering of the Perfect Human, the goal and endpoint of all human development. Feats such as teleportation have not been unknown among those who have aspired to this state, and a summary is presented of the subject with particular attention to recent developments in modern physics.)

Preliminary Notes on Terminology

The nature of man has traditionally been held to be tripartite. In addition to his outer being, the body (Greek *soma*), his inner existence has been conceived as having an "I", ego, self, or soul (Sanskrit *Atman*, Greek *Psyche,* Hebrew *Nefesh,* Arabic *nafs*) and a spirit (Latin *Spiritus,* Greek *Pneuma,* Hebrew *Ruach,* Arabic *ruh*). The spirit is the difference between a living body and a dead one, i.e., that which animates the body, and is considered to survive after bodily death; in other words, the phenomenon of death is nothing but the decoupling or *dégagement* of the spirit from the body. The self, I, or soul, on the other hand, is the seat of (self-)consciousness; in a loose analogy, the spirit is to the soul as a fruit is to its core or kernel—the two are inseparably connected.

Now the soul and the spirit were considered to be different and distinct entities in both early Hebraism and early Christianity. Yet with the passage of time, the two became confused, so that today the soul, the spirit, and the psyche are considered synonymous, and it is not always

281

clear in usage which of the two aspects one is referring to. This situation derives from the fact that both the spirit and the soul survive after death, as well as from the fact that they both mean "breath" in various languages (see the equivalents given above). As we shall see below, however, the distinction between them is a useful one to maintain. In what follows, therefore, the "self" has been consistently used for the "soul" to avoid confusion, and this terminology is adhered to at least throughout this chapter. Also, to avoid cumbersome language, the male third-person represents both the male and female genders, as before. Needless to say, Sufi sainthood is open to women as well as men, of whom the archetypal example was Rabia al-Adawiya.

Introduction

In his famous mystical poem, *The Conference of the Birds,* the Sufi poet Fariduddin Attar depicts the search of a company of birds for the legendary arch-bird, the *Simurgh.* This name, meaning "thirty birds," simultaneously represents the number of birds in the flock, which is also thirty. (Actually, the original name of the poem, *Mantiq al-Tayr,* can also be translated as "The Reasoning of the Birds." Like the Greek *Logos,* which stands for both "Word" and "Reason," the Arabic word *mantiq* signifies both "speech" and "logic.")

After traveling through seven valleys and experiencing many arduous adventures, the birds finally come face to face with the incomparable Simurgh. The climax of the story is also one of the most moving pieces to be found in the poetry of mysticism. Here are a few sample lines, in the unforgettable translation of Edward Fitzgerald:

> *All you have been, and seen, and done, and thought,*
> *Not you but I, have seen and been and wrought...*
> *I was the Tajidar[204] who led the Track:*
> *I was the little Briar that pull'd you back...*
>
> *Come, you lost atoms, to your Centre draw*
> *And be the Eternal Mirror that you saw;*
> *Rays that have wander'd into darkness wide*
> *Return, and back into your Sun subside.*

Now the search of the birds for the Simurgh is none other than the human search for God, or Absolute Reality. And the seven valleys they have to traverse are the seven stages, or "stations," of the self.²⁰⁵ Only at the final stage can the veils fall from one's eyes, revealing a vision of the incomparable splendor of divine majesty. This is an experience so amazing, so miraculous, so ineffable, that all those who have been graced with it agree that compared to it, there is nothing else worth living for. In the words of Misri, another Sufi poet, "If the ruler of the entire world heard of this, he would give his life for just a drop of it."

Our theme in this section, then, is the stages of the self as described in Islamic and Sufic sources. Happy the ones who, traveling from stage to stage, draw ever nearer to the source of all being and the sought-after goal of becoming the Perfect Human. And pity the ones who, lacking the drive and the diligence to work out their own salvation, remain stuck in the basement—the dungeon!—of the Base Self.

The Lord Almighty in His wisdom has sent down the secrets of His Essence from the invisible Heavens to the Earth, and has hidden those secrets in the essence of each human being in order to reveal His own Names and Attributes. But humans, sinking into the darkness of the egotistical self, have forgotten the values and perfections they possessed before coming into the physical world. When human beings leaned toward the external world and the compulsions of the self, they donned the attribute of ignorance and completely forgot their truth and homeland. Whereupon God sent them prophets and holy books to wake them from this heedless sleep, to guide them to the straight path, to purify and order their inside and their outside, so that they might finally sweep away the cobwebs of darkness and the veils of lust, discover the World of Light, remember their origin, and return to it. Who approaches God even an inch with this intent and desire, He will approach by a foot, and He comes running to those who merely walk toward Him.

As with the ancient Egyptians (*ba* and *ka*) and Chinese (*hun* and *p'o*) before them, Islamic scientists divided the human spirit into two parts. The first of these they called the *animal spirit,* and the second, the *human spirit.* What they termed animal spirit was a subtle spiritual substance that comprised the life, sentience, motive force, and will of the body, which man possessed in common with all animals. The self associated with this spirit is called—naturally enough—the *animal self (nafs al-haywani),* the carnal, egotistical, imperious, and impelling *Base Self.*

All the distinguishing higher faculties of man were grouped by the scholars of Islam under the heading of human spirit. The self associated with this spirit they called the *speaking/reasoning self (nafs al-natiqa),* and it is this self which is capable of evolving to the higher stages of selfhood: *accusing, inspired, serene, pleased, pleasing,* and *perfect.* But as the animal self is its substratum and the more exclusively human self cannot exist without this, the problem becomes one of taming the animal self and curbing its animal urges. It is only in this way that the more truly human—and divine—aspects of the self can emerge.

1. Self as Tyrant: The Base Self (Impelling Self)

In the *Arabian Nights,* Sindbad the sailor, during one of his many escapades, is shipwrecked and barely survives, dragging himself onto a strange island where he is washed ashore, and falls asleep in exhaustion. When he wakes up, he finds that an ugly pair of legs are entwined around his neck, and that they belong to a drunkard. From that day on, Sindbad becomes the slave of that debaucher, who never relaxes his stranglehold and beats our poor hero on the head until his every whim is satisfied.

Sindbad eventually escapes, of course, but the rest of the story is not our immediate concern. It has been remarked that the *Arabian Nights* contains elements of Sufism, and there is no better example in support of this than the drunkard's deadlock described above; for it is one of the best descriptions in world literature of the essential nature of the Base, or evil, Self.

Nor, however, is this all. In mythology and fairy tale, in epic and science fiction, we can trace the footprints of the lower self of humans: from the seven-headed Hydra (note the number seven!) to the dragon of St. George, from Mary Shelley's Frankenstein to cyborgs, androids, and killer robots—always, it is the despicable, impulsive, or compulsive self who is the villain, the ogre, the monster. And as mythologist Joseph Campbell aptly pointed out, he who conquers this Minotaur of a self is the hero, as in his title *The Hero with a Thousand Faces.* Always it is the same universal story that is retold, under a myriad of appearances and guises. The stories do not usually explain who the villain symbolizes, though this does not detract from their interest or enjoyment; but Campbell has given away the whole show. The enemy is not outside, but within: as the comics character Pogo once remarked, "We have met the enemy, and he is us."

But wait! Where there are dragons, there also are beautiful damsels and buried treasure. Where there is the "dragon of a thousand coils," there also is the Golden Fleece. So what is to be gained by tackling this adversary? Nothing less than something so valuable, so precious, that people of all times and climes have compared it to the hand of a princess or to priceless treasure hoards—not indeed because this was literally true, but because their imagination fell miserably short in attempting to describe what is really involved and could only allude to reality by such metaphors.

It is not simply in myth or sci-fi that we encounter the compulsive self, but also in contemporary literature, theater, and cinema—the arts, in short. We see it in Picasso's *Minotauromachy* ("Struggle Against the Minotaur") and *Guernica;* Hermann Hesse's *Steppenwolf,* which character is part wolf and part human; Oscar Wilde's *Portrait of Dorian Gray,* which becomes uglier as Dorian's misdeeds accumulate; Kafka's portrayal of a man's *Metamorphosis* into an insect, gigantic and revolting; Eugene Ionesco's *Rhinoceros,* which begins with a solitary beast that proliferates like Albert Camus's *Plague* until it encompasses the whole populace, charging to and fro—all are depictions of the domineering self. Modern and postmodern writers and artists, the antennae of society, are drawing attention to a psychic malaise which is so widespread that it is now also social—for religion has never been disclaimed to the extent that it has been in the twentieth century.

Perhaps psychology—*psyche-ology,* or "knowledge of the self"—should properly be dealing with this subject, but a recognition in modern psychology of the pharaonic aspects of the self are confined to the subconscious or id, to which all our meaner impulses are relegated. This is, of course, important: that the capricious self should have a subconscious component, extending like the roots of a tree under the ground beyond visibility and frustrating our attempts at conscious control, is certainly a significant discovery. But beyond this, cognizance of the despotic self is scarcely to be found. As for the higher levels of the self and the possibility of evolving to such levels, these lie entirely beyond the imagination of current psychology. Only very rarely in the West does one come across attempts to conceptualize the stages of the self.

One reason for this is that we in the West have been taught that the enemy, the arch-villain, is the flesh, or our instincts, or—in more recent times—the subconscious. These mistaken diagnoses have veiled the true source of strife from our eyes.

The motto of the carnal self is simplicity itself. From Rabelais's *Abbey of Thelema* to occultist Aleister Crowley's, "Do what you will shall be the whole of the law." This, however, overlooks a very simple yet dangerous fact: the more the vagabond self is given free rein, the more it tends to grow. The little squirming worm first becomes a king cobra, then a colossal, fire-breathing dragon. Prometheus unbound becomes Frankenstein unshackled. Looking at the male and female serial murderers of our day, who abuse, torture, and dispose of dozens of people without batting an eyelid, one can see the results of the dominating self run rampant, and since things are going from bad to worse, one can only shudder for the future. Newspapers report that cannibalism has revived—not in the dark jungles of Africa, but in Russia. *The Terminator* and *Alien* have nothing on them; as in the case of the armed person—to all appearances entirely ordinary—who enters a random store or restaurant one day and opens indiscriminate fire, the oppressive self dictates, first, the destruction of all others within its purview, and finally the destruction of its own self. Robots, mechanical men programmed to kill from whom all feelings of compassion and mercy have been removed, are the end result of this process.

These are, to be sure, extreme examples. So what about the rest of us ordinary human beings? Well, in the dark recesses of each person's psyche there lurks a Minotaur, patiently biding its time, waiting to pounce. It may be under wraps, we may be unaware of its presence, but it is there nevertheless. The Minotaur (not to mention all the other mythical images) is a symbol for a core complex of egotistical drives. And the "damsel in distress" that awaits salvation is the spirit. The choice is between our spirits and our egos; both cannot be free simultaneously. If the inferior self is given free rein, it chokes the spirit. The ego can suppress evidences of the spirit to such an extent that we begin to think we are soulless machines. Hence, in order to elevate and liberate our spirits, we must constrain and confine our egos. Only then is spiritual progress possible, only then can the spirit soar.

The containment of the egotistical self has taken on an added urgency in our day. Thanks to the spin-offs of science and technology, even the humblest person now enjoys privileges undreamt of by even the pharaohs and emperors of yesteryear. "Magical boxes" bring voices and images from the other side of the globe; "self-propelled carriages" transport even the poor at speeds no king or queen ever achieved in a lifetime. An African Bushman can communicate with the four corners of the planet. This progressive equalization of previously unheard-of opportunities and goods can only be applauded, and one can hardly think of it as bad.

Yet there is a catch. For the containment of the egotistical self is relatively easy in conditions of scarcity, but difficult in an environment of affluence. Because of the tendency of the inferior self to mushroom in such circumstances, our very luxury may prove our unforeseen undoing.

An ecological perspective is germane here. Not maximal, but sustainable consumption; adherence to the principle of the Golden Mean; taking no more than one's needs even when standing beside a vast ocean—this is how we can keep the commanding self at bay, sustain our standards of living, and contribute to the further democratization of available resources (sharing with others the common wealth of our world) in the midst of plenty.

At the first, entry level, the human or speaking/reasoning self has been subdued by the carnal self and is stuck at this level. It commands and impels to evil, for which reason it is termed the commanding or *impelling self*. Its characteristics are bad habits such as ignorance, miserliness, greed, conceit, self-adulation, lust, jealousy, bad manners, useless activities, making fun of and hurting and scolding others.

The impelling self is a burden on a human being. It is like an alcoholic son who does every iniquity and leaves his father to mop up behind him. Now the self, or "I," is a product of God's infinite grace. But it has become defiled by being attracted to the world and its intense interest in its own desires. It has come under the influence of animal urges which are pure lust, has become bound to lust and thus, to animality. It has exchanged its own admirable qualities for the lowly traits of animals, until its only remaining difference from them is outward form. Even Satan gains strength from it. This ugly self is an enemy within us. It is tyrannical and imperious, like a dictator. Furthermore, it emerges from under whatever stone it is lurking at the least expected moment, when we think we have vanquished it, and forces us to fulfill its despicable demands. Only after everything is over do we realize what has happened.

As Ahmed Sirhindi, a saint of great renown, says:

"In its state of impulsiveness, the self always strives to be superior—to be a leader, an authority, and greater than its peers. It desires that all creatures should be dependent on it and that they should obey its commands and prohibitions. It refuses to acknowledge its dependence on and debt to others. This is nothing but a claim to divinity, and association of itself with God. Indeed, the self with this quality of compulsion, miserable and distant from happiness as it is, will not settle even for partnership with God, but desires to subjugate even Him, to enslave all that exists. It is for this reason that aiding and abetting this self, the enemy of God, so that it may attain the leadership and authority it is greedy for, is the greatest of follies and disasters."

This gremlin can be tamed only by self-restraint. Give the impulsive self its rights, but deny it its pleasures. "The rights of the self," says Abdulqader Gilani, one of the greatest saints, are as follows:

> the needful amount of food, drink, clothing, and shelter. Its pleasures are the things it likes, and its lusts and caprices. Give it its rights in accordance with the measure of the Holy Law. Always feed it with what is Allowed or clean, never that which is Forbidden or tainted. Be content with little, as long as it is allowed. Accustom your self to this.

> If you desire liberation, oppose your self where obedience to your Lord is concerned. If your self tends toward obeying Him, concur with it. If it inclines toward sin, oppose and struggle against it.

> Do not remove the stick of struggle from the back of your self. Do not be fooled by its tricks. It will appear to sleep; do not be

taken in. Neither would you be off your guard in the presence of a carnivorous beast that feigns sleep and drowsiness. For it is seeking for a chance all the while that it seems lethargic and somnolent. It is in its predatory nature to do so.

Now the self is just like a predator. It acts as if it were sleepy and drowsy, yet the moment it finds its opportunity, it strikes. This self makes a show of external obedience, docility, and compliance with what is good; yet it is hiding the exact opposite within. So be very careful with it in matters where it appears submissive.

Try to heal your self. Say to it: "Whatever good you do is to your own benefit, and what evil you commit is to your suffering. Whatever you do, whether good or ill, will return to you."

Struggle against your self. For God has said: "Whoever struggles for Our sake, We shall surely guide to the straight path" (29:69), and also: "If you aid God in His religion, He will aid you" (47:7).

Never give the self any room, never tolerate it. Do not obey its demands. Only then will you find salvation and liberation. Never condescend to smile at it. If it tells you a thousand things, answer only one, until you are sure that its behavior is rectified and it is quiescent. If it requests anything belonging to its pleasures and capricious desires, always postpone it, saying: "Wait until Paradise." Accustom it to the patience of want. Never accept a word of what it says. For its propensity is always towards evil. What it wants you to do is evil, without the shadow of a doubt. If you must answer it, let your reply always be negative. Opposition to the self is the road to its edification.

Patience on this path has an end. Patience is temporally finite, yet its fruits are infinite.

The Devil

Enter the devil.

The devil is the principle of evil that exists in the external world. He is not directly perceptible to the physical senses, but as with many other things, we infer his existence through his effects. Rather than being an abstract principle, however, he is personified, for the Koran and the previous sacred books tell us that he is a fallen angel who, out of spite for humans, always tries to cheat them out of their rightful destiny, which is to attain Paradise and the friendship of God. Unlike other religions, though, the devil in Islam does not possess any great supernatural power, and his abilities are restricted to deceiving those who heed his misadvice. For this reason, he is termed "the Whisperer" in the Koran.

One of the cleverest ploys of the devil is to convince people that he does not exist. In this way, he can work his ways on unsuspecting people, and continue his task undisturbed. Further, since everything is known by its opposite, denial of the existence of the devil, who is evil, leads to the tacit denial of the existence of goodness, and of God. Once this point is reached, one is thrown into a moral turmoil where good cannot be distinguished from evil, and hence the tendency to do evil is magnified manifold, since one does not guard against it.

Within humans, the devil finds his natural ally in the animal self—the self that "always impels to evil." If one heeds the devil's whisperings and falls into his trap, the exterior principle of evil becomes interiorized. External torment becomes internal torment.

When the traveler is at the stage of the impelling self, the devil approaches him and attempts to thwart him from the path, bombarding him with the following suggestions:

"What business have you with this path? All those who have entered it are dead. Only their words and their books remain. I know you want to enter the Path of Truth. But who is there to guide you? Show me, where are the people of lofty attainment, of great Struggle and Observation, who are able to work miracles? That was in the past. Nowadays, you cannot find even one of their kind. The best thing for you is to remain with the Holy Law, be content with it, and seek help from the dead saints."

Deception, untruth, is the essence of the devil, and here he is trying to conceal a fact. Perfect Humans, mature masters and teachers, exist in every age. Mohammed combined two aspects in his person: Prophethood and Sainthood. Although he is the Seal of the Prophets, and hence no further prophet will be forthcoming, his attribute of Sainthood (the Friendship of God) will continue until the end of the world.

Now if the traveler heeds this advice of the devil, he will reduce his efforts and struggle in the path of the Spiritual School, his enthusiasm will cool, and a timidity in continuing the journey will come over him. In that case, the devil next comes to him and says:

"God is forgiving. He loves those who act with License toward permitted things. Stop treating your self cruelly. Treat it with tenderness, so that it may obey you."

License (*ruhsah*) is the opposite of Restraint (*azimah*), which is to exercise inhibition in performing things that are Allowed (*halal*). If the traveler does this, his notion of what is permitted and what is Forbidden (*haram*) begins to get confused, and he begins to approach the border of prohibitions as a result. As doubts increase, darkness invades the person's heart, and he finally winds up yielding to prohibitions.

If, however, God comes to the rescue, the traveler will be able to discern that all these delusions are from the devil, and say: "To pursue License is for the lazy. To act according to it is for weaklings. It is necessary to follow the manners dictated by Divine Law and the principles of the School." If the traveler can do this, the self will rise to the second stage, the stage of the Critical Self. From the prison of the carnal self, it takes wing to the space of divine spirit. In the end, that Seeker's pride is transformed into humility, hatred into love, callousness into tenderness, and lust into chastity.

2. The Critical Self

The second station of the rational self has been called "critical," "reproachful," or "soul-searching," because it repents of commanding evil and blames itself. Some traits of the compelling self still survive in this stage, but it has the ability to discriminate between truth and falsehood, between good and evil. It is disturbed by the bad traits it finds within itself, but is incapable of completely ridding itself of these. It loves the Sacred Law and the spiritual schools, however, and it has many good deeds to its credit, such as Prayer, fasting, and charity. Still, covert hypocrisy remains mixed in with them.

The possessor of this self wants his good works to be known by other people. S/he does them both for God's sake, and for show. S/he is revolted by this habit, however, and cannot find solace, but is also unable to get rid of it.

Those in this station have, of their own choice, decided to die to their selves and to exist with God, and have entered the path of dying by their own volition before physical death overtakes them. The Prophet said: "Die before you die," that is, try to kill your selves. Moses said the same thing to his people: "Slay your selves" (2:54). What is meant by "self" here is the ego—namely egotism, self-aggrandizement, and egocentrism. Suicide is definitely not implied.

It is necessary to continue on one's way without tarrying in this station. For there is great danger and an eroding weariness at Stage 2. Those who remain there cannot find comfort or salvation. The two dangers of this stage are arrogance and anger. Of these, anger is composed of the same fire that Satan was made of. Indeed, when his wife Aisha was angry, the Prophet said: "This is the fire which has been called 'the place of Satan.'" This state of fury is an extremely dangerous and accursed enemy for its owner. And the essence of this bad habit is arrogance. To eradicate this conceit from one's self is the best of all cures.

Anger and conceit have three antidotes:

1. When conceit is gone, it will be found that anger has vanished of itself. As long as the cause of conceit remains, it cannot be expelled. The cause of conceit is a full stomach. This strengthens conceit, and anger reaches the zone of depravity. Hunger and sleeplessness should therefore be cultivated, and conceit should be uprooted with hunger.

2. The best antidote for the stimulus of anger is to think of one's self as weak, and thus to consider oneself unjustified in attacking another. One must threaten one's self with the bitter fruits of anger and the retribution of God. Kindness, affection, and gentleness are necessary, but overcoming anger is even more necessary.

3. Another antidote for anger is this: If you are standing when you get angry, sit down; if you are sitting, stand up. If possible, take a Washup

(ablution), lie down face upwards, and recite the following prayer: "My Lord, enrich me with knowledge, decorate me with gentleness, grant me worship and fear of You, bestow well-being and health upon me. Amen."

Remember too that all beings envy the wayfarer, and try to prevent him from the presence of God. In return, that person should not favor anything or be afraid of anyone.

The devil makes one's actions appear lovable to a person in this station, and thus introduces feelings of self-love into his heart. Then he appears to side with truth, and says: "You have now learned everything. From now on, you have no need either to learn further knowledge, or to join the discussion groups of the wise and knowledgeable or to listen to the sermons of preachers. If only that man of knowledge or preacher would advise his own self, and perform even a tenth of your deeds!" As a result of this deceit, the person becomes so conceited that he does not heed a single advice of the sage. He does his worship according to his own mind, and is wasted away in the darkness of ignorance.

As can be seen, the tricks and deceptions of the devil are legion. He will wreck the deeds of the traveler if he can; and if he cannot, he will then instill a better deed in the seeker's heart—so superior to his works that he will be incapable of performing it. He praises this deed to the disciple and forces him to attempt it, so that in his struggle to achieve this higher goal the wayfarer forsakes even his lesser accomplishments. Thus, he loses both.

For example, the devil may suggest to the disciple that he perform the Pilgrimage, in spite of the fact that he lacks the means to do so. The disciple sets out on the road with little or no preparation, and becomes destitute. His heart begins to darken, he postpones his Prayers, and starts to gossip, swear, and engage in other ill deeds. Whereas he was a light-hearted, good-natured person at home, who comported himself with gentleness and regarded others as superior to himself, he now begins to criticize people and regard them as inferior because of these travails. He becomes ill-mannered, his heart becomes troubled, his self miserly, covetous, and critical of others. The devil thus achieves his goal.

If God's grace and salvation reaches out to this disciple and protects him from such devil-inspired delusions, that person can be raised to the third station by diligently practicing the etiquette of the Sacred Law and the requirements of the mystical orders.

3. The Inspired Self

The self in the third station is called *inspired* because it receives inspirations from the Lord without any intermediary. Although superior to the reproachful self, this too is a dangerous station and needs the guidance of an enlightened master to handle it. Otherwise, it is to be feared that a relapse to the previous stage will occur.

The aspirant should confess all desires and errors to his guide when they are alone, and should not hide anything from him. Whenever he feels like denying or opposing his teacher, he should tell him this without hesitation or holding anything back, and repent. For as long as one's faith in one's teacher remains firm and strong, his heart will be protected against delusions, and his ascent in the divine world will be assured. If someone wholeheartedly attaches himself to a mature guide, tells him all the good and bad thoughts that occur to him, if he accepts the remedies this guide offers and practices them with diligence, if one is pleased in his heart with this master—spiritual elevation is speeded and one reaches the fourth station quickly.

The fact is that this station, while superior to the preceding two, is still not secure against the inspirations of the devil and the ego. Because it also receives inspirations from God, it confuses the one with the other.

The efforts of the ego and Satan at this stage are geared toward dissolving the ties between the student and his master. In the guise of a divine inspiration, they try to make the master appear in a bad light in the seeker's eyes. But since the master is actually a mirror to people, the ugly characteristics that the disciple projects upon him are none other than his own. The lifesaver that the student must cling to on these stormy seas is the Holy Law. In particular, the Prayer must be performed with great care for its details. If this gives rise to arrogance and feelings of superiority in the disciple, s/he cannot rise to the rank of those close to God, and remains only in the rank of the good. But if the Seeker intentionally discontinues Prayer, s/he will be reproved, and deprived of the spiritual pleasures of Prayer. A condition of love is that the lover should obey every wish of the Beloved.

In this station, the traveler is prone to experiencing "loss-of-self." While in this state, the disciple forgets everything he knows, sees wrongly, understands wrongly, and is mistaken in general. The sense organs convey erroneous impressions and perceptions to the disciple at this stage. This state has nothing to do, however, with the "extinction in God" (*fana fi-Allah*) experienced at a later stage, and should not be confused with it.

The devil is still in hot pursuit of the traveler in the third station. Appearing to side with truth, he says: "You have now seen, heard, and understood everything. You have become a sage. Why should you need to perform all these arduous deeds any longer? From now on, what becomes you is this: Leave all the worship and work that belong to outer appearance to the externalists. Try to invest your time with internal worship, with concentration and contemplation (contemplate God and try to see Him), which are more important and necessary than external worship."

If the disciple is taken in by these suggestions and abandons worship and struggle, his heart begins to darken and the devil gains a foothold there. Once he has achieved this, he again approaches the disciple and says:

"You are the truth of your Lord, and He is your truth. You have now become a saint. All the observances and limitations incumbent upon mortal servants have been lifted from you. Therefore, you can do whatever you please or desire. Everything is permitted for you. You will not be held accountable." This is one of the most insidious deceits of the devil. For—to paraphrase Dostoyevsky—everything can be permitted only if one denies God.

When this happens, the veils of darkness engulf the physical and spiritual sight of the disciple to such a degree that he becomes completely incapable of seeing the truth. He does not hesitate to commit any iniquity, such as theft, treason, fornication, or drinking. The Seeker's faith is corrupted entirely, and s/he ceases to fear God, becoming such a plaything of the devil that s/he leaves God aside and takes the devil as a leader. Such is the sorry end of anyone who heeds the words of the devil.

If God's grace rescues this person, if s/he remains firm in worship and struggle with love and diligence, the self rises to the fourth station.

4. The Serene Self

The human or rational (speaking/reasoning) self in the fourth station is content, its heart is assured, and its sorrow dispelled by the speech of its Lord. This is why it is called contented, tranquil, or *serene.*

The disciple does not show the slightest deviation from the Holy Law in this station. He takes pleasure in practicing the moral conduct of the Prophet, his heart is contented by following his example in actions and behavior. Everything he says is in harmony with the Koran and the Traditions. Therefore, those who listen to this seeker never tire of listening, for the truths and subtleties poured into his heart by the Lord come alive in his words. This disciple enlightens those around him, and occupies himself with worship and invocation most of the time. He has won most of the approved qualities, and become invested with generosity, trust in God, surrender, patience, hope, righteousness, kind-heartedness, cheerfulness, thanksgiving, hiding others' shames, forgiveness, and joy of heart. He does not care for the paranormal feats that may manifest from him, and binds himself to God who is the true source of such phenomena. He knows that being partial toward these is shameful and leads one astray. Perfect Humans do not know the psychic achievements exuding from them, and if they do, they don't attach importance to them; they try to hide them, and don't tell them to anyone.

For the perfect person truly in love with God, all thoughts that do not accord with the Sacred Law are in error. For the Folk of the Inner have found internal perceptions that violate the external world to be perverse. *Every external decree of the Holy Law has a secret—an internal—counterpart.* But one who does not abide by its clear, outer precepts can become neither a saint nor perfect. The hidden treasures of the Divine Law remain locked to that person. S/he may even become faithless and perverse.

But the person who has attained the fourth stage has, after great struggle and hardship, finally been able to overcome the devil. He abides by God's Commandments and the Prophet's Way in every move and deed. These two are the only lifesavers and branches to hold on to in tempestuous seas. Hence the traveler reaching this station has definitely beaten the devil, and the hazards of the earlier stages no longer exist at this level. From now on, it is much easier to progress to subsequent stages. The

Koran has underlined this ease with the verses: "*Contented* Self, return to your Lord, you *Pleased* with Him and *Pleasing* to Him" (89:27-28).

The devil cannot approach a person of this maturity, and even if he does, he can't find a way into that heart or sway that disciple from the path. Indeed, the devil once approached the great sage Gilani and said: "Abdulqader, I am your Lord. I now Permit you what I had previously Forbidden. You can do whatever you wish." But the saint only replied: "You're lying. You are the devil. For the Lord never wants His Prohibitions to be done, and will never order anyone to do them."

5. The Pleased Self

The human self in the fifth station is called the *pleased* self because it has achieved mature pleasure in all respects: it remains pleased with God no matter what befalls it. The characteristics of the self in this stage are: to avoid Prohibitions, to love with a pure heart, peacefulness, psychic aptitude, surrender, and to leave and forget everything except God. The person accepts every event in the world with calmness and placidity, without objections. Because s/he is in control of the self, s/he does not approach forbidden or objectionable things. God never turns down this Seeker's prayers and always accepts them. But an excess of shame and humility prevents him from praying; he is ashamed to request anything of God, prays only in an emergency, and his prayers are sure to be accepted. Honored in the sight of the Lord, s/he is seated on such a throne in the inner world that the whole outer world awaits his or her command.

6. The Pleasing Self

The rational self in the sixth stage is called the *pleasing* self because it is pleasing to God. The person at this echelon is clothed with the morality of God, has departed from human desires, and become fair-mannered. S/he forgives sins, hides shames, and always thinks well. S/he is kind, generous and altruistic towards everyone, loves and tends toward people, trying to rescue them from the prison of nature—and the darkness of the ego—into the light of the spirit. This love is only for the sake of God, which is why it is valuable. The pleasing self combines the love of creatures with the love of God.

The owner of this station is moderate in everything, neither exceeding nor falling short. This temperate attitude is apparently easy, but very difficult to achieve in reality. Everyone wants to possess this wonderful asset but few ever do, because it is an extremely difficult state to maintain. It is a grace and boon belonging to those in this station alone.

To the mature person in the sixth stage, the first good signs of the great viceregency begin to appear. At the end of this process he is dressed in all the regalia of that rank. The servant knows all the subtle secrets of things through the knowledge given him by the Lord. God has informed His servants of these secrets with the proclamation: "I taught Adam the names of all things." There are secrets associated with this stage that cannot be expressed in words. It is impossible for anyone not possessing this state to comprehend these, for they do not have correlates in the external world to which they might be compared.

7. The Perfect, Pure, or Complete Self

The human self that has risen to the seventh station is called the *perfect self* because it has reached the pinnacle of maturity, and the purified or *pure self* because it has become completely purified. The seeker can rise to the sixth stage by struggle, but the seventh can only be bestowed by the grace of God.

The seventh station is the highest and most exalted of all the stations. The Inner Kingdom (the Kingdom which, as Jesus said, "is within you") has reached perfection, and the struggle is finished. The Perfect Human, the Islamic/Sufi Saint, is in full bloom. Such a person comprehends the loftiest reaches of Sufi mysticism, not through theoretical knowledge but through direct experience. Asceticism and self-compression are no longer necessary. It is enough to observe medium conduct in all things. The possessor of this stage has no desires left, for they have all been granted. He still continues, however, to wish for the pleasure of his Lord.

The actions of the perfect human being in this stage are all goodness and worship. His sweet breath is power and grace, his gentle speech is knowledge and wisdom, sweetness and light. His blessed face radiates peace and joy.

The person at this stage is never without worship, not even for a moment, worshiping with all the bodily organs, with tongue, hands, and feet or solely with the heart, and is never heedless of the Lord.

Such a person repents frequently, is extremely humble, and the tendency of people to God pleases him greatly. He is sad and offended if others neglect God, loving those who desire and love God more than his own child. Both his love and anger are not for his self, but for God alone. Everything he does is right. He acts with justice in everything. His every wish is in accord with God's wishes.

Solving the Riddle of the Universe

Sainthood, elevation to higher levels of self, is hard work. This is both a challenge and a promise. It is a challenge, in that only the most diligent can attain it. It is a promise, in that nobody is barred from it for whatever reason—being human is enough to qualify for application. The only obstacle is the lack of struggle and effort on our part.

Not all of us, perhaps, can attain the highest levels of sainthood. It would suffice us all, however, to struggle as much as we can against our lower selves, for no matter how far we progress, it is to our good—and to the greater good of society.

What we have described above can only be a very abstract and general guide to comprehending the Book of the Universe. Actually experiencing the reality of these descriptions is something else again. The Lord Almighty has informed human beings in the Koran that there are many portents in observable entities. Indeed, every word spoken by a person has a meaning that is modified according to the words preceding and succeeding it. In a similar way, there is a secret in each entity or event, and this appears differently to everyone. Direct, naked perception of it is very rare and difficult. God has revealed such secrets only to His wise servants who know their selves, and has hidden them from the ignorant.

This very book you are reading—isn't it the same? People of knowledge who read it perceive its meaning. But when ignorant people look at it, they can neither read nor understand it, nor can they take pleasure from it. They can only see the printed lines of the book. The world of nature is similar. But to read, to decipher, the Book of Nature is much more difficult than reading this book. It is not for everyone to read, or having read to comprehend, the vast Book of the Universe.

Spacewarps, Timewarps

To our technological age, preoccupied with science and its fruits, it may come as a surprise that teleportation and time travel, which still lie in the realm of science fiction, were paranormal feats performed by Sufis hundreds of years ago. The subject is such an engrossing one that it merits separate treatment in itself.

The instantaneous spatial transfer of matter is claimed to be one of the routine accomplishments of the Friends of God (i.e., Saints). It is said that the teleportation of many of the great sages in the twinkling of an eye was a frequent event. According to one such account, for instance, the great sage Abdulqader Gilani instantly crossed thousands of miles to be present at a student's funeral. A better-known example concerns the Prophet of God. When he informed his people of his Ascension (*miraj*), his detractors would not believe him, and demanded that the Prophet tell them the number of entrances of the temple at Jerusalem (*masjid al-aqsa*—"the Farthest Mosque"), which he had visited on the first leg of his spiritual journey. The Prophet could not remember this, having naturally been occupied with more important things than counting doorways at the time. At this point God caused the entire temple to appear before the Prophet's eyes, and he was able to answer the question simply by counting the portals.

Since the cultivation of paranormal feats is frowned upon and belittled in Sufism, the justification for raising the subject in a book such as this lies not in its sensational aspect, but in the insight that may be afforded by contemplation and reasoning about it. Perhaps we can look beyond a naive belief in the miraculous to the underlying—and unsuspected—scientific principles that are involved.

What we have, for want of a better word, called "teleportation" here, the Sufis call *tayy al-makan*. Now our initial instinct might be to think that this term refers to some such meaning as "flying through the air."

However, it does not. We are in for a staggering surprise—staggering, that is, only if we are familiar with the insights of contemporary physics. For the dictionary meaning of this term is: "the folding of space." Now why have the Sufis preferred such a counterintuitive, technical concept to some familiar term, such as flight? To discover how truly extraordinary the Sufic employment of this term is, we need look only at some basic discoveries of modern mathematics and physics.

According to Einstein's Theory of Relativity, three-dimensional space is not rigid but plastic—it can be curved. Although, according to that theory, only very large masses are able to produce such curvature, its possibility—the bending of space itself, not of objects—is inconceivable in terms even of nineteenth-century physics.

Teleportation, with or without the bending of space, has been extensively used as a theme in science fiction. Finally, physicists Kip S. Thorne, et al., in the United States have brought this venerable science-fiction topic into the realm of sober physics. According to their view, a "short-circuit" or "wormhole" can connect two points in space, such that anything can instantly pass from one point to the other without traversing the intervening space. In effect, a wormhole is nothing but a miniature spacewarp.

Let us try to visualize how this happens by the simplest of examples. Suppose we take a piece of white paper and place a mark on each of its two ends, calling the first mark "Point A" and the second, "Point B".

The sheet of paper in our hands is a surface—that is, a two-dimensional space. Remaining within that space, we can go from Point A to Point B by various routes. None will be shorter than its "geodesic," or shortest distance, which happens to be a straight line. No matter how close A and B are, there still is a finite distance between them.

Now we take this piece of paper and *bend* or *fold* it *through a higher (i.e., third) dimension* in such a way that points A and B coincide. Although we cannot eliminate the distance between them no matter how hard we try as long as we remain in two-dimensional-space, we can reduce it to nil by bending their space within a space of higher dimension.

Now if we imagine what has just been said for two-dimensional-space in terms of three-dimensional-space, we shall immediately understand what the Sufis and the physicists are driving at. It is singularly noteworthy that we can appreciate the depth of meaning contained in *tayy al-makan* only by making use of the concepts of modern physics and mathematics. This raises an interesting prospect: Perhaps the dreams of modern physics were, even hundreds of years ago, the realities of Sufism.

Time Travel

Nor is this all. For tales are frequently recounted of Sufis that play havoc with our ordinary conception of time. One of the best-known of these concerns the famous sage, Shihabuddin Suhrawardi. He once invited the Sultan of Egypt, so the story goes, to dip his head into a bowl of water. Having done so, the Sultan found himself transported, all of a sudden, to a faraway land and time. He lived there for years, got married, had children; and then one day he jumped into the sea to take a swim—and surfaced to find himself in his original palace in Cairo, to the accompaniment of the smiling presence of Suhrawardi.

No tale can underscore the total relativity of space and time better than this. The Ascension of the Prophet, too, presumably occurred in a contraction of time, for it is said that he caught on his return a pitcher that had just begun to topple at his departure, so the water in it was not spilled.

Time travel is perhaps the most overworked topic of science fiction. It was dismissed for a long time by serious physicists, up until 1991, when the first scientifically respectable theory involving time travel emerged. This is how recent scientific interest in time travel is.

Now it so happens that Sufis have a technical term referring to time travel as well. They call it, however, by a different name: *tayy al-zaman,* or "the folding of time," similar to the folding of space. And indeed, according to Einstein's Theory of Relativity, time is a dimension inseparable from the ordinary three spatial dimensions; to paraphrase Hermann Weyl, space in itself and time in itself have ceased to exist, and the two have become welded together in a single spacetime continuum. Once time is seamlessly attached to space in this way, it becomes possible to think that it, too, may share the plasticity of space. And if "the folding of time" is a fact, than Islamic Sufism is not just a science; it is a *super* science. For in terms of modern science, such a possibility has only recently become conceivable, let alone realized.

The Koran, which is the constitution or genetic code of the universe, explicitly stated fourteen centuries ago that teleportation is a possibility. When King Solomon desired to bring the throne of the Queen of Sheba to Jerusalem from South Arabia, his vizier, Asaph ben Berhia (not named in the Koran but rather in Islamic tradition), accomplished the feat in a split-second (27:40). The distance involved is almost a thousand miles. Of course, the Koran does not explain in detail exactly how Asaph managed to do this. Our age, however, has witnessed the continual transfer into the scientific domain of feats that perennially had been regarded as belonging to the miraculous. (This does not, of course, obviate the possibility of miracles, but rather justifies Arthur C. Clarke's famous observation that "Any sufficiently advanced technology is indistinguishable from magic.") The knowledge that spacetimewarps are possible *at all* is, perhaps, more important in the final analysis than that they may have occurred miraculously in the past. If the Koran says something is possible, it's possible; if not, then it's not, whether by miraculous or scientific means.

The Flowering of the Perfect Human

God has given humans everything—has exalted us above all else—but He has not given us His Divinity, His Godhood. As the Prophet of God said, the highest station is the station of being a servant of God. The Koran counsels us to "call on Him humbly, with fear and longing" (7:55-6). Obedience to God and humility are our best tools on this path.

The Perfect Human is not God—heaven forbid!—but rather, the viceregent of God on earth. As such, although he is a human being, and although there is little to distinguish him from other people in his outward appearance, yet in his inner, spiritual life, he is invested with exceptional qualities that set him apart from ordinary human beings. These superior qualities are in principle available to all ordinary mortals by virtue of their being human (though some may be more gifted than others). The Perfect Human differs from others only in that he has undergone special training to enhance or develop these qualities, endured the hardships of the Way, and emerged triumphantly on the far shore of Realization.

For example, the Koran states of the prophet Idris: "We raised him to a lofty station" (19:57).[206] The great Sufi sage, Ibn Arabi, has explained in his *Fusus* that Idris and Noah were both raised to the sphere of the sun. In classical astronomy, the nine principal spheres denoted a series of nested, concentric transparent spheres surrounding the earth, on which the orbit of each heavenly body resided. Before we dismiss these as fantasies of the ancients, however, we might pause to consider the possibility that these spheres can also be taken to mean something quite in accord with modern astronomy—namely, the spheroid shapes of the heavenly bodies themselves. "The sphere of the sun" can then be understood as "the sun disk," or simply "the sun." Noah's and Idris's Ascension and establishment in the sun must have a very profound meaning in terms of the relationship between the human species and the cosmos, yet its exact meaning escapes us, and in such a case silence is preferable to misleading speculation. Still, we should strive to get out of the tiny walnut-shell of our brains, and take spiritual wing to the Milky Way.

We have indeed looked into the depths of the universe, perhaps all the way to its very borders, but we have not yet solved its riddle. Our sight is confined to visible light, which occupies a narrow slit in the electromagnetic spectrum. We cannot see energies that fall outside its range. We cannot see things that are too near, too far, too big, or too small. We do not see deeply enough. We do not see clearly enough. We do not yet see.

Every outward travel brings us back to ourselves. Perhaps, when we look deeply enough into ourselves, we shall discover the treasure hidden within. Then we shall know the answer. Perhaps we shall not know *all* the answers. But we shall know the one answer that counts—the solution to the riddle. Beyond this point, words fail us.

✹

In this chapter, we have reviewed the various methods employed by Sufis as they carefully guide the adept through the various stages of the self and the various worlds as the psychic centers open one by one and new challenges arise. We have also reviewed how time and space are conceptualized and traversed using Sufi techniques. The final stage is, of course, the glorious state of becoming The Perfect Human, the ultimate goal of the seeker.

Epilogue:
Finding the Heart of Islam

------------ ✄ ------------

If it were lawful for me to relate
Such truths to those who have not reached this state,
Those gone before us would have made some sign;
But no sign comes, and silence must be mine...
And I too cease: I have described the Way—
Now, you must act—there is no more to say.

—FARIDUDDIN ATTAR, *THE CONFERENCE OF THE BIRDS* (FINALE)[207]

Picking my way through the maze that is our world, I came upon something for which I was wholly unprepared. At the heart of a religion much maligned for the antics of its sometimes demented followers, I found a priceless jewel. Effendi, my Master, was fully illuminated by the jewel in this heart. I would be shirking my debt to humanity if I were to pass over in silence what I had found. Had I encountered that heart elsewhere, I would not have hesitated to report its existence wherever else it might have been found. But, unlikely as it may seem, I discovered it in Islam and nowhere else.

That gift is still there. And it will always be there, for those who are able to set aside their prejudices and take an earnest look.

To find the heart of Islam is, at the same time, to find the heart of all religion. Because I arrived at the Master by a roundabout route, I was not unaware of other religions and wisdom traditions. A long search had led me to him—"Seek, and you shall find." It is my awareness of all those other religious traditions, plus what I encountered in Effendi, which leads me to say that Islam is not the religion of yesterday, but the perfect religion for tomorrow. This may sound like an exaggerated claim, but it is not, as any careful reading of this book will demonstrate.

Those who find fault with Islam are justified to the extent that they see only its external, legalistic trappings when they look at it. Here, the fault lies with many Moslems themselves. Islam seems prone to a kind of fossilization that views the Koran and the Way as historically fixed entities buried in the past, rather than living ones that should be realized anew in each era and in each Moslem's life. It is Islam's adherents who are going to refresh it—no one else can do it for them, nor would they accept it even if someone did. But neither should that result look anything like what the world has been watching in horror in recent years. A little more effort is called for on the part of Moslems, to demonstrate the beauty of their religion to everyone, by themselves conforming to the noble conduct it invites us to. "You would reform the world? Begin with yourself, brother!" Don't try to change the world, society, the state, and so on, try to improve yourself using the tools your religion has placed at your disposal. And this goes for the adherents of other religions as well, for the thread of wisdom, the beckoning of the divine, runs through them all. No matter what your religion is, if you can conform better to its high ideals, it's a win-win deal—you win and the world wins, too.

The Heart of Islam beats eternally and it is the greatest mistake to view it as a religion of the past, as though we had somehow missed the "golden era." The brightest era of Islam is yet to come, since humankind has the greatest opportunities at hand due to phenomenal developments in technology—if we can only develop ourselves in parallel.

Religion properly deals both with the inward and the outward. Islamic Sufism covers the esoteric and the exoteric, fusing them into a single whole that is breathtaking in its implications. To this combination, the Master referred to it as "Islam" and I have sometimes referred to it as "Sufism" in this book. The Master's use is the more correct form, because any religion should combine the spiritual and external aspects.

More than any of its predecessors, Islamic spirituality has charted the deep ecology of the human odyssey, taking a rigorous—I would use the word "scientific"—approach to the higher levels of selfhood and realms of the spirit that lie within the reach of us all. It has drawn attention to the greatest potential that remains buried in our selves. And this potential was fully realized in Effendi. He was the living, breathing example of what it means to be a Perfect Human—something as far beyond the ordinary human condition as the latter is above the beasts. I saw it, I was and am his witness.

But if this possibility were open to only a single human being, it would be solely of limited interest. We would marvel at the example of the Master and perhaps a few other saints, and pass on to other things. On the contrary, however, this chance is available to us all. Having been born human, we are all faced with the deepest challenge: *to realize what we have the potential to become.* And this is the true calling of religion. It beckons to us, saying: "Come on, don't tarry, don't waste time, stop wallowing in the mud, and rise to the stature that you really are." Because we were born human, this greatest of gifts, the possibility of becoming a Perfect Human Being, is denied to none of us—unless we choose to deny it ourselves.

> *I fled Him, down the nights and down the days;*
> *I fled Him, down the arches of the years;*
> *I fled Him, down the labyrinthine ways*
> *Of my own mind; and in the mist of tears*
> *I hid from Him...[But in the end God said:]*
> *"Ah, fondest, blindest, weakest,*
> *I am He Whom thou seekest!*
> *Thou dravest Love from thee, who dravest Me."* [208]

APPENDIX A

Ah, Courtesy

——————— ✄ ———————

(The following sayings regarding "courtesy," or splendid moral conduct, have been culled from the Traditions of the Prophet and the aphorisms of the great saints. It was a sheet often distributed by the Master.)

"My Lord made me courteous, and endowed me with the best courtesy."

"If a person has no trace of courtesy, s/he is not human."

"The difference that sets humans apart from the animals is courtesy."

"A mind unadorned with courtesy is a hero without a weapon."

"Courtesy is the outer appearance of intelligence."

"Courtesy is to be in control of one's hand, one's tongue, and one's loins [sexuality]."

"Who visits with courtesy will return laden with gifts."

"The beginning of all courtesy is to speak little."

"Courtesy is the guide and sign of the Friends of God. It is the cause of communion with God."

"Without courtesy, nobility is naught."

"Courtesy is a weapon that kills the devil."

"Courtesy is the greatest art. It is food for the road that leads to God."

"Courtesy is the beginning of everything. The whole of Sufism is courtesy."

"Courtesy is the first requirement of perfection."

"One who abandons courtesy is not wise."

"Fortify courtesy, renounce all else."

"Those who lack courtesy are driven from God's doorstep."

"Who lacks courtesy has no trustworthy knowledge."

"Truth is nothing but courtesy."

"True courtesy is to renounce the lower self."

"Cloak your shame with courtesy."

"True beauty is beauty of knowledge, and courtesy."

"The adornment of a human being is that person's courtesy in its entirety."

"An orphan is not one whose parents have died, but one who lacks knowledge and courtesy."

"Those who fail to teach courtesy to their children will please their enemies."

"Spiritual elevation is only possible with courtesy."

"The intelligent person learns courtesy from the discourteous."

"With the honor of knowledge and courtesy, Adam was raised above the angels."

"Satan was banished from God's presence because he abandoned courtesy."

"Discourteous acts interrupt enlightenment, and drive their owner from the heart of the King."

"The discussion [of sages] is a body. The spirit of that body is courtesy."

"In order to attain Truth, one needs Knowledge of Certainty; for Knowledge of Certainty, one needs sincere deeds; for sincere deeds, one needs to perform the Obligations of God; for this, one needs to follow the Way of the Prophet; and in order to do that, one needs to observe courtesy."

"Courtesy is to possess the knowledge and principles that protect one from all error."

"One who has not been trained by the Sufis cannot understand the truth of courtesy."

"Everything loses value as it increases. But when courtesy increases, it becomes more valuable."

"Courtesy is: not to overvalue one's superiors, and not to belittle one's inferiors."

"One who does not adopt the courtesy of one's Master cannot adopt the courtesy of the Prophet's Way and Traditions. And one who does not adopt these cannot adopt the courtesy of the Koran and its sacred verses."

"Those who enter their Master's presence with courtesy will earn boundless enlightenment."

"Those who serve their Master courteously earn stations as high as the Throne."

"As long as one does not adopt the courtesy of Masters, it is not possible to gain anything from them."

"Beauty of courtesy frees a person from the need for relatives."

"Courtesy makes a person sincerely loved."

"Courtesy is the power that protects a person from shameful things."

"Courtesy is to act in accordance with the Prophet's Way."

"There is no honor higher than courtesy."

"The least of the rules of courtesy is for one to stop when one senses one's ignorance and to remedy it."

"One who would learn wisdom should act courteously."

"One who seeks to possess good deeds should seek to learn knowledge courteously."

"As long as the People of Love possess goodwill in the matter of love, their courtesy will increase."

"Courtesy is to train the self as necessary and to decorate it with beautiful morals."

"Courtesy is the absolute source of virtue for a human being."

"The stations of Paradise are earned by good works and courtesy."

"The friends of courtesy are: Modesty, Sincerity, Submission, Love, Intention, Obedience, Striving, Discussion, and Service."

> *I sought admission to the Assembly of Knowledge;*
> *Knowledge was left behind—courtesy, just courtesy.*

> *It covers the shames of humanity;*
> *What beautiful clothing is the garment of courtesy.*

> *I sought admission to the People of the Heart;*
> *Every aptitude has value, but first place goes to courtesy.*

> *Courtesy is a crown made of the light of God;*
> *Wear that crown, and be safe from all calamity.*

APPENDIX B

Our Prayers

————————— ✻ —————————

(This is a combination of three prayers: what the Master called the "Peace prayer," a prayer by the Grand Saint Abdulqader Gilani, and a prayer of the Prophet, in that order. These were distributed either singly or in combination, as below, by the Master for many years.)

These prayers are the common property of all mankind. They can be recited either after Formal Prayer, or at any other time. Remember us, too, in your prayers.

Dear God, our Creator, thanks and praise be to you.
May God's blessings and peace be upon Mohammed and his family.
In the name of God, the Compassionate, the Merciful:

I

Dear God, grant that we may sow peace wherever we go. Let us be reconcilers and unifiers, not sowers of dissent. Allow us to disseminate love where there is hate, forgiveness where there is injury, faith where there is doubt, hope where there is despair, light where there is darkness, and joy where there is sorrow.

Dear Lord, help us to be not of those who see the failings of others, but of those who hide them; not of those who seek consolation, but those who console; not of those who wish to be understood, but those who understand; not of those who crave to be loved, but those who love.

313

Grant that we may become like the rain, which bestows life without discrimination wherever it flows; like the sun, which enlightens all beings everywhere without distinction; like the earth which, though everything steps on it, withholds nothing and bestows its fruits on everyone; like the night, which hides all shames from view and allows the world to rest.

Grant us the destiny to join the ranks of those who give rather than receive, those who are forgiven because they forgive, those who are born in Truth, live in Truth, die in Truth; and those who are born again in eternal life. Amen.

II

My God, may your peace and blessings on Mohammed, his dynasty, and his loved ones be numerous as your creatures, in proportion to your pleasure, weighty as the Highest Heaven, and in the amount of the ink spent on words.

My Lord, make me one of those whose hearts belong to you and who place their trust in you. We are poor servants, enrich us; we are weak, fortify us; we are sinners, forgive us. Maintain our constancy on the path of the religion with which you are pleased.

My God, I wish in this world for the opportunity to worship and the wisdom to avoid sins; and in the afterworld for your Paradise, the sight of your countenance and safety from your chastisement.

O refuge of the derelict, true friend of the forlorn, you are my confidant and beloved in both this world and the next. Reclaim my soul as a Moslem at my death, rectify my self. You are the final arbiter in all worries and complaints. You are the ultimate purpose of all desires. Please have mercy on the tears of this petitioner. To whom shall I turn for help, when you are the sole possessor of all? In whom shall I take refuge, when you are the sole benefactor, vast in generosity and grace?

My Lord, give us the ability to perform deeds with which you are pleased. Grant us life through our worship of you.

My God, do not turn down my prayer. Do not leave me to my own devices. Have mercy on my impotence, take pity on my weakness and wretchedness. Do not mete out to us the treatment we deserve. Protect our hands from reaching out to someone else just as you protect us from prostration to others.

My God, may your blessings and peace be upon Mohammed, his family, and his companions: such blessings as will save us from all kinds of fears, afflictions, and similar ills; will ensure our security against all troubles, plagues, and disasters, worries and misfortunes; will cleanse us from all shames and shortcomings, sins and rebellions; and will result in a pardon for all our sins and an answer to all our prayers. Amen.

III

My Lord, I take refuge from your chastisement in your forgiveness and pleasure; from you, I take refuge again in you. I cannot exalt you as you have exalted yourself.

My God, keep me as far from sins as you have distanced East from West.

My Lord, give me a faith and certainty that does not end in unbelief; bestow on me a mercy that will earn me your honor in this world and the next.

My God, grant us a fear that will serve as a barrier between us and our sins, an obedience that will win for us your Paradise, and a faith that will ease the burden of worldly ills.

My Lord, make my life an occasion for the increase of all that is good, and my death the means for liberation from all that is evil.

My God, I take refuge in you from the fearless heart, the insatiable ego, the knowledge that is useless and the prayer that remains unanswered.

My Lord, number us among those who are saved and who bring salvation to others.

We take refuge in you from a wasted life, senility, miserliness, and poverty.

Help us in worshiping, remembering, and giving thanks to you.

My Lord, you are forgiving, you love to forgive; hence, forgive us too. Amen.

Most Merciful of mercifuls, protect me from the Fire, save me from severe chastisement. Amen.

APPENDIX C

Put Your Trust in God

—— ✿ ——

(The following poem is by the famous Sufi, Ibrahim Hakki of Erzurum, whom my Master also counted in his chain of transmission. It has the interesting effect that it will elevate you from any mood—depressive or otherwise—after a few readings, and the Master recommended it for this express purpose. Translated by the author.)

1.

Bad things to good, God modifies
Think not He does otherwise
Always watched on by the wise—
What God will ordain, let us see
Whatever He does, well does He

2.

In God you should put your trust
Surrender yourself, find rest at last
With everything He does, be pleased
What God will ordain, let us see
Whatever He does, well does He

3.

Put in your heart of His strength a
   dose
Recognize what He doth dispose
Abandon what you propose
What God will ordain, let us see
Whatever He does, well does He

4.

He is the Compassionate Creator
He is the Benevolent Provider
He is the Wise and Divine Author
What God will ordain, let us see
Whatever He does, well does He

5.

The Final Judge in any claim:
Direct your prayers toward Him
Let go of your personal whim
What God will ordain, let us see
Whatever He does, well does He

6.

Don't crave after a thing or cause
Don't be stubborn if one occurs
It's from God, do not refuse
What God will ordain, let us see
Whatever He does, well does He

7.

Since matters are in God's hands,
vain
Is any confusion or pain
He unfolds Wisdom divine
What God will ordain, let us see
Whatever He does, well does He

8.

All His deeds are superior
And in tune with each other
Everything He does is proper
What God will ordain, let us see
Whatever He does, well does He

9.

Keep sorrows distant from your
heart
Find comfort instead in your Lord
Just leave everything to God
What God will ordain, let us see
Whatever He does, well does He

10.

Don't deem justice to be malice
Surrender, don't burn in the Blaze
Don't give up or give in—patience!
What God will ordain, let us see
Whatever He does, well does He

11.

Do not say: "Why is this so?"
It is good that it is so
Look, see how the end will go
What God will ordain, let us see
Whatever He does, well does He

12.

Look down on no one, nor slight
Don't give offense, don't break a
heart
With your ego never side
What God will ordain, let us see
Whatever He does, well does He

13.

A believer's deed is never vice
A wise man's way is never strife
A sage's speech won't agonize
What God will ordain, let us see
Whatever He does, well does He

14.

His patience is a grace on me
His ruling, my security
The Lord God is my deputy
What God will ordain, let us see
Whatever He does, well does He

15.

His name resounds in every call
His remembrance in every soul
His rescue is for one and all
What God will ordain, let us see
Whatever He does, well does He

16.

Just when your hopes are down to
nil
Suddenly He parts a veil
He grants solace from every ill
What God will ordain, let us see
Whatever He does, well does He

17.

In each moment to each servant
Whether wrathful or beneficent
He's at a task each instant
What God will ordain, let us see
Whatever He does, well does He

18.

Now Complier and now Preventer
Now Harmer and now Benefiter
Now Debaser and now Upraiser
What God will ordain, let us see
Whatever He does, well does He

19.

Now He makes His servant a sage
Now malignant, now virtuous
Over every heart He rules
What God will ordain, let us see
Whatever He does, well does He

20.

Sometimes He makes your heart
    empty
Or fills your spirit with beauty
Or makes you His loving devotee
What God will ordain, let us see
Whatever He does, well does He

21.

Simple one time, complex the next
Sometimes He makes your heart
    perplexed
Happy one moment, sad the next
What God will ordain, let us see
Whatever He does, well does He

22.

Sparingly eat, sleep, and drink
Give up carnality, it is junk
Settle in the rose garden of the
    heart
What God will ordain, let us see
Whatever He does, well does He

23.

Yourself with His creatures do not
    strain
Nor with your ego remain
You and your heart, keep close the
    twain
What God will ordain, let us see
Whatever He does, well does He

24.

With what is past, fall not behind
What is yet to come, don't mind
Even in the present, don't reside
What God will ordain, let us see
Whatever He does, well does He

25.

Unceasingly His name recite
Cunning and shrewdness, cast
    aside
Admire Truth, Truth articulate
What God will ordain, let us see
Whatever He does, well does He

26.

Isn't it time you were amazed
Discover Him, yourself forsake
Cast away sleep, become awake
What God will ordain, let us see
Whatever He does, well does He

27.

Every word contains advice sound
Every object is much adorned
Every action is a godsend
What God will ordain, let us see
Whatever He does, well does He

28.

A symbol and portent are all
    things
A sign of good news are all things
A fountain of grace is everything
What God will ordain, let us see
Whatever He does, well does He

29.

Lend ear to anyone who speaks
Understand Him who makes him
    speak
And with all your heart accept
What God will ordain, let us see
Whatever He does, well does He

30.

The languages of things proclaim
"Truth, O Truth!" they all exclaim
Creation's courtesy ascertain
What God will ordain, let us see
Whatever He does, well does He

31.

Yes, He has done very well
Of course He has done very well
Indeed He has done very well
What God will ordain, let us see
Whatever He does, well does He

—IBRAHIM HAKKI OF ERZURUM

APPENDIX D

Universal Law, Human Rights, and God's Commandments

(This Appendix belongs to the chapter, "Islam and Democracy." It covers a comparison between the Ten Commandments we all know and the Twelve Commandments of Islam, demonstrating how both democracy and human rights are firmly rooted in the monotheistic religions.)

The 1789 Declaration of Human Rights has been taken from the Ten Commandments in the Old Testament, according to Jacob Kaplan.[209] And this, in turn, brings to mind the following question: Could it possibly be the case that the basis for modern law, human rights, and such concepts as freedom and equality, has been derived from religions?

As everyone knows, the Ten Commandments, revealed by the Lord to Moses and his people, occur in the Torah (part of the Old Testament). The "Twelve Commandments" revealed to Moslems, on the other hand, are to be found in the Koran. Let us initiate this analysis with a comparison between the two.

The Ten Commandments

The Ten Commandments, given in more detail in *Exodus*, 20:2-14, are summarized in *Deuteronomy*, 5:6-21, as follows:

1. I am the Lord your God. You shall have no other gods before me.

2. You shall not make for yourself an idol (graven image).

3. You shall not make wrongful use of the name of the Lord your God.

4. Observe the sabbath day and keep it holy.

5. Honor your father and mother.

6. You shall not kill.

7. You shall not commit adultery.

8. You shall not steal.

9. You shall not bear false witness against your neighbor.

10. You shall not covet your neighbor's wife.

The Twelve Commandments

As outlined in the Chapter of the Night Journey (17:23-37) in the Koran, the Twelve Commandments of Islam may be summarized as follows:

1. Do not set up another god with God.

2. Respect and be good to your father and mother.

3. Help your relatives, travelers, and the poor.

4. Do not squander, nor be miserly.

5. Do not kill your children for fear of poverty.

6. Do not go near fornication or adultery.

7. Do not kill wrongfully.

8. Do not approach (pillage) the property of orphans.

9. Be as good as your word.

10. Be honest in measures and weights.

11. Do not pursue what you have no knowledge of.

12. Do not tread on the earth with vanity and pride.

Comparison

Upon inspection, it can be seen that both sets of commandments start with the same injunction. For ease of reference, the Ten Commandments will be referred to as "10C" in this section, and the Twelve Commandments as "12C." In addition, note that 12C-1 covers 10C-2. 10C-5 is repeated in 12C-2. The order not to kill in 10C-6 occurs a bit differently in 12C-7 because the former makes no allowance for self-defense. 12C-6 covers both 10C-7 and 10C-10. Similarly, 12C-9 is the more general form of 10C-9. 12C-5 is included in 10C-6. 12C-10 is the more finely-tuned version of 10C-8. Indeed, while 10C-8 prohibits theft, 12C-10 forbids even the slightest intentional mismeasure.

As can be seen, eight of the Ten Commandments are covered in some way in the Twelve Commandments. There remain only articles 3 and 4, of which the latter is specific to Jews and Christians.

Half of the Twelve Commandments, on the other hand, do not occur in the Ten Commandments at all. Articles 12C-3, 4, 5, 8, 11, and 12 are nowhere to be found in 10C, except, perhaps, for 12C-8, which with a little effort might be included in 10C-8. The other articles are Islam's free gift to humanity.

The 1789 Declaration of Human Rights

Let us now take a look at the definition of liberty in the French Declaration of the Rights of Man of 1789:

> *Art. 4. "Liberty consists in the ability to do whatever does not harm another."*

As can be seen, a very concise definition of freedom has been given here, but nothing is said about the content of "whatever does not harm another." What, then, are the things that harm others? The Commandments of God given above describe what these are.

The French Declaration of the Rights of Man is based on the Judeo-Christian religious and cultural tradition. The terms it defines may be novel, but these have not developed in a conceptual vacuum; they have a historical background. They did not simply fall out of the sky. It is for this reason that the Ten Commandments constitute an explanation of and commentary on the French Declaration of Human Rights. And the Twelve Commandments of Islam are a more detailed and comprehensive version of the former. Both human rights and the precepts of universal law, therefore, find their origin in the Commandments of God.

It is noteworthy that both sets of Commandments begin with faith in God and not associating any other gods with Him. The reason for this is that the remaining Commandments are all predicated on this one. A person may embrace the other Commandments without believing in God, but he will feel free to interpret them and put them into practice as he pleases. Only if he believes in the existence and unity of God, and that these Commandments come from Him, will he act with greater trepidation and constrain himself to obeying them more carefully.

The second point that calls for attention is this: the points outlined in these Commandments are serious crimes deserving serious sanctions in all sytems of law. Indeed, only when a legal code replaces "You shall not kill" with "You shall kill," "You shall not steal" with "You shall steal," "You shall not fornicate" with "You shall fornicate," and "You shall not lie" with "You shall lie"; only when it substitutes insult and cruelty to parents in exchange for honoring them, will it become independent of— and in fact diametrically opposed to— religion, God, and the Koran. And then it will no longer be Law, but the very essence of injustice and oppression. Otherwise, no law can be independent of religion. Because God had already revealed His Commandments to human beings before legal codes ever saw the light of day, and these lie at the foundation of all legal systems worthy of the name.

APPENDIX E

Warning: A Call to Peace

— ✻ —

(Among his multifaceted activities in the service of humanity, Master Ahmet Kayhan was also active in the field of peace. Up to his death, he and his friends drafted four invitations to world peace in opposition to weapons of mass destruction, of which the third is reprinted below. The second, titled "Invitation to Peace" (1987), was sent to major heads of state and influential people and received wide acclaim. Respondents in favor of the message included Pope John Paul II, the President of France, and the President and Prime Minister of Israel.

It was the Master's firm conviction that if humankind is to have a future, all weapons of mass destruction must be abolished. Their existence poses an ongoing threat, and unless this is done, Doomsday will sooner or later be brought about through humanity's own hands. As the world again begins to look like a dangerous place after September 11, 2001, this is an admonishment we neglect at our peril. The only way to prevent weapons of mass destruction

(WMD) from being used in the future, whether by states, terrorists, or anyone else, is to abolish them completely. There is no other way.

This message has been drafted in collaboration with a select group of retired professors who share the concern expressed hereunder and who, taking pity on the human race, have seen it fit to issue this declaration. We of the Republic of Turkey, out of compassion for all humanity, and all creatures vegetable and animal—having seen clearly that this material

and spiritual hellfire, the atom, will incinerate the whole world and reduce it to ashes—have issued this plea for peace as against nuclear warfare, to be delivered to the United Nations and all governments aspiring
to human rights. This is not to say that we ignore, or condone, the use of
other toxic weapons, the perils of the peaceful atom (such as the radioactive emissions from Chernobyl), or indeed any toxic releases into the
environment of whatever amount or kind. The atom has already killed
people without any bomb being thrown: did human beings come into
this world to destroy each other?

This message is an admonition to and an onus on all human beings.
We leave the final decision to the United Nations, beginning with the
United States of America.

Fittingly, the message was prepared between July 16 and August 6,
1995, the anniversary of Hiroshima.

August 6, 1995

That date is the fiftieth anniversary of the bombing of Hiroshima. It
is the semicentennial of the first use against human beings of the weapons that are going to destroy mankind. It is the anniversary of the first
rehearsal of doomsday.

With the delivery of that bomb, a new age opened in human history.
In this age, human beings constantly live under the shadow of a disaster
that will strike suddenly and without warning. In spite of important
steps taken in recent years in the direction of peace, we are not yet free
from the shadow of that threat.

Ever since the fall of the Berlin Wall and the Soviet empire, we have
entered a relatively more peaceful and relaxed environment. It is also true
that some significant advances have been made in the direction of nuclear
disarmament. But in spite of this, we are still very far from where we
ought to be.

Forgetfulness is an affliction of human memory. How soon have we
forgotten that we had been living on the brink of "Mutual Assured Destruction" (aptly shortened to MAD) until just yesterday? Have nuclear
weapons, perchance, all gone off to another planet? Or have we shown
the effort necessary for their eradication, and been successful therein?

The truth is that none of these have happened. What has happened is that we have all become immersed in a deep complacency and heedlessness. Some among us have even prophesied "the End of History." We all seem to think that the danger of a Third World War is gone forever.

But we are deeply mistaken. Even in these carefree days, aren't wars being fought and genocide practiced in Bosnia, in Rwanda? Do we seriously think that mankind, which has failed to make war in only three hundred of the last fifty-six hundred years, has given up its penchant for war forever? On the contrary, it is much more probable that we will continue to spend ninety-five percent of the following years in warfare.

Global annual arms expenditures have passed the one-trillion-dollar mark and are continuing to increase, in spite of the fact that the cold war is over. How many children could not be fed with those one trillion dollars, how many sick people could not be cured, how many countries not developed?

No one can guarantee that two small countries will not confront each other tomorrow. Nor can anyone guarantee that larger ones will not be sucked into the conflict. When that day comes, the weapons of mass destruction, now sleeping silently by the thousands in their silos and by the tens of thousands in submarines, on airplanes, military vehicles, or in their protective igloos, will be waiting for us—or our children—just around the corner. By then, it will be too late for remorse over the fact that we failed to get rid of them while we still had the chance.

Do not imagine that the horrifying nature of these weapons will prevent them from being used forever. When he invented dynamite, Alfred Nobel was elated because he thought that he had found a weapon terrible enough to dissuade people from waging war. But people went right on fighting, this time using dynamite. You probably know that the Nobel Prizes stem from the disillusionment and guilt of the man who instituted them. As for the First World War, in which dynamite was used more than ever before, its perpetrators called it "the war to end all wars." The exact opposite happened.

Yet, now is just the right time. A golden opportunity is at hand. While a more or less peaceful atmosphere prevails, while time is plenty and circumstances favorable, we must act quickly to do away with weapons of mass destruction before they do away with us. Individuals, organizations, and societies should do everything within their power to achieve this end. (If you can't do anything else, tell a friend who's uninformed.) If we miss this golden opportunity, we may not get a second chance.

But you may be saying: "What's all the fuss about?" In these days when we are living through a springtime of peace, perhaps the winter of war, even a "nuclear winter," seems very remote to you. But if we do not make preparations during the spring and summer, our chances of surviving that winter are nil. And the first and most important thing to be done is to destroy—without exception—all weapons of mass destruction.

What will happen otherwise?

Then you haven't heard, or perhaps you have forgotten. In that case, if you wish, let's crack open the gates of Hell and take a look inside.

The Beginning

Although Hiroshima was the first example of the use of atomic weapons against human beings, it wasn't the first atomic bomb to be exploded. The world's first atomic bomb, with a destructive force of twenty kilotons (equivalent to twenty thousand tons of TNT) and code named "Trinity," was detonated three weeks before, on July 16, 1945, at Alamogordo in the United States of America. "Trinity" here does not refer to the Christian Trinity, but rather to the triad of bombs comprised by this bomb in addition to those dropped on Hiroshima and Nagasaki. There is deep symbolic significance in the fact that this first bomb was exploded near the village of Oscuro ("dark") at the vicinity called Jornada del Muerto ("death journey").

A distinguished group of visitors was present that day to witness the explosion from a distance of sixteen kilometers. Their first impressions are important to any understanding of the dimensions of the phenomenon.

Among the visitors were military and government officials, as well as scientists who had worked on the manufacture of the bomb. These were not religious people. In fact, most were devoid of any religious inclination whatsoever. And yet, it is striking that all, in relating their impressions later on, felt the need to use expressions taken from the domain of religion. One of the generals present, for example, said:

"The whole country was lighted by a searing light with an intensity many times that of the midday sun...Thirty seconds after the explosion came, first, the air blast pressing hard against the people and things, to be followed almost immediately by the strong, sustained, awesome roar which warned of doomsday and made us feel that we puny things were blasphemous to dare tamper with the forces hitherto reserved to the Almighty. Words are inadequate tools for the job of acquainting those not present with the physical, mental, and psychological effects. It had to be witnessed to be realized."

Physicist J. Robert Oppenheimer, known as "the Father of the Atomic Bomb," was reminded of verses from the Bhagavad Gita, the sacred book of the Hindus: "I am become Death, shatterer of the worlds."

These are the words of eyewitnesses watching the event from a distance of sixteen kilometers. Let us now take a look at those who experienced the Bomb at closer range—the survivors of Hiroshima.

"The details and the scenes were just like hell."

"And when we looked back it was a sea of bright red flame."

"I saw fire reservoirs filled to the brim with dead people who looked as though they had been boiled alive."

"They looked like boiled octopuses."

As the internal organs of those at a distance of one kilometer boiled away, they were seared to smoking black char in the fraction of a second. The skins of those further away were blistered by the thermal pulse, the shock wave tore their skins off their bodies; with their skins hanging off them like threads they threw themselves into the rivers, hoping to cool off. Little did they know that the rivers themselves had been heated to the boiling point. As people evaporated, the blinding light bleached everywhere on the walls behind them except where their shadows had been. Go see for yourself, those shadows are on those walls to this very day. Birds ignited in midair. "Doctor," a patient was saying a few days later, "a human being who has been roasted becomes quite small, doesn't he?"

Seventy thousand men, women, and children, the great majority of whom were civilians, died in the very first instant of the explosion. One-hundred-and-thirty thousand more died of radiation poisoning and burns within the next few months. Another two-hundred-and-twenty thousand had died within five years. More than half the population of Hiroshima perished, and two-thirds of the city was razed to the ground. Almost nothing above knee-level was left.

Now consider the fact that the bombs thrown on Hiroshima and Nagasaki were mere firecrackers compared to those of our day. The hydrogen bomb, discovered in the succeeding years, is a hundred to a thousand times more powerful than an atomic bomb. During the arms race they entered in the years of the cold war, America and Russia produced tens of thousands of these weapons. They now sleep silently in their silos, several mounted on each missile, waiting for the day when they will strike you, your children, or your grandchildren. That day those missiles will fulfill the purpose for which they were designed, hurtle thousands of miles in fifteen to twenty minutes, and rain universal death everywhere.

The Effects of a Nuclear Bomb

There is no end to the list of the destructive effects of nuclear (and thermonuclear) weapons, which have no purpose of existence other than to wipe out humanity and human civilization. Yet at first count, these can be summarized under four major headings. They are: 1. the initial nuclear radiation, 2. the heat pulse, 3. the blast wave, and 4. radioactive fallout. Other more insidious effects, such as the electromagnetic pulse, the destruction of the protective ozone layer of the earth, and the "nuclear winter" effect, were only discovered decades afterwards.

Sober scientists have investigated these effects in great detail and have amassed data that fill many volumes. Space does not permit us to summarize all of these here. Still, we intend to describe the effects of a nuclear explosion, if only in outline. A one-megaton device, equivalent to the destructive force of one million tons of TNT, is a medium-size weapon in today's nuclear arsenals. We shall take this value—equal to eighty Hiroshima bombs—as a yardstick.

At the instant of detonation, an incredibly hot, bright fireball is formed. The temperature of this fireball is millions of degrees centigrade, and its pressure is millions of times greater than ordinary atmospheric pressure. All unprotected humans are killed and everything is destroyed within a circle of fifteen square kilometers, with "Ground Zero," the point directly below the explosion, as its center. This is the initial nuclear radiation.

The second effect is the heat pulse. This is a wave of searing light and intense heat. If the fireball is close to the ground, and touches it, it instantly vaporizes or incinerates everything within it. The heat pulse lasts ten seconds and inflicts second-degree burns on persons at a distance of fifteen kilometers. Its sphere of influence is greater than seven hundred square kilometers.

As the fireball expands, it creates a blast wave expanding in all directions. This is the third effect of a nuclear bomb. This shock front is a wall of compressed air which moves away from the center at supersonic speeds, dragging winds that move at three hundred kilometers per hour behind it. It flattens almost all buildings within a radius of seven kilometers and an area of one hundred square kilometers, and severely damages all buildings in an area of three hundred and twenty square kilometers and a radius of thirteen kilometers. The blast wave lasts for a few seconds and destroys buildings by surrounding them in all directions. Three kilometers from Ground Zero, wind speeds reach six hundred and fifty kilometers per hour and at six kilometers from Ground Zero, they reach three hundred kilometers per hour.. At a distance of sixteen kilometers, they hurl broken glass and sharp objects at lethal velocities.

As the fireball burns, it rockets skyward and reaches a height of ten kilometers. For ten seconds it cooks the city beneath it. People at a distance of fifteen kilometers now receive third-degree burns and most probably die on the spot. Those closer catch fire and perish instantly. In a circle of fifteen kilometers radius and seven hundred square kilometer area, flammable materials such as paper and dry leaves are ignited, giving rise to mass fires.

As the fireball rises, a mushroom cloud is produced due to the condensation of water vapor in the air. If the explosion has occurred near the ground, a great crater is formed and the bomb throws tons of debris and earth into the air. This mixture later rains down in the form of a fine ash. This phenomenon, called radioactive fallout, is the fourth effect of a nuclear bomb, and comprises about three hundred different kinds of radioactive isotopes. This fallout lethally contaminates an area of twenty five hundred square kilometers, "lethal contamination" being pedantically defined, in the present context, as the amount necessary to kill off half the able-bodied young adult population.

Let us now suppose that a one-megaton bomb is detonated two and a half kilometers above the city you live in or a city close by, and that you are standing at a point about three kilometers distant from Ground Zero. Your physical body could not survive, of course, so we assume you are present "in spirit." What would you see?

First, the blinding white light of the fireball lasts about thirty seconds. Simultaneously, searing heat melts windows, automobiles, lampposts, and everything made of glass and metal as though they were made of butter. People in the street are instantly ignited and, within a very short time, transformed into puddles of tar. Five seconds after the light, the blast wave hits. Some skyscrapers are crushed as if squeezed by a giant fist, while others are torn off their foundations and hurled through the air like matchsticks. Meanwhile, the fireball has been burning in the sky for ten seconds. A little later, everything is engulfed in thick clouds of smoke and dust. The mushroom cloud, which happens to have a diameter of twenty kilometers, cuts off the sunlight, and day turns into night. Within a few minutes, the heat pulse ignites broken gas mains, as well as gas and oil tanks. Fires begin spreading in the dark. A radioactive rain may fall in the meantime, as a result of the extraordinary weather conditions produced. Before long, all the individual fires combine to produce one gigantic fire. In such a mass fire the temperature reaches one thousand degrees centigrade, melting glass and metal and burning ordinarily fireproof materials. Depending on the condition of the winds, either a conflagration or a "firestorm" occurs. In the first case, the whole city is simply burned to the ground. Otherwise, winds being sucked into the center create a huge firestorm, forming a single fire of great heat. Because both kinds of fire consume the oxygen in the air and produce noxious fumes, people in the shelters are choked to death at the same time that the heat pulse is turning the shelters into pressure cookers. In this vast theater of events, all the agony and death scenes of Hiroshima are relived, with the difference that the death count now reaches millions instead of merely hundreds of thousands.

The Present Situation

During the long winter years of the cold war, America and Russia held the world on the brink of a precipice. There were only two good things about this "Balance of Terror": One, by the undeserved grace of God we were spared a nuclear war, and two, the parties kept their nuclear weapons and materials under stringent control.

In time, England, France, and China also became members of the "Nuclear Club," but they too were able to keep their materials under control.

But things didn't end there. Israel developed nuclear weapons, too. So did India. And because of India, so did Pakistan. Iraq, which tried to develop the Bomb because Israel had it, was stopped for the time being. Other, lesser nations began to stand in line.

It is obvious that there is no end to this process of proliferation. Anyone who does not possess nuclear weapons feels insecure toward those who do, and attempts to arm himself in the same way. The greatest obstacle in the way of success lies not in the difficulty of building a nuclear weapon, but in the difficulty of procuring uranium and plutonium, the materials necessary to make a bomb. But in time, as nuclear reactors are used, not with peaceful purposes for generating electricity, but for plutonium production, this obstacle too will be bypassed.

With the demise of the Soviet Union, serious gaps appeared in Russia's control over its nuclear weapons. Even if it has not happened yet, the possibility of nuclear material and bombs being smuggled in order to be sold to countries that crave them is a subject for serious concern. Another possibility is that these should fall into the hands of terrorist organizations. As evidenced in the recent example of Japan, a sufficiently fanatical terrorist group will not shrink from using weapons of mass destruction against innocent human beings. Considering how widespread terrorism is in today's world, it is not difficult to realize what this means.

(When speaking of weapons of mass destruction, biological and chemical weapons are also included in addition to nuclear arms. Space does not permit detailed analysis of these weapons, in spite of their equally disastrous effects, but the present treatment is intended to cover them as well.)

As if the two generations of nuclear weapons—atomic bombs and hydrogen bombs—were not enough, the superpowers were trying to spawn third and later generations of these weapons toward the end of the cold war. Here, the purpose is to selectively enhance one or more of the destructive effects of the atom. Indeed, the nuclear tests conducted by the great powers have only one purpose: to build a more advanced, i.e., worse, nuclear weapon.

In fact, the progress in high-energy physics will only be put to the misuse of building even more terrible weapons in the end, difficult as this may be to conceive. With atomic fission and fusion, physicists had unleashed the energy that powers the sun. Not content with this, they now aim to achieve the energy levels present at the creation of the universe. When that happens, it will be possible to disintegrate not merely the atom, but the fundamental particles of existence, and the way will be open to the manufacture of weapons powerful enough to melt down the entire landmass of the planet.

The superpowers recognized long ago that the destructive force accumulated in their hands would be sufficient to destroy the world many times over. It was then that they initiated the exploration of space. The actual, though unstated, purpose behind this exploration was (and still is) to ensure that the one or two persons who would propagate the human race after the world had been annihilated would be "one of our boys." This is the truth that lies behind all the space stations and the attempts to colonize Mars. And thus we are faced with a phenomenon, the like of which has been encountered only twice before in the entire history of mankind: the third Adam.

The Third Adam

Adam was the ancestor, the progenitor of the human race. When humankind was wiped out in a deluge of water, Noah became the second Adam. And now, unless we take the necessary measures, humanity will be destroyed this time by a deluge of fire, and the human race will start anew with a third Adam.

During the days he gave the order to bomb Hiroshima, President Truman wrote in his diary: "We have discovered the most terrible bomb in the history of the world. It may be the fire destruction prophesied...after Noah and his famous Ark." This Biblical prophecy (2 *Peter* 3:10) is referred to as "Judgment Day" and "Doomsday" in the Koran. Unless we beware, we shall have fulfilled the forewarnings of the sacred books of the world by our very failure to take precautions. For it has been stated in a Holy Tradition: "We will not destroy men; rather, they will destroy themselves by their very own hands."

You who are reading or hearing this, do you find any solace in the knowledge that your race will continue from a third Adam? Does the notion of a third Adam comfort you in the face of the fact that you, your children, or your grandchildren will be vaporized in unspeakable agony, the entire biosphere of the earth will be annihilated, the oceans will evaporate, and the very crust of the earth will be melted?

What Should Be Done?

Today, a Godsent opportunity is at hand. In today's atmosphere of relative peace, while the Soviet Union is safely out of the way, let us dismantle the Doomsday Machine, let us abolish all weapons of mass destruction. Let us block all the means that would lead to their manufacture. Perhaps we cannot put an end to war. But we can prevent the destruction of humanity as a result of war. Tomorrow, when hostilities resume between nations, it will be too late and cooperation, impossible.

The only solution is that no weapons of mass destruction—including, preferably, missiles and delivery systems—should be left in the hands of any nation whatsoever. Because if even only one country has them, the rest will want to possess them as well.

The START agreement on arms reduction is a step in the right direction, but only a very small one. Because it still leaves enough weapons to annihilate each other ten times over in the hands of both sides. This is all or nothing. And it is now or never.

The permanent members of the United Nations must first bring all weapons of mass destruction under strict international control. The continuing experience of the United States, and of the USSR before its demise, proves that such controls and verification can be effective. Later, the present process of disabling and "scuttling" mass destruction weapons should be continued universally.

An Appeal to Everyone

If you are religious, we say to you: the heart of all religions is love. Hatred does not cease by hatred, hatred ceases by love. If you are not, we leave the word to Albert Einstein and Bertrand Russell, two of the most eminent scientists and philosophers of our time: "Remember your humanity, and forget the rest." What true religion ever ordered the murder of innocent human beings? And what loyalty, ideology, or hate is great enough to justify the annihilation of all men, women, and children, of all the winged and four-footed animals of the earth, of all its plants, its fishes, its unicellular organisms? Have you no pity for even your own children, your own grandchildren?

The time to act is here and now. If we do not do now what we have to do, Behold: the final curtain of human history. See if you care to shoulder the responsibility.

Inferno

The time is an unspecified date in the future. The place is a planet called Earth. All except the smallest countries of the world possess nuclear and other mass destruction weapons. Men have turned their backs on the call of true religions and become progressively more ruthless. God has removed from them the capacity for compassion. They are therefore able to do even less than we are in a position to do today.

The end will begin near sunset. First, one nation will deliver a bomb on another. Suppose, for example, that America bombs England. England will retaliate. Then America will bomb China. China will bomb France. After these first four bombs, the whole international community will go berserk, everybody bombing everybody else in a thermonuclear free-for-all.

We said earlier that the Hiroshima and Nagasaki bombs were firecrackers compared to the bombs of our day. In comparison with an all-out attack of tens of thousands of bombs, the detonation of one nuclear device will, in turn, seem like a firefly. Tens of thousands of suns, each many times brighter than the sun itself, will light all the continents of the earth. In the areas first targeted, the great majority of people will be radiated, crushed, or burnt to death. Hundreds of millions will simply be vaporized. Tens of thousands of blast waves will sweep away the physical existence of the countries of the world like dust in the wind. Buildings, habitations, factories, installations already on fire will be shattered, blasted, or pulverized out of existence. Then, as the mushroom clouds bloom, day will turn to night. All the forests of the world will be set on fire. Because the whole world is burning, there will be nowhere to escape. As bombs that have not yet been invented but soon will be enter the scene, mountains will melt and be tossed like cotton. Both living and unliving things will be burnt to ashes. The oceans, while evaporating on one hand, will attack the melting landmass of the earth on the other. Everything will be reduced to a uniform sludge. This sludge will redistribute under the influence of the centrifugal forces of the planet, and, when it cools, will solidify like lava into a surface almost, though not quite, as smooth as glass. And then... And then, America, Russia, and Europe will all be as flat as a table. Only the natural curvature of the earth will prevent an egg stood on one end from being seen from afar (if an egg and a human being to see it could have survived).

While all this is happening, anyone with access to a spaceship will head for outer space. Some of their rockets will burst on the ground before they can escape. Others able to make it will, deprived of the natural life support systems and supplies of the earth, be able to survive in space for at most only five more years.

By the grace of God, only a single man will survive. He is the one who will be called "the third Adam."

All this will happen, have no doubt. Unless we take preventive steps now. Do not imagine that you, your children, or your grandchildren will be exempt from this fate.

And that is why...

As we sow, so shall we reap. Come, let us sow peace, not war. Let us douse fire with water. We are the stewards, the custodians of this planet. God has entrusted the Earth to us. Come, let us purge the world of this danger of betrayal, and hand it over to the generations who will succeed us. What needs to be done must be done now. Our children and grandchildren have the right to live at least as much as we do.

(This draws a pretty bleak picture, but here, too, the Master offered a solution. "Of the nearly two hundred nations now extant," he said, "one person who is wisest, most cultured, and who loves his country and nation should be chosen from each. Those chosen should love humanity and other nations as much as their own. From among these, the most intelligent seven should again be selected by examination, plus twenty or thirty members. These should compose the United Nations. Next, all weapons and all kinds of war should be prohibited. When war erupts anywhere, the representatives of the parties concerned should first try to resolve differences between themselves. If they prove unsuccessful, the rest should intervene to stop it.

"Next, hunger. After war, hunger too should be abolished. Whatever it takes should be done to achieve this. Without weapons and hunger, humanity will be able to maintain peace for a while. In time, smaller countries would join bigger nations [in regional alliances, somewhat in the manner of the European Community]. Small states would give way to large states, and in the absence of weapons the latter would live in peace. This means not just toxic weapons (nuclear etc.), but all weapons. This is the only solution. There is no other way."

This plan may be difficult to achieve. Yet it is elating to know that a way out is possible—if it can only be realized.)

Endnotes

1   Please note that in the Turkish tradition, various terms of respect may be appended to a name. "Effendi," for example, is Turkish for "master," and it is placed after the first name, and throughout this book I may refer to him variously as Effendi (pronounced F-N-D), Ahmet Effendi, Master Kayhan and Master. I may also refer to him as Grandpa, a term of affection many of his followers used.

2   Scholarly texts on Sufism are usually peppered with italicized Arabic originals of special terms. This is because the original words possess more depth than their English-language equivalents do. In a book such as this one, however, intended as it is for a general readership, it was considered superfluous to include Arabic words when perfectly good counterparts for them could be found in English, by choosing the closest sense in a given context. Hence, this translation contains a minimum amount of Arabic words, and the ones present are generally Sufic technical terms for which the presentation of the Arabic originals is a must. Diacritical marks have been omitted. Technical terms without their originals are indicated by italicizing them or by capitalizing their first letters, especially when they first occur in a text.

   In Arabic names, the suffix "-i" indicates "from" or "of," similar to the *von* in German. For example, Gilani means "of (the town of) Gilan," Arabi means "of Arabia," and Misri means "from Misir" (or Egypt—hence "Egyptian").

   Since they occur frequently, those parts of Arabic names denoting family relationships are summarized here for convenience: *ibn* or *ben:* "son of," *bint:* "daughter of," *abu* or *abou:* "father of," *umm:* "mother of."

3   Also, some material—though not much—from *The Station of No Station* is reproduced in the present book.

4   Louis Pasteur (attributed), following Benjamin Constant and Francis Bacon.

5   "Every scientist *must* invoke assumptions and rules of procedure, which are not dictated by sensory experience. To deny the presence, indeed the necessary presence, of metaphysical elements in any science is to be blind to the obvious." Professor Henry Margenau, *The Nature of Physical Reality* (New York: McGraw-Hill, 1959), pp. 12–13 (italics in the original).

6   Attributed. Arabic *habais* is the plural of *habis,* which also has the secondary meaning of "ugly, ugliness."

7   "True *Jihad*," http://www.wie.org/misc/jihad.asp, accessed 05/21/2002.

8   Former deputy prime minister of Malaysia. http://www.digitalnpq.org/archive/2002_winter/ibrahim.html, accessed 08/20/2002.

9   A recent article ably traces the influence of twentieth-century totalitarianism on the genesis of Islamism. In brief: Hassan al-Banna borrowed from fascism, Mawdudi from Marxism. Next, Sayyid Qutb borrowed from both Banna and Mawdudi to obtain "Leninism in an Islamist dress." Khomeini was then inspired by both Mawdudi and Qutb (that is, "Marxism-Leninism" or communism). See Ladan and Roya Boroumand, "Terror, Islam and Democracy," *Journal of Democracy*, April 2002, pp. 5-20, http://www.journalofdemocracy.org/Boroumand.pdf. See also Francis Fukuyama and Nadav Samin, "Can any good come of radical Islam?" *Commentary*, Sept. 2002, pp. 34-38, available at http://www.opinionjournal.com/forms/printThis.html?id=110002251. Also refer to footnotes 19 and 20.

10   See the last chapter of their *Vision of Islam,* London: I.B. Tauris, 1996; p.334. Shariah or sharia is the Holy Law or Divine Law of Islam.

11   Using the Jacques Berque translation. http://www.internatif.org/EspMarx/Islam/LP299BERQ.pdf, accessed 08/15/2002. Among English translations, Arberry uses "oversee," Yusuf Ali uses "manage their affairs" and Muhammad Asad has (lit.) "no power over them." Each of these adds a different shade of meaning that deepens and enriches our understanding of the verse.

12   Many people confuse Islam with Islamism. It is important to maintain the distinction between them.

13 W. Chittick and S. Murata, *The Vision of Islam,* p. 332.

14 Philip Ball, "Physics Bans Cloning," http://www.nature.com/nsu/ 020520/020520-1.html, accessed 05/23/2002.

15 "He created you (all) from a single soul, then created from it, of like nature, its mate" (4:1, 39:6). The rest of humanity then descended from Adam and Eve.

16 Or: strangers.

17 Sunnis are the followers of the Prophet's Way (*sunna*). Out of their great love for Ali, the Prophet's cousin and son-in-law (also the fourth Caliph), Shiites have developed some different concepts and practices (*shia* means "party," so they belong to the "party of Ali").

18 Olivier Roy, "Search for a Perfect World of Islam," *Le Monde Diplomatique,* May 2002. (Translations from the German and Italian (April) editions have been used in the text.)

19 For the connections between the terrorists' version of *jihad,* Marxism and postmodernism, see also Waller R. Newell, "Postmodern Jihad: What Osama bin Laden learned from the Left," *The Weekly Standard,* Vol. 7, No. 11 (11/26/2001), http://www.weeklystandard.com/Utilities/printer_preview.asp?idArticle=553&R=51A5AB2B. Also refer to footnotes 9 and 20.

20 Malise Ruthven, "Cultural schizophrenia" (27 September 2001), http://www.opendemocracy.net/forum document_details.asp? CatID=98&DocID=686&DebateID=150, accessed 07/20/2002. On this point, notably with reference to Iran, see Daryush Shayegan, *Cultural Schizophrenia: Islamic Societies Confronting the West,* Syracuse, NY: Syracuse University Press, 1997. See also footnotes 9 and 19.

21 For excerpts, see www.usdoj.gov/ag/trainingmanual.htm, accessed 07/ 30/2002.

22 Roy, "Search…"

23 In a 1993 *Foreign Affairs* article, Samuel Huntington claimed that the clash of civilizations, especially between Islam and the West, would dominate world politics.

24 Olivier Roy, "L'Islam de Ben Laden," in "La Guerre des Dieux," special issue of *Nouvel Observateur,* January 2002, p. 20. Being based on the denial of civilization, bin Laden's "modernity" is actually anti-modern at its core, because modernity is a recent phase in the march of civilization.

25 From the German play *Schlageter* (1933) by Hanns Johst. The phrase is sometimes also attributed to Joseph Goebbels, the Nazi propaganda minister.

26 Christopher Hitchens, "Let's not get too liberal," *Guardian,* September 21, 2001.

27 Pippa Norris and Ronald Inglehart, "Islam & the West: Testing the 'Clash of Civilizations' Thesis," http://ksghome.harvard.edu/ ˜.pnorris.shorenstein.ksg/ACROBAT/Clash.pdf, accessed 04/28/ 2002.

28 Extracts from Al-Jihad leader Al-Zawahiri's new book (regarded as his "last will"), *Knights Under the Prophet's Banner,* published by the Arabic daily *Asharq al-Awsat* of London, 2-12 Dec. 2001. http:// www.fas.org/irp/world/para/ayman_bk6.htm, accessed 03/03/2002.

29 http://www.fas.org/irp/world/para/ayman_bk11.htm, accessed 03/03/ 2002.

30 In the eyes of some Islamic youth, he has become a romantic guerilla leader, an Islamic Che Guevara.

31 "Officials Reveal Bin Laden Plan," *Los Angeles Times,* May 18, 2002. http://www. latimes.com/templates/misc/printstory.jsp?slug=la-051802masoud.

32 Quoted in http://www.fas.org/irp/world/para/ladin.htm, accessed 07/ 06/2002.

33 Some people claim that the caliphate is Koranically based. But this is erroneous. The *khalifa* mentioned in the Koran is the viceregent of God, i.e. Adam (and later the Perfect Human), not the political "successor" of the Prophet. The former is the caliph of God, the latter is the caliph of the Prophet in his function as leader (one of many such functions). Abu Bakr, the first Caliph, pointed this out very clearly when he said, "I'm not the caliph of God, I'm the caliph of His Prophet."

34 Ideally, politics should be *informed* by morality, and hence religion. This means that a political actor should act in accordance with ethics. In reality, however, politics is all too often divorced from morality and religion is misused as an instrument of politics. Religion, an end in itself, becomes a means serving political ends. Under such circumstances, the best recourse is to decouple politics from religion entirely, since the politician has already accomplished this unilaterally to the detriment of religion.

35   Stephen Dedalus in James Joyce's *Ulysses.*
36   J. Schacht, "Law and Justice," *Cambridge Encyclopaedia of Islam,* vol. II, pt. VIII/chpt. 4, pp. 539*ff.* Further details about the Holy Law can be found in the chapter on "Islam and Democracy" below.
37   See e.g. Thomas L. Friedman's series of columns in the *New York Times,* June 16, 23, 26, and especially June 19, 2002.
38   Rosalind Gwynne, "Al-Qaida and al-Qur'an: The 'Tafsir' of Usamah bin Ladin," http://web.utk.edu/~warda/bin_ladin_and_quran.htm, accessed 05/17/2002.
39   "Khatami's view: The refreshing voice of moderate Islam," *The Economist,* November 24, 2001.
40   Hassan Mneimneh and Kanan Makiya, "Manual for a 'Raid,'" *The New York Review of Books,* January 17, 2002.
41   Seyla Benhabib, "Unholy Politics," http://www.ssrc.org/sept11/essays/benhabib_text_only.htm, accessed 05/18/2002.
42   André Glucksmann, "Penser le 11 Septembre," *Le Nouvel Observateur,* No. 1940 (Jan. 10, 2002); *Dostoïevski à Manhattan,* Paris: Robert Laffont, 2002.
43   Because of this, they are not *conscious* nihilists.
44   *Spiderman* (2002).
45   http://www.mii.kurume-u.ac.jp/~leuers/zizek-welcome_ to_ the_desert_of_the_real.html, accessed 05/18/2002. See http://www.inthesetimes.com/issue/25/24/zizek2524.html for a slightly different version. I have made use of both.
46   In Greek mythology, Ariadne gave Theseus a ball of thread so he could find his way out of the Labyrinth.
47   Edward W. Said, "Impossible Histories," *Harper's Magazine,* July 2002, p. 70.
48   Prince Charles, "Islam and the West," http://www.furman.edu/~ateipen/pr_charles_speech.html (27 Oct. 1993).
49   George Saliba, "Greek Astronomy and the Medieval Arabic Tradition," *American Scientist,* Vol. 90, No. 4 (July-August 2002), pp. 360-67.
50   Fritjof Schuon, *Christianity/Islam,* 1985, pp. 174-5, 177-8.
51   Edward Gibbon and Simon Ocklay, *History of the Saracen Empire,* London, 1870, p. 54.
52   *Mohammad and Mohammadanism,* London, 1874, p. 92.
53   *Histoire de la Turquie,* Paris, 1854, Vol. 11, p. 277.

⁵⁴ John Davenport, *Muhammad and Teachings of [the] Quran*, 1869, pp. 61-2, 70-71.

⁵⁵ *Time* magazine, July 15, 1974.

⁵⁶ *The 100: A Ranking of the Most Influential Persons in History*, New York, 1978, p. 33.

⁵⁷ Karen Armstrong, "The curse of the infidel," *The Guardian*, June 20, 2002.

⁵⁸ For comparison, in Catholicism the ultimate authority is the Church; in Protestantism it is the Bible. In Islam, it is the Koran plus the example (the Way) of the Prophet.

⁵⁹ Neither did it in Christianity, originally. Nothing in Jesus' teachings contains anything about Original Sin; this concept was added by St. Augustine in the 5th century A.d.

⁶⁰ In this book, wherever the word "evil" is used, it should be understood in this sense, not in the Christian sense of the term.

⁶¹ "Synergy: Some Notes of Ruth Benedict," *American Anthropologist*, 72 (1970) 320-333. Quotation from p. 325.

⁶² *Ibid.* 329.

⁶³ Jeff Madrick, "The Power of the Super-Rich," *The New York Review of Books*, July 18, 2002.

⁶⁴ Ignacio Ramonet, "Saving the Planet," http://mondediplo.com/2002/08/01edito, accessed 08/15/2002.

⁶⁵ In the later Sufi section of this book, "The Spiritual Journey of the Sufi," I will address the importance of the guide or master (*murshid* or Enlightener).

⁶⁶ I am indebted to Lewis Mumford and Paul Johnson for some of the ideas discussed below.

⁶⁷ Not Arabic but *Rab*-ic, where *Rab* stands for "Lord."

⁶⁸ A principle of Sufi masters based on the Koran: "There is no compulsion in religion" (2:256).

⁶⁹ Or "transrational" (Ken Wilber).

⁷⁰ A wealthy businessman who hated the Prophet.

⁷¹ An uncle of the Prophet who became his enemy.

⁷² Normally, justice demands retribution, which is sanctioned. But the Koran teaches that if one can do it, forgiveness is higher. The conduct of the Prophet in such cases is very difficult for others to emulate. As Asghar Ali Engineer has observed, "Retaliation is human, to forgive is divine."

73   The Kaaba was considered a holy sanctuary from time immemorial. First built by Abraham and his son Ishmael, in Mohammed's time it was filled with the idols of the polytheists before the Prophet cleared them out.

74   Chosroes was the ruler of Persia, Negus of Ethiopia.

75   Making other deities equal to Him, or even making Him chief God in a pantheon among lesser gods. He is One and Only, with no associates whatsoever. There is no god but God. That is the basic item of the covenant.

76   In fact, mental health is their prerequisite. The mentally ill and children who have not yet reached the age of puberty are under no obligation to perform them.

77   http://jews-for-allah.org/Jews-and-Muslims-Agree/Jews-prayed-like-Muslims.htm reproduces the postures, first published in Hayim Halevy Donin, *To Pray as a Jew: A Guide to the Prayer Book and the Synagogue Service,* New York : Basic Books, 1991 [1980].

78   According to classical Islam, animals, plants and even inanimate matter possess spirit, which is ultimately derived from God's spirit.

79   This is the true meaning of the superstition that one who breaks a mirror will suffer seven years' bad luck, for the heart is comparable to a mirror—it mirrors God's light.

80   *Haqq* is one of God's names, which can be translated as Truth, Reality or the Real. This is why Truth is capitalized here.

81   Since Dirac, symmetry has continued to play an important role in modern physics (such as supersymmetry, symmetry breaking, "duality," etc.).

82   *Scientific American,* May 1993, p. 62, quoted from *ibid.,* May 1963.

83   In preparing this chapter, I have relied heavily on articles concerning "reform in Islam" in Ahmet Kayhan's Turkish-language anthology, *I Found What I Was Seeking* (1991).

84   If it be claimed that Moslems are engaged in some sort of "jihad," the reply is that nowhere in the world are Moslems currently engaged in a war declared on others (although some misguided groups seek to declare it). If you want to fight, officially declare war first. Neither, however, should this be misread as an endorsement of atrocities perpetrated against Moslems anywhere.

85   In the case of Iran, the causes are different but the end result is the same.

86   This may not be the initial impression of a reader. Further study and

meditation, however, will resolve any problems, which usually result from mistranslation or insufficient commentary.

[87] As mentioned earlier, war is justified in Islam only in self-defense or when the Faith is under assault.

[88] Not everyone has to marry (marriage is not compulsory), but the Prophet encouraged marital life.

[89] For women, the veil is not a Koranic attire. It is sufficient that they dress modestly.

[90] The transmission and interpretation of Revelation does not require a church. Sacred scripture on the one hand and the Prophet's example on the other cannot be used to justify the existence of a church, when Islam has been able to preserve both in the absence of a church for 14 centuries. In Islam, the "sacred deposit" (The Koran and the Prophet's Way) has been entrusted to the community as a whole, not to a separate ecclesiastical organization. If an excommunicatory authority had existed in Islam, this book—and many books like it—could never have been written.

[91] It might be argued that the example of Iran violates this statement. But it is in fact an exception, spanning less than one-seventieth of Islam's history, and the Shiites constitute less than a tenth of the present world population of Moslems. As I have said repeatedly because it is so important, where the role of the Prophet's Way is diminished, other authorities rush in to fill the void. This is one of the reasons for its importance, and many will agree that the results of its absence leave much to be desired.

[92] Some Western sources have recently begun to speak of the "separation of mosque and state," as if the church and mosque were comparable. But the mosque is not a religious institution. It is a building of worship, a temple pure and simple.

[93] Not to be confused with "Gnostic," a member of one of several heretical Christian sects in the second century.

[94] This short list begins with Turkey, and even here there are doubts. Some would extend this to Bangladesh, others would—with even greater reservations—add Iran.

[95] Webster's Bible. Or: causes an offense.

[96] J. Schacht, "Law and Justice," *Cambridge Encyclopaedia of Islam*, vol. II, pt. VIII/chpt. 4, pp. 539ff. See the Prologue for more details.

[97] Malise Ruthven, *Islam in the World*, Harmondsworth: Penguin, 1991

[1984], pp. 157-8.
98 *Ibid.* p. 158.
99 *Ibid.* pp. 160-1.
100 *Ibid.* p. 179.
101 http://cogsci.ucsd.edu/~sereno/wArabichtml, accessed 07/11/2002.
102 Alexis de Tocqueville, *Democracy in America,* George Lawrence (tr.), New York: Harper and Row, 1966 (single-volume edition), p. 444.
103 And absolutely not anti-Semite. As a matter of fact, both Arabs and Jews are of Semitic stock—they belong to the same race.
104 Bernard Lewis, *The Political Language of Islam,* Chicago: University of Chicago Press, 1988, p. 30.
105 *Ibid.* p. 31.
106 An unjust law is not a law. Hence, this cannot be misread as "Islam upholds injustice."
107 *The Economist,* "Survey: Islam and the West," August 6, 1994, p. 10.
108 Tocqueville, p. 268.
109 *Ibid.* p.269.
110 *Ibid.* p. 271.
111 *Ibid.* p. 287.
112 *Ibid.* p. 409.
113 After "the self always impels to evil" (12:53).
114 In *Thus Spoke Zarathustra,* Nietzsche called the state "the coldest of cold monsters," which was perhaps the inspiration for Joseph Campbell's coinage, "the monster state."
115 In one Tradition, "those in authority" is related to "scholars of *fiqh*," which would again underscore the law-abiding nature of Islam.
116 E.g. Keith Ward (Professor of Theology at Oxford University), in an article published in August 1994 in Britain's respected daily *The Independent.*
117 See also Appendix D.
118 Note that this is exactly the claim, full of pride and contempt, that led to the downfall and expulsion of Satan: "I am better than he" (7:12), which all human beings must do their utmost to avoid, not just in racial terms but in every respect.
119 Robert A. Dahl, *Democracy and Its Critics,* New Haven: Yale University Press, 1989, pp. 85-6.
120 Tocqueville, p. 411.
121 G.K. Chesterton, *What I Saw in America* (1922), Chapter 19.

[122] Paul Johnson, *A History of the Jews,* London: Weidenfeld and Nicholson, 1987.

[123] *Ibid.* p. 40.

[124] *Ibid.* p. 156.

[125] Norman Mailer, the *Sunday Times* interview on 9/11 (8 September 2002), also available at http://www.
counterpunch.org/pipermail/counterpunch-list/2002-September/022469.html.

[126] Lewis Mumford, *The Condition of Man,* New York: Harcourt Brace Jovanovich, 1973 [1944], pp. 322-3 (italics added).

[127] I have outlined some of this Sufic wisdom in my book, *The Station of No Station,* and will elaborate on it in later chapters of this book.

[128] Biological differences can lead to differences—and thus different needs—in the other two areas. See e.g. a report on "Brain Differences in Males and Females," which states: "Contrasts in [brain] morphology translate into behavioral and attitudinal differences in the two genders." http://www.tarleton.edu/~sanderson/Brain Differences.doc, accessed 07/24/2002. Some differences, such as better verbal skills in women, do not seem related to brain anatomy.

[129] "In general, men are taller and heavier than women. In sports, men tend to outperform women in strength and speed. Women seem to have greater endurance." J. Bland, "About Gender: Differences," (1998) http://www.gender.org.uk/about/00_diffs. htm, accessed 07/24/2002.

[130] Karen Armstrong, *Muhammad: A Western Attempt to Understand Islam,* London: Victor Gollancz, 1991, p. 240.

[131] *Ibid.* p. 198.

[132] Quoted in e.g. http://www.jamaat.org/islam/unjust.html, accessed 08/02/2002.

[133] *Ibid.*

[134] That is, barring adultery or Illicit Lust. Otherwise, some women and men must be practicing *de facto* polyandry.

[135] A.J. Arberry, *The Koran Interpreted,* London: Oxford University Press, 1975 [1955].

[136] Again, God is referred to as "He" in English, but this does not mean that God is a man—for the Lord transcends both male and female.

[137] *Maitreya 4* (1973), pp. 12-13, quoted from Wynne-Tyson, *The Philosophy of Compassion* London: Centaur Press, 1970, p. 271.

138 Armstrong, p. 239.

139 Quoted *in Zaman*, 1.12.1994, p. 15.

140 The term "folk Islam" also has a derogatory tone to it, especially when implying such ignorant practices as "tomb worship."

141 Reason does have its limits, though, beyond which lies the transrational or surrational. As Pascal remarked, "The heart has its reasons that reason knows nothing of." See the chapter on "Moses, Jesus and Mohammed," subsection "Weakly Coupled Religions," and also "The Secret That is Love" chapter.

142 Quotations are from J.L. Borges, "The Aleph" (tr. Anthony Kerrigan), in *A Personal Anthology*, London: Picador, 1972, p. 113-125.

143 In the Koran, "heavenly wine," which is pure and not comparable to earthly wine, is mentioned in 47:15, 76:21, and 83:25.

144 As I have suggested earlier in this book, the derivation and implementation of a legal code over society is distinct from this, and more properly called *fiqh*.

145 Is this one reason why Lamarck's "inheritance of acquired characteristics" was opposed so vehemently, and Darwin's "natural selection through random mutation" championed?

146 "Tenets of Sunni Islam," in *Country Studies: Turkey*, Washington, D.C.: Library of Congress, 1987 (www.loc.gov).

147 See the chapter on Hermeticism below for a plausible, imaginative account of Hermetic initiation.

148 See the section "Spacewarps, Timewarps" in the last chapter.

149 The undesired (and undesirable) disintegration of the self—leading to loss of contact with reality, schizophrenia, and other forms of mental disorder—is not what is intended here.

150 The Koranic verse: "He created the seven heavens" (65:12) may be relevant in this context.

151 Peter D. Ouspensky, *In Search of the Miraculous*, New York: Harcourt, Brace & World, 1949, pp. 44-49.

152 *Ibid.*, p. 50; italics in the original.

153 Annemarie Schimmel, *Mystical Dimensions of Islam*, Chapel Hill: University of North Carolina Press, 1975, p. 237.

154 See the chapter "The Spiritual Journey of the Sufi," Method 3: Spiritual Connection with the Master.

155 Reported by Philip Cohen in *New Scientist*, 8 November 1997.

156 Keith Campbell *et al.*, *Nature*, *380* (1996) 64-66.

157 *Discover,* September 1994, pp. 27-8; *Scientific American,* September 1997, pp. 9-12. An alternative explanation, called "hypermutabil-ity," has been advanced based on randomness.

158 Attributed.

159 Shakespeare, *As You Like It,* II, 1.

160 The term that is given to this process, "Unification" (*Tawhid*), is of-ten misunderstood as a kind of levelling process that somehow blends all differences into some more bland admixture. The reality, however, is that of One being reflected in the many. This also guards against the danger of attributing Divinity to the things themselves. At all times this higher vision—of unity in diversity in unity—must be kept in mind, particularly if, to use the language of the mystics, we are to assert the *seamlessness* of the One.

161 In *Megatrends 2000* and in *The Post-Capitalist Society* (1993), respec-tively. For a summary of Drucker's observations concerning the knowl-edge society, see P.F. Drucker, "The Age of Social Transformation," *Atlantic Monthly,* November 1994, pp. 53-80.

162 For more on the scientific achievements of Islamic civilization, see Seyyed Hossein Nasr's *Islamic Science: An Illustrated Study* (1976) and *Science and Civilization in Islam* (1968).

163 Quoted in David Jay Brown and Rebecca McClen Novick, *Mavericks of the Mind,* Freedom, CA: Crossing Press, 1993.

164 F. Rosenthal, *Knowledge Triumphant,* Leiden: E.J. Brill, 1970, 1-2.

165 *Ibid.,* 240.

166 *Ibid.,* 309-10.

167 *Ibid.,* 311.

168 *Ibid.,* 333.

169 *Ibid.,* 334.

170 *Ibid.,* 340.

171 *Ibid.,* 30.

172 *Ibid.,* 105.

173 V. Havel, "Faith in the World," *Civilization,* May 1998. Havel is the Czech president and former dissident playwright under the Com-munist regime.

174 I prefer the term "archetype" to god here.

175 J. Godwin, "The Hermetic Tradition," *Lapis, 1,* 1 (1995).

176 Albert Champdor, *The Book of the Dead,* New York: Helix Press, 1966, p. 43.

177 I have made use of the on-line version—the G.R.S. Mead translation—of the *Corpus Hermeticum,* available (as of June 1998) at www.hermetic.com/caduceus/hermetica/index.html through the good offices of John Michael Greer. I have edited and simplified the language, and used the numbering given therein for convenience.

178 Greer comments: "'The Good,' in Greek thought, is also the self-caused and self-sufficient, and thus has little in common with later conceptions of 'goodness'" (Intro. to Chapter 6). Another such meaning in Greek is that the good of any being is that being's necessary goal (Intro. To Ch. 2). These meanings bring Plato's "Good" much closer to God.

179 The on-line *Corpus* is incomplete, so I have supplemented this with the Everard translation and indicated such use with **bold** numerals. The printed copy I use is *The Divine Pymander* (ed. P.B. Randolph), Rosicrucian Publishing Co., 1871, reprinted by the Yogi Publication Society, Des Plaines, IL (no date). Please note that the ordering of chapters and the numbering differ from Greer's.

180 One is reminded of William Blake's remark: "If the doors of perception were cleansed, everything would appear to man as it is, infinite."

181 This is meant both in the ordinary and the esoteric senses.

182 The ancients associated these with the planets, but this need not be the case.

183 Harold Waldwin Percival, *Masonry and Its Symbols in the Light of 'Thinking and Destiny'.*

184 Those who are still in doubt about this can consult Frithjof Schuon's *The Transcendent Unity of Religions.*

185 Inspiration to Sheikh Abdelqader Gilani, *Treatise on Divine Aid (The Holy Bestowal).*

186 From a poem by Niyazi Misri. Truth: the Real, or Absolute Reality, i.e. God.

187 See e.g. Ibn Arabi's writings.

188 Gilani, *The Mystery of Mysteries.*

189 Gilani, *Treatise on Divine Aid.*

190 Holy Tradition (a saying of God uttered through the Prophet's mouth that is not included in the Koran).

191 From the teachings of Master Ahmet Kayhan.

192 Gilani, *Mystery.*

193 *Ibid.*

194 This point was reached only gradually in ancient Egypt. Until the

"grand synthesis," practically every god was worshiped as the supreme creator at one time or another—a process called "henotheism."

195 Aspirants were mostly males.

196 Champdor, *Book of the Dead,* p. 25.

197 The *Abjad* ("ABCD") calculations in Islam assign a value to each letter in a word or sentence, and attempt to find deeper correspondences on the basis of these numerical values. Although similar to numerology in its popular and vulgar use (e.g., fortune-telling), the more sophisticated applications seek deeper truth from numerical equivalents. Adepts sometimes used it as a code that yielded profound meaning when deciphered. The decorative tulips on porcelain in mosques, for instance, are symbolic of God, because the numerical values of "tulip" and "God" in Arabic are equal. The decorations therefore constitute a pictorial calligraphy.

198 Rory Howlett quoting from *Nature, 391* (1998) 76 in *New Scientist,* 20 June 1998.

199 Noted for his books on the philosophy of science, such as *Personal Knowledge,* Polanyi is a chemist by profession.

200 As in the Jewish and Christian traditions, Pharaoh is an archetype of evil power in Islam.

201 Spiritual poverty (*faqr*) denotes that state in which one is emptied of everything except God. This leads to extinction or annihilation (*fana*) of the little local self (in God).

202 Although Blake's Fourfold Vision does not refer to the four ontological worlds of the Sufis, I believe it is a valid poetic description thereof.

203 The figure is intended to be representative rather than definitive.

204 Lit. "crowned." In translations, the phoenix or hoopoe symbolizing the Sufi master.

205 While the seven valleys the birds pass through do not correspond to the stages of the self as described in this chapter, the sevenfold metaphor still holds.

206 Sometimes identified with Enoch, Idris is also confused with Hermes, due to the similarity between the spectacular heavenly journeys experienced by the two.

207 Quoted from http://www.shobak.org/islam/birds.html (Translation by Afkham Darbandi and Dick Davis).

208 Francis Thompson, "The Hound of Heaven." Dravest: Drove away.

209 In *Revue des Sciences Morales et Politiques,* No. 1 (1989).

Index

------- ✴ -------